Approaches to Teaching Tolkien's *The Lord of the Rings* and Other Works

Approaches to Teaching World Literature

For a complete listing of titles, see the last pages of this book.

Approaches to Teaching Tolkien's *The Lord of the Rings* and Other Works

Edited by

Leslie A. Donovan

The Modern Language Association of America
New York 2015

Printed in the United States of America

Library of Congress Cataloging-in-Publication Data

Approaches to teaching Tolkien's The Lord of the Rings and other works / edited by Leslie A. Donovan.
pages cm. — (Approaches to teaching world literature, ISSN 1059-1133 ; 136)
Summary: "Offers pedagogical techniques for teaching Tolkien's *The Lord of the Rings*, *The Hobbit*, and *The Silmarillion* in undergraduate and graduate classes. Topics include race, gender, sources, environmental sustainability, interdisciplinarity, learning communities, science, epic, pastoral, and reception. Includes syllabus suggestions, information on editions, reference works, biographies, film adaptations, and online resources"— Provided by publisher.
Includes bibliographical references and index.
ISBN 978-1-60329-205-4 (hardback) — ISBN 978-1-60329-206-1 (paper) —
ISBN 978-1-60329-207-8 (EPUB) — 978-1-60329-208-5 (Kindle)
1. Tolkien, J. R. R. (John Ronald Reuel), 1892–1973—Study and teaching.
2. Tolkien, J. R. R. (John Ronald Reuel), 1892–1973—Criticism and interpretation.
3. Fantasy fiction, English—Study and teaching. I. Donovan, Leslie A., 1957– editor.
PR6039.O32Z555 2015
823′.912—dc23
2015016037

Approaches to Teaching World Literature 136
ISSN 1059-1133

Cover illustration of the paperback edition: Caspar David Friedrich, *Mountain Peak with Drifting Clouds*, c. 1835. Oil on canvas, 9 13⁄16 x 12 1⁄16 in. (25 x 30.6 cm.). Kimball Art Museum, Fort Worth, Texas.

Published by The Modern Language Association of America
85 Broad Street, suite 500, New York, New York 10004-2434
www.mla.org

CONTENTS

Preface ix

Acknowledgments xiii

PART ONE: MATERIALS

Leslie A. Donovan

Tolkien in Context 3

Editions

The Lord of the Rings 9

The Hobbit 11

The Silmarillion and Other Works from the Legendarium of Middle-earth 12

Works of Short Fiction 13

Scholarship and Other Nonfiction Works 16

Translations 17

The Instructor's Library

Historical and Biographical Resources on Tolkien's Life and Times 18

Reference Works 19

Literary Criticism 20

Languages and Linguistics 21

Journals and Periodicals 22

Resources for Teaching 22

Multimedia Aids for Teaching

Music 23

Audio and Video Recordings 24

Visual Aids 25

Charts and Maps 25

Films 26

PART TWO: APPROACHES

Introduction: Seed of Courage Not So Hidden 31
Leslie A. Donovan

Teaching the Controversies

The Perils of the Tolkien Course: Reading the Readings 36
Craig Franson

Teaching the Critical Debate over *The Lord of the Rings* 44
James McNelis

Tolkien's Other Works as Background

Eucatastrophe and the Battle with the Dark 50
Verlyn Flieger

Why Teach *The Silmarillion*? Tolkien's Mythology of the Abject Hero 56
Jane Chance

Child of the Kindly West: Innocence and Experience in *The Hobbit* 65
Brian Walter

Using *The History of Middle-earth* with Tolkien's Fiction 75
Yvette Kisor

Connections to the Past

Presenting Tolkien's Pasts 84
Robin Chapman Stacey

Teaching the Oral Tradition in *The Lord of the Rings* 92
Leslie Stratyner

Becoming Tolkien: Reading His Anglo-Saxon and Boethian Sources 97
Liam Felsen

Tolkien as Nation Builder: Teaching *The Lord of the Rings* in an Epic Literature Class 103
Melissa Ridley Elmes

Conceptions of the Pastoral in *The Fellowship of the Ring* 108
Philip Irving Mitchell

Modern and Contemporary Perspectives

Teaching Tolkien in the Context of the Fantasy Tradition 114
Christopher Cobb

Tolkien and the Modern: Reading the Canon through *The Lord of the Rings* 126
Sharin Schroeder

The Tower, the Sausage Maker, and the Soup: Teaching Tolkien in a Postmodern Classroom 137
Thomas L. Martin

Teaching Tolkien and Race: An Inconvenient Combination? 144
Dimitra Fimi

Women Students and *The Lord of the Rings*: Showing Them Where They Fit In 150
Shelley Rees

Language, Culture, Environment, and Diversity in *The Lord of the Rings* 157
Deidre Dawson

Interdisciplinary Contexts

Starting with the Film: Jackson as a Way Back to Tolkien on Heroism and Evil 165
Christopher Crane

Tolkien and Faith: An Interdisciplinary Approach 172
Nancy Enright

Melkor, Moon Letters, and Menelmacar: Middle-earth in the Science Classroom 177
Kristine Larsen

Tolkien and Environmental Sustainability in the Science Curriculum 183
Justin Edward Everett

Classroom Contexts and Strategies for Teaching

Tolkien in the First-Year Literature Survey Course 191
Anna Smol

Team-Teaching Tolkien in a Large Lecture Class: Challenges and Opportunities 200
Julia Simms Holderness

England's Mythmaker? A Tolkien Learning Community 207
James R. Vitullo and Keith W. Jensen

"[T]hings That Were, and Things That Are, and Things That Yet May Be": Teaching Tolkien's *The Lord of the Rings* Online 214
Judy Ann Ford and Robin Anne Reid

Morals and Malice in Middle-earth 219
James Gould and Ted Hazelgrove

Tolkien Immersion: Why a Three-Week Intensive Course Works 225
Cami D. Agan

The Council of Elrond, All Those Poems, and the Famous F-ing Elves: Teaching the Hard Parts of Tolkien 231
Michael D. C. Drout

Fellowship and the Rings: Intellectual Sociability and Collaborative Learning among Tolkien and the Inklings 237
Michael Tomko

Notes on Contributors 243

Survey Respondents 249

Works Cited 253

Index of Works Written, Edited, or Translated by J. R. R. Tolkien 273

Index of Names 275

PREFACE

Testifying to the phenomenal popularity of *The Lord of the Rings* among general audiences, several turn-of-the-millennium reader polls identify the prominent place J. R. R. Tolkien and his fantasy epic hold for audiences. In 1997, a reader poll conducted by Waterstones booksellers and the BBC ranked *The Lord of the Rings* as the greatest book of the twentieth century (Shippey, *J. R. R. Tolkien* xx); in 1999, an *Amazon.com* poll named *The Lord of the Rings* the favorite "book of the millennium" among readers in the United States (O'Hehir); in 2002, a BBC poll of the one hundred "greatest Britons" of all time included Tolkien ("BBC Reveals"); in 2003, the BBC's "Big Read" survey found *The Lord of the Rings* to be the "Nation's Best-loved Book"; and, in a 2006 poll taken by the Museums, Libraries and Archives Council, librarians across Britain placed *The Lord of the Rings* third on their list of the thirty books all adults should "read before they die" (Pauli). More recently, in 2011, *The Lord of the Rings* appeared in the number one spot on NPR's "Top 100 Science-Fiction and Fantasy" survey (Weldon).[1]

Beyond evidence for Tolkien's popularity among general readers provided by such polls, academic interest in Tolkien and his works has developed well beyond the peripheral study of a popular culture phenomenon to a field of substantial critical inquiry. The online database of the *MLA International Bibliography* lists sixty-six publications on Tolkien or his works that appeared between 1960 and 1969. Between 1970 and 1979, that number grows to 154 publications, and to 359 between 1980 and 1989. However, at least half the publications in these decades are short pieces by amateur scholars and students in books from minor presses and non-peer-reviewed journals. The same bibliography lists 428 publications on Tolkien between 1990 and 1999, but in this decade the trend shifts, and a strong majority of works are clearly by professional scholars. The online *MLA International Bibliography* cites at least 793 works on Tolkien during the first decade of this century, of which more than three-fourths represent serious academic scholarship. A random sampling from the 2011 bibliography in the *Tolkien Studies* journal shows publications on such diverse topics as ecological interpretations, source studies, postmodernism, Norse themes, linguistic studies, Christian spirituality, structural analyses, onomastic strategies, astronomical themes, historical contexts, and issues of race and culture. The rapidly increasing number of publications and variety of subjects over the last fifty years confirm that Tolkien scholarship is both a viable and a rich field for new literary discoveries and academic inquiry.

More important for the present volume than the rise in scholarly interest about Tolkien's works is the growth in courses that incorporate his works, from a few scattered experiments taught by especially dedicated high school English teachers in the 1960s and 1970s to numerous courses now offered in many different disciplines at secondary and postsecondary schools across North America and Britain. Whether these courses study *The Lord of the Rings* primarily for its medieval traditions, use of epic conventions, perspectives on spirituality, or literary place in the genre of modern fantasy, Tolkien's work offers a variety of materials and perspectives for students and teachers to consider. The current educational interest in Tolkien's works, grounded in the recognition that his Middle-earth fiction continues to hold lasting value for readers from varied backgrounds and experiences, motivated the preparation of this project.

The goal of *Approaches to Teaching Tolkien's* The Lord of the Rings *and Other Works* is to provide the broadest possible array of methods and options for teaching Tolkien's works. It is intended to be useful across a diverse range of institutional settings to experienced Tolkien teachers and those considering teaching his works for the first time. Through varied approaches, strategies, pedagogies, curricular models, and student assignments, this book is designed to enhance the educational experiences of current and future Tolkien teachers as well as many generations of students.

Although this project discusses Tolkien's other works, it focuses on *The Lord of the Rings* in order to highlight the most common pedagogical concerns teachers face. Like other volumes in this series, this one began with an online survey distributed as widely as possible to those who teach Tolkien's works primarily in college-level courses. The survey gathered information on both typical and distinctively innovative practices teachers use. Data from this survey not only identified the information most useful to teachers but also established the factors critical for choosing essays most likely to aid their efforts.

Basic trends in the data gathered from 102 survey responses indicated that *The Lord of the Rings* is taught in both lower- and upper-division courses that focus exclusively on Tolkien's works (about 81% of respondents) or that incorporate them among works by several authors (nearly 61%). While many respondents confirmed that medieval works known to Tolkien feature prominently in their courses (slightly more than 54%), a healthy number of respondents (around 38%) integrate historical and literary materials contemporary with Tolkien's own time. Teachers responding to the survey were particularly interested in how interdisciplinary topics such as race, gender, religion, environmentalism, science, and linguistics might play more substantial roles in their courses. Respondents also expressed a strong desire for approaches to inserting Tolkien's works into courses taught in disciplines other than English literature. Finally, a number of teachers wanted new options for integrating Tolkien's works into already existing curricula and for developing stand-alone courses to serve a greater diversity of student populations.

These surveys have shaped a volume that brings together a broad spectrum of teaching materials and pedagogical perspectives relevant to teaching Tolkien's texts. The "Materials" section compiles and summarizes basic resources for studying *The Lord of the Rings* and some of Tolkien's other works. It emphasizes materials whose relevance to teachers will not soon be superseded by future scholarship. Resources discussed in this section provide the foundations on which students and teachers can build more extensive expertise and knowledge for themselves.

The "Approaches" section contains 29 essays selected from the 102 proposals submitted by 83 survey respondents. These essays best address the myriad pedagogical needs requested in the surveys. They collect a rich assortment of ideas and methods for teaching *The Lord of the Rings* and other works by Tolkien, and they represent the range of pedagogical contexts reported in the surveys, including perspectives from various school types, class formats, and student populations.[2] These essays are grouped into six loosely defined categories: "Teaching the Controversies," offering the essential critical contexts for teaching *The Lord of the Rings*; "Tolkien's Other Works as Background," presenting approaches to Tolkien's wider corpus that may be studied in conjunction with *The Lord of the Rings*; "Connections to the Past," exploring relationships between *The Lord of the Rings* and earlier literary and historical documents; "Modern and Contemporary Perspectives," focusing on teaching such topics as race, culture, and gender in the context of *The Lord of the Rings*; "Interdisciplinary Contexts," featuring courses that incorporate less commonly expected materials or disciplines; and "Classroom Contexts and Strategies for Teaching," discussing specific course structures (such as team-taught, summer, and online courses) and methods for teaching central aspects of the text. While the essays in each category build on the previous ones and lead into those that follow, teachers will also make useful discoveries by reading the essays independently from one another. Several essays within and across sections further complement or converse with one another in addressing Tolkien's works.

Regardless of the order in which the essays are read, *Approaches to Teaching Tolkien's* The Lord of the Rings *and Other Works* draws together patterns from which teachers may design their own pedagogies. This volume's objective is not to prescribe how Tolkien should be taught by college-level teachers but to make available resources from which they may choose for themselves how best to supply their students with full and empowering learning experiences. By presenting resources in "Materials" and perspectives from experienced Tolkien teachers in "Approaches," this collection offers teachers practical and reflective solutions to help students better appreciate the influences, methods, and craft of Tolkien's works. In addition, since these works are certain to carry popular currency in the future, this volume seeks to aid teachers in understanding the distinctive pedagogical advantages and challenges involved in teaching them.

NOTES

[1] Tom Shippey cites other polls between 1996 and 1999 in which *The Lord of the Rings* ranked highly (*J. R. R. Tolkien* xx–xxi).

[2] Essays were chosen to represent as much diversity as possible among courses taught in large and small schools, public and private universities, community colleges, and undergraduate- and graduate-degree-granting institutions, as well as among varied geographic locations primarily throughout the United States but also in Canada and Great Britain.

ACKNOWLEDGMENTS

At times in this project, I imagined what Tolkien might have felt when the work at hand, so deeply important, came to fruition too slowly because of the myriad distractions of professional duties and an undoubtedly overzealous desire to make sure all the details were correct. Yet, even so, preparing this volume was always immensely inspiring and exciting. It was a joy to work with so many dedicated teachers who gave this project their time, patience, and a humbling constellation of pedagogical innovations. While my foremost gratitude is owed to all of them, Jane Chance, Michael D. C. Drout, and Verlyn Flieger provided especially crucial advice along the way.

Too many members of the Mythopoeic Society to name offered information, kindness, and ideas that benefited this project, but I offer them my gratitude nonetheless. Special thanks goes to James Hatch, MLA acquisitions editor, for his unflagging patience with me throughout this entire process and to the MLA Publications Committee and editorial and production staff for their careful attention to this project. Most appreciated was the encouragement of my colleagues from the Honors College and Institute for Medieval Studies at the University of New Mexico (UNM). Most important, my own Tolkien students as well as members of the UNM Hobbit Society constantly reminded me why this project mattered.

The hard work and attention to the tiniest of details that my editorial assistant, Zach Watkins, so generously provided make this an infinitely better book than it would have been otherwise. Any errors that remain are my own. Also, Jeanell Pelsor, always my brightest light in all the darkest places, kept me going when the workload threatened to crush.

Finally, I wish to honor and acknowledge the debt of thanks all of us involved in this project owe to The Professor. May his beacon blaze always so brightly.

Part One

MATERIALS

Tolkien in Context

J. R. R. Tolkien (1892–1973), a British author, never intended to write immensely popular literature that would challenge traditional ideas about the nature of great literature and would be worthy of study in colleges across the world; instead, he set out only to write a great story, the kind of story he and his friends would enjoy reading,[1] a story to represent the core of his English culture. While he wanted his stories to attach themselves to people's hearts and minds, he cared much more about establishing them as important in themselves than in launching his career as a writer of fiction. Above all, he considered himself a philologist and a medieval scholar, a lover of words and the stories of earlier peoples, a teacher of past glories and sorrows still meaningful in the modern world. He perceived *The Lord of the Rings* and his other Middle-earth fiction as natural extensions of his professional life, which itself reflected ideas and images that were dear to him personally. Until the initial popularity of *The Lord of the Rings* reached its height late in his life, it is doubtful that Tolkien ever conceived of his fiction as more than pure and pleasurable entertainment, that he ever envisioned arguments in which its literary value or questions of canonicity would be discussed.

Tolkien was born to British parents on 3 January 1892 in Bloemfontein, the capital of what is now the Free State Province of South Africa, and named John Ronald Reuel Tolkien. When his father, Arthur Reuel, the manager of a South African branch of a British bank, died of a brain hemorrhage in 1896, his mother, Mabel, returned to England with the four-year-old Tolkien and his younger brother, Hilary. The family settled in the Birmingham area of the West Midlands until Mabel died of complications resulting from diabetes in 1904. Father Francis Xavier Morgan, a Roman Catholic priest with whom Mabel had been friends, became the guardian of the Tolkien boys. The rural areas surrounding the Birmingham of Tolkien's childhood formed his most happy memories and became the basis for the landscapes and people he created later for the Shire. The Roman Catholic faith instilled by his mother and Father Francis, and which Tolkien preserved throughout his life, also profoundly affected his literary works.[2]

Tolkien attended King Edward's School in Birmingham and then Exeter College in Oxford, where he studied languages, classics, and English and Germanic literatures. The admiration for medieval narratives and mythological themes that he developed throughout these educational experiences inspired the beginnings of his fiction and set him on the path to his career as a medieval scholar and teacher. In 1908, he met another orphan, Edith Bratt, whom he married when he was twenty-four. Remaining especially close throughout their lives, they were married fifty-five years until Edith's death in 1971. Tolkien viewed their love as akin to that of his characters the mortal Beren and Elven Lúthien, the couple whose heroic love story he recounts in various forms in his legendarium. Shortly after marrying Edith, he was shipped out to the western front in March 1916 as a junior officer in the British army, where he served in the Somme offensive of World War I. Most of his close friends were killed in that war, and he was sent home after contracting trench fever. He served out the rest of World War I in Britain.[3]

After the war, because of his education in language and literature, Tolkien was hired as a lexicographer for what would become the *Oxford English Dictionary*. In 1920, he took a position teaching English language at the University of Leeds, then returned to Oxford in 1925 with the prestigious appointment of Rawlinson and Bosworth Professor of Anglo-Saxon. Despite the common conception that his scholarly output was small because he preferred to spend his time writing fiction, he produced a number of important works of scholarship before retiring from Oxford in 1959. Although he has fewer academic publications than some other scholars of the time (such as his friend C. S. Lewis), those Tolkien published demonstrate meticulous research and highly original analysis that set standards still respected today. During his time at Oxford, he made connections with other writers and thinkers in a group called the Inklings,[4] at whose gatherings he shared early drafts of *The Lord of the Rings* and received feedback instrumental to the final version of that work.[5]

While in his twenties, Tolkien began working with ideas he would later develop into the mythology and heroic legends of Middle-earth. He expanded and revised many of these stories throughout his adult life. He considered much of the popular appeal of *The Lord of the Rings* to be based on its allusions to these legends and myths, "to the glimpses of a large history in the background: an attraction like that of viewing far off an unvisited island, or seeing the towers of a distant city gleaming in a sunlit mist" (*Letters of J. R. R. Tolkien* 333). His son Christopher, with the assistance of Guy Gavriel Kay, eventually compiled the notes, fragments, and multiple versions of Tolkien's mythological tales into *The Silmarillion*. Through these mythologies and legends of Middle-earth, Tolkien sought to create what Humphrey Carpenter, his early biographer, called "a mythology for England" (*J. R. R. Tolkien* 67) in order to evoke a sense of admiration for the foundations of his country. In much the same way that Greek, Roman, Celtic, Scandinavian, and even Finnish mythological literature furnished cornerstones for their cultures to admire and value, Tolkien wanted his fiction "to restore to the English an epic tradition and present them with a mythology of their own" (*Letters of J. R. R. Tolkien* 231).

Tolkien's first widely read work on Middle-earth, *The Hobbit*, was published in 1937. The British success of this children's fantasy novel led to its sequel, *The Lord of the Rings*. A work that Tolkien called a tale that "grew in the telling" (*Lord* xxii; foreword), *The Lord of the Rings* was written largely between 1937 and 1950, though revisions to the text and negotiations with his publisher, Allen and Unwin, about the form the book would take lasted another four years before the work saw print. To keep costs down for producing what the publishers initially perceived as a prestige publication that would most likely lose money,

The Fellowship of the Ring and *The Two Towers* were published as separate volumes in 1954, followed by *The Return of the King* in 1955, after a delay while Tolkien was completing the appendixes. Since its first publication, *The Lord of the Rings* has had a particularly complicated and confused publication history.[6]

At first, these new additions to the story of Middle-earth were read primarily in small circles of devoted fans in both Britain and the United States and achieved only modest sales. But in 1965, interest in Tolkien's work skyrocketed when Ace Books in the United States produced immense quantities of a highly affordable but unauthorized and non-royalty-paying version, using new technology to print paperback books. Tolkien's publishers responded to this copyright infringement by producing a second edition of *The Lord of the Rings* in an authorized paperback version through Ballantine Books. The authorized edition was supported by an extensive grassroots publicity campaign against Ace's version that featured a new foreword in which Tolkien asked that readers "who approve of courtesy (at least) to living authors will purchase it and no other" (xiii). The demand inspired by Ace's low-cost pirated version, along with the response from protective and outraged fans to Tolkien's plea, brought more attention to *The Lord of the Rings* than it would likely have received otherwise. As Tolkien himself noted, "I expect my 'authorized' paper-back will in fact sell more copies than it would, if there had been no trouble or competition" (*Letters of J. R. R. Tolkien* 364). Before this controversy, books published in paperback form had been considered cheap and second-rate, but the conflict surrounding *The Lord of the Rings* catalyzed the potential of mass-marketed paperback books to revolutionize the printing industry. As Joseph Ripp explains in "Middle America Meets Middle-earth":

> The controversy with Ace Books, then, inadvertently "democratized" the book through both increased public awareness of *The Lord of the Rings* and the manufacture of an abundance of inexpensive pocket book copies. As the publishing world was increasingly coming to recognize, paperback publication potentially revolutionized the interaction of readers with texts. (259)

Motivated by the Ace controversy, paperback sales of *The Lord of the Rings* rose exponentially, largely because college students appreciated the portability and inexpensiveness of the format.[7] In turn, *The Lord of the Rings* evolved into what has become known as a cult object, a status reaching its height in the late 1960s and early 1970s, "when the focus of American culture generally became increasingly fixed on youth," and *The Lord of the Rings* became frequently associated with the "latter stages of Beatlemania and the incipience of hallucinogenic culture" (Ripp 247–48).

Media attention during this time centered on the popularity of *The Lord of the Rings*, especially among young people in their late teens and early twenties, instead of on the work itself. Although many readers of all ages were actually reading Tolkien's novel, reporters and reviewers focused almost exclusively on what they perceived as the crazy obsessiveness of young people's attraction to it. In a *New York Times Magazine* article typical of the time, Philip Norman reported that a Berkeley campus bookstore manager said, "This is more than a campus craze; it's like a drug dream." Norman continued:

> In the U. S. hobbits have quite replaced Salinger and Golding as "in" reading. Tolkien seems to promote a mild kind of intellectual hooliganism. But his supporters argue (overwhelmingly) that, on the contrary, it does everyone good to stay in the Tolkien world, where things are still green; there is hope for people and pleasantness. (101)

As many since have noted, the interest of young, rebellious, and radically thinking Americans in a book by an elderly British Oxford don who was devoutly Catholic and never visited the United States seemed not only puzzling but even phenomenal. Ripp poses a likely explanation for this appeal:

> For young readers inured to witnessing the effects of harsh reality all around them—whether war abroad or social conflict at home—it is fundamentally predictable that they should have flocked by the millions to Tolkien's fantastic vision of a world not simpler, but more pure and more mysterious. A world in which Tolkien's own experience of World War I was translated into a high valuation of "fellowship," deep satisfaction in simple pleasures, a hatred of mechanization, and a delight in untainted natural and artistic beauty. It is indeed perfectly logical that Tolkien's values would resonate with the college generation of the 1960s. (268)

Although many young people, especially in the United States, enthusiastically embraced *The Lord of the Rings*, closer attention to sales figures and book reviews indicates that Tolkien's novel also gained wide readership among other audiences, including such older literati as the eminent poet W. H. Auden and the novelist and philosopher Iris Murdoch. From early in its history, Tolkien's work was also well received among readers in the science fiction community (Anderson, "Mainstreaming" 301).

Yet, much as the works of Charles Dickens a hundred years earlier had earned their author during his lifetime unprecedented popularity among both well-read literati and commonly educated readers but not always among other writers and critics, so too *The Lord of the Rings* secured Tolkien both widespread acclaim among varied populations and mixed response from literary critics. Where earlier fantasy writers, such as William Morris and George MacDonald, had the support of literary communities to lend credibility to their works, early critical response to *The Lord of the Rings* was divided. Some reviewers praised *The Lord of the Rings* for its unique mixture of heroic perspectives and rustic philosophies; others simply could not get past its being "something like half a million words in length, unabashedly, willfully archaic in style, and thematically fixated on sacrifice and loss" (Ripp 247). Many critics reacted with suspicion to an imaginary world in which goblins, elves, wizards, and little people with furry feet battled one another in a war between good and evil. They regarded Tolkien's work not only as simplistic but also as intentionally escapist and thus unworthy of serious literary study. The excessive length of *The Lord of the Rings*, its fictive critical apparatus, invented languages, and "strange combination of extreme conservatism and mythic recasting of modern dilemmas" (245–46) added to their confusion.

As heated as some early debates over the literary value of *The Lord of the Rings* became, and the question is still heated in some circles today,[8] Tolkien's novel is now generally ranked among the most influential works of the twentieth century. This status results from the popular phenomenon it generated, its central role in the development of the genre of modern fantasy literature, and its powerful juxtaposition of the medieval past and the modern present. Although other prominent twentieth-century authors—George Orwell, William Golding, and John Steinbeck, to name a few—incorporated medieval themes and conventions into some of their fiction, they were not medievalists by profession. As a medievalist, Tolkien was "deeply conscious of the strong continuity between that heroic world and the modern one" (Shippey, *J. R. R. Tolkien* xxviii), unlike other authors who employed medieval conventions as tools convenient for their modern purposes but not as inseparable parts of that purpose.

Like *Beowulf*, the Old English poem he studied so deeply, *The Lord of the Rings* is at its heart a "work of mediation," whose purpose is to reconcile "what appear to be incompatibles: . . . escapism and reality, immediate victory and lasting defeat, lasting defeat and ultimate victory" (xxxii). The role of monsters, the relationship between fate and free will, the centrality of personal honor, and the burdens of ancestral heritage are among the features of many medieval texts that find their modern response in *The Lord of the Rings*. By anchoring the work in such mythic and historical traditions, Tolkien imbues his secondary world with a veracity of cultural experience from our own real, primary world that most earlier fantasists lacked. In the world of Middle-earth described in *The Lord of the Rings*, he "did not reject a tradition, but transformed it into something so new that the act of its forging obscured the materials used. Tolkien's legendarium speaks eloquently of his century to our own, and his meditations on triumph and loss are only made more, not less, applicable by their mythic sheen" (Mortimer 127). Tolkien's innovative use of ancient and medieval constructs in his fantasy epic contributed much to its tremendous response from readers, but it was his unusually moving integration of medieval conventions with modern perspectives that rapidly made *The Lord of the Rings* a foundational classic.

In our politically and personally complex world of the twenty-first century, as in the twentieth century in which it was written, the connections embedded in

The Lord of the Rings between the medieval and modern worlds come vividly alive to readers exposed to any number of national and international discussions about the uses and misuses of power, the existence of evil, the necessity of self-sacrifice, the protection of beloved homelands, the collaboration of untraditional allies, the nature of good, and the meaning of friendship. Arguing that *The Lord of the Rings* deserves consideration as a modernist work alongside the works of authors such as T. S. Eliot and James Joyce, Patchen Mortimer explains that Tolkien "faces the horrors of his age, especially the ravages of war, head on. He examines the modern condition as effectively as any laconic Hemingway protagonist. His use of fantasy is not escapist, but a strategy for articulating the awful and inexplicable" (121). Despite critics who viewed the medieval context surrounding Tolkien's work as archaic and irrelevant to the concerns of modern people, recent studies[9] find *The Lord of the Rings* rich with such modernist concerns as the quest for identity, passive resistance as an answer to violence, and the impact of human ambition on the natural world.

Tolkien's works, *The Lord of the Rings* in particular, are important not only for the connections they make between medieval and modern concepts but also for their contribution to the development of modern fantasy literature. In fact, while many authors before Tolkien wrote works of fantasy, today it is widely acknowledged that the modern "literary genre of fantasy for adult readers emerged only after the success" of *The Lord of the Rings* and that it "provided both the theoretical and the literary underpinnings of the genre" (Ringel 160). Tolkien's attention to detailed world building, including maps, invented languages, and internal mythologies, set the example for later fantasy works. As Raymond Feist, a best-selling fantasy author, confirms, *The Lord of the Rings* serves as "the touchstone against which all of us in the fantasy field are struck to test our mettle" (7). Where earlier works managed story lines in which magic was powerful and fantastical creatures were frequent, modern works following Tolkien are expected to offer plausible rationales for the existence and use of such elements. Even more significant, modern fantasy literature after Tolkien is required to go beyond stories of witches and unicorns to "reveal not just the reality behind the appearances, but the ultra-reality behind the reality, . . . the meaning of human life and our presence on the planet" (Flieger, "What Good" 221).

In the end, leaving aside all discussions of Tolkien's popular achievements, academic merits, intricacies of publication history, and modern or medieval concerns, the attraction of *The Lord of the Rings* likely rests most solidly on the kind of book it is—the kind of book many people read multiple times, shed tears over, give as special gifts to family, and lend to friends freely and with excitement. This book, often identified as the most popular and influential of the twentieth century, carries a bankable mass appeal that fills commercial bookshelves with other works vying for even a small share of Tolkien's reward. Yet, for most of us readers, scholars, and teachers who so deeply cherish *The Lord of the Rings*, Tolkien's work brings about the "[f]ar more powerful and poignant . . .

effect in a serious tale of Faërie" that occurs in "such stories when the sudden 'turn' comes [and] we get a piercing glimpse of joy, and heart's desire, that for a moment passes outside the frame, rends indeed the very web of story, and lets a gleam come through" (Tolkien, "On Fairy-stories" 87).

Editions

The Lord of the Rings

Initially, Tolkien had planned *The Lord of the Rings* to be published as a single volume along with a second volume containing much of the mythological material that later became incorporated into *The Silmarillion*. However, even though he viewed his sequel to *The Hobbit* as a single work consisting of six books, his original publisher, George Allen and Unwin, published it from 1954 to 1955 as three volumes to lower printing costs. The three-volume format quickly caused Tolkien's fantasy to be inaccurately identified as a trilogy, a classification modern scholars still seek to correct. The tradition of printing *The Lord of the Rings* as three volumes continues, even though one-volume editions are now also commonly published. Today, all of Tolkien's works are published by HarperCollins in Britain and Houghton Mifflin in the United States. In addition to publishing separate editions of *The Lord of the Rings*, both publishers have agreements to publish Tolkien's works with several trade and mass-market publishers or subsidiary companies, such as Ballantine, Del Rey, and Mariner.

The complex publishing history of *The Lord of the Rings*, along with Tolkien's "concern for the textual accuracy and coherence of his work" (Hammond and Scull, "Note" xix), has led to several editions, revised editions, and a wealth of impressions or reprints. These feature different redactions that attempt to revise inconsistencies found by Tolkien himself or brought to his attention by readers, as well as to correct errors made in the printing process. Similar changes were made after Tolkien's death by his son Christopher and later editors. As one researcher notes, the minor discrepancies among various editions and printings of *The Lord of the Rings* "arise in part from the conditions of the publishing and printing industries in the 1950s and subsequent decades, but the unfamiliarity of Tolkien's invented languages, landscapes, and peoples coupled with his habit of tinkering endlessly with details on his writing have added to the difficulties" (Oberhelman 640).

Following his father's death in 1973, Christopher Tolkien assumed responsibility for maintaining the textual integrity of his father's work and assisted in preparing the second edition, revised impression. Many scholars in the United States cite this three-volume version, published in hardback format by Houghton Mifflin in 1987, as the standard edition for *The Lord of the Rings*. Apart from some minor corrections in a few later printings, those who consider this the most definitive version argue that it remains the final primary authority for Tolkien's editorial intentions because it represents the emendations and corrections overseen directly by Tolkien himself before his death.

Another important version of *The Lord of the Rings* is the fiftieth anniversary edition, closely supervised by Christopher Tolkien but prepared by Wayne G. Hammond and Christina Scull, preeminent scholars of historical and bibliographic matters related to Tolkien and his works. Published in 2004 and corrected in 2005, with several reprintings since then, the fiftieth anniversary edition appears in both one- and three-volume formats. It contains "between three and four hundred emendations [that] have been made following an exhaustive review of past editions and printings" (Hammond and Scull, "Note" xviii).[10] The intention of those involved in its preparation was to compile all corrections from the many printed versions and from Tolkien's various hand-corrected typescript copies to construct a text as close as possible to what Tolkien himself would have expected in a definitive edition of his work.

Although constructing definitive modern editions of literary works from all historical time periods has been a laudable professional pursuit, recent discussion of contemporary editorial practice has called into question the usefulness and reliability of such standard editions. Some criticize standard editions for homogenizing texts in ways that may occlude variants essential for certain types of examination, particularly in the case of modern texts for which multiple manuscript revisions may exist. The value of texts that reflect changes in authorial perspective over time has been discussed regarding authors such as Tolkien. The extended time throughout which he wrote *The Lord of the Rings* and revised the mythological works in his legendarium affords significant opportunities for analysis of the evolution of his views and intentions.

The teachers surveyed to prepare this volume indicate that editions used for classroom purposes vary widely. In fact, no single edition or reprinting of *The Lord of the Rings*, in one or three volumes, is considered standard for college courses. Instead, the surveys confirm that teachers typically assign any number of inexpensive and widely available trade and mass-market editions of *The Lord of the Rings*. Although sometimes respondents noted that they select certain versions to avoid cover designs that feature movie actors or poorly conceived images, the surveys show plainly that teachers' choices of editions are based largely on cost to students and bear no relevance to course content or pedagogical approach.

Further complicating the issue of which version of *The Lord of the Rings* best serves teachers is the recent rise of e-books. Reports show that e-book sales continue to increase among all populations, including college students. Since the fiftieth anniversary edition of *The Lord of the Rings* is now commonly available in several print formats and is the only version currently available as an e-book, the present collection keys its references from *The Lord of the Rings* to the one-volume version of this edition.[11] Supporting this decision is the fact that the 1987 second edition, revised impression, in hardback, which was long considered the standard for scholarship, is no longer in print.

The Hobbit

Tolkien said that the genesis of *The Hobbit* began when he was grading examination essays, probably in 1928, and suddenly its first line came into his head: "In a hole in the ground there lived a hobbit" (Carpenter, *J. R. R. Tolkien* 181). He scribbled this line on a page left blank by a student, which he tucked away until he later began to craft it into a story for his children. When *The Hobbit* was published in 1937, Tolkien neither planned to write a sequel nor had he yet imagined its connection to various mythological materials he had been working on intermittently for nearly twenty years. He expected *The Hobbit* to be a single, discrete work of children's fantasy and was surprised by its dramatic and immediate success—its first printing in Britain sold out in about three months. Such reader response caused him to write in a 1937 letter to his publisher, "At the moment I am suffering like Mr Baggins from a touch of 'staggerment'" (*Letters of J. R. R. Tolkien* 24).

Setting into motion a chain of publications that would eventually lead to the massive worldwide interest in Middle-earth that continues today, the success of *The Hobbit* motivated Allen and Unwin to request a sequel. This sequel, of course, grew into *The Lord of the Rings* and outgrew the genre of children's fantasy that characterized *The Hobbit*. Yet, in the process of writing *The Lord of the Rings*, Tolkien felt compelled to reconsider parts of *The Hobbit*. As a result, he substantially revised the portion of the text involving Gollum for the 1951 second edition of *The Hobbit* to make it fit new material in its longer sequel.[12]

After several later editions and corrected reprintings, the basic text of *The Hobbit* has remained relatively stable, and its publication history is much less complex than that of *The Lord of the Rings*. Various anniversary versions of *The Hobbit* have been released, which usually include its original illustrations by Tolkien himself and a lengthy foreword by Christopher Tolkien concerning the history of his father's text. Most recently, a seventy-fifth anniversary edition of *The Hobbit* in a digital format incorporates not only Tolkien's original illustrations but also pages from his manuscripts and audio content of his reading or singing portions of the text.

The edition scholars consider the most definitive in matching Tolkien's intentions, however, is *The Annotated Hobbit*, compiled and edited by Douglas A. Anderson. First published in 1988 and then revised and expanded in 2002, it documents Tolkien's sources and influences, the history of corrections and changes to the manuscripts, and a host of reference material on the work's historical context. While Anderson's text is not commonly used in college classrooms because its illustration-rich format requires additional printing expense, it has quickly become the standard for references to *The Hobbit* in scholarship.

Like *The Lord of the Rings*, *The Hobbit* is available in a variety of inexpensive trade and mass-market editions. Overall, teachers responding to the survey for the present work based their choice on availability and cost, even though a few preferred a printing that features cover art by Tolkien.

The Silmarillion *and Other Works from the Legendarium of Middle-earth*

The Hobbit and *The Lord of the Rings* present stories from the history of Tolkien's subcreated world of Middle-earth, which itself is surrounded by a larger mythological history or legendarium that Tolkien constructed over more than sixty years. A few of the individual stories in this legendarium originated early in his life and reached relative completion without substantial alterations in focus, structure, or thematic character. However, most of his mythological tales include portions that he struggled to bring to definitive form throughout his life, often radically revising or even abandoning them later. Some of these works are composed as prose narratives, others appear as poetry, and still others are recorded in annalistic form or as scribal notes. A few stories are rendered into both poetry and prose. The immense mythopoeic[13] structure that Tolkien worked to create grew from his desire to establish "a body of more or less connected legend, ranging from the large and cosmogonic, to the level of romantic fairy-story—the larger founded on the lesser in contact with the earth, the lesser drawing splendour from the vast backcloths—which I could dedicate simply to: to England; to my country" (*Letters of J. R. R. Tolkien* 144).

Tolkien initially planned to publish his mythology at the same time as *The Lord of the Rings*, but only a handful of selections from these works were published during his lifetime. The scope of the works, the numerous manuscripts and pages of scribbled notes, and his frequent changing of material when new inspiration arose made daunting the task of unifying the various stories, legends, and mythologies into a cohesive form. Yet, after his death, his son set out to accomplish exactly that. With the assistance of Guy Gavriel Kay, Christopher Tolkien gathered, compiled, and edited his father's notes and stories "to work out a single text, selecting and arranging in such a way as seemed . . . to produce the most coherent and internally self-consistent narrative" (*Silmarillion* viii; foreword). This work was published in 1977 as *The Silmarillion*.

Later scholars sometimes criticize the choices Christopher Tolkien made to bring a cohesive narrative shape to the materials his father had left in varying and sometimes opposing stages of development in his precomputerized era. Yet the value of *The Silmarillion* to the body of Tolkien's work cannot be disputed. Most teachers surveyed for this project assigned at least portions of *The Silmarillion* in courses designed primarily around Tolkien's works. Those seeking detailed information about the choices Christopher Tolkien made when constructing *The Silmarillion*, as well as alternative possibilities he might have made, are advised to consult Douglas Charles Kane's *Arda Reconstructed: The Creation of the Published* Silmarillion.

Apart from the stories published in *The Silmarillion*, other collections of Tolkien's writings about the mythological and cultural history of his invented world are useful to teachers, students, and scholars. The most significant of these is the twelve-volume *History of Middle-earth*, published between 1982 and 1996 and edited by Christopher Tolkien, which gathers together and explicates details from Tolkien's drafts, revisions, and notes on Middle-earth's mythology, legends, and history. David Bratman describes this impressive achievement in the *J. R. R. Tolkien Encyclopedia* as a "longitudinal study of the development and elaboration of Tolkien's legendarium through his transcribed manuscripts, with textual commentary by the editor" ("History" 273). Although material related to the development of *The Hobbit* is not represented in *The History of Middle-earth*, these volumes provide a treasure trove for uncovering the development of Tolkien's thoughts and authorial choices as his works progressed. Because of its length and complex critical apparatus, only a few teachers surveyed used this work in courses on Tolkien. When teachers included *The History of Middle-earth* in their syllabi, most often they chose the first volume, *The Book of Lost Tales, Part I*, alone or sometimes paired with the second volume, *The Book of Lost Tales, Part II*. Yet even teachers who omitted *The History of Middle-earth* from their syllabi often reported using excerpts from it to expand class discussions or enhance their lectures. A particularly useful resource for navigating the work is the *History of Middle-earth Index*, published by HarperCollins in 2002 and reissued in 2010. This thirteenth volume integrates the indexes from the first twelve into one large index.

Stories from Tolkien's larger legendarium have also been published as single-volume texts. In 1980, Christopher Tolkien published a volume by his father titled *Unfinished Tales of Númenor and Middle-earth*. Although much of the material in this collection is reproduced in the *History of Middle-earth* volumes, a number of teachers surveyed included *Unfinished Tales* in their courses because it offers highly readable and relatively cohesive versions of several essential stories from Tolkien's mythological material, even though Tolkien never completed these texts to his satisfaction. In 2007, Christopher Tolkien published *The Children of Húrin*, which collects various versions of material previously published in *The Silmarillion*, *Unfinished Tales*, and *The History of Middle-earth* in what many consider Tolkien's most tragic tale. Several teachers reported that they incorporate this text into courses on Tolkien because they appreciate the pedagogical benefits of including a shorter but fully developed and self-contained narrative that relates a straightforward chronology of events.

Works of Short Fiction

Although none have achieved recognition approaching that of his major works on Middle-earth, Tolkien also wrote short works of fantasy fiction for children.

While the surveys reported that these stories are not often taught in college courses, teachers wishing to consider the breadth of his corpus may find helpful brief descriptions of his stories for children.

Roverandom was written in the mid-1920s but not published until 1998, when it was edited by Scull and Hammond. It has remained available in several trade formats ever since. This illustrated story by Tolkien tells of a dog named Rover who is turned into a toy by a wizard and who undertakes a series of adventures to earn his way back to becoming a real dog again. *Roverandom* is the only text for young children to be collected with other short works by Tolkien in the expanded 2008 version of the collection *Tales from the Perilous Realm*. Another story he told to his own children, *Mr. Bliss*, was written probably in 1928 and first published in 1982. Appearing in an illustrated manuscript housed at Marquette University, *Mr. Bliss* tells a whimsical and ironic story of the eccentric Mr. Bliss, who has a penchant for wearing very tall hats, finds a creature called a girabbit living in his garden, and experiences trying encounters with both human beings and animals. This text was republished by HarperCollins in 2011 in a new trade paperback format. *The Father Christmas Letters*, first published in 1976, is a lavishly illustrated work featuring images of letters that Tolkien, in the persona of Father Christmas, wrote to his children between 1920 and 1943. Edited by Baillie Tolkien, Christopher Tolkien's second wife, the revised edition published in 1999 as *The Letters from Father Christmas* contains materials not previously published. A further revision of this text, published in 2004 and reprinted several times since, generally is considered the most complete edition.

Tolkien also wrote several short works not strictly for children that are sometimes taught in Tolkien courses. Among these, *The Adventures of Tom Bombadil* is the only text directly related to Middle-earth. In this collection of sixteen poems by Tolkien, only the first poem, from which the collection takes its title, and the second, "Bombadil Goes Boating," feature the character who saves the hobbits from Old Man Willow in *The Fellowship of the Ring*. The remaining pieces are short poems written by Tolkien on a variety of subjects in several styles, including three excerpted from *The Lord of the Rings*.[14] *The Adventures of Tom Bombadil* was first published in 1962 under Tolkien's direction and has been reprinted several times since. When it is assigned, teachers generally use the version found in one of the popular collections of Tolkien's shorter works.

In contrast to *The Adventures of Tom Bombadil*, four of Tolkien's short works regularly appear in courses. Even though these works have no direct connection to *The Lord of the Rings* or Middle-earth, they present themes such as Faërie, magic, the nature of heroism, the consequences of pride, and the tragedies of conflict and war. These works are *Farmer Giles of Ham*, *Smith of Wootton Major*, "The Homecoming of Beorhtnoth Beorhthelm's Son," and "Leaf by Niggle."

Written in the 1930s and first published in 1949, *Farmer Giles of Ham* tells the humorous story of a farmer who becomes a hero and eventually king. This novella-length story set in a time long ago and in a fantasy land evocative of medieval Britain features a conniving dragon named Chrysophylax and a talking dog named Garm. The fiftieth anniversary edition of this work, edited by Scull and Hammond in 1999, is the most complete and reliable. Along with the text in two stages of its development, it contains Tolkien's fragmentary notes for a never-completed sequel to the story.

Tolkien began work on *Smith of Wootton Major*, the last of his works to be completed and published before his death, in 1964 and published it in 1967. It is the story of a boy who swallows a fairy star in a slice of cake during a community celebration and grows up to encounter some of the perils and marvels of the realm of Faërie. This text, which Tolkien described as "an old man's book, already weighted with the presage of 'bereavement'" (*Letters of J. R. R. Tolkien* 389), offers a poignant reflection on the nature of imagination and creativity as well as on the relationships between human beings and the Faërie otherworld. The most definitive edition of this text is the 2005 extended one, edited by Verlyn Flieger. It includes Tolkien's early draft of the story, a discussion of its genesis, a chronology of its development, an alternative ending to the story, and a lengthy essay by Tolkien on the nature of Faërie.

In "The Homecoming of Beorhtnoth Beorhthelm's Son," Tolkien constructed a short drama in alliterative verse based on the fragmentary Old English heroic poem *The Battle of Maldon*, which relates a battle between Anglo-Saxons and Vikings in 991. The play is introduced by Tolkien's essay "Beorhtnoth's Death" and followed by another essay titled "Ofermod," an Old English term that means overconfidence or excessive spirit and that can be equated with the concept of overweening pride. Tolkien wrote these three works before 1945 and published them as a unit in 1953; the play was produced as a radio drama in 1954 and 1955. In his commentary on the consequences of misplaced pride, Tolkien critiques the relationships between wartime leaders and those they lead. This work has been reprinted in several collections with other works by Tolkien, but it has not yet been published separately in a widely available edition.

Despite Tolkien's famous comment that he "cordially dislike[d] allegory in all its manifestations" (*Lord* xxiv; foreword), Tolkien's short story "Leaf by Niggle" is commonly considered an allegorical text, or at least a metaphor in fictional form, that expresses Tolkien's views about his own creative process and puts into a narrative form his philosophies on the writing of fantasy. Tolkien wrote this story between 1938 and 1939 and first published it in *The Dublin Review* in 1945. Along with his essay "On Fairy-stories," "Leaf by Niggle" later became part of his 1964 *Tree and Leaf*. To these two works, Christopher Tolkien added the poem "Mythopoeia" in the 1988 revised second edition. In 2001, the volume containing "Leaf by Niggle" was expanded yet again as *Tree and Leaf, Including the Poem "Mythopoeia" [and] "The Homecoming of Beorhtnoth Beorhthelm's Son"* in a version that now serves as the standard edition for these works.

Most of these minor works of fiction appear separately in editions considered definitive by current scholarship, but teachers assign these texts almost exclusively from one of two popular and easily available anthologies of Tolkien's short works: *Tales from the Perilous Realm* and *The Tolkien Reader*. The expanded 2008 edition of *Tales from the Perilous Realm* contains Tolkien's short works *Roverandom*, *Farmer Giles of Ham*, *The Adventures of Tom Bombadil*, *Smith of Wootton Major*, "Leaf by Niggle," and "On Fairy-stories." It features an introduction by Tom Shippey, a notable Tolkien scholar. However, the greatest number of teachers surveyed used the frequently reprinted and widely available *The Tolkien Reader*, a collection that includes "The Homecoming of Beorhtnoth Beorhthelm's Son," "Leaf by Niggle," "On Fairy-stories," *Farmer Giles of Ham*, and *The Adventures of Tom Bombadil* as well as an introduction by Peter S. Beagle, a fantasy writer, titled "Tolkien's Magic Ring."

Although published too late to be recorded in the surveys for this project, three additional works edited by Christopher Tolkien are starting to be incorporated into courses that emphasize the medieval influences on Tolkien's fiction. *The Legend of Sigurd and Gudrún*, published in 2009, presents Tolkien's freely rendered poetic translations of Old Norse legends from the *Saga of the Volsungs* and *The Poetic Edda*. It features an introduction taken from one of Tolkien's lectures as well as Christopher's thorough notes and commentary. Published in 2013, *The Fall of Arthur* offers Tolkien's fragmentary epic poem based on Arthurian legends and a substantial essay by Christopher discussing it in the context of his father's medieval sources. Most exciting to contributors are the teaching possibilities afforded by the 2014 publication of Beowulf: *A Translation and Commentary*. It contains a prose translation of the Old English text that Tolkien completed in 1926, along with two poetic versions of his "The Lay of Beowulf," that he intended to be sung.

Scholarship and Other Nonfiction Works

During his academic career at Oxford, Tolkien held two prestigious appointments: the Rawlinson and Bosworth Professorship of Anglo-Saxon (1925–45) and the Merton Professorship of English Language and Literature (1945–59). These appointments encouraged him to pursue his interests in Old English, Middle English, and Old Norse literature. Much of the scholarship he produced while at Oxford was highly influential during his lifetime and continues to be widely read today. For example, his posthumously published translation of *Sir Gawain and the Green Knight* is currently one of the versions of the Middle English poem most used in undergraduate courses. Further, his essay "Beowulf: The Monsters and the Critics" (first presented as a lecture in 1936) was instrumental in changing the direction of literary criticism on the Old English epic and continues to be one of the most frequently anthologized works of *Beowulf* criticism. More than seventy-five years after it was written, most college students pursuing degrees in Old English language and literature read this essay before they graduate. Similarly, his essay "On Fairy-stories," presented originally as an invited lecture in 1939 and published in 1947, is still considered a foundational work for studying fantasy, myth, and fairy tales.

Teachers who offer courses exclusively on Tolkien's works typically assign some of his scholarship or otherwise incorporate it into lectures and class discussions. Tolkien's translation of *Sir Gawain and the Green Knight* appears in a consistently reprinted volume of his medieval translations, *Sir Gawain and the Green Knight, Pearl, and Sir Orfeo*, edited by Christopher Tolkien and first published in 1975. This work provides highly readable translations of these three Middle English poems.

Most essential to teachers are Tolkien's essays "Beowulf: The Monsters and the Critics" and "On Fairy-stories." Although teachers most commonly use the text published in *The Tolkien Reader*, which is the version cited throughout the essays section of this volume, the definitive edition of "On Fairy-stories" used by scholars is the 2008 version edited by Verlyn Flieger and Douglas A. Anderson as *Tolkien: "On Fairy-stories."* The most comprehensive edition of Tolkien's "Beowulf: The Monsters and the Critics" is titled Beowulf *and the Critics*. While "On Fairy-stories" appears in the popular collections of Tolkien's short works, "Beowulf: The Monsters and the Critics" appears mainly in specialized anthologies of Old English scholarship. As a result, teachers most often assign the version in *"The Monsters and the Critics" and Other Essays*, edited by Christopher Tolkien. Published in 1983 and frequently reprinted, this collection offers seven essays by Tolkien that are relatively accessible to general readers. In addition to "Beowulf: The Monsters and the Critics," it contains Tolkien's lectures and essays "On Translating Beowulf" (published in 1940), "English and Welsh" (a 1955 lecture published in 1963), "On Fairy-stories," "A Secret Vice" (a 1931 lecture), "Sir Gawain and the Green Knight" (a 1953 lecture), and "Valedictory Address to the University of Oxford" (a 1959 lecture).

Translations

Tolkien's major works have been published in more than fifty languages. Some texts occur in multiple versions of the same language—for instance, at least nine Russian translations of *The Lord of the Rings* exist. Other languages his works have been translated into are Armenian, Basque, Chinese, Dutch, Esperanto, Faeroese, Finnish, French, German, Greek Indonesian, Latvian, Macedonian, Portuguese, Serbian, Spanish, Swedish, Thai, and Turkish. In addition, *The Lord of the Rings* and *The Hobbit* appear in Latin, Middle English, Quenya, and Sindarin. Both *The Lord of the Rings* and *The Hobbit* are also available in braille.[15]

The Instructor's Library

Instructors also may benefit from other materials commonly regarded as essential to the study of Tolkien and his works. This selective list recommends the resources that survey respondents offered as most useful for teaching and studying *The Lord of the Rings* or the larger contexts of Tolkien's corpus. It summarizes materials that meet the varied needs of both experienced and novice teachers. Book-length works and collections are preferred over individual essays simply because they generally cover topics more comprehensively. Also, while few teachers in this century can be completely unaffected by the influences of popular culture on contemporary response to *The Lord of the Rings*, the works included here focus on Tolkien's literary texts rather than on their adaptations in other media.

Historical and Biographical Resources on Tolkien's Life and Times

Researchers have available several crucial sources for considering Tolkien's life experiences and the historical contexts in which these experiences developed. *The Letters of J. R. R. Tolkien*, edited by Humphrey Carpenter with the assistance of Christopher Tolkien, contains 354 letters from Tolkien to his friends, family, publishers, colleagues, and fans. Although more recent biographical efforts have been published, Carpenter's 1977 *J. R. R. Tolkien: A Biography* remains the definitive study of Tolkien's life, largely because of Carpenter's access to private papers that no editor since has been granted.

Works discussing the geography and landscapes of the Britain in which Tolkien lived offer insights into his ideas as well as into his fictional geography of Middle-earth. Among those commonly cited as most useful are *The Roots of Tolkien's Middle Earth* and *Tolkien's Oxford*, both by Robert S. Blackham. These picture books provide past and present-day photos along with chronological text detailing places from Tolkien's life. Alternatively, teachers wishing for images related to Tolkien's life in Oxford may consult online "JRR Tolkien's Oxford," which employs interactive panoramic photographs of places in Oxford well known to Tolkien in conjunction with a time line of events in his life.

Despite a variety of available approaches to Tolkien's life, the secondary studies most noted by survey respondents focus on his experiences in World War I. Foremost of these is John Garth's *Tolkien and the Great War: The Threshold of Middle-earth*, which details the ways in which Tolkien's experiences as a second lieutenant in the British army influenced the characters and events in his literary world. Another frequently cited resource, Janet Brennan Croft's study *War and the Works of J. R. R. Tolkien* not only documents connections between Tolkien's war experiences and his fiction but also includes particularly valuable chronologies of war-related events in his life and the lives of his family members.

Also important for biographical study of Tolkien is his involvement with the Inklings. An informal group of male writers and scholars loosely associated with the University of Oxford, the Inklings met regularly between 1930 and 1949 to discuss primarily works of fantasy fiction written by their members.

Most famous among the Inklings were Tolkien, C. S. Lewis, Charles Williams, and Owen Barfield, though several others were regular members or occasional visitors over the years the group met. Drafts of works such as *The Lord of the Rings*, Lewis's Narnia books, and Williams's *All Hallows' Eve* were read and critiqued at Inklings meetings. While a number of studies explore the relationships among the personalities, literary works, and chronological events associated with the Inklings, the works most immediately accessible for this facet of Tolkien's life are *The Inklings: C. S. Lewis, J. R. R. Tolkien, Charles Williams, and Their Friends*, by Carpenter; *Tolkien and C. S. Lewis: The Gift of Friendship*, by Colin Duriez; and *The Company They Keep: C. S. Lewis and J. R. R. Tolkien as Writers in Community*, by Diana Pavlac Glyer. Carpenter's 1978 study, though early, remains one of the standard explorations of the Inklings overall, while Duriez's work focuses specifically on the friendship between Tolkien and Lewis that grew out of the interactions within the group. Glyer's 2007 investigation examines the ways in which Inkling writers such as Tolkien knit together a larger community experience through similarities in writing practices.

Reference Works

Several works published in the first decade of this century provide particularly helpful reference materials for the study of *The Lord of the Rings* and other works by Tolkien. Published in 2006, the *J. R. R. Tolkien Encyclopedia: Scholarship and Critical Assessment*, edited by Drout, offers contributions by more than one hundred scholars that discuss topics fundamental to Tolkien's life, his works, important themes, sources and influences, historical information and contexts, and central works of scholarship on Tolkien. Its concise and clear summaries of material make it a valuable resource for scholars, teachers, and students alike.

Well-researched bibliographic resources documenting Tolkien's works have been available since the early years of the field. *J. R. R. Tolkien: A Descriptive Bibliography*, published in 1993 by Hammond with Douglas A. Anderson, catalogs details of Tolkien's published work. Although not always available because it has been partially superseded by more recent efforts, this work is still essential for those wishing a comprehensive record of Tolkien's publications. Less comprehensive but more available for nonspecialists is Åke Bertenstam's online *A Chronological Bibliography of the Writings of J. R. R. Tolkien*. One of the most inclusive early bibliographies of criticism on Tolkien's works is Judith A. Johnson's *J. R. R. Tolkien: Six Decades of Criticism*, published in 1986. Johnson's work provides annotations of more than 1,600 reviews, articles, essays, books, and other commentary about Tolkien's works. An article published in *Envoi* in 2000 by Drout and Hilary Wynne titled "Tom Shippey's *J. R. R. Tolkien: Author of the Century* and a Look Back at Tolkien Criticism since 1982" lists works of Tolkien criticism between 1982 and 2000. Since 2004, annual bibliographies of scholarship have been published in the *Tolkien Studies* journal.

Without doubt, the most authoritative reference work to date is The Lord of the Rings*: A Reader's Companion*, by Hammond and Scull. The authors present detailed chapter-by-chapter annotations discussing the text's literary and historical influences, relationships to other works and to Tolkien's life, critical problems in the texts, and unusual features of language and style. Even more ambitious and broader in scope, *The J. R. R. Tolkien Companion and Guide*, also by Scull and Hammond, provides extensive description and analysis of topics involving Tolkien and his works. The first volume of this latter work, titled *Chronology*, compiles a massive time line of the details surrounding dates linked both to the composition of Tolkien's creative and scholarly works and to the historical events of his life. The second volume, *Reader's Guide*, is composed of alphabetically arranged essays on central topics such as biographical aspects of Tolkien's life, the history and structure of his works, influences on his writings, and his philosophies and views.

Teachers responding to the survey also recommended several less exhaustive reference works to assist their students. One of these, Michael W. Perry's *Untangling Tolkien: A Chronology and Commentary for* The Lord of the Rings, chronicles more than 1,400 years of the fictional, internal history of the narratives of Middle-earth. The most often cited aid for students, however, was Robert Foster's work, now published under the title *Tolkien's World from A to Z: The Complete Guide to Middle-earth,* which gives alphabetically organized references for characters, places, objects, and events of Tolkien's fictional world. Another work mentioned by survey respondents is *A Tolkien Compass*, edited by Jared Lobdell, a frequently reprinted collection of early articles on Tolkien's fiction suitable for students. Teachers also reported using two other concise reference guides for their students: Colin Duriez's earlier guide, which recently has been replaced by his *J. R. R. Tolkien: The Making of a Legend*, and J. E. A. Tyler's *The Complete Tolkien Companion*.

General information on Tolkien and his works also may be found online. The Tolkien Society in Britain, the oldest Tolkien organization in the world, serves as the main international clearinghouse for news and resources related to Tolkien and his works. Its Web site provides many excellent resources and should always be consulted for accurate general information. Two other quite trustworthy fan-generated sites offer general information that may serve as starting points for research: *The Encyclopedia of Arda*, an illustrated online resource containing more than four thousand entries and several interactive reference tools, and *The Tolkien Gateway*, a wiki-based site written and maintained by volunteers.

Literary Criticism

The enormous output of literary criticism, especially concerning *The Lord of the Rings*, provides a wealth of interpretations and perspectives for understanding Tolkien's work. Among the most notable and frequently referenced literary critical works are two works by Shippey, *The Road to Middle-earth* and *J. R. R. Tolkien: Author of the Century*. In *The Road to Middle-earth*, Shippey examines the sources of, inspirations for, and evolution of Tolkien's works on Middle-earth, especially *The Hobbit* and *The Lord of the Rings*; in *Author of the Century*, he constructs an argument for Tolkien's enduring popularity by analyzing the complex mythological and moral underpinnings of his fiction. In their lists of most used secondary sources, survey respondents included Jane Chance's The Lord of the Rings*: The Mythology of Power*, which explores the modern and mythological implications of the interaction among power, politics, and language in Tolkien's works, and Verlyn Flieger's *Splintered Light: Logos and Language in Tolkien's World*, which analyzes the image of refracted light as a metaphor for the languages, peoples, and history of Middle-earth. Elizabeth A. Whittingham's *The Evolution of Tolkien's Mythology: A Study of the History of Middle-earth* was also commonly cited as a useful work on the development of Tolkien's overall mythology of Middle-earth. Yet the work of literary criticism that teachers most commonly found essential for the study of *The Lord of the Rings* in college classrooms is a collection of classic and more recent essays titled *Understanding* The Lord of the Rings*: The Best of Tolkien Criticism*, edited by Rose A. Zimbardo and Neil D. Isaacs. Another collection of essays popular among teachers is The Lord of the Rings, *1954–2004: Scholarship in Honor of Richard E. Blackwelder*, edited by Hammond and Scull.

Apart from these general works of literary criticism, one of the most common topics for critical exploration of Tolkien's work is the study of his sources and influences. Particularly useful studies mentioned in the surveys that link Tolkien's fiction with medieval works are *The Keys of Middle-earth: Discovering Medieval Literature through the Fiction of J. R. R. Tolkien*, by Stuart D. Lee and Elizabeth Solopova; *Perilous Realms: Celtic and Norse in Tolkien's Middle-earth*, by Marjorie Burns; *Tolkien the Medievalist*, a collection of articles edited by Chance; and *Tolkien's Modern Middle Ages*, edited by Chance and Alfred K. Siewers. Another collection edited by Chance, *Tolkien and the Invention of Myth: A Reader*, contains discussions of classical and medieval influences on Tolkien. *Tolkien and Shakespeare: Essays on Shared Themes and Language*, a collection edited by Croft, explores connections between Shakespeare's plays and Tolkien's fiction.

Languages and Linguistics

In addition to being a fiction writer and medieval scholar, Tolkien was a devoted philologist and linguist who even invented his own languages. In fact, he wrote that his subcreated world of Middle-earth was "*fundamentally linguistic* in inspiration. . . . The invention of languages is the foundation. The 'stories' were made rather to provide a world for the languages than the reverse" (*Letters of J. R. R. Tolkien* 219). Words from or allusions to at least eight of these invented languages appear in *The Lord of the Rings*. The Elvish languages of Quenya and Sindarin were Tolkien's most fully developed linguistic creations, even though he never completed them.

Besides appendix F, "The Languages and Peoples of the Third Age of *The Lord of the Rings*," several valuable resources for the study of Tolkien's languages exist. Although they have been criticized for using outdated approaches, the linguistic works most commonly referenced are *The Languages of Tolkien's Middle-earth*, by Ruth S. Noel, and *A Gateway to Sindarin: A Grammar of an Elvish Language from J. R. R. Tolkien's* Lord of the Rings, by David Salo. Excellent online resources are *The Elvish Linguistic Fellowship* (*E. L. F.*) (Hostetter) and *Ardalambion* sites. Those wishing the most up-to-date linguistic studies will find helpful Carl F. Hostetter's history of the study of Tolkien's invented languages in "Tolkienian Linguistics: The First Fifty Years" as well as publications by various authors and editors from two *E. L. F.* journals featuring advanced studies of Tolkien's languages, *Parma Eldalamberon* and *Vinyar Tengwar*.

Journals and Periodicals

Tolkien Studies, the first peer-reviewed academic journal devoted exclusively to scholarship on Tolkien and his works, had its inaugural edition in 2004. Since then, this annual journal has published new Tolkien scholarship in such varied fields as linguistics, medieval studies, religious studies, and literature as well as book reviews, bibliographies, reference works, and previously unpublished works by Tolkien. *Mallorn*, an annual journal published by the Tolkien Society, and *Mythlore*, a journal published twice a year by the Mythopoeic Society, also publish significant research on Tolkien and his works. Other journals that occasionally publish articles on *The Lord of the Rings* and other works by Tolkien include the *Journal of the Fantastic in the Arts*, *The Lion and the Unicorn*, and *The Journal of Inklings Studies*. Instructors may also find useful for some teaching purposes less scholarly publications such as the Tolkien Society's *Amon Hen* bulletin and the Mythopoeic Society's newsletter *Mythprint* and literary magazine *Mythic Circle*.

Resources for Teaching

Many Web sites feature reliable general information about Tolkien and his works, but a few deserve special mention. Houghton Mifflin's *Lord of the Rings* site offers teacher's guides and curriculum assignments designed primarily for K–12 students that may be profitably adapted for college audiences (http://hmhbooks.com/hmh/site/hobbit/home/LOTR). The Tolkien Society site provides a section for K–12 and college educators. *Waymeet*, a peer-reviewed online project, publishes syllabi, assignments, and other pedagogical materials for teaching Tolkien's works primarily at the college level. Housed on the *MLA Commons*, *Waymeet* began as an outgrowth of the present volume and makes available many resources discussed in the Approaches part of this volume.

Multimedia Aids for Teaching

Abundant resources are available to teachers who wish to expand classroom study of Tolkien's works to include multimedia. Music, audio and video recordings, and visual art created by Tolkien himself exist, and later artists and filmmakers have extended his vision into adaptations of his works. In fact, several survey respondents reported that using nonliterary works associated with Tolkien's fiction made teaching the subject a richer, more interdisciplinary venture for both teachers and students than is possible in most typical literature courses.

Music

Teachers and scholars alike have studied the poems in *The Lord of the Rings* and *The Hobbit*. While some consider the bulk of these poems to be amateurish in style, others acknowledge that, intended as song lyrics, they add to the sense of completeness and authenticity with which Tolkien imbues Middle-earth. For seven poems, Tolkien collaborated with Donald Swann, a British singer and songwriter, to construct the song cycle *The Road Goes Ever On* (1967). Swann wrote the music for six poems from *The Lord of the Rings* and one poem from *The Adventures of Tom Bombadil*. The 1993 third and latest edition of *The Road Goes Ever On* includes several poems by Tolkien along with the original song cycle and two additional songs in a book accompanied by a CD. The book features pages decorated with handsome illuminations and some text in Elvish script by Tolkien, sheet music for each song, notes and commentary, and translations for Elvish lyrics. The CD records Tolkien's recitations of the poems and Swann's performance of each song to piano accompaniment. The music for one song, "Namárië," Galadriel's farewell lament to Lothlórien, is based on a tonal pattern Tolkien himself composed, which has similarities to Gregorian chant. "Namárië" is also one of Tolkien's longest examples of the Quenya language. An online essay titled "Music in Middle-Earth," by Gene Hargrove, discusses issues surrounding the music of Tolkien's peoples and cultures and provides links to several Web sites.

Apart from the musical compositions Tolkien supervised for Swann's collection, numerous other songwriters and performers have sought to capture the airs of Middle-earth by creating their own music for Tolkien's lyrics. Most notable among these is the Tolkien Ensemble, a Danish group who produced four recordings between 1997 and 2005 of their musical interpretations of Tolkien's songs and poems. Unlike other Tolkien-inspired music, the Tolkien Ensemble's project was approved by the Tolkien family and HarperCollins. In bringing this project to completion, the Tolkien Ensemble succeeded in creating a complete body of musical compositions for all songs and poems from *The Lord of the Rings*. Their four recordings were released as a set in 2006 under the title The Lord of the Rings*: Complete Songs and Poems*. Even more prevalent than musicians who compose music for the world of Middle-earth are groups who reference Tolkien's fiction in music set in the modern world. From the instrumental Celtic ballads of Enya to the British hard rock sounds of Led Zeppelin, musicians across the globe have alluded to Tolkien's literary stories in songs they hope will speak to their own audiences. An exhaustive discography of such music may be found online at *The Tolkien Music List*.

Audio and Video Recordings

Audio and video recordings by Tolkien or about him and his works are also available to teachers wishing to supplement more traditional course materials. Foremost among these are a group of recordings made in 1952 by Tolkien himself on a tape recorder (a then-new technology), in which he reads selections from *The Hobbit* and *The Lord of the Rings*. Although these recordings have been released in several formats under various titles, one of the most widely available today is a set of four CDs published as *The J. R. R. Tolkien Audio Collection* (Tolkien and Tolkien).[16] It includes Christopher Tolkien reading a few selections from *The Silmarillion*. Links to a handful of these recordings are included in some e-book formats of the seventy-fifth anniversary edition of *The Hobbit*. Although these are early amateur recordings, the sound quality is reasonably good. Students find particularly captivating Tolkien's dramatic readings of scenes such as Bilbo's encounter with Gollum, the chapter "The Ride of the Rohirrim," and his poem "A Elbereth Gilthoniel" in Sindarin. Professional audio recordings in many popular formats of *The Lord of the Rings* and other works by Tolkien performed by well-known actors are also widely available. The most comprehensive list for ordering Tolkien's works recorded by himself or by others may be found online at *LearnOutLoud.com*.

A wealth of other digital materials by or about Tolkien's life and works now exists online. Video and audio lectures and documentaries related to Tolkien studies are available from *LearnOutLoud.com*, both free and for purchase in several popular downloadable formats. In addition, by searching materials on *YouTube*, teachers can find not only the expected host of ubiquitous (though often well-constructed and informative) slide presentations created by fans but also important archival footage of several interviews in which Tolkien discusses his life and writings.

Visual Aids

A large number of visual aids are available to complement classroom discussions of Tolkien's literary works. Many photographs of Tolkien at various points in his life, of his family, and of places important to him are viewable on several Web sites found easily through any common search engine. Teachers frequently use such photographs to portray the personal character of Tolkien.

While crafting his stories into literature is obviously Tolkien's primary achievement, he was a quite competent visual artist who deeply enjoyed drawing and painting scenes, especially landscapes, from his works. Original illustrations exist for much of his fiction; and, for several topics from *The Lord of the Rings* and *The Hobbit*, we have multiple versions that show changes in his thinking about his stories over time. *J. R. R. Tolkien: Artist and Illustrator*, by Hammond and Scull, provides a comprehensive study of Tolkien's art. Illustrated with many color plates, their examination of his visual creativity discusses the history and development of images he created in connection with *The Hobbit* and *The Lord of the Rings* as well as works he did in his youth, drawings for his children's picture books, and the many heraldic patterns he created for the noble houses of Middle-earth. Many of these images are reproduced in anniversary versions of *The Hobbit*, including e-book formats of the seventy-fifth anniversary edition. *The Art of* The Hobbit *by J. R. R. Tolkien*, also produced by Hammond and Scull, provides complete and beautifully rendered images by Tolkien for that work. Further, a great many artists have made substantial careers by illustrating Tolkien's works through paintings or drawings. Among the most highly regarded contemporary artists whose works are readily available are John Howe, Alan Lee, and Ted Nasmith.[17]

Charts and Maps

Several survey respondents found especially helpful the maps, genealogies, and charts that Tolkien or his son Christopher created. Because of the care Tolkien took to ensure the accuracy of such materials in relation to his stories, teachers use these tools to highlight his efforts in creating a world as complete and authentic as possible and to organize some of the complex details of Tolkien's world into more easily comprehended visual formats.

Most important among these materials are those that appear in all editions of *The Lord of the Rings*. Survey respondents mentioned most often the ancillary charts of various types compiled by Tolkien or Christopher Tolkien in the text's appendixes, such as time lines, genealogies of important families in the texts, the

Shire calendar, and alphabets for some of Tolkien's invented languages. Similar materials appear in *The Hobbit* and in some editions of *The Silmarillion*.

A highly useful visual resource for studying Tolkien's works is the online *LOTR Project*. Begun by Emil Johansson, a Swedish photographer and chemical engineer, this exhaustively detailed project incorporates several interactive and interrelated areas, including an ever-expanding genealogy and a historical time line of Middle-earth. Eventually, the genealogy portion intends to chart the family histories of Middle-earth in their entirety for every character mentioned by Tolkien. The time line of events spans all four ages of Middle-earth's history and is linked to routes on a map that are color-coded to main characters. A testament to what dedicated Tolkien fans can achieve, the *LOTR Project* further functions as a statistical experiment recording continuously updated data about the populations of Middle-earth according to factors such as race, gender, and even life expectancy.

All editions of *The Lord of the Rings* and *The Hobbit*, as well as some editions of *The Silmarillion*, contain maps of Middle-earth. As many researchers have noted, the verity of Middle-earth was so important to Tolkien when constructing his texts that he spent considerable time and effort plotting out geographic distances and scales; he even revised portions of his texts to match his concepts about the lands of Middle-earth. However, although Tolkien and his son Christopher are largely responsible for drawing the maps appearing in early editions of *The Hobbit* and *The Lord of the Rings*, teachers should be aware that maps have been redrawn by others in several more recent editions of these works. Information on the development and revision process of the original maps for *The Lord of the Rings* in Christopher Tolkien's descriptions appears in the *History of Middle-earth*.[18] Quite a few survey respondents said that they also rely heavily on Karen Wynn Fonstad's *The Atlas of Middle-earth*. For this work, Fonstad, a cartographer, created her own maps and compiled details of Tolkien's Middle-earth geographies into highly readable descriptions. Featuring more than one hundred maps, her *Atlas* contains the most comprehensive set of Middle-earth maps yet published, along with a useful index of all place-names in Tolkien's Middle-earth fiction.

Films

Along with the worldwide readership Tolkien's fiction has gained, *The Lord of the Rings* has been adapted into one of the most successful film sequences in Hollywood's history. The three *Lord of the Rings* films, produced and directed by Peter Jackson and released between 2001 and 2003, were so well received that they not only won seventeen Academy Awards but also hold the current record for the highest-grossing film trilogy (surpassing other popular film trilogies, such as the original *Star Wars* and *The Godfather* films). Many survey respondents use clips from these films in their courses on Tolkien either to dramatize key aspects of his narratives or to point out radical differences between the film version and Tolkien's literary text. While several works of scholarship discuss these adaptations in terms of film studies scholarship, two collections contain studies that consider more directly the relationships between these films and Tolkien's texts: *Tolkien on Film: Essays on Peter Jackson's* The Lord of the Rings, edited by Croft, and *Picturing Tolkien: Essays on Peter Jackson's* The Lord of the Rings *Film Trilogy*, edited by Janice M. Bogstad and Philip E. Kaveny.

Jackson's films have overshadowed other attempts to portray Tolkien's texts on film, but teachers should be aware of earlier films. Ralph Bakshi's 1978 *J. R. R. Tolkien's* The Lord of the Rings used rotoscope technology in combination with animation and live-action footage to tell the first half of Tolkien's story on film. Although critical response to Bakshi's film was mixed, most fans and critics at the time agreed the technology lent the film a stunning and original visual appeal. Unfortunately Bakshi never pursued the sequel to his film to finish the story. A 1980 animated version of *The Return of the King* was produced as a television special by Arthur Rankin, Jr., and Jules Bass. The highly stylized animation of this film marked it as intended for children, much like its predecessor, the 1977 Rankin and Bass version of *The Hobbit*. A simplified version of Tolkien's story, Rankin and Bass's seventy-seven-minute *The Hobbit* was also first released for television. Few survey respondents mentioned incorporating clips from these less popular films into their courses.

NOTES

All citations of *The Lord of the Rings*, unless otherwise noted, come from the one-volume fiftieth anniversary edition (2005).

[1]Walter Hooper once said about C. S. Lewis and Tolkien that "[t]hey merely wrote the sort of books that they liked, which turns out to be the sort of books that many other people like" (Pearce, *Tolkien: A Celebration* 192–93).

[2]While Humphrey Carpenter's biography of Tolkien remains the standard work on Tolkien's life, the details of all known chronological events associated with Tolkien's life appear in Scull and Hammond's *J. R. R. Tolkien Companion and Guide*.

[3]The most comprehensive study of Tolkien's World War I experiences is Garth, *Tolkien*.

[4]Useful discussions of the Inklings may be found in Carpenter, *Inklings*; Glyer.

[5]Manuscripts of *The Hobbit*, *Farmer Giles of Ham*, and *The Lord of the Rings* are preserved in the Raynor Memorial Library Collection of J. R. R. Tolkien's Manuscripts at Marquette University in Milwaukee, Wisconsin. Tolkien's academic works and other literary manuscripts are held by the Bodleian Library at the University of Oxford in Great Britain.

[6]Only the barest outline of the complex publication history of *The Lord of the Rings* is given here to convey some of its essential facts for teachers. Those wishing detailed information are encouraged to consult Hammond and Scull, The Lord of the Rings*: A Reader's Companion*; Scull and Hammond. In addition, an especially useful summary of the work's early publication history within the context of social history appears in Ripp.

An accessible discussion of changes made in the published versions appears in recent editions of *The Lord of the Rings*, in front-matter notes by Anderson and by Hammond and Scull.

[7]The rise of paperback sales in the 1960s and 1970s finds interesting publishing industry parallels today in the rise in sales of digital books, for similar reasons of portability and affordability.

[8]Curry, "Tolkien," provides a lengthy analysis of and defense against the many past and present criticisms that have viewed Tolkien's works negatively.

[9]Apart from Mortimer, quoted above, other important discussions of Tolkien as a modern writer appear in Weinreich and Honegger, vols. 1 and 2.

[10]A complete list of changes made in the fiftieth anniversary edition, as well as the differences between reprintings of this edition, may be found on the Web site of Hammond and Scull at www.hammondandscull.com.

[11]The one-volume version was chosen over that in three volumes because many teachers prefer this format as the most economical for students.

[12]John Rateliff's two-volume *The History of* The Hobbit provides a thorough and detailed history of the work's composition process and publication history. Rateliff's work (undertaken and published with permission from Christopher Tolkien) fills the void left by the omissions of material about *The Hobbit* in *The History of Middle-earth*.

[13]"Mythopoeia," which means "mythmaking," is a term Tolkien was particularly fond of; he explicated its significance in his lengthy poem of the same name. The various stories composing his legendarium reflect his efforts to construct a corpus of mythological tales supported and connected by his mythopoeic vision of the kinds of stories he wished existed in the cultural history of his own country.

[14]The three poems included in this collection and published in *The Lord of the Rings* are "The Man in the Moon Stayed Up Too Late," "The Stone Troll," and "Oliphaunt."

[15]Lists of translations of Tolkien's works into other languages may be found in Scull and Hammond, and online at the Tolkien Library Web site.

[16]Other common titles under which these recordings have been released are *The Tolkien Audio Collection* and *Essential Tolkien CD*.

[17]Lee's art appears in illustrated editions of *The Hobbit* and *The Lord of the Rings*, while Nasmith has illustrated *The Silmarillion*. Howe's art is featured on the covers of several printings of Tolkien's works. Howe and Lee also helped create much of the artwork appearing in Peter Jackson's film adaptations of *The Lord of the Rings*. Information about many other artists popular for their visions of Tolkien's works may be found in Beahm; *Realms*.

[18]Hammond and Scull's The Lord of the Rings*: A Reader's Companion* also provides a useful discussion of the early development of Middle-earth maps (lv–lxvii).

Part Two

APPROACHES

Introduction: Seed of Courage Not So Hidden

Leslie A. Donovan

During its first rise in popularity in the mid-1960s, teachers, particularly in the United States, sought to use *The Lord of the Rings* to advance a wide spectrum of educational objectives. As early as October 1966, an article advocating teaching Tolkien's work was published in *English Journal*, the primary professional publication of the National Council of Teachers of English. "Fantasy in and for the Sixties," by Merle Fifield, an English teacher at Ball State University, concludes its impassioned argument thus:

> Fantasies, like Tolkien's often ignored work, can provide plausible themes for this our brave new world. Admittedly their use would require adults to abandon their own ideal of youth, to accept the young as neither romantic idealists nor practical realists, but rather as sceptical pessimists. But adult failure to make such a sacrifice of faith condemns the next generation to read in boredom and abandons them to live in aimless apathy. (844)

While records are silent about whether Fifield's article helped ignite other teachers of his time to follow his example, several articles about teaching Tolkien's work in United States high schools and colleges were published over the next ten years.[1] The survey data for this volume consistently confirms that teachers today still consider *The Lord of the Rings* an ideal text to prepare students to negotiate our even braver new world of the twenty-first century through the study of literature.

Certainly, most literature sets out to accomplish the same goal: inspiring readers to view their lives differently. Abram Van Engen argues that "literature is important" because "our lives are implicated in the lives we read about" (8, 11). *The Lord of the Rings* is a significant work precisely because readers recognize themselves in its characters and yearn to find their own meaning and purpose through their example. Yet the main difference between other literary works and *The Lord of the Rings* is that Tolkien's narrative offers characters who not only matter to readers but matter in ways that manifest intensely in the classroom. Because of both the nature of this work and the vast community of people for whom it is special in a highly personal way, *The Lord of the Rings* encourages readers to feel that they too matter, and matter profoundly. The contributors in the Approaches section of this volume write about the joys and challenges of teaching a subject that typically generates powerful responses from readers of many different ages, cultures, personal values, and life experiences. Their experiences confirm that Tolkien's text speaks to readers in their seventies and preteens, Republicans and Democrats, neopagans and orthodox Catholics, as well as soldiers, nurses, and computer software engineers. They find that teaching Tolkien to such diverse student populations is dramatically rewarding but also demands specific planning and pedagogy.

Among the challenges teachers face when teaching *The Lord of the Rings* are students' unusual familiarity with the text, the text's length, and students' deeply personal connections to the text. The medieval tenor of the work, with its frequently archaic style and plethora of strange names, combined with Tolkien's invented framework of authorial or scribal intrusions on the story, such as appendixes and a historical introduction to the culture of Hobbits, further complicates the work of teaching *The Lord of the Rings*. Nevertheless, many teachers report that managing such issues leads to their most compelling interactions with students.

Perhaps unique among the unexpected pedagogical experiences for teachers is that most students in courses devoted largely to Tolkien have read *The Lord of the Rings* before such courses ever start. Students, already familiar with the major content, enroll because of their knowledge and appreciation of the text. Such a statement cannot be made of any other commonly studied work of Western literature, except perhaps the Bible. Where most college students register for courses because they are committed to learning new subjects, students sign up for Tolkien courses generally because they are eager to expand old friendships. Although the 2001–03 film versions of *The Lord of the Rings* have attracted some students to Tolkien courses, informal evidence from teachers indicates that most of those courses continue to be populated primarily with students who have read the original books by Tolkien. Many have read *The Lord of the Rings* more than once. Tolkien teachers report that it is common for students to read it at regular intervals in their lives.

Although some teachers hesitate to fit such a lengthy text as *The Lord of the Rings* into a course syllabus containing many other texts, most students do not view the book's nearly 1,200 pages as a burden. Survey respondents noted that their students rarely complain about the amount of reading in Tolkien courses, probably because their prior familiarity with the texts fosters strong levels of comfort with the material and confidence in their understanding of it. Of course, because so many students already know the text, they may sometimes neglect reading assignments. Even with that neglect, their previous investment in *The Lord of the Rings* usually enables them to participate fully in day-to-day classroom activities. Contrary to what might be expected, teachers note that students with extensive prior knowledge so relish the opportunity to study Tolkien's text formally and with others that they rarely fall behind in reading assignments.

Most students have read Tolkien's main works before the course begins, but some enroll mainly because they want a chance to earn college credit for reading the book on which their favorite films are based. The reading load of a Tolkien course can surprise and even overwhelm such students. To counter the extensive reading required, several teachers in this volume require that students read *The Hobbit* and *The Lord of the Rings* before the first day of class. Such a requirement would be unthinkable in any other literature course but seldom meets with objections from students.

In addition, students' previous exposure to Tolkien's work gives teachers the opportunity to foster in-depth discussion earlier than is normally possible in other courses. In most literature courses, teachers must delay such discussion, because students need time to work through new reading material before they can delve deeply into the subject. Survey respondents typically reported that Tolkien students are eager to discuss significant ideas early in the course, even on the first day. Students not only know Tolkien's works before the course starts but also love them deeply and wish to share their delight in them with others. Their abiding love for Tolkien's world tends to exceed the feelings that most other works of literature or popular culture generate in students. They care so much about Middle-earth and its peoples that the challenge for teachers becomes not how to engage them in the subject but rather how to encourage them to view the works objectively and think about them critically. Some survey respondents mentioned that occasionally students are so strongly attached to Tolkien's world that they respond to its details and nuances with an almost fanatical intensity. Many of these students get so passionately caught up in Middle-earth that teachers frequently need to remind them that its events and characters are fictional. Such overenthusiasm and uncritical appreciation can hinder their ability to learn and to accept new perspectives. The challenge for teachers is to find approaches that shift such intensely protective and reactive energy about the subject into new avenues for serious academic inquiry as well as personal reflection. Regardless of the challenges that responses like these pose for teachers, the powerful personal responses of students to *The Lord of the Rings* result in an extraordinary eagerness that makes teaching this subject so rewarding. Students' initial excitement about the people and places of Middle-earth gives rise to a sustained, concentrated engagement with a global community of dedicated readers that extends well beyond the college classroom and select circles of literary critics and scholars. Membership in such a community affords students not only an enriched understanding of Tolkien's works but also a stronger appreciation of literature in general. Robin Hobb, a well-known fantasy writer, describes how studying Tolkien affected her education: "English teachers had sought in vain to instill in me some appreciation for 'literature.' Required reading lists and formulaic book report requirements hadn't done it. But with one shot J. R. R. Tolkien had injected it straight into my heart" (95).

Teachers find that Tolkien's works aid students like Hobb to understand not only the general nature of literature but also the merits of early literary history. Although many students harbor a popular fascination with dragons, knights, and castles, they are often reluctant to study medieval literature in college courses, unless they intend to specialize in the field. They judge such texts to be filled only with archaic beliefs and practices, difficult idioms and language usage, and stereotypical characters. Yet, survey respondents reported that connecting *The Lord of the Rings* to the narratives of early cultures helps teachers make the past less distant and more relevant to their students. When students learn that Tolkien's text derives much of its fabric from a medieval heritage, they more readily begin to appreciate the works of the Middle Ages that Tolkien valued so highly. In addition to establishing for students a bridge to ancient and medieval traditions of literature and culture, Tolkien's works provide insight into the tension between the present and past. *The Lord of the Rings* echoes postmodernist concerns that grapple with "mourning the past while facing the future, and transcribing the modern age with tools of the past" (Mortimer 126).[2] Many survey respondents balance Tolkien's epic motives and medieval tropes with how these speak to the contemporary search for individual identity, the struggle against alienation and despair, and the consequences of industrialism. As Melissa Thomas notes, fantasy texts such as Tolkien's offer teachers "a metaphor for the human condition—[that is] ripe with mythic structures, heroic cycles, and social and religious commentary" (60). Several teachers commented that their students discuss how to apply the lessons of *The Lord of the Rings* to such modern issues as the political abuses of dictators, individual perseverance, human responsibility, greed, racial alliances, and class conflicts. In his essay "On Fairy-stories," Tolkien addresses the attraction of an imagined past for modern people when he asserts that we need not be ashamed

> of preferring not [only] dragons, but horses, castles, sailing-ships, bows and arrows; not only elves, but knights and kings and priests. For it is after all possible for a rational man, after reflection . . . to arrive at the condemnation . . . of progressive things like factories, or the machine-guns and bombs that appear to be their most natural and inevitable . . . products. (81–82)

By offering such a sane response to the experience of both hope and despair, fantasy literature like *The Lord of the Rings* often gives students astounding insights into themselves and their world. Thomas writes, "[W]hat is most important about fantasy, what separates it and frees it from the boundaries of other genres, is that it is an undistilled version of human imagination—momentary worlds and magic that may be at odds with the rational truth, yet continue to reflect our culture and times" (64). Students in Tolkien courses tend to draw sharp parallels between contemporary heroes on the television news and the medieval literary heroes on whom Tolkien modeled some of his Middle-earth characters and about whom he writes that they "found a potent but terrible solution" to their own monsters "in naked will and courage" ("Beowulf" 26). If students can recognize, though not always articulate, the contemporary necessity of reconciling such forces in order for our culture to survive, then it is no wonder that Tolkien's text provides them with such a bright beacon.

Teaching Tolkien's works creates a bond between teachers and students. It is not only students who are passionate about *The Lord of the Rings*, who see themselves in its characters, and who gain knowledge and support from a global community of similarly appreciative readers; teachers share those same experiences. As several of the essays in this volume describe, Tolkien teachers gain a classroom experience like no other through interactions with their students, many of whom can talk about Tolkien's texts with as much confidence and nuance as their teachers. Animated and targeted discussions that grow naturally from a thorough familiarity with the texts as well as advanced and willing critical thinking are commonplace in such courses. Teachers and students come to realize through courses like those discussed in this volume that their own lives and thoughts matter to a larger fellowship of both scholars and general readers; although they themselves may seem insignificant, as in the example of Frodo and his companions, their participation in such a community can exceed all expectations.

Despite the need for uncommon resources and brave new pedagogies, those of us who teach Tolkien come to understand quickly the joys that are possible in such courses. We discover that our first professional dream of sharing the love of one piece of literature and of making a difference in the lives of others is not futile or hopeless. Our hearts leap to find that teaching contains hidden marvels that low salaries and depressing news stories about higher education cannot suppress. Much as the "seed of courage hidden (often deeply, it is true) in the heart of the fattest and most timid hobbit, waiting for some final and desperate danger to make it grow" (*Lord* 140; bk. 1, ch. 8), takes root in Frodo, so too the seeds planted in Tolkien courses can yield fruit that is unexpectedly whole, healthy, and sweet. Such an old, quaint fantasy text of nearly 1,200 pages can achieve precisely that, with a courage that is not so hidden anymore.

NOTES

[1] Articles from this time most relevant to the present discussion are Crossley; Roos; Stanton; Taylor.

[2] On postmodernism in Tolkien's works, see S. Hughes; Nagy, "Medievalist"; Reid and Ford.

The Perils of the Tolkien Course: Reading the Readings

Craig Franson

Teachers of J. R. R. Tolkien's writing face a unique classroom challenge. While all literary works draw students of varied ability and interest, no other works are subject to quite the same combination of cultic appeal and popular appropriation. Students of modernism seldom express outrage when a peer complains that "Ash Wednesday" is a dull poem. Second-language students of Shakespeare rarely show up to class having read all the plays in Korean. High school drama students do not hang posters of Tony Kushner in their dorm rooms, and there is no such thing as a Caryl Churchill fan-fiction site or a *Real Inspector Hound* role-playing game. The same cannot be said of Tolkien. Though I have only once encountered a pair of students who taught themselves Old English after watching Peter Jackson's film version of *The Fellowship of the Ring*, I rarely teach Tolkien's works in a classroom where at least one student does not know a smattering of Elvish. Students in my Tolkien courses frequently have read not only *Beowulf* but also portions of the Eddas and the *Kalevala*. Many have perused Tolkien's essays or letters. Some have read Tom Shippey, Verlyn Flieger, and Patrick Curry. Always a few know Tolkienian adaptations of cartoons, comics, and video games. A handful of students even confess (eventually) to posting fan fiction and playing MERP (Middle-earth Role-Playing).

Students with such intense emotional and intellectual investments guarantee instructors lively classroom discussions, but they also contribute to a classroom dynamic that can become difficult to manage. Driven by a passionate identification with Tolkien's invented world and sometimes prone to digressive elaborations of corpus minutiae, these students can push their classmates into oppositional stances. Before long, the pedagogical space can turn into a rhetorical arena where hostile camps of readers struggle to authenticate their own textual interpretations, using Tolkien's works to reify their ideological practices, reaffirm their cultural values, and advance their social interests. This type of instructional space can be uncomfortable at times, but it can also be enlightening, for the peculiar social dynamic that often forms in the classroom restages in microcosm the contentious scene of Tolkien's historical reception. Moreover, it dramatizes a theme that recurs throughout his writing: the agency and the interactive nature of reading. Thus conflicts between Tolkien's student readers are much more than pedagogical problems to avoid or eliminate; they are also the manifestation of a particular sociohistorical and theoretical problematic—something the cultural historian or critical theorist can analyze, understand, and even harness in the classroom.

In my experience, students with great expertise in Tolkien are rare, yet their enthusiasm and confidence give them an outsized classroom influence. Just as substantial, however, can be the influence of advanced English majors in the room. To the dismay of the first group, students in this second group frequently assert their authority through disparaging remarks about Tolkien's genre fantasy, which they contrast with serious literary classics by authors like Milton or Joyce. Dismissing their laudatory peers as mere fans, the more vehement of these students can become open foes of Tolkien's fiction. To make matters worse, these foes have access to a methodology that gives them a critical edge over the fans. Any time a fan cites a passage from Humphrey Carpenter's biography or from *The History of Middle-earth*, a foe can dismiss the gesture as intentionalism or mere origin hunting. As the classroom factionalizes, students who know Tolkien square off against students who know the discipline.

Caught in the middle is a third group: students who have only passing familiarity with Jackson's films and who thought the class would be a fun diversion and an easy A.[1] They are shocked by their peers' cultic knowledge and off-putting jargon. Expecting the sensationalism of Hollywood or the accessibility of *Harry Potter*, they often balk at the difficulty of Tolkien's writing. When they find what they perceive to be a long, alienating, fragmentary mess of a text, they can grow cool to the whole endeavor. Marginalized by both the freakish fans and the elitist foes, they recuperate their authority by queering any kind of passionate investment. Situating indifference as normal, they can grow more and more distanced even as the larger classroom becomes more and more engaged.

Having these three separate audiences—fans, foes, and self-proclaimed non-freaks—in a single classroom can provide an instructor with the exceptionally demanding challenge of preparing an approach suited to the needs and appetites of each. One option is to give different material to each camp. The fans get the source work and biography they crave, the foes get a historical or critical context into which they can assimilate Tolkien, and the others get a basic critical vocabulary and a chance to dissect popular movies. Teaching becomes a balancing act, and the instructor's key task turns into strategizing about when to deliver which piece of information. Such a classroom is inevitably knowledge-rich, and one can trust that many students will expand their interests and learn much they might never have sought out on their own.

Another approach is to make classroom factionalization itself a subject of critical attention. Rather than ignore or diffuse tension, an instructor can arrest and attend to it, allowing the class to analyze its own disputes. This approach makes the classroom a cultural laboratory, giving students a concrete scene of reception to analyze. Classroom factionalization can dramatize the cultural conflicts that shaped Tolkien's historical reception, giving representative faces to the different programs that have valorized, vilified, and commercialized Tolkien's writing across the last half century. With only a little context and reflection, students come to see their personal reactions to Tolkien's writing as part of a larger historical moment. The fans see their adulation reflected by early proponents, such as C. S. Lewis and W. H. Auden, whose defenses of Tolkien's artistry and moral vision double as principled critiques of modernity (Lewis, "Dethronement"; Auden, "Quest Hero"). The foes see their criticism reflecting positions argued by Edmund Wilson, Raymond Williams, and (more recently) Harold Bloom, whose charges of Tolkien's immaturity, nostalgia, and idiosyncrasy represent an ideological struggle over the English literary canon (Edmund Wilson, "Oo"; Williams; Bloom, *J. R. R. Tolkien* 1–2). Students in the middle see their initial indifference as that of a public conditioned by an entertainment-driven commodity culture—one needing Tolkien's books to be reworked into action films, religious homilies, or political propaganda. At the same time, they come to see the strange classroom conflict in front of them as part of a sociohistorical context that they cannot simply dismiss as a feud between two camps of nerdy college kids. For each group, reading becomes recognizable as a socially conditioned practice, with fairly determinate causes and effects—something, in other words, to be read.

When an instructor adopts this explicitly reflective approach, the act of reading takes on a visible form in every discussion, gaining the kind of density more typical of a course in critical theory. Abstractions like aesthetic perception, textual hermeneutics, cultural identification, and ideological appropriation become palpable things—the matter not just of instruction but also of perception—and the instructor is enabled to teach advanced concepts to students who rarely get to consider them. Students come to see the classroom as a field of cultural conflict in which competing readers struggle to craft three distinct versions of *The Lord of the Rings*: an authorial magnum opus, a complex cultural artifact, and a rollicking adventure story. Construed in this way, these perspectives map roughly onto the classical rhetorical triangle, with each of the factions honing in on a single theoretical component (authorship, textuality, and readership).

In a Tolkien-centered course, such theoretical concerns are matters of no small importance. Tolkien's writing never ceases to interrogate the operations of language and form. Further, his thinking on these matters is more complex than some readers realize. Although many critics note Tolkien's work as a philologist, few note the tangled web of theories that compose his view of philology (see Shippey, *Road*; Flieger, *Splintered*). Working through his scholarship, lectures, and letters, one finds elements that correlate with semiotics, psychoanalysis, folklore, pure sound theory, New Criticism, Russian formalism, and structuralism. His notion that readers half create the meaning of a text links him to aesthetic theories of both Romanticism and poststructuralism.[2] Meanwhile, his concern with the interplay among language, race, and power gives his work resonance with cultural materialism (see esp. Tolkien, "Sigelwara Land" and "English"). How texts are crafted and consumed are questions that recur throughout his writing, the fiction no less than the scholarship. Indeed, the recurrent figure of the Ring instantiates a metafictional reflection across all the novels—one that overlays the narratives with a sustained meditation about how artifacts affect the world, culturally, politically, psychologically, and morally. By focusing on reading conflicts that unfold in the classroom, teachers can bring students inside the very debates that situate and structure all of Tolkien's writing.

The degree to which I foreground the act of reading in my Tolkien course varies greatly, depending not only on the dynamic of a particular classroom but also on the structure of the course. I have taught works by Tolkien in three different college course formats—the theme based survey, the dual- and triple-author course, and the single-author course. In my experience, each takes a different approach. For theme-based surveys, where a single work by Tolkien appears among an assortment of texts, I treat him much as any other author—though, because his major texts are intensely interdependent, I am careful with my choices.[3] In a more intensive, dual- or triple-author course, I foreground the work of reading frequently, situating authors in dialogue so that works by each implicitly respond to the others.[4] Finally, in a course exclusively devoted to Tolkien's works, I treat language and reception theories as integral to all that we study. In these single-author courses, students enter thinking they will learn a little about *The Lord of the Rings*, but they exit having learned a great deal about philology, hermeneutics, deconstruction, and reception aesthetics.

Anytime I teach Tolkien's works in depth, I open with extended consideration of philology, treating both its principles and its institutional history. *The Hobbit* provides a ready framework for lessons on both etymology and medieval literature, and it is easily supplemented with accessible, scholarly articles. Along with these, I always assign Tolkien's "On Fairy Stories" and "Beowulf: The Monsters and the Critics," which we work through carefully, detailing his arguments about the social function of literature and the nature of poetic language. At the same time, I connect our work to the critical practices of Tolkien's contemporaries by situating it within the political and intellectual context of the 1920s through the1940s (Shippey, *Road* 1–27; Tolkien, "Valedictory Address"). Moving into *The Lord of the Rings*, we linger over the framework provided by the foreword and prologue. The foreword stakes out authorial claims regarding the text's proper context and use while inviting readers to extend its "applicability" to new contexts (*Lord* xxiv). The prologue, meanwhile, as an elaborate work of invented scholarship, situates the novel proper as a reassembled text, not unlike *Beowulf*—one that challenges readers to find a lost reality beyond the scope of its representations even as it calls that reality into question by comically overplaying its hand. These documents give us entry to biographical considerations, and we examine carefully both the World War I and World War II contexts of Tolkien's writing, feeling out the extent to which the fiction sustains links (as expression, allegorical representation, and symptom) to his life. We also examine language use by the narrator or narrators and by the characters, seeking the peculiarities of expression through which characters gain identities grounded in an age, class, culture, race, gender, expressive range, objective, and ethos. As we advance into the narrative, I emphasize scenes that add to the theme of reading, reciting, or storytelling. We uncover theories of language and social ideologies implicit in each of these scenes, connecting them to the fictional societies of the narrative and then to historical societies of our own world. We use such scenes as measures of our reading, attempting to situate our critical practices within the logic of the narrative.

My pedagogical approach hinges on these reflective practices. At select moments in the term, we look back through the scenes to ask what needs have been served by all these acts of language, and we look to ourselves to ask what needs are served by our own acts of reading. What are we doing with this textual Ring that has come to us? What is this Ring doing to us each time we try it on? Are we using it to hide ourselves or to dominate others? Is there a will in it, prompting us to read in certain ways? What is the source of that will? The author? an original historical context? our private needs or the needs of our culture? a potent rhetorical trope? And what can it mean that the text wants the Ring to be destroyed?

This reflective work leads us naturally to consider the endless hoards of artifacts that have been made of Tolkien's *The Lord of the Rings* since its publication in the 1950s. So, as my students finish reading the work, we turn to its popular reception. Jackson's films provide a natural starting point for this conversation, since they act as both an adaptation and appropriation of the text. I emphasize the profound differences between film and novel, trying to convey the distance between Tolkien's mid-century countermodernism and Jackson's turn-of-the-century postmodernism. One element I stress is the gothicism of Jackson's vision, which my students typically see as the natural way to represent Tolkien's novels, since they are after all full of monsters, magic, ruins, misty landscapes, and medieval battles. This murky, violent, wraith-filled nightmare, I tell them, has little resemblance to readings from the text's early decades.

To make my point, I lead students through visual representations of Tolkien's world, starting with the outlandish cover art for the first American editions and working through representative selections from the Tolkien calendars.[5] Each image, I argue, is a personal vision but one suited to the expectations and conventions of a particular moment in history. The popular folksy illustrations of the Brothers Hildebrandt and Jimmy Cauty resonate strongly with their context in the mid-1970s, though each views Middle-earth through very different lenses. The Hildebrandts' vivid, blocky, and cartoonish paintings situate Tolkien nostalgically in a childhood world of comic books and Disney films. By contrast, Cauty's brooding, monochromatic drawing sets Tolkien in a bleaker (if also stranger) historical landscape—one filled with piled corpses and framed by teetering towers of goblins. Both visions respond to threats of ascendant communism and a looming atomic apocalypse, yet each makes Tolkien's world do different cultural work. Similarly, the epic realism of Ted Nasmith, the iconic monster styling of John Howe, and the moody landscapes of Alan Lee respond to the shifting cultural and political landscapes of the 1980s and 1990s, just as the sprawling, cinematic productions of Jackson speak directly (if often accidentally) to their post-9/11 context. As the succession of images makes clear, different decades call for different readings, but also different readings call out to one another, developing a complex, cross-cultural, multimedia conversation with history.

In a class devoted significantly to Tolkien's writing, I take several weeks to work students through a succession of these tertiary readings, dropping in short lessons as we move through *The Silmarillion*. My aim is to give students the analytic tools for original archival work on popular applications of Tolkien's writing—a practice that allows them to experience and interrogate "the freedom of the reader" that Tolkien valorizes (*Lord* xxiv; foreword). To do this, I assign an optional research project in which students situate any Tolkien-inspired artifact into a historical framework of their own construction. I urge them to select an artifact no one has studied yet (a video game, action figure, board game, work of fan fiction, even a motif reworked by another novelist, whatever calls out for analysis) and then to situate it in a narrative that tracks how such a reading of Tolkien's work became possible. As an example, I juxtapose two texts that pose a dramatic conceptual problem. We view Jackson's nightmarish depictions of Weathertop, the Paths of the Dead, or Minas Morgul, noting his intense deployment of gothic imagery and horror conventions. Then we view Leonard Nimoy's absurd beach video "The Ballad of Bilbo Baggins," with its campy lyrics and psychedelic sensibilities.[6] How in the world, I ask them, did we get from Nimoy to Jackson?

After discussing the medium, audience, context, and aim of each of these creative readings, I pose my own speculative answer: Led Zeppelin. Moving from the 1969 "Ramble On" to the 1971 "Battle of Evermore," I demonstrate how the iconic band translates Tolkien to speak first to a hippie culture of pastoral folk music and free love and later to a gothic culture of heavy-metal music, existential dread, and mounting fears over the quagmire in Vietnam. While Led Zeppelin is derivative in both their folk and heavy-metal readings, the band amplifies Tolkien's prominence in and beyond both countercultural movements. They help make Tolkien's writing a resource not only for rock-and-roll musicians but also for comic book artists, game developers, and filmmakers. With each of these new readings established, Jackson's now worldwide audience is primed for the cinematic reading Jackson offers.[7]

Although I rarely share it with my students, I take the framing for these intertextual lessons and assignments from a mix of theoretical approaches. These include the dialogical criticism of Roland Barthes, the reception aesthetics of Hans Robert Jauss, and the critical theory of Walter Benjamin—especially as Benjamin has been developed by poststructuralist readers.[8] For a number of reasons, his writing also proves instructive in the larger framing of my Tolkien courses. Not only does Benjamin share some of Tolkien's linguistic presuppositions and critical orientations, he also articulates a theory of the literary work's historical afterlife that helps explain how generations of readers have continued to reactivate and creatively remake Tolkien's fiction, translating it across disparate languages, cultures, and decades, while also transmitting its various readings around the globe.[9]

By turning a critical lens on reading conflicts that develop in the classroom, instructors can prompt illuminating discussions of Tolkien's historical reception and launch student-led explorations of the "tricksy" work of reading. Establishing such a focus also helps sustain long-term participation among student groups. This final advantage is crucial because the unfolding complexity of Tolkien's corpus drives many students into awed passivity. Saturated with veiled allusions, rich with sources, ambiguously connected to philology, conflicted in form and politics, and out of step with normative literary history, Tolkien's writing seems to beg for a master to step in and sort it all out. This demand, akin to what Tolkien called the "purposed domination of the author" (*Lord* xxiv; foreword), finds reinforcement in the publication empire that has amassed around the Tolkien name—an empire that drives scholars to become disseminators of an ever-expanding hoard of arcane lore.[10] Faced with a resistant text and a daunting archive, new students of Tolkien often pressure instructors to relieve their anxiety and resolve their uncertainty. Focusing on the imaginative work of reading, an instructor can arrest this drive toward passivity and bring students into the spirit of Tolkien's writing. Alerting students to the perils of language and the powers of reading, an instructor can prompt them to resist the authorial domination they have been taught to desire—a domination Tolkien's fiction would seek to destroy.

NOTES

[1] In the immediate wake of Jackson's *The Lord of the Rings* film trilogy, many in this third group had deep knowledge of the cinematic texts. Jackson fans memorized Elvish dialogue, tracked online debates, and often read the novels. This group has since grown away from the films, which they now tend to equate to *Harry Potter*, *A Game of Thrones*, or any other cinematic epic fantasy.

[2] For Tolkien on reading, see Rosebury, *Tolkien* 182–92. For poststructuralist resonance, see Curry, *Defending*.

[3] In a general education course on war literature, I taught Tolkien's *Children of Húrin* as a stand-alone text—something I would not recommend. Too reliant on *The Silmarillion*, the novel alienated many students. It also left them too dependent on me to provide them with sufficient background.

[4] Two complementary sets of works, for example, are J. K. Rowling's *Harry Potter* novels and Joss Whedon's *Buffy the Vampire Slayer* television series. Each acts as a historically situated rereading of Tolkien's take on maturation, friendship, morality, modernity, historical agency, catastrophe, and (centrally) death.

[5] Tolkien was appalled by the Ballantine cover of *The Hobbit*, writing of its bizarre vignette, "[W]hat has it got to do with the story? Where is this place? Why a lion and emus? And what is the thing in the foreground with pink bulbs? I don't see how anybody who had read the tale . . . could think such a picture would please the author" (*Letters of J. R. R. Tolkien* 362). For a representative spectrum of images, see *Tolkien's World*. For design images from Jackson's films, see Russell. Other images are widely available on the Internet.

[6] Nimoy's "Ballad of Bilbo Baggins" appeared 28 July 1967 on the short-lived ABC variety show *Malibu U*, now easily found through *YouTube*.

[7] For Tolkien's early American reception, see Walmsley. For treatment of Tolkien's subsequent appropriation across pop culture, see Mathijs.

[8] For a comprehensive theorization of reading, see Iser.

[9] Benjamin and Tolkien overlap in their understandings of poetic language and positions regarding the untranslatability of poetry. For comparison, see Tolkien, "On Translating." Additionally, Benjamin's rejection of Marxist realism and his valorization of engaged, Romantic formalism speak to Tolkien's critical and creative rejections of realism. For Benjamin's dispute with Marxist realism, see Adorno, Benjamin, Bloch, Brecht, and Lukács. For Tolkien's argument, see "On Fairy-stories."

[10] For critical treatment of author-centered scholarship in Tolkien studies, see Drout, "Towards a Better Tolkien Criticism." For a recent defense of source criticism, see Fisher.

Teaching the Critical Debate over *The Lord of the Rings*

James McNelis

My J. R. R. Tolkien course is a lower-division introduction to literature, taken primarily by nonmajors. As with other lower-division English courses, the general-education goal is to teach good argumentative writing applicable to other academic disciplines. Such a focus on argumentation works especially well in a course on Tolkien. In fact, I have been more successful teaching criticism, and critical debates, to the nonmajors in my Tolkien course than to students in my courses for English majors. Although this success may result largely from students' preexisting knowledge of and passion for *The Lord of the Rings*, I am convinced it also has to do with the gulf between pro and con critical perspectives. Like W. H. Auden, I find it hard to think of any other major book regarding which the contested space is so clearly marked and vigorously fought over.[1] When I introduce students to the literary debates on *The Lord of the Rings*, they become caught up in a titanic and now nearly sixty-year-old donnybrook, and they learn something of the commitment that professional literary critics feel. It almost seems that a parallel discipline of English literature is functioning in this single course, a discipline that has a student body far more diverse and with a greater range and vigor of participation than majors have in a traditional English program.

To begin our focus on critical perspectives of Tolkien's major works, I assign a comparison of Edmund Wilson's "Oo, Those Awful Orcs!" with W. H. Auden's "The Hero Is a Hobbit." For this assignment, I ask students to write a short response paper evaluating the merits and demerits of both critics' arguments. They are not allowed to simply say, "I agree with one [Auden] and hate the other [Wilson]." The assignment starts students thinking about the very beginning of the critical wars; drives home to them the seemingly unbridgeable gulf between those who like and those who dislike *The Lord of the Rings*; and illustrates a concept we see again and again as the course progresses, that these two opposing critics sound as though they are not even discussing the same book. The students are greatly interested and (mostly) make a good effort on the papers, and these papers form the basis of a lively and extended discussion on the day they are brought to class.

However, the pro-Tolkien bias of many students who have chosen my course among others is usually so strong that they find it difficult either to appreciate the qualifications in Wilson's arguments or to recognize the care with which Auden expresses his own critical judgment. They tend to be quite incredulous that Wilson's daughter could have appreciated *The Lord of the Rings* at the age of seven (even after being told that their own professor read it at that age). Beyond that, many students have difficulty noticing that Wilson bends over backward to write about how much he likes *The Hobbit* and fantasy and adventure literature as a genre, even though he cannot swallow *The Lord of the Rings* as an adult novel. At the same time, they tend to gloss over the constraint of Auden's praise, such as his categorization of the book as a genre work, his relatively mild celebration of its value as a Christmas present, and his personal delight in it as a reader. They ascribe stronger and more unqualified support for the book to Auden than he actually expressed at that time—certainly, when compared with his eventual thunderous proclamation, after two years of "violent" debates, that Tolkien "has succeeded where Milton failed" ("At the End").

I generally have to walk students through Wilson's points one by one to help them see that several seem well founded and are carefully stated—even if not all meet with the students' personal approval. I stress his bewilderment that a book that began as a linguistic exercise is to be taken seriously. This is one of our first digressions on language versus literature, the great war between philology and criticism that caused the fundamental rift in twentieth-century literary studies and continues to figure heavily in the disciplinary crisis of English that remains to this day.

I point out that Auden was one of Tolkien's students, who personally loved Tolkien and his lectures. Today, we would consider it a conflict of interest if a reviewer did not disclose his personal connection to the author of the work reviewed. In class, we address the nature of literary-critical backlash to other instances of fulsome praise, such as the references to Ariosto and Spenser on the dustcovers of early editions of *The Lord of the Rings*. We also discuss an example of a far greater potential conflict of interest: an early, unsigned review by Tolkien's friend C. S. Lewis, which famously proclaimed *The Lord of the Rings* to have come like "like Lightning from a clear sky" ("Gods" 1082). Because Lewis was known to be the author of this review and because the British intelligentsia had a widespread dislike of him, Tolkien's books were regarded negatively in such circles. Also, Auden's blithe assignment of the book's appeal to readers from twelve to seventy years of age starts my class discussing Tolkien's "On Fairy-stories" and children's literature, the expectations of age-appropriate reading levels (something Tolkien always dismissed), and related issues of genre and critical evaluation. This is a good jumping-off point to address the traditional critical contempt for children's literature. It is helpful here to bring in the example of the *Harry Potter* series, which many students argue vigorously (and effectively) should not be pigeonholed as children's books, an argument that can be enhanced by introducing the controversy over *The New York Times*'s exclusion of the *Harry Potter* books from their adult best-seller list.

This first assignment, comparing the early reception of Tolkien's work from Wilson and Auden, establishes the foundation for a later paper on critical reception and also sets up the concept of genre, a standard topic for introductory literature courses. When *The Lord of the Rings* debuted, reviewers could not be sure what it was in a genre sense, which created confusion, the expectation being that critics must begin with a genre classification before they can evaluate a text. Students may not know that adult fantasy as a literary category essentially did not exist on the shelves of bookstores before *The Lord of the Rings* (though the fantasy works of earlier writers such as H. Rider Haggard, Robert E. Howard, and others must be discussed). This discussion of the setting for critical response to *The Lord of the Rings* leads to good papers on genre, reader response, conventions of criticism, the vexed question of the books' popularity, and other topics (including the literary-critical trinity of race, class, and gender, which are particularly important in *The Lord of the Rings*).

I introduce the concept of genre with an in-class exercise, for which I ask that the students tell me a story. After their ensuing silence, I frequently qualify my request by saying, "Tell me a fairy tale." If need be, I ask them how a fairy tale begins. They typically answer en masse: "Once upon a time." Then I make lists on the board as I question them: What characters commonly occur? What events? locations? How does the story generally go? And how does it end—with what event? (a wedding) with what words? ("Happily ever after"). Finally I ask them how they know all this. Their answers include children's fairy tales, bedtime tales, and inevitably Disney films.[2]

From this grounding, I provide a handout that gives brief descriptions of various genres relevant to *The Lord of the Rings*: fable, fairy tale, mythology, epic, folktale, romance, modern fantasy, science fiction, and the novel. Once we all understand what these genres are, we go on to the meaning of genre fiction. I present genre fiction in any number of ways. One possibility is discussing the various characteristics of "guy movies" versus "chick flicks," which is always lively and accompanied by some hilarity. Or I might focus on the western movie. From the classic clichés of white hats versus black hats and the climactic gunfight, through later developments in the genre such as *The Ox-Bow Incident*, *High Noon*, *High Plains Drifter*, and *The Unforgiven*, I might underscore the factor of genre expectations, the eventual need for variation and for the confounding of expectations for audiences who have them, and the critical tradition of categorizing any genre fiction as second-rate literature. The Academy Awards's snubbing of fantasy films until the wins by Peter Jackson's *The Lord of the Rings* offers an example here. This range of genre topics in Tolkien's work provides much material about issues surrounding genre formation and tradition that students can develop more fully in later papers.

The first version of each formal paper I assign is peer-reviewed in class, and all students get written revision directions from me about sources suitable for their topics. I demonstrate the MLA database in class and point students to *Tolkien Studies*, *The Lion and the Unicorn*, and *Mythlore* as promising sources for up-to-date research on fantasy literature. I have found the use of a class Web page to be essential, in that when I place password-protected or restricted-access PDF files of scholarly articles or excerpts of book chapters on such a page, my students more readily read them. Once they start working with a source I have excerpted in this way, they are much more likely to look at the original from which it came in the physical library. This strategy is the best I have yet found for getting students over the threshold of our library. In fact, for the most recent term in which I taught *The Lord of the Rings*, *Tolkien Studies* tied for my college's most frequently accessed online journal for the semester.

For their formal paper assignment, students may select from several topic areas related to my course's focus on Tolkien's critical reception. One of these topics asks them to evaluate whether the popularity of *The Lord of the Rings* should have a bearing on critical response. They have surprising difficulty in writing good papers on this topic because they tend to start from the position that because a book is very popular, it must also be very good, so what is there to talk about? Yet even papers based initially on such uncritical judgments can be worked through to end up resulting in more thoughtful reactions.

In the context of my focus on critics and criticism, I also bring up race in Tolkien's works as a possible topic for a formal paper. My students are nearly all Midwestern whites who are reluctant at first to discuss the arguments about race in *The Lord of the Rings*. They tend to start from the opinion that the books are self-evidently not racist and that therefore race in these texts (or in literature and popular culture in general) is irrelevant. Nowadays most students have never heard of, for example, the Jar Jar Binks controversy from *Star Wars: The Phantom Menace* (see "Entertainment"), nor do they know the history of racist portrayals of black characters such as Lincoln Perry's Stepin Fetchit in American films (see Hurst). Similarly, they find it hard to understand criticisms of the Jackson films from this perspective. I often ask them to write a response to John Yatt's *Guardian* article "Wraiths and Race" as an opening gambit on this topic; usually they think the critic is "reading too much into it." Showing them some of the relevant scenes on the DVDs helps them begin to understand. Here useful scenes, for example, are Saruman's creation of the obviously dreadlocked Uruk-hai, the prominence given in the films to the Orc officer Gothmog, and the bloodlust of the Mûmak driver as his beast mows down the Rohirrim—as well as the cinematic emphasis on each of these villains' richly deserved death at the hands of the heroes and the evident expectation that the audience will delight in it.

Yatt writes that "the races that Tolkien has put on the side of evil are . . . given a rag-bag of non-white characteristics that could have been copied straight from a BNP leaflet." On a hunch that the British National Party might well in fact have had something to say about the Jackson films, I did a Web search that rewarded me with the discovery of an actual BNP pamphlet on the racist virtues of both the films and the books.[3] This invaluable piece of propaganda, including excerpts from John Rhys-Davies's much-criticized interview comments regarding Islamic immigration into Europe (see Ballinger), demonstrates that racists read the book and film differently from others. More recently, in 2011, the anti-immigrant Norwegian mass killer Anders Breivik was reported to have cited Tolkien in his manifesto and to have played *The Lord of the Rings* film soundtrack on his iPod to drown out the cries of his victims.[4] In class discussion as well as in paper-revision comments, I challenge students to explore the simple question, How is it possible for racists to think Tolkien's book is racist and for nonracists to think the opposite? Once the concepts and critical discussions sink in, several students always take an interest in writing papers on race issues in the book version.

In contrast, students are not reluctant to write final paper topics involving feminist criticism. I am surprised at how often both male and female students find feminist issues in the text interesting and write papers on them—and not all of their papers argue that the anti-Tolkien angle is without merit. These arguments can be developed by reference to scholarly and popular press articles addressing the roles of female characters in the books as well as the adaptations of those roles in the film version. I challenge the students to bring their arguments into sharper focus by responding to Tolkien's provocative response to criticism that his books contained "no Women"; his defense was that this point "does not matter, and is not true anyway" (*Letters of J. R. R. Tolkien* 220). While students are receptive to his second point, analysis of the first has an obvious bearing on Tolkien's own assessment of this line of criticism. His insistence, for example, that the "rustic" love between Sam and the all-but-absent Rosie is in fact "essential" should be considered when a student writes about this topic (161).

Tolkien's critical reception by creative writers is another topic some students select to explore in their formal papers. The overwhelmingly positive view of *The Lord of the Rings* from readers who are themselves professional writers of fiction has always contrasted with the stark divide among literary critics. I suggest that students develop an argument to explain this difference. As a starting point, I direct them to Karen Haber's *Meditations on Middle-earth*, which contains essays by authors such as Ursula K. Le Guin and Orson Scott Card detailing Tolkien's role in inspiring them to write fiction as well as in their choice of subjects.

As with the topic of race in Tolkien's works, it can be difficult at first to get students to explore critical consideration of Jackson's films in a formal paper: they find it hard to take seriously indictments of the films' shortcomings. A common response is, "It's just a movie, so what do you expect?" David Bratman's "Summa Jacksonia" provides more than enough well-substantiated argumentation to inspire a student paper that responds by arguing the opposite case, but it is often necessary to walk students through his points to draw them into developing specific and thoughtful answers to his criticisms. Another source, Janice M. Bogstad and Philip E. Kaveny's *Picturing Tolkien*, is a welcome addition to scholarship on the films; its essays are both interesting and provocative. In other publications provided for the students' reference, prominent critics take both the pro and con sides in discussing the films.

Current and early criticism of *The Lord of the Rings* offers a means through which I can achieve another of my core goals for the course: to ensure that students understand Tolkien's linguistic project and how it could produce the most popular British novel of the twentieth century. As a medievalist myself, I unapologetically grandstand for the glories of philology and medieval studies in these class discussions. At the same time, I stress Tom Shippey's points in his article "Fighting the Long Defeat: Philology in Tolkien's Life and Fiction" about the implications of Tolkien's success for the long-standing crisis in modern literary studies (*Roots* 139–56). In particular, Wilson's bafflement at Tolkien's writing a book founded on a linguistic exercise[5]—the class encountered it in "Oo, Those Awful Orcs!"—leads us to an introduction to philology and historical linguistics. In seeking to understand the view held by Shippey, and many others, that philology is the key to literature as well as the way forward out of what has hampered much literary scholarship in recent decades, we come face-to-face with the modern crisis in English. To enlarge on the implication of this discussion for the importance of language and linguistics to the study of literature, I bring up examples from other popular works. For example, many students are familiar with the Klingon language from various *Star Trek* books, films, and television series, as well as the Na'vi language from the film *Avatar*. These examples allow a consideration of constructed languages and of what they teach us about the joys of philology. In addition, they help demonstrate the unique strength of Tolkien's constructed languages, which unlike Klingon or Na'vi demonstrate historical evolution through realistic sound changes.

Critics skeptical of the quality of Tolkien's work have often attributed the enthusiasm of his readership to a childish naïveté, concomitant with a lack of competence in the critical evaluation of literature. In fact, the more students read and respond to professional scholarly criticism of Tolkien, the more firmly grounded and emphatically developed their appreciation becomes. As they come to accept some qualification and shading in their assessment of *The Lord of the Rings*, their foundation for considered response continues to develop and to enhance the judgments and preferences they are now able to present and defend. Far from secondary, the critical literature plays a fundamental role in adding enduring value to students' ability to read and enjoy Tolkien's work.

NOTES

[1]"I rarely remember a book about which I have had such violent arguments" (Auden, "At the End").

[2]This exercise was created by Sean Taylor.

[3]This pamphlet from the British National Party, titled "Stand, Men of the West," was apparently withdrawn from the BNP Web site. But, as of 8 July 2013, it was accessible from the archive listing for 9 August 2007 at web.archive.org/web/20070809085441/http://www.bnp.org.uk/pdf_files/lotr.pdf.

[4]Discussions of this horrifying news story may be found in Gianluca; Gysin, Sears, and Greenhill.

[5]Wilson wrote, "[A] philological curiosity—that is, then, what *The Lord of The Rings* really is."

Eucatastrophe and the Battle with the Dark

Verlyn Flieger

Faced with a classroom full of expectant students, most of whom have read *The Lord of the Rings*—some many times—before signing up for the course, teachers of J. R. R. Tolkien's work should have clearly in mind what aspects of that multivalanced work they want to emphasize. Will it be the completeness and integrity of Tolkien's subcreated world? the medieval roots of his narrative? its surprising modernity? its relation to the world of modern fantasy? While all these aspects are valid, and I take care to include them in the course, my own special goal is to help students discover what gives the book its extraordinary ability to move its readers, why they keep coming back again and again to a story that the author himself called "complex, rather bitter, and very terrifying" (*Letters of J. R. R. Tolkien* 136). For me, the gateways into *The Lord of the Rings* and the keys to its power are to be found in his two great essays, "On Fairy-stories" and "Beowulf: The Monsters and the Critics."

The essays are contradictory: they mark the opposite poles of Tolkien's creative imagination, one celebrating the magic of fairy tales and their archetypal happy ending, the other exalting the heroic *Beowulf*ian battle with the dark that ends in defeat. Yet while they seem both emotionally and philosophically at odds, they also exist in a curious kind of creative tension with each other. The same man wrote both essays, understood and believed both points of view, and made both part of his fiction. The tension between these extremes is what gives *The Lord of the Rings* much of its energy and its power to move the reader. In any course on Tolkien that I teach, my path into his work is through these essays, and though it is a winding way, I have found that following it results in a richer appreciation of the books than my students and I might otherwise arrive at.

Starting off a course with these two essays, however, is a challenging beginning, for it throws students in at the deep end and requires them to swim. That many students are already more or less familiar with Tolkien's fiction makes little difference to their experience of the essays, which are predicated on a level of knowledge about literatures—myth, folklore, fairy tale, and early English epic—rarely offered these days in English class syllabi. Thus teachers must not only translate the occasional phrase from Greek or Anglo-Saxon but also explain and contextualize the two contrasting genres of epic and fairy tale as well as fill in the history of scholarship in both fields.

Written in 1938, at the time of transition from *The Hobbit* to *The Lord of the Rings*, Tolkien's fairy-story essay should be read in two contexts. The first is the necessary background history of the myth and folklore movement, which shows where Tolkien was coming from and how he was entering the debate. The second context is that of the essay's importance as a working explication of his creative process. In terms of the latter, "On Fairy-stories" sets up a number of concepts easy to recognize in Tolkien's work—faerie, enchantment, subcreation, the secondary world, fantasy, the inner consistency of reality. I am not alone in having discussed these at greater length in other works, so I will just say here that once we have got past the problem of definition (what is or is not a fairy story and how one knows this) and the questions of origins and importance (where fairy stories come from, why they are good reading, whether they are for adults as well as children), the key concept in the essay is the notion of faerie, which leads to all the others.

My class spends some time on the derivation of the word *faërie* from Old French *fae* or *fée* ("fairy"), its suffix *-ery* or *-erie* extending the root noun to a process or state, as fay-*ery*, the practice of enchantment or the state of being enchanted. Tolkien calls this state the secondary world, the otherworld of fairyland, which readers experience when they read such stories. Further etymology adds a darker aspect by tracing the word back to Latin *fāta* ("the Fates"), plural of *fātum* ("fate"), explaining why Tolkien calls Faërie a perilous realm and illuminating his treatment of the otherworlds of his fiction from Mirkwood to the Old Forest to Lothlórien to Fangorn Forest. The Hobbits' encounters with Old Man Willow, with Tom Bombadil and Goldberry, with the Elves of Lórien, are journeys into Faërie in both its light and dark aspects.

These characters and scenes are fantastic in that they represent no part of the observable real world yet preserve in the secondary world the inner consistency of reality that makes them believable. Old Man Willow is a tree, and his character extends only a little beyond what trees really do. He puts out obtrusive roots, his leaves flutter and murmur, the great cracks in his trunk have the mysterious terror of a child's nightmare. His nemesis, Tom Bombadil, defies definition, but Tom's benevolent nature, as well as Tolkien's specific comments about him in his letters, allies him with the vanishing English countryside, whose loss Tolkien mourned. Moreover, Tom's indifference to the Ring defines the nature of its power, which is to dominate others—an indifference not characteristic of the natural world. Of all the otherworlds, Lórien in its timeless elven beauty is the most purely faerie-like, the most enchanting.

Students enjoy applying the theory of Tolkien's essay to the practice of his fiction, seeing both in action, so to speak, and coming to understand his use of his working model. By the "On Fairy-stories" definition, *The Lord of the Rings* takes place in a secondary world, so in effect it is a fairy story—one unquestionably writ extra large but a fairy story nonetheless. Yet, in a sense, all this is window dressing or a prologue to what is the heart of the matter for Tolkien (and must be for students): the use of fairy stories in terms of the rewards that they give their readers. Tolkien lists these rewards as escape, recovery, and consolation, with special emphasis on the happy ending, the final reward. In this respect, *The Lord of the Rings* both conforms to the essay and transcends it. Students find escape (entry into a secondary world) and recovery (seeing the familiar as if it were new) easy enough to apply, and they come to the consolation of the happy ending, expecting it to be equally easy.

Then we tackle eucatastrophe, the "good catastrophe," the turn that takes the story from dark to light, from potential disaster to the happy ending. The influence of "On Fairy-stories" on *The Lord of the Rings* becomes complicated here, for the turn, which Tolkien calls "a sudden and miraculous grace: never to be counted on to recur" ("On Fairy-stories" 86), depends for its effect on the imminent dyscatastrophe that generates the very real possibility that no happy ending will come. It is not so much the escape as the hairbreadth narrowness of the escape that achieves the effect. The "sudden and miraculous grace" cannot be a god from the machine but must fit into the credibility of the world and the events. It is easy to recognize in Tolkien's both stunning and extraordinary climax the one-two punch of Frodo and Gollum at the Cracks of Doom that saves Middle-earth. Tolkien's insistence that fantasy must have the "inner consistency of reality" comes into play here (68). Given the circumstances, Frodo cannot do otherwise than what he does. Given the circumstances, Gollum cannot do otherwise than what he does. The actions of both together move the narrative with startling suddenness from the dyscatastrophe that is Frodo's claiming of the Ring to the eucatastrophic turn of Gollum's attack and the Ring's consequent destruction. Both lead to the happy ending. Tolkien departs, however, from the "On Fairy-stories" model at this point, for it is a qualified and bittersweet happy ending. The story suddenly swings from fairy story to the opposite pole of Tolkien's imagination, which is discussed in the *Beowulf* essay, and shifts from eucatastrophe to actual, not narrowly escaped, tragedy and the fate of being human.

Differing in scope and subject matter ("On Fairy-stories" is a wide-ranging discussion of a genre, the *Beowulf* essay a narrowly focused examination of a single work), Tolkien's two essays yet employ the same strategy of argument: previous scholars' misreading of a text is presented as background for why Tolkien's reading is the correct one. Since today's students are rarely conversant with early *Beowulf* scholarship, in my class we first explore why Tolkien's reading of *Beowulf* is important, how his defense of the monsters as central to the poem's theme not only revealed the poem to be a coherent work of art but in the process also dramatically redirected *Beowulf* scholarship. The essay's emotional and critical positions lead straight to *The Lord of the Rings* and to Frodo's struggle with the monsters, both Gollum and the Ring itself. The heart of Tolkien's essay and the key to his art are revealed in his focus on "that battle with the hostile world and the offspring of the dark which ends for all, even the kings and champions, in defeat" ("Beowulf" 18). His statement that "*lif is læne: eal scæceðleoht and lif somod*" (19; "life is loan: all perishes, light and life together" [my trans.]) captures the essence of what the poem meant to him.

In class, we read "Beowulf: The Monsters and the Critics" as a guide to Tolkien's reading of *Beowulf*, a two-part meditation on the theme of courage and defeat. The young warrior's victory over Grendel is balanced against the final defeat of the death-ripe old king in the fight with the dragon. But *The Lord of the Rings* is a long and multilevel book, and only when students have read it in the light of the essay can they connect Tolkien's understanding of the Old English poem with the sense of doomed heroism and inevitable loss that permeates his own book. After making that connection, we read *The Lord of the Rings* not as a fairy story but as a tragedy, the tragedy of Frodo, whose struggle against his inner monster (externalized as both the Ring and Gollum) ends in defeat. Gollum's unforeseen but inevitable attack at the Cracks of Doom turns the dyscatastrophe of Frodo's capitulation to the Ring into an ending that is happy for everyone except the hero, since Middle-earth benefits in general and Aragorn, Faramir, Éowyn, Merry, Pippin, Sam benefit in particular. Yet Frodo, although he has been freed from the power of the Ring, does not benefit: stuck in the dyscatastrophe, he pays a high price for everyone else's joy. Tolkien's uncompromising honesty (based almost certainly on his own experience of war and its aftermath) will not permit Frodo to emerge unscathed from his struggle with the dark. Instead, Tolkien goes back again to the statement in *Beowulf* that he finds so compelling: *Lif is læne: eal scæceð leoht and lif somod*. Frodo is wounded, traumatized, bereft of his health, his home, as well as the most important thing in his life—the Ring.

Tolkien called the structure of *Beowulf* "essentially a balance, an opposition of ends and beginnings" (28). So too we discuss in my Tolkien courses how the structure of *The Lord of the Rings* rests on a balance—not so much chronological as thematic—of light against dark, faerie and enchantment against loss. This balance is most movingly manifest in what happens to Frodo over the course of the book as he moves from fairy tale to tragedy. Reading *The Lord of the Rings* through Tolkien's *Beowulf* essay allows students to see in his fiction the same perspective Tolkien found in the Old English poem, "a new perspective [on] an ancient theme: that man, each man and all men, and all their works shall die" ("Beowulf" 23). Such a perspective helps prepare students for what really happens to Frodo—no fairy tale happy ending but unhealed wounds and the loss of all he holds dear. Tolkien does not have Frodo die, but what he arranges for his Hobbit hero is in many ways a crueler fate. We have only to note Frodo's recurrent illness, or hear his words to Gandalf: "I am wounded with knife, sting, and tooth, and a long burden. Where shall I find rest?" (*Lord* 989; bk. 6, ch. 7); later to Sam: "I am wounded . . . wounded; it will never really heal" (1025; bk. 6, ch. 9); and, most poignant of all, his words to Farmer Cotton: "It is gone for ever . . . and now all is dark and empty" (1024).

This is a bitter pill for some readers to swallow, and there are students who refuse to accept it, who argue in the teeth of the evidence that the story really *is* a fairy tale, that there *is* a happy ending, that Frodo succeeds in his quest and lives happily in some post–*Lord of the Rings* ever after. In some pretty intense class discussion, students passionately defend one position or the other and talk to one another instead of to me (an action I applaud and encourage). Students often resist the citation of Tolkien's letters that the quest "was bound to fail" (*Letters of J. R. R. Tolkien* 234), that Frodo "failed" (252, 326), that "the power of Evil in the world is *not* finally resistible by incarnate creatures, however 'good'" (252), and that Valinor is "a purgatory" (328) rather than a version of Heaven. I usually let the debate run for a while before announcing that I will simply put the question on the final exam or make it part of the final paper assignment and invite students to argue pro or con, insisting only that they support their position with evidence from the book and both essays. If they make a good case, which often turns on interpretation of the word "fail," I give them full credit.

Since both essays demand a knowledge of history and scholarship beyond the classroom experience of most undergraduates and both are dense with references and allusions, a good way to begin is by inviting students to air their difficulties with the essays. Their responses will give the teacher cues as to where and how to engage them with the material. Ignorance and confusion are useful springboards, and revealing them enables students to discover with relief that they are not alone and gives them courage to express their opinions. My exams draw evenly from both essays and from what comes up in discussion. They are open-book and open-notes, because my objective in giving exams is not to test students' memory but to foster the learning process by inviting students to read carefully, think deeply, and write in an informed manner. A midterm might ask them to identify and write on quotations from the essays—for example, "as in a little circle of light about their halls, men with courage as their stay went forward to that battle with the hostile world and the offspring of the dark which ends for all, even the kings and champions, in defeat" ("Beowulf" 18), or, "I will call it *Eucatastrophe*. The *eucatastrophic* tale is the true form of fairy tale, and its highest function" ("On Fairy-stories" 85). Another question might be, "What are Tolkien's chief criteria for fairy stories, and how well do they fit his own work? Where and how do you see evidence of faerie in *The Lord of the Rings*?" A final exam or final paper assignment might be:

> In his biography of Tolkien, Humphrey Carpenter described him as "a cheerful almost irrepressible person with a great zest for life." But Carpenter also said he was "capable of bouts of profound despair [and] a deep sense of impending loss. Nothing was safe. Nothing would last" (39). Write an essay exploring the relevance of Carpenter's statements to *The Lord of the Rings*.

or:

> In "On Fairy-stories" Tolkien writes that "the sudden, joyous 'turn' . . . does not deny the existence . . . of sorrow and failure." In fact, he says, "the possibility of these is necessary to the joy of deliverance" (86). Discuss "deliverance" and "sorrow and failure" as opposing themes in *The Lord of the Rings*. Is the balance between them even?

It is important for students to realize that studying Tolkien results not in right or wrong answers but in understanding how he expressed his view of the human condition and its paradoxical union of joy and beauty with loss and pain. This paradox, not just in his general treatment but also in his specific treatment of Frodo, is what gives the story its poignancy and power. I do not say Tolkien reconciled the paradox, for I believe that the contradiction is in the man as well as in the works and remains unresolved. *The Lord of the Rings* combines final defeat and eucatastrophe, *Beowulf* and fairy story in interconnection and interdependence, and this lack of resolution gives students the framework within which to understand the extraordinary depth of Tolkien's vision. Frodo does not and cannot live happily ever after, and his alienation from home and friends is the final defeat through which the tragic ethos of the *Beowulf* essay opposes, though it does not negate, the joy of "On Fairy-stories." The tension between tragedy and eucatastrophe is what keeps this "complex, rather bitter, and very terrifying" (*Letters of J. R. R. Tolkien* 136) story alive. I want my students to know that.

Why Teach *The Silmarillion*? Tolkien's Mythology of the Abject Hero

Jane Chance

Most intriguing, yet problematic, for students in my J. R. R. Tolkien course at Rice University—majors, nonmajors, and some graduate students enrolled in a directed reading with me—is how and why two odd, mythical, half-pint Hobbits become such important, if unlikely, epic or fairy-tale heroes by the end of *The Hobbit* and *The Lord of the Rings*. By nature uninterested in the pursuit of adventures of any sort, Hobbits generally prefer to occupy holes and smoke tobacco. And yet, even when Bilbo appears to fail in his quest, or lacks the means of overcoming an insuperable adversary or difficult obstacle, he is aided almost magically by a benefactor who appears at just the right moment, whether this is Gandalf, the shape changer Beorn, or the Eagles, much as Frodo is similarly aided by Tom Bombadil, Gandalf, or the Elves. Although *The Hobbit* has rarely been studied as a mythological work per se, the intrusion of magical figures into the narrative at points of heroic failure opens a window into Tolkien's mythology of magic in his fantasy of Middle-earth. To understand how that mythology and its aspects explain the differences between Tolkien's antiheroes and medieval heroes, students need to read at least portions of *The Silmarillion*.

A book difficult to read and follow and never published (or even finished) during Tolkien's lifetime, *The Silmarillion* is even more difficult to teach. For many years I did not teach it at all and used it primarily as a background resource on the outside reading list. It is a dense mythological epic and chronicle of Middle-earth and the history of the Elves; its chapters are drawn from diverse sources, frequently unrelated to one another; and it lacks a single, narrative-unifying protagonist, even though the conflict between Ilúvatar and Melkor continues throughout as a theme (later extended into *The Lord of the Rings* by Morgoth's servant Sauron). So why even teach *The Silmarillion*, especially when there is not enough time in a semester course to include all Tolkien's other significant works—and when it remained incomplete at the time of Tolkien's death?

Only *The Silmarillion*, in the space of one collection of stories, contains the key to Tolkien's mythology, as the initial work in what has been called the "Silmarilliad": the chronological trilogy of *The Silmarillion*, *The Hobbit*, and *The Lord of the Rings*. As a key, it unlocks Tolkien's taxonomy of cosmic being in Middle-earth, from which most of the narrative events and characterization flow. Most important, *The Silmarillion* answers questions about Tolkien's concepts of the nature of good and evil; the power of chance, fate, or providence when set against the individual's own will; why Tolkien, a Roman Catholic, created his fantastic universe at all; and the reason he so emphasizes the ordinary or even antiheroic hero—"abject," in the Kristevan sense. By my juxtaposing works by Tolkien (these and others) during class discussions, as well as in two exams and two papers, my students are reminded constantly to look back at *The Silmarillion* and *The Hobbit* while reading *The Lord of the Rings*. As a result, the course creates its own palimpsest—a written-over manuscript scraped and rescraped—of layers of intertextuality within Tolkien's canon, including those medieval works he adapted in his own fiction and interpreted in his scholarship.

To begin with, Tolkien's own letters are especially helpful in explaining his idea of the hero as the ordinary man: in letter number 213, he confesses, with his typical multilayered irony, "I am in fact a *Hobbit*" (*Letters of J. R. R. Tolkien* 288). But Tolkien's preoccupation with flawed heroes of whatever type (such as a Hobbit) and why such heroes cannot or will not behave heroically surfaces as early as his King Edward's School debates on the Finnish orphan Kullervo.[1] The Oxford medievalist reveals to Christopher Bretherton on 16 July 1964 in letter 257 that "[t]he germ of my attempt to write legends of my own to fit my private languages was the tragic tale of the hapless Kullervo in the Finnish *Kalevala*" (345). Certainly, Tolkien projects Kullervo into *The Silmarillion* in the construction of the antiheroes Aulë, Feänor, Thingol, Túrin Turambar, and Eärendel, among others, not to mention Bilbo, Frodo, Gollum, and Saruman. All these characters represent some strain of the cosmic failure incarnated in Melkor and bear resemblance to Sigurd, the Old Norse failed hero similar to Kullervo, whose story Tolkien himself retold in verse as *The Legend of Sigurd and Gudrún*.

In Tolkien's other works inspired by medieval literature, such as his dark sequel to the Old English *Battle of Maldon*, "The Homecoming of Beorhtnoth Beorhthelm's Son," and his scholarly interpretation of the Old English epic in "Beowulf: The Monsters and the Critics," heroism is a vexed concept that is both culturally and socially constructed, as his excursus on the word *ofermod* ("pride") that follows "Homecoming" surely testifies ("Homecoming" 21–27).[2] The Anglo-Saxon *comitatus* lord Beorhtnoth courteously decides to allow the Danes to cross to solid ground before undertaking battle, which may suit his noble station but results in the loss of his retainers. Their self-sacrifice out of loyalty to him, in accord with their supportive but socially inferior role within the tribe, appears morally superior. The hero in *The Battle of Maldon*—an old "companion" named Byrhtwold—is "abject," or other, in this case, because he *is* old (presumably battle-weary), and yet ready to offer his life to his leader:

> I am old of years, but yet I flee not;
> Staunch and steadfast I stand by my lord,
> And I long to be by my loved chief. (Gordon 76)

A helpful definition of the abject hero appears in Melissa Ruth Arul's gendered postcolonial analysis of Elven alterity as based on Julia Kristeva's theory of the abject. For Arul, the abject hero, such as Fëanor in *The Silmarillion*, suffers from a self that is damaged, pitched against the world. She argues that the Noldo Elf's sense of inferiority, reinforced by the early loss of his mother, Miriel, results in a desire to make himself whole by means of the creation of the Silmarils, or what Arul identifies as his "fetish." She explains that the "abjection of his kin and the Kinslaying were caused by his failure to integrate into the Symbolic order." Arul broadens the context of her discussion of Elven identity to explain the differences among the various tribes, chiefly, between the Caliquendi and the seemingly inferior and abject Moriquendi.

While *The Silmarillion* is key for students to grasp the nature and origin of the abject hero in Tolkien's mythology of Middle-earth, some preparation is necessary before tackling Tolkien's most Joycean work, especially in relation to the author's early life and writings as well as to his frequent focus on the medieval ignoble hero in his scholarship. In the first major section of my course syllabus, "A Mythology for England: *The Silmarillion*," I assign several important early short stories and poems by Tolkien to reveal the work's metastructure as a journey, or cycle of journeys, some escapist and some restorative, during different loops of history, following what Tolkien terms a "Fall" or "Doom" that involves an antihero. A simplified structure for Tolkien's mythology might be called "The Story of Early England and Aelfwine/Eriol the Mariner," in that the history of Middle-earth is an Orosian universal history, a *historia mundi*, beginning with the prerecorded mythological history of England and ending with our historical present. Yet Tolkien also projects into his mythological history events that he experienced after the death of his mother when, at the age of twelve, he became an orphan and, in both a metaphysical and a literal sense, homeless.

In this section, we discuss how the foundational meeting with his future wife, Edith Bratt, and their relationship up to their marriage was crucially important for Tolkien because of his early loss and alienation, as reflected in his fantasy poem "The Cottage of Lost Play, which Introduceth [the] Book of Lost Tales" (1916–17) (*Book of Lost Tales I* 1–39). In this work, the city of Kortirion[3] is the fair city of Tol Eressëa, the Lonely Isle of the Elves (or Faërie) to which the mariner Eriol ("One Who Dreams Alone"), the son of Eärendel, journeys "from the lands to the East of the North Sea" (that is, from England), apparently before the Anglo-Saxons invaded Britain. To understand the geographic location of the city of Kortirion in the mythology of Middle-earth is to discover its ancient legendary location in Warwickshire (*Kor-* and *War-* being related etymologically): that is, near Edith, who lived there until they were married, and then after their marriage in Great Haywood, near Tolkien's camp, before he left (exile-like) for France and after he returned from battle in World War I.[4] Indeed, Tolkien began writing what scholars now call *The Silmarillion* during the years of World War I.

If the Eriol story represents the germ of Tolkien's mythology, that does not mean its influence is simple, which students often assume. As Christopher Tolkien notes in his "Commentary on 'The Cottage of Lost Play,'" "The 'Eriol-story' is in fact among the knottiest and most obscure matters in the whole history of Middle-earth and Aman" (*Book of Lost Tales I* 13). Tolkien wrote down notes and outlines about the "Story of Eriol's Life" in a little notebook to relate it to the invasion of Britain in the fifth century by Hengest and Horsa and to the figure of Hengest in *Beowulf*.[5] Of course, Tolkien changed the relations between recorded English history and his own mythological history several times. As Christopher Tolkien emphasizes:

> [I]n *The Cottage of Lost Play* Eriol comes to Tol Eressëa *in the time after* the Fall of Gondolin and the march of the Elves of Kôr into the Great Lands for the defeat of Melko, when the Elves who had taken part in it had returned over the sea to dwell in Tol Eressëa; but *before the time* of the "Faring Forth" and the removal of Tol Eressëa to the geographical position of England. This latter element was soon lost in its entirety from the developing mythology. (*Book of Lost Tales I* 18)

Equally important for students in understanding Middle-earth's kernel mythology is Tolkien's penultimate version of the pseudo-historical and Anglo-Saxon frame story of "Ælfwine of England" (1920) in "The History of Eriol; or, Ælfwine and the End of the Tales" (*Book of Lost Tales II* 318–40). Here, Tolkien renames Eriol "Ælfwine" ("Elf-Friend"), who comes from Anglo-Saxon England to Tol Eressëa. Ælfwine relays the important story of Eriol, or Eärendel the Mariner, who redeemed the Doom of the Noldor.[6] There is, thus, a (pseudo)historical witness to this event, recording the link between the Anglo-Saxon Ælfwine and the mythical Hobbits Bilbo and Frodo.[7]

Given the overarching resultant narrative of dissidence, rebellion, and recuperation in several such tales, isolating Tolkien's interest in the Elven hero, fallen or victorious (or both), brings into focus for students the larger cosmic pattern that endures throughout all Tolkien's work. To help them recognize this focus, I ask my students to read only the "framework" of *The Silmarillion*, which includes the first several chapters and introduces Tolkien's archetypal abject hero, Melkor; Fëanor's creation of the Silmarils; the tales of the heroic couple Beren and Lúthien and Lúthien's antiheroic father, Thingol; the fallen hero Túrin Turambar; and the final apotheosis of the redeemer, Eärendel.

Over a week and a half, we read and discuss the myth of creation and the fall of the Valar and Maiar, namely, the significant establishing myth in "Ainulindalë" (*Silmarillion* 15–22) and "Valaquenta" (25–32), along with Tolkien's defining letters on the history of Middle-earth (letters 131, 165, 186, 297). Then, we turn to the central Elven myth of Feänor and the Fall of the Noldor in "Quenta Silmarillion: The History of the Silmarils" (*Silmarillion* 35–90), accompanied by additional pertinent Tolkien letters (letters 178, 180, 181, 211, 247). Finally, we look at the tales of Beren and Lúthien and of Túrin Turambar (*Silmarillion* 162–87, 198–226), examining the former as a paradigm for love relationships in *The Lord of the Rings*—but also as reflective of how Tolkien described his love for his wife. We read the tale of Túrin side by side with the Finnish tale of the reprobate orphan Kullervo from the *Kalevala* (Turgon 337–89), whom

Tolkien uses as a model for his antihero (West). We finish the section on *The Silmarillion* with the redemptive voyage of the Noldo hero Eärendel (246–55).

That Tolkien places semidivine and mortal dissonance and failure within a cosmos in which both magic and mysticism prevail and triumph by means of mortal victory, however muted, attests to his successful transmogrification of medieval and religious materials into the masterpiece of *The Lord of the Rings*. Most important in *The Silmarillion* is the figure of Melkor, Tolkien's equivalent of the fallen angel Lucifer, who, with his twisting of and dissidence toward the divine plan of the One, creates evil in spite of his magical being as a Vala at the same time that he also provides a model and theorization for later, more ontologically degraded continuations of evil by the Maia Sauron and other lesser figures throughout Tolkien's major works. Melkor is also the best example of Tolkien's antihero, because he is potentially so perfect a creation of Eru's thought. If instructors can encourage students to understand what makes Melkor both perfect and flawed, students may begin to comprehend not only the failed heroism of so many of Tolkien's protagonists but also the special cosmic magic in his mythology that adjusts and balances for mortal imperfection.

Working through *The Silmarillion* in this way leads students to central questions about Tolkien's mythology, such as, Why does Melkor rebel against the music of the One? Why does Aulë create the Dwarves, in direct disobedience of Eru and without consulting his own consort, Yavanna? Why does Fëanor create the Silmarils by stealing the light of Valinor from the Trees and in their creation seal the Doom of the Noldor? Why does Thingol forbid Beren to marry his daughter Lúthien and by this refusal set in place a series of tests for Beren to capture a Silmaril, which will end disastrously? And, finally, why does Túrin Turambar make such foolish decisions? Even Noldo Eärendil, who succeeds in convincing the gods of Valinor to rescue the Exiles and grant the peoples of Beleriand mercy, suffers the destruction of his home by the sons of Fëanor and, at least initially, the loss of his Telerin wife, Elwing, descended from Lúthien, when she casts herself and a Silmaril into the sea. Yet, it is these abject heroes—Eärendil the Blessed, apotheosized as a star, and Elwing, descended from the Teleri at Alqualondë through her great-grandfather Elwë and transformed by Ulmo into a bird—who work for the good of the whole of the community of Elves and of Middle-earth. From their sons Elrond and Elros, the later heroic Elves and Men descend.

For students to decode the Tolkienian origins of what might be termed evil and, therefore, to understand by contrast the much more difficult abstract concept of good, a helpful discussion involves a close reading of the first several paragraphs of "Ainulindalë: The Music of the Ainur" (*Silmarillion* 15–22). When Ilúvatar first thinks, the "offspring of his thought," or the Ainur, sing to him, each contributing to a "Great Music" until the void is full of music and until one of them, Melkor, rebels and wishes his own song to vie in power with the music of his brethren (15–16). After Melkor's different notes deepen into discord, Ilúvatar creates a first, second, and third theme, at which time the

Music ceases and Ilúvatar offers instead a vision of a new world in which the Music contains each Ainur's being: "[N]o theme may be played that hath not its uttermost source in me, nor can any alter the music in my despite. For he that attempteth this shall prove but mine instrument in the devising of things more wonderful, which he himself hath not imagined" (17).

What exactly does Ilúvatar mean by his reminder that all that exists and happens comes from him? He means that individual discord is only a part of the whole Music, which supersedes it in value and wonder, and that he determines it to be so. Whatever harm is intended to Ilúvatar's plan will result only in positive, "more wonderful" consequences through the agency of the dissident. Through a close reading of these two pronouncements of Ilúvatar, the major theme of *The Silmarillion* emerges. From this passage the rest of Tolkien's mythology flows.

Further discussion of the first several paragraphs of "Ainulindalë" involves Tolkien's choice of the metaphor of music to convey the thought of Eru and why harmony is such a key concept for his purposes. We explore how the Ainur, as the "offspring of his thought" (*Silmarillion* 15), learn to sing, too:

> But for a long while they sang only each alone, or but few together, while the rest hearkened; for each comprehended only that part of the mind of Ilúvatar from which he came, and in the understanding of their brethren they grew but slowly. Yet ever as they listened they came to deeper understanding, and increased in unison and harmony. (15)

The Ainur each represent only a part of Eru's mind: alone, they draw away from the understanding of his mind, which has been increased by their working together.

If students select key words in this first chapter that appear to carry positive connotations—*harmony*, *power*, *beauty*, *song*, *music*, *the Imperishable Flame*—they can then set these against more negative words (the blackboard helps here)—*alone*, *void*, *discord*, "*of his own*," *singular*, *dark*, *uproar*, *loud*, *vain*, *clamorous*—to define by contrast, again, the origin of evil, as represented by dissident individual Melkor. What he never understands is that he himself has been thought by Ilúvatar and that, therefore, the One has a part in him: Melkor is a part of a much greater whole although, in Kristevan terms, an "abject hero." In this passage, in contrast to the abstract presentation of other Ainur, Melkor is portrayed in Tolkien's mythology as other because of his lack of self-understanding, wisdom, and good judgment as well as his inability to listen: to be silent, to hear or appreciate, what the other Ainur sing, say, or think. He is other because he is unwilling to become part of the larger community in which he shares. To accept his role as one of many Ainur, with a specific obligation to oversight of the cosmic community—as students soon realize through class discussion—Melkor would need to subordinate himself to the One and perform his designated role, that which makes him unique as a Thought. If he had done so, he would have remained as a god, a divine being with magical powers, in the service of Eru. That is, throughout his seminal legendarium, Tolkien historicizes Faërie as a "Perilous Realm" ("On Fairy-stories" 38) in which magic is natural and derives from God, only for God he uses the name Eru, the One, or Ilúvatar. What is imperative for students to visualize as a backdrop to their later reading of *The Hobbit* and *The Lord of the Rings* is Tolkien's Neoplatonic and Stoic hierarchical genealogy of essential being in his mythology, which extends from Eru to the Valar, Maiar, Istari, Elves, and Men (and even Hobbits, who have generally set themselves apart from others). This community of being from which Melkor isolates himself becomes most apparent in the sequence of these three early chapters of *The Silmarillion* (and in readings from *Unfinished Tales* on the Istari and Palantiri).[8]

Similarly, when Ilúvatar creates the Children of the World (the Elves and Men), students benefit from seeing how these beings fit together philosophically as part of the third theme to people the communities of Middle-earth in the cosmos of Arda, the Earth (*Silmarillion* 18–19). The class explores the passage in which Ilúvatar sends the Imperishable Flame to Arda, along with any Ainur who choose to go there, so that the World might come to exist as Eä. Those Ainur who go become known as Valar, the Powers of the World, otherwise known as gods (*Silmarillion* 20). According to the "Valaquenta," these seven Valar and seven Valier (their queens) represent a hierarchy of different powers of the Earth and its regions and inhabitants—air, stars, water, gems, fruits, spirits, the Dead, time, visions, healing, and lamentation (25–32). Chief among these Valar is Manwë (the air and winds), associated with the Elves and joined by Varda, or Elbereth (the stars). Next comes Ulmo (the water), and then Aulë (the gems of earth), who creates the Dwarves and is joined by the consort Yavanna (giver of fruits).

Throughout his mythology Tolkien privileges the Valar and the Maiar associated with Manwë and Varda (air and stars) because they are physically and materially highest in Middle-earth, just as he diminishes those associated with Aulë (the gems of the earth)—and, hence, physically and materially lowest. But when discussing the early sections of *The Silmarillion*, students learn that in Tolkien's cosmos, to privilege some is not to create beings that are, in effect, ontologically superior. That is the mistake Melkor, Aulë, and Sauron make about their own power. Not only is Sauron a servant of Aulë, but when Aulë creates the Dwarves in secret, in disobedience to Ilúvatar and without the knowledge of his wife, Yavanna, Ilúvatar punishes him by means of the Dwarves' long sleep during the First Age. In addition, the Elves, like the Valar, divide into groups of greater and lesser being. During the First Age, Ilúvatar creates two groups of the Firstborn, or Quendi ("Those that speak with voices").[9] The first of these is the Eldar, "People of the Stars," who accept Manwë's summons to make the Great Journey to Aman and are made better by their life there as the Elves of the Three Kindreds (Vanyar, Noldor, and Teleri). The second group, the Avari, refuse the summons, stay where they are, and become the lesser Silvan (Wood)

Elves. Once these Silvan Elves are killed or die of grief, they retreat to the halls of Manos (never to return to Middle-earth). Close reading of the mythological materials enables students to understand that if the Avari are lesser, it is because they *choose* their fates and not because of any intrinsic inferiority.

By extricating these and other mythological patterns in *The Silmarillion*, students become aware of how they are repeated in *The Hobbit* and *The Lord of the Rings*. They see that because the gods—the Valar—do not reinforce and dominate fate in Middle-earth, there is balance in Tolkien's cosmos among the human, the magical, and the divine. Free will among Men, Hobbits, and Elves allows for choice, but the Valar provide a safety net should any balancing act fail. When the abject hero Frodo reaches out on the top of Mount Doom for the Ring on the finger that Gollum has just bitten off, is he impelled by greed or self-sacrifice? Whatever his motive, his alter ego Gollum also has a will, no matter how diminished and corrupted, perhaps bent on service to the Master by means of the rescue of Frodo and Middle-earth at his own expense, or perhaps once more driven by Sauron's enslavement of him or his own greed. So, too, the Ring itself has a will of its own, imbued as it is with some of Sauron's power. That these antiheroes Frodo and Sam are rescued from death and despair by the Eagles—signs of Manwë—suggests a higher power whose obligation is to protect the Children of Middle-earth despite themselves and their failures and abjection. Once students learn to recognize this pattern of magic set against mystery, as it is established in *The Silmarillion*, the mythology shines through many scenes in Tolkien's Middle-earth fiction to illuminate even this pivotal epic scene of failure as redemptive.

NOTES

[1] At the 1992 exhibit for King Edward's School, a placard relayed Tolkien's interest in "scandalous heroes"—Kullervo, in particular—in one of his preserved debates from the Debating Society.

[2] Convenient for teaching translations of medieval texts contemporary with Tolkien (such as *The Battle of Maldon*, edited by Tolkien's own professor, E. V. Gordon, in 1937) is the collection edited by Turgon; the translation available to Tolkien that Turgon includes (69–76) is that of Cosette Faust and Stith Thompson (1918).

[3] Kortirion is also celebrated in a poem titled "Kortirion among the Trees" (1915), which follows "The Cottage" (*Book of Lost Tales I* 25–37).

[4] See Christopher Tolkien's notes on the importance of Kortirion (*Book of Lost Tales I* 12–19).

[5] See J. R. R. Tolkien, *Finn and Hengest*. The most significant treatment of the relation between Anglo-Saxon history and Tolkien's mythology, aside from Christopher Tolkien's commentary, is Drout's "A Mythology for Anglo-Saxon England."

[6] Perhaps the best treatment of Ælfwine is Flieger's "The Footsteps of Ælfwine."

[7] Flieger has published some important work on the witnesses, or recorders, of Tolkien's mythological history, including Ælfwine, Bilbo, Frodo, and even Sam: see "Tolkien and the Idea of the Book."

[8]On the Istari, see "The Istari" (*Unfinished Tales* 388–402). When I ask students to read these sections on the Istari in conjunction with Gandalf's battles with Saruman and Sauron, I also refer them to letter 246 (*Letters of J. R. R. Tolkien*, esp. 332–33).

[9]See Christopher Tolkien's gloss on "Quendi" in the "Index of Names in *The Silmarillion*" (*Silmarillion* 313–54). Although the term was originally intended by Oromë to refer to all the Elves, it came to be used only for the Eldar and not for the Avari, "The Unwilling, the Refusers."

Child of the Kindly West: Innocence and Experience in *The Hobbit*

Brian Walter

Teaching *The Hobbit* in my course on children's literature and film opens up several profitable avenues into the book's treatment of J. R. R. Tolkien's signature creation, the hobbit. To ground discussions throughout the semester, we pose two overarching questions at the beginning of the course that can apply meaningfully to all the works studied:

> What does it mean to be a child within the world of _____?
> How will _____ appeal particularly to a child reader?

The Hobbit stands out immediately from the other books in the course, such as *Alice's Adventures in Wonderland* and *The Wonderful Wizard of Oz*, because it technically has no child characters to use in addressing the first question. Instead, my students and I address the way in which Bilbo Baggins, the hobbit of the title, stands in for the typical child protagonist of the other texts. Still more profitably, we work to illuminate what it is about him that can appeal to the child reader, for whose enjoyment some kind of vicarious identification with a character within the narrative is central.[1] In exploring that revised version of our first grounding question, then, my students and I necessarily engage another topic that occupies us throughout the course but takes on extra weight with Tolkien's book: the relation between innocence and experience.

On this topic, Bilbo and his dwarf companions prove generously instructive. The Dwarves, in fact, treat Bilbo as something of a helpless child for much of the book, dismissing him as useless or something even worse: a detriment to their revenge/treasure quest. Even though the dwarves' opinions of him change in the course of their deadly adventures, the new authority and leadership Bilbo eventually assumes remain rooted in his comparative innocence of the world, ultimately achieving the status of a spiritual truth, and not just for Bilbo. On his deathbed after the Battle of Five Armies, Thorin Oakenshield not only recants the abuses he has recently heaped on Bilbo but also uses telling terms to exalt the hobbit's simple outlook above the stubborn pride and jealous prerogative that motivated him and the other dwarves in their quest: "There is more in you of good than you know, child of the kindly West. . . . If more of us valued food and cheer and song above hoarded gold, it would be a merrier world" (348). Thorin's judgment crucially redeems Bilbo's earthy practicality and enduring innocence.

My class approaches *The Hobbit* through the manifold implications of Bilbo's status as a quasi-child, a naïf bracingly, even dangerously, abroad in the world, who may learn important lessons in his adventures but who, as a hobbit, more importantly embodies a curiously and obstinately vital innocence. Through discussion questions, essay prompts, and analysis of various visual interpretations (including the author's own illustrations and the 1977 Rankin-Bass animated television movie), my students engage a fundamental question: What does Bilbo—as a hobbit, a quasi-child, an innocent—lend to the heroic dragon-slaying quest of *The Hobbit*? Such a question lends itself more broadly to a fundamental issue for those who have struggled to move from *The Hobbit* and *The Lord of the Rings* to the Hobbit-less *Silmarillion* and other writings from Tolkien's legendarium: What makes a hobbit so important to the popular success of Tolkien's grander vision of Middle-earth? The answer for Bilbo resembles the answer for Frodo and his companions in *The Lord of the Rings*: the hobbits remain open to a greater world full of unknowns even as their deep roots in their homeland of the Shire help them heroically resist the darker forces of Middle-earth that beset them in their journeys.

As we address these issues and questions, my students and I focus our discussions on the hobbit's innocence, invoking passages from Tolkien's book and drawing on other relevant sources. The questions I ask the students often revolve around practical storytelling concerns: Why introduce this character at this point? Why send the dwarves and Bilbo to this place on the heels of the last adventure? How do the hobbit's words and actions work together with the twists and turns of the plot to emphasize the author's defining themes? With such questions, we construct an image of hobbits in general, and Bilbo in particular, as remarkably compelling embodiments of a strain of philosophical conservatism—an insistence on a foundation of moral beauty beneath the inherent and inevitable corruption of matter in Middle-earth—that runs through Tolkien's work.

For example, when we discuss in class the forms Bilbo's innocence takes, we start by examining the playful narrative tone of *The Hobbit*, which depends, to a telling degree, on Bilbo's endearing cheeriness, itself rooted in his status as a hobbit who has remained predictably sheltered from the world at large. These traits shape both his speech and his actions, a connection that would seem hardly worth mentioning in the work of such a resourceful scholar of languages as Tolkien was, but one that might surprise in the light of the vast differences between *The Hobbit* and *The Lord of the Rings*. As Tom Shippey has noted, Tolkien's conception of Middle-earth was decidedly limited during the composition of the earlier work; the term "Middle-earth," in fact, hardly ever appears in *The Hobbit*. Nor does *The Hobbit* fill Middle-earth with names the way *The Lord of the Rings* does, suggesting that *The Hobbit* did not exist at the same level of specificity in Tolkien's mind as it did in the later work.[2] My goal in class discussions is not just to get students to read *The Hobbit* on its own terms (avoiding the temptation to blend it misleadingly with its very different sequel) but also to suggest how deeply speech informs character for Tolkien, because Bilbo's innocence finds delightful form in his speech as much as in his actions.

I begin by asking my students leading questions about Bilbo's opening encounter with the mysterious stranger, who turns out to be Gandalf. The goal of these questions is to help students see how this encounter establishes both the parameters of the hobbit's provinciality as well as a verbal dynamic that prevails for much of the book, one in which the wizard, a veteran wanderer of Middle-earth, serves as the hobbit's playful, sometimes almost mocking instructor, showing the master of Bag End how little he comprehends even the simple implications of the terms he uses. In effect, Bilbo offers up his innocence for Gandalf to expose and educate, a process that begins with Bilbo's cheery, thoughtless greeting: "Good Morning!" (32). The greeting itself probably matters less than the implied explanation that follows, the third-person narrator substantiating Bilbo's first words in the book with a reference to the surrounding conditions: "The sun was shining, and the grass was very green." I work with my students to make sure they recognize that such minor, routine details put the hobbit in a good mood—according to the narrator, at any rate—and also set him up for Gandalf's complicating response: "'What do you mean?' he said. 'Do you wish me a good morning, or mean that it is a good morning whether I want it or not; or that you feel good this morning; or that it is a morning to be good on?'" Bilbo again responds cheerily ("All of them at once" [32]), but the wizard's continued wheedling soon leaves him cross, at which point Bilbo attempts to use precisely the same phrase to dismiss the increasingly amused wizard. The shift in Bilbo's intentions for the "Good morning!" phrase suggests that he recognizes the power of speech but also that he cannot easily wield its power in contest with others, especially not at this early point. The power or powerlessness of Bilbo's speech constitutes an important theme throughout his adventures. Often in his travels, Bilbo finds himself on one end of a trying conversation with creatures or people entirely outside his experience and for whom he is equally exotic and unprecedented. Tolkien presents him very much as a simple soul abroad, and the outcomes of his adventures often spring from his verbal self-presentation as provincial hobbit—from his poor showing with the dwarves in Bag End to his deadly riddle game with Gollum to his importantly effective taunting of the Mirkwood spiders and finally to his remarkably ingenuous conversation with the Elvenking when he hands over the Arkenstone. Tolkien clearly uses Bilbo to convey his unmistakable delight in the deep connections between language and character.

As we examine the relation of Tolkien's text to other works of children's literature, my students and I also decide that it is not plausible to characterize *The Hobbit* as a bildungsroman. While Bilbo certainly acquires a great measure of knowledge and even some wisdom in the course of his adventures, that knowledge only underscores the soundness of his arresting delimitations as a hobbit. On the book's final page, when Gandalf and Balin visit the master of Bag End many years after the quest, the wizard and Bilbo together emphasize not only the inability of experience to alter the hobbit in meaningful ways but also how experience only confirms his humble status. Gandalf says, "You don't really suppose, do you, that all your adventures and escapes were managed by mere luck, just for your sole benefit? You are a very fine person, Mr. Baggins, and I am very fond of you; but you are only quite a little fellow in a wide world after all!," to which Bilbo replies, laughing, "Thank goodness!" (362–63). Nevertheless, the question of Bilbo's education remains a profitable one, because it points up the complexities of his relationships with his dwarf companions and others he encounters.

We also carefully consider the Arkenstone gambit near the end of the book. Asking students simple questions about this bold move tends to open up a remarkable complex of perceptions and motives in the hobbit:

> Why does Bilbo take the Arkenstone in the first place?
> What does his thievery contribute to the story?

These questions prove instructive for students because they expose the technical superfluity of the Arkenstone. Neither the first plot climax (the confrontation with and eventual death of Smaug) nor the secondary plot crisis of the Battle of Five Armies depends at all on Bilbo's ploy. Nothing in the way the dragon dies or the battle unfolds would change if Tolkien omitted the Arkenstone altogether—with one notable exception: the final reconciliation between Thorin and Bilbo.

It would seem, then, that Tolkien uses the Arkenstone at least in part to bring Bilbo and Thorin's relationship to a breaking point, to reduce each character to his core values in such fundamental opposition to each other that only death can heal the rupture. The reconciliation allows Thorin to redeem himself, offsetting all his ugliest traits, which led to his killing rage when he learned that Bilbo gave the Arkenstone to the Elvenking and Bard. But the reconciliation also endears Bilbo's humble, peaceful, and simple philosophy of life as a hobbit while attaching all kinds of qualifiers and costs to his triumph. Bilbo takes no joy in Thorin's deathbed recantation and praise. The immediate and total forgiveness of the hobbit, which Tolkien self-consciously emphasizes, serves as an example for readers who might otherwise judge Thorin's ingratitude more harshly. The child of the kindly West wins, validating the narrator's unabashed admiration of and love for him throughout the book. Nevertheless, Bilbo's victory comes at a cost, a pattern that prevails throughout Tolkien's work and that usually requires characters to accept some kind of sacrifice to achieve victory, as with the Arkenstone.

I then ask:

> Why does Bilbo decide to give the stone away?
> What benefits does he hope to realize?

I point out that Bilbo has no underlying motive when he first takes the Arkenstone; he simply cannot resist the beauty of the gem. Still more revealing, it makes Bilbo uncomfortable to consider his (selfish) motives for taking it in the first place.It is telling that Bilbo's political instincts are perfect (he realizes that the immovably stubborn Thorin would compromise himself to recover this precious family heirloom), but his political abilities remain starkly amateurish. When Bilbo hands the Arkenstone over to the Elvenking and Bard, Tolkien again notes the gem's simple but potent allure for the hobbit, so that his giving it up for the sake of a greater good honors him all the more. Bilbo takes the Arkenstone not as a bargaining piece but willingly relinquishes it by heeding his better conscience. At this point in the discussion, I ask the students how Bilbo's use of the Arkenstone compares with what the narrator characterizes as his bravest, most heroic deed: his decision to proceed down the tunnel alone to Smaug's lair the first time. Which is more admirable, to face Smaug alone or to sacrifice this one gem he loves and even covets in the hope of avoiding battle and the death of his beloved companions?

The Arkenstone gambit lends a kind of wisdom or even clairvoyance to innocence. Bilbo takes the Arkenstone with an innocent's greed, desiring the bright gem for its beauty alone, but he just as innocently gives it up for a greater good. He proves unable to bear Thorin's wrath on the discovery of the jewel. He clearly feels guilty—like a child caught in a lie—when Thorin continually demands the source of the jewel. Bilbo's guilt is not only that of a child but also that of a peacemaker: it motivates his confession and his effort to come between Thorin and the embassy to take the dwarf's ire on himself. Bilbo clearly hopes to spare his friends (the dwarves, the men of Laketown, and the elves) from needless and inevitably bloody conflict. In addition, he seeks to heal the rifts that separate them. When he hands the Arkenstone over to the Elvenking and Bard, he is bravely risking his relationship with Thorin and the dwarves for the sake of a greater good.

I ask students to consider a further benefit of the Arkenstone exchange: it subtly validates and even redeems the elves, the superior creatures in Middle-earth. Tolkien poses a considerable challenge to himself in the characterization of the elves in *The Hobbit*, for they remain unfriendly toward Bilbo's friends the dwarves but still must possess the noble qualities of the elder children. Because they remain fundamentally uncorrupted in Tolkien's conception, they have a natural affinity with the innocent hobbit, who has become close to the dwarves in their travels but remains always an outsider. Hence, before allowing Thorin his best sentiments on his deathbed, Bilbo's gambit spurs the Elvenking to declare that the simple hobbit is more worthy to wear the armor of an elven prince than many others who look more splendid in it. He invites Bilbo to stay with the elves, not only out of genuine affection and delight but also in the fear that Bilbo's life will be in peril once the jewel is revealed. Subsequent events show the Elvenking to be right.

Whatever the risk to himself, Bilbo must return to the dwarves, because they are his friends and he promised to wake Bombur at midnight. Given the magnitude of the stratagem Bilbo has just played, his return seems almost absurdly inconsequential, but it demonstrates the hobbit's deep-rooted honesty and sense of duty. He may have been dishonest in service of a greater good by giving over the Arkenstone, but he will keep the less important promise he made at the beginning of the story. In so doing, he bears out the dwarves' faith in him. At this point, I ask:

> How do the worldly-wise leaders who accept the Arkenstone respond to Bilbo's gesture, and why?

The words and actions of Bard, the Elvenking, and Gandalf during the transfer of the Arkenstone emphasize the harrowing love in Bilbo's actions. When Bilbo warns them of the approach of a hostile dwarf army led by Dain of the Iron Hills, dour Bard, in particular, distrusts and misreads his gesture: "Why do you tell us this? Are you betraying your friends, or are you threatening us?" (330). The prospect of innocent good will and sacrifice in the midst of war preparations requires the dwarves' foes, especially Bard, to rethink their goals and intentions. Tellingly, the Elvenking catches on more quickly (suggesting again the kinship between elves and hobbits indicated in Bilbo's joyful arrival in Rivendell), and his appreciation turns immediately into concern for Bilbo's safety should Bilbo return to the dwarves. Recognizing innocence at work, the Elvenking offers to protect and honor Bilbo, again validating the hobbit's simplicity, especially in comparison with the materialistic motivations of the dwarves.

The response of Gandalf, the fourth party present at the Arkenstone transfer, works to enshrine the innocence of the hobbit and to attribute its success to factors beyond the control of anyone present. Gandalf conceals himself to allow Bilbo his moral triumph free from any guiding influence; regardless of what happens afterward, Bilbo has, acting entirely on his own, clearly and superbly repudiated Bard's cynicism. Gandalf restrains himself as a loving parent might, the authority figure who wishes to see his child pass the moral test that complicated (and dangerous) circumstances have set before him. Ironically, the moral test takes the form of Bilbo's simply regressing to his core practicality as a hobbit, which dictates that beautiful objects such as the Arkenstone have no intrinsic value. As his ominous follow-up comment to Bilbo suggests, Gandalf knows more than even Bard and the Elvenking about the dangers that will soon beset all elves, men, and dwarves massed in and around the Lonely Mountain. The hobbit's simple sacrifice will not ensure the hoped-for peace, yet Gandalf recognizes and celebrates his actions, affirming more deeply than could the Elvenking or Bard the hobbit's virtue.

In class, we evaluate how Bilbo's leadership in the latter stages of the quest confirms his defining innocence. The narrator's comment toward the end, that Bilbo has become the leader of the group (9), shows that Bilbo's experiences in their travels have made his innocence less helpless. By rescuing the dwarves from the spiders and then from imprisonment in the dungeons of the Elvenking, Bilbo demonstrates remarkable resourcefulness and wins the respect of his companions. Yet innocence trumps experience through the hobbit's luck. Although *The Lord of the Rings* develops this theme in greater depth,[3] the earlier work sees good luck less as an accident than as a reward for those who trust in forces greater than themselves. Gandalf originally chooses Bilbo to serve as the lucky number for the dwarves, and the trials they endure in the quest bear out Gandalf's choice, for it is the hobbit's differences from the dwarves that consistently enable the hobbit to offer them otherwise unlikely, even unimaginable, rescue and services. Good luck applies especially to his discovery of the Ring, for Bilbo, the small, slow hobbit, must ride on the back of one of the dwarves as they flee through the tunnels of the goblins, an arrangement that enables his separation from the dwarves and eventual encounter with Gollum. Similarly, he could not rescue the dwarves from the Mirkwood spiders without his superb, Shire-fostered accuracy as a stone thrower. Finally, if he had not been a complete unknown, Bilbo probably would not have survived his interview with Smaug; instead, he beguiles the great dragon with riddles until Smaug reveals the fatal flaw in his armor. Bilbo is the lucky number for the dwarves and their quest precisely because he is an innocent abroad in a world full of dangers and deadly hostilities. As the universal unknown, Bilbo consistently befuddles or delays the various enemies of the dwarves in their often feckless attempts to win back their own.

Bilbo's experience in the Battle of Five Armies also demonstrates his fundamental innocence as it incorporates and eventually outweighs his experience to enable his survival. An outsider among the dwarves throughout the quest, he finds himself on the sidelines when the battle gets under way: cast out by Thorin but hardly in position to join up with either the elves in the Elvenking's army or the men in Bard's army. The narrator's description of Bilbo's decision to take a stand with the elves emphasizes the simplicity of the hobbit's thought processes and allegiances, particularly his instinctive love of elves. His ability to see the eagles arriving similarly springs from his marginal status, for he literally detaches himself from the battles and looks up at the sky (instead of focusing on the goblin and warg forces) with his keen hobbit's eyes to spot their rescuers. When Bilbo finally reappears after the battle, Gandalf cements the connection between the hobbit's survival and his innocent good fortune: "'Baggins!' he exclaimed. 'Well I never! Alive after all—I *am* glad! I began to wonder if even your luck would see you through!'" (347–48).

Finally, I discuss with my students the connection between Tolkien's narrative tone and Bilbo's innocence. Tolkien first told the story that would eventually become *The Hobbit* to his own children,[4] and the finished version still reveals the tale's roots in a thoughtful, playful parent's attempts to entertain, excite, and reassure his beloved audience. The relationship between the narrator and the imagined reader in *The Hobbit* bears out Vladimir Nabokov's description of the gamesmanship that characterizes the author-reader relationship, in which the author, anticipating the reader's concerns and surmises, acts as a kind of inspired tour guide who takes joy in simultaneously creating in the reader expectations and fulfilling them.[5] In this relationship, Bilbo must serve as the vehicle for an innocent reader's fears and delights. The narrator consistently follows the latest plot development by turning to its effect on the hobbit, anticipating the reader's instinctive question, "What about Bilbo?" Bilbo is, in many ways, the younger, rather helpless sibling in constant danger of being left behind by the more worldly, more experienced, more able dwarves, a fear to which any child can relate. Through the kindly narrator, Tolkien milks this anxiety, building suspense and alleviating it.

The first encounter with the wargs illustrates the narrative touches that subtly establish an undertone of playfulness, which in turn creates a reassuring distance between an innocent reader and the dangers that beset the vulnerable little protagonist. After the avalanche delivers the troupe into the dell, where they will soon climb up trees to escape the wargs, the narrator includes the hobbit in a parenthetical aside that both associates him with and distinguishes him from his companions: "The dwarves (and Bilbo) were feeling far from happy" (144). Such a simple side reference to the hobbit rewards readers who automatically worry about Bilbo. Tolkien makes it clear that Bilbo may travel with them but still has special needs and sensibilities, precisely honoring children's sense of simultaneous belonging to and difference from the adults on whom they depend. The narrator frequently includes Bilbo in just this fashion, as an afterthought who will be anything but an afterthought for the children readers inclined to identify with the hobbit.

For another example, Bilbo, the least hardy and most wary of the troupe, asks, "Must we go any further?" He then proceeds to complain (like a child incapable of appreciating adult imperatives in the face of simple bodily urges) that he needs to stop, danger or no danger. Gandalf responds to Bilbo's whining just as a parent might: "A bit further." The payoff comes at the beginning of the next paragraph, in which the narrator injects his own perspective in a way that insinuates Bilbo's simpleminded unhappiness: "After what seemed ages further . . ." (144). The narrator is not only constantly aware of Bilbo's perspective but also caters to the innocent reader's concern for Bilbo, who cannot negotiate predicaments along with the wizard and the dwarves. A few paragraphs later, when the beleaguered party hears the wolves howl, the narrator again plays to the reader's concern for the hobbit:

> There were no wolves living near Mr. Baggins' hole at home, but he knew that noise. He had had it described to him often enough in tales. One of his elder cousins (on the Took side), who had been a great traveller, used to imitate it to frighten him. To hear it out in the forest under the moon was too much for Bilbo. Even magic rings are not much use against wolves—especially against the evil packs that lived under the shadow of the goblin-infested mountains, over the Edge of the Wild on the borders of the unknown. Wolves of that sort smell keener than goblins, and do not need to see you to catch you! (145)

This digression carefully encourages the reader's affinity with hapless Bilbo, even anticipating the reader's likely protest that Bilbo has a magic ring now, which should protect him—no protection at all against this threat, the parental narrator points out. The exclamation at the end also serves to heighten enjoyable suspense while minimizing the danger: the wolves will only catch you, not kill or devour you. Almost every chapter of *The Hobbit* similarly invites the reader to detach subtly and momentarily from the plot and identify with the hobbit's plight, share in the hobbit's inexperience, enjoy the suspense created when obvious solutions for the hobbit will not work, even when the reader remains confident (another benefit of the narrator's kindly, playfully parental tone) that the hobbit will somehow survive.

To conclude our discussions of *The Hobbit*, I like to ask my students a question that seems to come out of the proverbial blue: How would they compare Tolkien's book with Lewis Carroll's touchstone children's text, *Alice's Adventures in Wonderland*? Inevitably, the students struggle to compare the texts, at which point I mention that Tolkien himself initially rejected the comparison before accepting it—with illuminating qualifications. In a 1937 letter to his publisher, Tolkien, as a university professor who was also a children's writer, objected to a book-jacket blurb that likened him to Charles Dodgson (who wrote under the pen name Lewis Carroll). There would seem to be little similarity between Dodgson, a mathematician, and Tolkien, a philologist. But on further examination, Tolkien allowed that comparing *The Hobbit* with *Through the Looking Glass* did convey some of the complexities of Bilbo's experience and characterization (*Letters of J. R. R. Tolkien* 20–22). In both *Wonderland* and *Looking Glass*, Carroll's Alice finds herself in a world where the rules she has observed during her young life prove largely useless. As she attempts to apply her experiences from conventional reality to the dreamscapes, she learns that the creatures and situations she encounters never quite yield to her sensibilities or perspective. She can function in the dream worlds, respond to questions and prompt responses to her own, affect the behavior of creatures she meets, and, in the end, successfully resist the will of the Red Queen, the most frightful figure she encounters. Ultimately, however, she wakes to conventional reality relatively unchanged, coming out of her dream in *Looking Glass* to find her cat Dinah reassuringly present. Alice learns little from her adventures, even though her experiences have shown the limitations in her perspective and upbringing. Still, she is the child at the end that she was at the beginning. The original volume of her adventures ends with a nostalgic reverie suggesting the author's (much more than Alice's) nostalgia for childhood innocence and the limits it imposes on Alice's actions even as it seems to spark her imagination (Carroll 125–27).

When I ask students to consider Alice from this perspective, they soon appreciate the comparison with Bilbo. Tolkien, of course, was not encouraging a point-by-point connection between his hobbit and Carroll's Alice, but as a hobbit, even at this early stage of the figure's development within Tolkien's work,

Bilbo embodies a stubborn innocence, an earthy, deep-rooted immunity to change (somewhat like Alice), despite the overwhelming qualities of his adventures. Tolkien clearly valued Bilbo's ability to resume his life at the end—with some changes certainly, but still more or less the same pleasant burgher's life of leisure he had established in Bag End before his journey. This steadfastness compares favorably not only with Alice's awakenings but also with the returns of Sam, Merry, and Pippin to the Shire in *The Lord of the Rings*. Our discussions thus return full circle to the question of innocence and experience and their roots in the landscape and languages that Tolkien imagined: Bilbo remains, in both his book and its sequel, a creature of his home and homeland, the child of the kindly West that Thorin names him—with all the limitations and gifts the description implies.

NOTES

[1]While a long-standing commonplace in studies of children's literature, the necessity of a child reader's identification with a book's protagonist has prompted considerable debate. For a brief, useful overview of this debate, see Lesnik-Oberstein, especially pages 27–28.

[2]For a fuller explanation of these key developments between *The Hobbit* and *The Lord of the Rings*, see Shippey, *Road*, especially pages 96–103 in the chapter "A Cartographic Plot."

[3]See Shippey, *Road*, especially pages 150–54 in the chapter "Interlacements and the Ring."

[4]See Douglas A. Anderson's introduction to *The Annotated Hobbit*, especially pages 8–10, which include a description by Tolkien's son Christopher of the author's reading early, unfinished versions of the story to his children.

[5]For a fuller description of Nabokov's characterization of this relationship, see B. Walter.

Using *The History of Middle-earth* with Tolkien's Fiction

Yvette Kisor

Thanks to the work of Christopher Tolkien in editing his father's papers, *The History of Middle-earth* provides a rare opportunity for students to engage in an author's creative process and trace the development of not only a work of fiction but also a world with its own history and languages. In addition, Christopher Tolkien's commentary, replication of different drafts, description and dating of manuscripts, determination of the order of composition, and other scholarly apparatuses expose students to the editorial tasks that go into the production of any authoritative edition. Of the numerous ways students can usefully engage these volumes in conjunction with J. R. R. Tolkien's fiction, two approaches are particularly useful.

One approach focuses directly on the individual volumes of *The History of Middle-earth* by having students work collaboratively, in groups of two or three, to become experts on their assigned volume.[1] I give this assignment early in the course, although students make their presentations after the midterm: the long lead time enables them to prepare for this demanding assignment. Since *The History of Middle-earth* presents a kind of reading they will likely not have encountered before, it is important that teachers emphasize that all students in the group need to read their volume thoroughly. The volumes include fragments of stories Tolkien never published, early drafts of familiar fiction, songs, poems, essays, maps, illustrations, genealogies, plot outlines, and links among items, all in various real and invented languages, and what might best be called private musings as he worked out relations among various elements of the world he was creating. All this text can confuse students, and their confusion may be increased by the editorial apparatus of Christopher Tolkien.

The language of the editor will be familiar to medieval scholars accustomed to descriptions of manuscript stemmata, scribal hands, and attempts to date different manuscripts but completely foreign to students. For example, the first volume, *The Book of Lost Tales, Part I*, opens with "The Cottage of Lost Play," which is prefaced by a brief introduction that includes references to "fair copy," "rough pencilled manuscript," and "date of the actual composition" (13). The text itself is followed by notes, a list of changes made to names (with accompanying explanations), and commentary, which is also footnoted. Technical descriptions and terms are used without explanation. Arguably, students can figure out what is meant by "hand" in an editorial context or decipher a description like "the text in ink was written over a draft in pencil that was wholly erased" (45), but teachers may want to introduce the vocabulary of editing first. Christopher Tolkien uses various designations to specify subsequent manuscripts (sometimes A, B, C or I, II, etc.; other times letters are derived from the title of the manuscript)[2] or to designate different versions of events.[3] These manuscripts can include penciled drafts, notes and outlines, fair copies in ink, typescripts, carbon copies, and other versions in at least three hands (Tolkien's; his wife's, Edith's; and even that of a young Christopher himself). On rare occasions, Christopher Tolkien uses untranslated Latin terms such as *ab initio* and *terminus a quo* without explanation (*Treason* 250; *Lays* 3).

I have found that a short introduction to the editorial apparatus generally accompanying a scholarly edition is appropriate, as is a discussion of the particularities of Christopher Tolkien's editorial work. The techniques and terminology used in dating manuscripts and constructing a stemma for the various manuscript witnesses, as well as the language used to describe manuscripts, should suffice. This brief introduction eases students into the work and gives them a better sense of the text they are encountering. The editorial apparatus of *The History of Middle-earth* also provides teachers with the rare opportunity to use a modern text to demonstrate how a work with a much longer history is edited. Christopher Tolkien's attempts to edit his father's manuscripts bring to bear the same techniques of many editors of medieval manuscripts—and in fact Christopher Tolkien was trained in such editing. Alternatively, since most of the editorial apparatus is logical, one advantage of not providing this introduction, of "throwing them in the deep end," is that students unfamiliar with these editorial techniques can discover for themselves the parallels between editor and investigator.

Students are required to provide a detailed outline of their assigned volume. This outline will be distributed to the class, so that students will all have a comprehensive listing of the contents of all twelve volumes, which may aid them in finding relevant texts for later projects. In addition, groups may find helpful Web resources such as "What's in the History of Middle-earth?" (Pettersson), which lists the contents of each volume and gives a brief description of them, along with their chronology and genre.[4] Students choose two items from their volume to present to the class in greater depth. Because the rest of the class will be unfamiliar with what is presented, some summarizing is necessary. The students presenting should discuss what light these texts shed on the other works by Tolkien that we read for class. The items chosen might be an earlier version of a work read in class or a different work altogether. Even a text like "The Notion Club Papers" (*Sauron* 145–327) or an essay like "Athrabeth Finrod ah Andreth" (*Morgoth's Ring* 301–63) has some relation to *The Lord of the Rings* or other elements of Tolkien's published works, through plot, theme, or character. Many students note elements of various stories in *The Silmarillion* that reflect themes and motifs of *The Lord of the Rings*. Students should elucidate such connections to the less polished material of *The History of Middle-earth* and ultimately answer the question: What did reading this volume of *The History of Middle-earth* add to your understanding of Tolkien's Middle-earth?

I tried this assignment originally in a one-semester course of twenty-six students who were mostly juniors and seniors majoring in literature. Success was mixed. Working in pairs with little oversight, many students did an exceptional job. Most understood the volumes they were assigned and offered real insights into the connections between these materials and Tolkien's published fiction. They became experts on various aspects of Tolkien's development and on specific features of the evolution of Middle-earth. They could provide commentary and analysis in unforeseen ways, making class discussions at times feel like a conversation among a community of Tolkien scholars. But some students got bogged down summarizing their assigned volume and lost sight of the larger questions: how their volume related to our readings in class (Tolkien's published fiction) and increased their understanding of Middle-earth. Summarizing is generally considered a lower-level skill, but these students found it difficult given the wealth of detail and the confusing state of some of the material. It was not unusual for them to produce handouts in excess of ten pages. My mixed success with this approach led me to revise the assignment to make the links to Tolkien's published fiction clearer and allow students to deal with smaller sections of *The History of Middle-earth*.

In this second approach, the volumes of *The History of Middle-earth* become ancillary to Tolkien's published fiction. As a result, not all of them are covered equally, and elements of them are presented according to their relevance to the published fiction. This relevance-based approach is clear in four of the volumes that trace the development of *The Lord of the Rings*,[5] but it is not so clear regarding the convoluted history of *The Silmarillion*. A great help here is Douglas Kane's *Arda Reconstructed*, which discusses Christopher Tolkien's work as editor of *The Silmarillion* and traces its sources in detail, often outlining paragraph by paragraph which manuscript each section of the published work comes from. Sections from *The History of Middle-earth* can therefore be assigned to specific students for presentation: various texts from *The History of Middle-earth* are paired with passages of *The Lord of the Rings* and *The Silmarillion*. Students read their assigned sections of *The History of Middle-earth* with care, provide a brief oral summary to the class, create a detailed written summary to distribute as a handout, and identify and explain one important divergence and convergence, as well as two of lesser importance, between their section and a published passage. Ultimately they must answer the question: What did reading these sections of *The History of Middle-earth* add to your understanding of Tolkien's Middle-earth? Table 1 displays a way to assign texts from *The History of Middle-earth* to individual students, indicating the corresponding part of *The Lord of the Rings*.

For the stories of *The Silmarillion*, the same kind of assignment can be constructed. Using Kane's *Arda Reconstructed*, the list of contents available online, and the volumes of *The History of Middle-earth* themselves, teachers can determine which sections of *The History of Middle-earth* volumes correspond to which stories in *The Silmarillion*. While this task is more complex than for *The Lord of the Rings*, particularly the stories that have a long and intricate history of composition,[6] the general outline of Tolkien's mythology contained in *The*

TABLE 1: THE RELEVANCE OF *THE HISTORY OF MIDDLE-EARTH* TO *THE LORD OF THE RINGS*

The Lord of the Rings	**Student**	***The History of Middle-earth***
Fellowship, bk. 1	1	"The First Phase" (*Return of the Shadow* 11–131 [chs. 1–7])
	2	"The First Phase" (132–229 [chs. 8–13])
	3	"The Second Phase" (233–305 [chs. 14–18])
	4	"The Third Phase" (309–87 [chs. 19–22])
	5	*The Treason of Isengard* (5–80 [chs. 1–4])
Fellowship, bk. 2	6	"The Story Continued" (*Return of the Shadow* 391–467 [chs. 23–25])
	7	*The Treason of Isengard* 81–206 (chs. 5–10)
	8	*The Treason of Isengard* 207–377 (chs. 11–18)
Two Towers, bk. 3	9	*The Treason of Isengard* 378–451 (chs. 19–26)
	10	"The Fall of Saruman" (*War of the Ring* 3–81 [pt. 1, chs. 1–6])
Two Towers, bk. 4	11	"The Ring Goes East" (85–226 [pt. 2, chs. 1–8])
Return of the King, bk. 5	12	"Minas Tirith" (229–322 [pt. 3, chs. 1–5])
	13	"Minas Tirith" (323–439 [chs. 6–14])
Return of the King, bk. 6	14	"The End of the Third Age" (*Sauron* 3–141 [pt. 1, chs. 1–11])

Silmarillion is as follows:[7] the earliest conception (begun 1916–17) is *The Book of Lost Tales*, in which the mariner Eriol (Ælfwine) voyages to Tol Eressëa, the Lonely Isle, where he hears the stories of the elves. Tolkien also composed long narrative poems of the "great tales," some quite lengthy but none complete (1920s). The next formulations of the mythology as a whole are the "Sketch of the Mythology" (1926), followed by the "Quenta Noldorinwa" (1930), and the incomplete "Quenta Silmarillion" (1937). Tolkien also constructed abbreviated versions in the earliest "Annals of Valinor and Beleriand" (early 1930s); these are revised as the later "Annals of Valinor and Beleriand" (mid to late 1930s) and finally the "Annals of Aman" and the "Grey Annals" (1950–51).[8] His final version of the annals, composed after *The Lord of the Rings*, coincides with his later "Quenta Silmarillion" (1951) and later versions of the "great tales" (1950s). In addition, his two time-travel narratives, *The Lost Road* (1936–37) and *The Notion Club Papers* (1945–46), recount the Fall of Númenor.

I identify for my students relevant sections of *The History of Middle-earth* for several stories found in *The Silmarillion* ("Ainulindalë," "Valaquenta," and "Akallabêth") as well as the three "great tales" found in the "Quenta Silmarillion" ("Of Beren and Lúthien," "Of Túrin Turambar" [or *The Children of Húrin*],[9] and "Of Tuor and the Fall of Gondolin"). I choose these six stories because they are the major tales in Tolkien's imagination, as judged by the amount of time he spent writing and rewriting them. Table 2 lays out one possible version of this assignment.

TABLE 2: THE RELEVANCE OF *THE HISTORY OF MIDDLE-EARTH* TO *THE SILMARILLION*

The Silmarillion	**Student**	***The History of Middle-earth***
"Ainulindalë"	1	*The Book of Lost Tales, Part One* (13–63 [chs. 1–2])
		"Ainulindalë" (*Lost Road* 155–66 [pt. 2, ch. 4])
		"Ainulindalë" (*Morgoth's Ring* 3–44)
"Valaquenta"	2	*The Book of Lost Tales, Part One* 64–93 (ch. 3)
		"Quenta Noldorinwa" (*Shaping* 76–79 [text], 166–67 [commentary]; ch. 3 ["The Quenta"])
		"The Earliest Annals of Valinor 0" (*Shaping* 262–63 [text], 270 [notes], 274–76 [commentary], 292–93 [text fragment])
		"The Later Annals of Valinor" (*Lost Road* 109–10 [text], 120–21 [commentary]; pt. 2, ch. 2)
		"Of the Valar" (*Lost Road* 199–208 [pt. 2, ch. 6, titled "Quenta Silmarillion"])
		"The Annals of Aman" (*Morgoth's Ring* 47–49 [text], 56 [notes], 58–59 [commentary], 64–66 [alternate text], 69 [alternate emendations]; years 1–4)
		"Of the Valar" (*Morgoth's Ring* 141–52 [First Phase], 199–205 [Second Phase]; pt. 3, titled "The Later Quenta Silmarillion")

The Silmarillion	Student	*The History of Middle-earth*
"Akallabêth"	3	*Letters of J. R. R. Tolkien* 213, 232, 347
		"The Fall of Númenor" (*Lost Road* 7–35 [pt. 1, chs. 1–2])
		"The Drowning of Anadûnê" (*Sauron* 331–440)
		"The History of the Akallabêth" (*Peoples* 140–65)
"Beren and Lúthien"	4	"The Tale of Tinúviel" (*Book of Lost Tales, Part Two* 3–68 [ch. 1])
	5–6	"The Lay of Leithian" (*Lays* 150–367)
	7	"Sketch of the Mythology" (*Shaping* 24–26 [text], 54–56 [commentary]; from ch. 2, "The Earliest Silmarillion"; Tolkien ch. number 10)
		"Quenta Noldorinwa" (*Shaping* 109–16 [text], 177–79 [commentary]; from ch. 3, "The Quenta"; Tolkien ch. number 10)
		"The Earliest Annals of Beleriand" (*Shaping* 300–01; from ch. 7; years 160–64)
		"The Later Annals of Beleriand" (*Lost Road* 134–35 [text], 151 [commentary]; from pt. 2, ch. 3; years 261–65)
		"Of Beren and Tinúviel" (*Lost Road* 292–306 [chs. 12–15]; pt. 2, ch. 6, titled "Quenta Silmarillion"])
		"The Grey Annals" (*War of the Jewels* 58–69 [text], 129–32 [commentary], pt. 1; years 460–67)
"Túrin Turambar"	8	"Turambar and the Foalókë" (*Book of Lost Tales, Part Two* 69–143 [ch. 2])
	9	"The Lay of the Children of Húrin" (*Lays* 3–130)
	10	"Sketch of the Mythology" (*Shaping* 28–32 [text], 58–61 [commentary]; from ch. 2, "The Earliest Silmarillion"; Tolkien ch. numbers 12–13)
		"Quenta Noldorinwa" (*Shaping* 122–31 [text], 182–87 [commentary]; from ch. 3, "The Quenta"; Tolkien ch. numbers 12–13)

The Silmarillion	**Student**	***The History of Middle-earth***
		"The Earliest Annals of Beleriand" (*Shaping* 303–06 [text], 322–25 [commentary]; years 173–99)
		"The Later Annals of Beleriand" (*Lost Road* 138–41 [text], 151–52 [commentary]; years 273–99)
"Túrin Turambar"		"Of Túrin Turamarth or Túrin the Hapless" (*Lost Road* 315–23 [ch. 17]; pt. 2, ch. 6, titled "Quenta Silmarillion")
		"The Grey Annals" (*War of the Jewels* 79–103 [text], 135–65 [commentary]; years 472–99)
		"Ælfwine and Dírhaval" (*War of the Jewels* 311–15 [pt. 3, ch. 2])
	11	"Narn i Hîn Húrin" (*Unfinished Tales* 6–7 [introduction], 57–162 [text])
	12	"The Fall of Gondolin" (*Book of Lost Tales, Part Two* 144–220 [ch. 3])
	13	"The Lay of the Fall of Gondolin" (*Lays* 144–49)
		"Sketch of the Mythology" (*Shaping* 34–37 [text], 65–67 [commentary]; from ch. 2, "The Earliest Silmarillion" [Tolkien ch. numbers 15–16])
"Fall of Gondolin"		"Quenta Noldorinwa" (*Shaping* 135–48 [text], 191–95 [commentary], 213–18 [app. 2, "The Horns of Ylmir," a poem fragment]; from ch. 3, "The Quenta"; Tolkien ch. numbers 12–13)[10]
		"The Earliest Annals of Beleriand" (*Shaping* 307–08, 326; years 206–07)
		"The Later Annals of Beleriand" (*Lost Road* 142, years 300–07)[11]
		"Of Tuor and His Coming to Gondolin" (*Unfinished Tales* 4–6 [introduction], 17–56 [text])

Each of these pieces of *The Silmarillion* has between three and ten textual antecedents in *The History of Middle-earth* and can be covered by one to four students, depending on the length and number of the relevant texts. For example, the story of Beren and Lúthien exists in several forms. The earliest version is "The Tale of Tinúviel," found in *The Book of Lost Tales*; this is followed by the "Lay of Leithian," a lengthy narrative poem begun in the 1920s and recommenced in the 1950s. Brief versions of the story are given in the "Sketch of the Mythology" (Tolkien ch. number 10), "Quenta Noldorinwa" (Tolkien ch. number 10), the earlier "Annals of Beleriand" (years 160–64), the later "Annals of Beleriand" (years 261–65), "Of Beren and Tinúviel" in "Quenta Silmarillion" (Tolkien ch. numbers 12–15), and the "Grey Annals" (years 460–67). These versions can be divided among four students: one covers the earliest version in *The Book of Lost Tales*; two cover the lengthy "Lay of Leithian" and its later continuation (a convenient break comes after canto 9, "The Defeat of Thû" [259]); and a fourth covers the six briefer accounts in the later material. This approach works especially well in a course focused on Tolkien, as it highlights the process of composition and reifies the concept of a life's work. Another possibility, in a course focused on fantasy, would be to illustrate the particular difficulties of creating an internally consistent secondary world.

Using *The History of Middle-earth* as the content for oral presentations gives individual students an intimate knowledge of a small portion of *The History of Middle-earth*, and it gives the class as a whole an overall sense of Tolkien's process of composition and the growth of his conception of Middle-earth over his lifetime. The volumes of *The History of Middle-earth*, of course, can be used as resources for a research paper. In such a paper, students might choose one element of Tolkien's legendarium and use *The History of Middle-earth* to trace its evolution over time. Fruitful material for such a project might be an entire tale, such as "Beren and Lúthien" or "The Fall of Gondolin," or some smaller piece, such as the creation of the Sun and Moon, or even the conception of a single character. The volumes of *The History of Middle-earth* encourage such examinations and offer myriad opportunities for following the author at his workbench. In *The Road to Middle-earth*, Tom Shippey states that "much of 'The History of Middle-earth' demands to be taken as 'ox-bones'" (290).[12] The publication of *The History of Middle-earth* has given us the rare opportunity to see the bones of the ox.

NOTES

[1] I also sometimes include *The Unfinished Tales*, published just before *The History of Middle-earth*.

[2] See *Book of Lost Tales II* 312, *Lost Road* 294–95, and *War of the Jewels* 103, 209, 214 for just a few examples.

[3] See, for example, the discussion of Gandalf's delay in *Treason* 10–15.

[4]Their assignment goes significantly beyond this listing of content, but it may provide a starting point (and in my experience students tend to find such online resources on their own).

[5]These are volumes 6 through 9 of *The History of Middle-earth*, also referred to as *The History of* The Lord of the Rings, parts 1 through 4.

[6]Tolkien's account of the creation of the Sun and Moon is found in ten texts in five of *The History of Middle-earth* volumes: "The Tale of the Sun and Moon" (*Book of Lost Tales I* 174–206 [ch. 8]); "The History of Eriol or Ælfwine and the End of the Tales" (*Book of Lost Tales II* 281–89); "The Earliest 'Silmarillion,'" "The Quenta," and "The Ambarkanta" (*Shaping* 20–21 [text], 49–50 [commentary], 97–99 [text], 170–72 [commentary], 237 [text], 254 [commentary]); "Of the Sun and Moon and the Hiding of Valinor" (*Lost Road* 239–45; pt. 2, ch. 6, titled "Quenta Silmarillion"; Tolkien ch. number 6); "Ainulindalë" 3–5 (introduction), 40–44 (text) (pt. 1 of *Morgoth's Ring*); "Sixth and Last Section of the Annals of Aman, 1495–1500: Of the Moon and the Sun: The Lighting of Endar, and the Hiding of Valinor" 129–38 (pt. 2, sec. 6); "Of the Sun and Moon and the Hiding of Valinor" 197–99 (pt. 3, ch. 1, sec. 8); "Myths Transformed" 367–90 (pt. 5, esp. texts 1–3, 5).

[7]A partial summary of this evolution, with special reference to the three "great tales," is given in app. 1, "The Evolution of the Great Tales," in *The Children of Húrin* (269–82).

[8]Related to these is "The Tale of Years," a chronology with small narrative content. It continues past the point where the Grey Annals breaks off after the story of Túrin; see *War of the Jewels* 342–56.

[9]An account of the relation between the versions of the Túrin legend given in *The Children of Húrin* and the "Narn i Hîn Húrin," found in *Unfinished Tales*, with reference to *The Silmarillion* and other texts containing elements of the story, is given in "The Composition of the Text," in *The Children of Húrin*, app. 2, 283–92.

[10]The opening paragraphs of chapter 17 of the "Quenta Noldorinwa" include elements of the story included in chapter 23 "Of Tuor and the Fall of Gondolin" of *The Silmarillion*. See *Shaping* 148–49, 151, 155n3.

[11]One could also include the relevant sections of "The Tale of Years," though it is debatable how much is added to the story in these brief accounts, typically little more than a sentence or two. See *War of the Jewels* 344–54.

[12]For discussion of Tolkien's use of the ox bones metaphor in "On Fairy-stories," see Flieger's essay in this volume.

Presenting Tolkien's Pasts

Robin Chapman Stacey

As a historian whose research focuses primarily on medieval Ireland and Wales, I have long been interested in the use of myth as a vehicle through which to explore and reshape the past. In a very real sense, myth is both embedded in tradition and a manufacturer of it. As such, it sheds powerful light on aspects of the past that historians otherwise never see. What J. R. R. Tolkien offers teachers of history is unique: the perspective of a thoughtful and reflective observer who not only was an expert in the mythologies of ancient Europe, an expert whose nature expressed itself about things most deeply felt in mythic form, but also possessed the talent to write mythologies himself. Tolkien was not the only man to be profoundly affected by his experiences in the trenches of World War I, nor was he the only writer to have invented languages and worlds of his own. Most assuredly, he was not the only academic to hear the siren call of folklore studies and historical linguistics and imagine their implications for the resurrection of ancient cultures. He was not even the only author to make use of medieval imagery in his reflections on war and sacrifice. But he was, unquestionably, the most potent mythmaker of the twentieth century, an era that witnessed two devastating world wars, a rural way of life choked by industrial development, and humankind set adrift in a cosmos that God no longer seemed to inhabit. Tolkien's voice as a writer is both unique and courageous in its refusal to cast his small golden scepter down and take refuge in nihilism and despair.[1] This voice is what I try to capture in my undergraduate course, Reading Tolkien, at the University of Washington.

Although I originally developed my course on Tolkien for the honors program, its usual home nowadays is the history department, which reflects my own approach to the subject. Probably the most important consequence of teaching Tolkien's works in a history course is that the class proceeds topically and, to a lesser degree, chronologically. It is thus important to me that students be able to reference Tolkien's major writings, from the beginning of our discussions, on topics such as predestination and free will, the nature of evil, or morality and the natural world. In addition, because my university uses the quarter system, we have only eleven weeks from start to finish. Were we to proceed sequentially through Tolkien's major works, students would simply not have enough time to familiarize themselves with what they need to read in order to tackle these subjects. Therefore I require all my students to read the entirety of *The Hobbit* and *The Lord of the Rings* before the class begins. When I first announced this requirement, it met with considerable skepticism from colleagues. But after several years of teaching the class in a variety of formats, I have yet to be disappointed. I get students who were virtually weaned on Tolkien side by side with those who had never heard of him until they chanced on Peter Jackson's movies. If a student ever failed to fulfill the requirement, I was not aware of it. Of course, we reread substantial portions of both works as we progress through the class, and I cannot always tell whether students have done the rereading. However, that we all start more or less on the same page has been a major factor in the success of the course.

We begin by covering Tolkien himself. Much of our early work is biographical, accomplished primarily through lecture on the first day and consolidated over following class sessions by readings in either Humphrey Carpenter's biography or Tolkien's own letters.[2] In the first class, I give students an exercise designed to underscore the extent to which Tolkien's academic and mythmaking personas cannot be easily separated from each other. At this point, few students know of his career as a philologist and specialist in the literatures of the ancient north—likely even fewer have any notion what such a person does on a daily basis to earn a living. Tolkien's ideas, steeped in ancient myth and beliefs about the power of language, are unfamiliar to the vast majority of students today. With this in mind, I design an exercise to help them share in the excitement he may have felt when a word or name, briefly glimpsed, opened up hitherto unimagined fictional worlds.

I divide the class of thirty-five students into four groups, giving each group a list of English place-names together with their Anglo-Saxon roots and translations. I explain that these words are place-names as Tolkien, in his work as a philologist, would have seen them: rendered transparent by his intimate knowledge of the language. I ask the groups to imagine that all these names exist in proximity to one another (in fact, all are in Oxfordshire) and to invent a myth explaining to the rest of the class the connection among them. Two groups work separately on each list, so that two different myths are told for each list of names. Since I choose names with suggestive elements, such as "elf," "burial mound," "carrion birds," "holly wood," and the like, the stories almost always have thematic similarities that transcend their dissimilarities in structure and plot. Once the groups have finished presenting their myths, we discuss the similarities and differences, trying to understand how language itself can suggest particular plots and themes to the mind. Students are skeptical at first, but when they see how their group's words generated story lines and guided their imaginations in certain ways, they begin to grasp what it means for Tolkien's tales to have been inspired by and grounded in language rather than the other way around.

Also in the early weeks of the class, I establish the historical context within and about which Tolkien was writing. Although initially I give this context through lectures, these become more infrequent as the course progresses, while reading and discussion increasingly take center stage. Early lectures focus both on the emergence of historical linguistics and philology as fields of intellectual endeavor and on the rise in folklore and fairy-tale studies in the eighteenth and nineteenth centuries. We discuss Romantic nationalism and talk about the boundaries that often so thinly separate traditions found (works discovered in the archives or collected in the field, such as the Finnish *Kalevala*) from traditions invented (the Ossian poems of James Macpherson and the "druidic" works of Iolo Morganwg).[3] Students begin to grasp what was at stake in the disagreements between folklorists and comparative philologists such as Max Müller, Andrew Lang, and George Webbe Dasent and to recognize, when they read Tolkien's "On Fairy-stories" in the second week, the novelty of his approach and the intellectual problems to which his essay was responding. Reading Tolkien's poem "Mythopoeia" alongside "On Fairy-stories" enables students to probe further his ideas about myth and, especially, to appreciate the extent to which Tolkien perceived his own work as participating in a mythological and spiritual tradition larger than himself. This portion of the course helps students understand how the devoutly Catholic Tolkien can speak longingly of elves as though they might be real and why he takes such care in his tales to make room for Atlantis, Ragnarök, and other ancient mythological truths. Students familiar with his ideas about spirituality and myth, and with the debates about language and ancient cultures that preoccupied intellectuals in his time, are able to better contextualize his passionate desire to create a new yet also ancient-feeling mythology for his beloved England.

Other historical lectures follow at intervals throughout the term. However, because reading and discussion are my main teaching modes after the first few weeks, these lectures serve mainly to introduce topics that we relate to excerpts from Tolkien's works. Since many students know little about World War I, when we talk about Tolkien's views on war, I not only lecture about this particular war but also show a film documentary on the trenches to communicate the horror of what Tolkien and his peers experienced. The episode called "Slaughter" in the PBS series *The Great War and the Shaping of the Twentieth Century* is a bit dated but conveys both the pressures attendant on men of that era to join up to fight and the horrors of the Battle of the Somme, in which Tolkien participated. These presentations on World War I are followed by the first paper assignment, which asks students to choose a work by a recognized war author (loosely conceptualized) and compare its principal themes and preoccupations with those of Tolkien. Students may choose authors writing during or in the wake of either World War I (e.g., Wilfred Owen, Siegfried Sassoon, Robert Graves, T. S. Eliot) or World War II (e.g., William Golding, George Orwell, Kurt Vonnegut, Joseph Heller, Ursula K. Le Guin). In my first incarnation of this assignment, I had students choose different authors on which they gave short presentations to the class. I still insist that students explore a wide range of authors, but instead of a formal presentation I run a common discussion about these ideas on the day students hand in their papers. Organizing a discussion for which there is no common reading apart from Tolkien can be challenging. However, once students realize how many themes the works of these war authors share—for instance, the nature of man, the presence or absence of God, free will, the origins of evil, the wasteland—the conversation typically becomes quite animated.

Later lectures consider Tolkien in the context of other twentieth-century movements and developments. So that students see the often ideologically hostile context in which Tolkien and other contemporary Christian authors wrote, I lecture on the Inklings as well as on the rising popularity of philosophies trumpeting the death of God and the meaninglessness of traditional notions of order (Nietzsche, Dada, existentialism, and the like). In addition, since at least some of my students come into the class out of an interest in religion or C. S. Lewis in particular, we read excerpts from Lewis's works and highlight in our discussions the similarities and differences between his and Tolkien's treatments of such issues as predestination, free will, and the nature of evil. Previously, I used excerpts from *The Lion, the Witch and the Wardrobe* and *The Screwtape Letters* for this purpose; more recently, I have begun using *Perelandra* in response to student complaints that the other two works were too easy. Our discussions of Tom Bombadil, the ents, Saruman, and Tolkien's views on technology and science are prefaced by a presentation on industrialization and its environmental consequences. Similarly, a lecture on women and domestic life at Oxford in Tolkien's day prepares us to consider the historical contexts surrounding issues of women and the female in Tolkien's works. In honors classes, where longer reading assignments are expected, Brenda Partridge's "No Sex Please—We're Hobbits" usually generates the sort of skepticism among students that can lead to passionate discussion. Alternatively (or additionally), the tale "Aldarion and Erendis" (Tolkien, *Unfinished Tales* 167–209) provides a good foundation for debates about women and gender in Tolkien's work generally, especially within similarly structured marital relationships (e.g., the ents and entwives, Eärendil and Elwing, and others).

One last historical topic introduced by lecture and then pursued over the course of several discussions is the reception of Tolkien's works by different constituencies over the past several decades. Most particularly, Tolkien's detractors have often accused his works of sexism and of racism, and here, too, we try actively to come to grips with the problem of historical context. On these issues especially, it seems to me essential to allow students to determine for themselves where both they and Tolkien stand. To encourage them toward this kind of discovery, I read a couple of the most inflammatory characterizations of Tolkien's works in these contexts (e.g., John Yatt's "Wraiths and Race") and let discussion follow naturally to address such commonly raised questions as, Is Tolkien's treatment of evil implicitly racist? Are his women merely ciphers, or is the essence of heroism in this world service rather than mastery, as Jane Chance has argued ("Tolkien and the Other")? Should we as persons living more than half a century after the publication of Tolkien's major works judge Tolkien on issues of race and gender? Or, by doing so, are we applying historically anachronistic standards to what is, after all, a literary work of the past rather than a modern political manifesto?

When discussing these perspectives, we also consider whether Jackson's movies constitute a reception of sorts. We ask such questions as, How does Jackson understand Tolkien? Where do their theological priorities intersect, where do they differ, and what do these differences tell us about each artist and the period in which he lived? Finally, we examine how Tolkien came to perceive his own past and, specifically, how he decided to focus his energies more on his literary work than on his scholarship. We ask, How are his perspectives on his own life and choices translated into myth? Given that for him subcreation is a spiritual act, what do his later works reveal about his internal struggles?

So far in this essay, I have presented Tolkien in the context of nineteenth- and twentieth-century developments. But, by profession, he was a medievalist, as am I, and one of my course goals is to show him in active negotiation with the medieval as well as with the modern past. For me, it is important that students come to know firsthand at least some of the medieval vernacular and Latin works he knew and loved. Depending on the level of the class, I assign all or portions of "The Wanderer," "The Seafarer," *Beowulf*, *The Prose Edda*, *The Saga of Heidrek the Wise*, and *The Kalevala*.[4] If there is time, I find it useful to add to our discussions a few short Celtic works and sometimes have students read the Welsh *Cad Goddeu* ("Battle of the Trees"), when we are reading about the ents; the Irish sovereignty goddess tale "The Adventures of the Sons of Eochaid Mugmedón," when we are discussing Bombadil and Goldberry; or an Irish "riddle death" tale (e.g., "The Death of Diarmait Mac Cerbaill"), when we talk about Éowyn's slaying of the Witch-King.[5]

My purposes in having students read these medieval originals are many. I want to give students a way to contextualize the world of, say, the Rohirrim, with its emphasis on kinship, honor, and heroic values. But my larger goal is to keep before them always the idea of Tolkien as a mythmaker working within a long historical (and, he would argue, spiritual) tradition. Therefore we discuss how he appropriates and reshapes the mythic structures and themes of this early literature. Students are almost always drawn at first to the obvious borrowings of dragons, riddle contests, significant artifacts, and the like. Soon, however, they consider deeper thematic similarities and divergences, such as those in Tolkien's thought-provoking reflection on war, "The Homecoming of Beorhtnoth Beorhthelm's Son," which he conceptualized as a continuation of the Anglo-Saxon poem *The Battle of Maldon*. We read and discuss both these texts together.

Although I seldom assign any of Tolkien's scholarly work apart from "On Fairy-stories," his essay "Beowulf: The Monsters and the Critics," when read in conjunction with a translation of the original Anglo-Saxon poem *Beowulf*, casts precious light on what for students are often some of the darkest and most mysterious aspects of his fictional work. Tolkien famously remarked in his letters that *The Lord of the Rings* "is about Death and the desire for deathlessness. Which is hardly more than to say it is a tale written by a Man!" (*Letters of J. R. R. Tolkien* 262). Most of my students are too young to feel the weight of those words directly, but *Beowulf* gives them a sense of the tragedy of the passage from youth to old age, enabling them to appreciate in new ways the personal and theological magnitude of individual sacrifice. Tolkien's essay on *Beowulf* offers them a glimpse of how Tolkien layered himself into the poem as a critic and as a man: how he felt about death, about the courage each of us displays when, day in and day out, we do the right thing even though we know that we, too, like the Norse gods at Ragnarök, must inevitably die. My experience has been that Tolkien's heartfelt delineation of the "Northern courage" ("Beowulf" 20) can make the textual legacy of the European Middle Ages seem urgent and pressing even to the least historically inclined of students.

The medieval Latin sources I use also raise issues that cut to the quick of things students care deeply about in their own lives. The nature and origins of evil, the omnipotence of God, the possibilities and limitations of the individual human will are problems they debate willingly far into the dormitory night. Such issues arise naturally from discussions about characters like Sauron, Saruman, and Gollum. Student reflections on these characters can be brought into sharper focus by brief readings from classics such as Augustine's *City of God* and Boethius's *The Consolation of Philosophy*, which deal with matters that those with little knowledge of Christian theology might easily miss: sin, repentance, and grace. Even students who care nothing about religion often will disagree passionately about whether particular characters in *The Silmarillion* or *The Lord of the Rings* fall because of their own flaws or because of a twist of fate for which they ought not to be held responsible. Augustine's treatment of the fallen angels (*City of God* bk. 11, chs. 11–13) seems to imply that the good and bad angels received more or less grace according to God's foreknowledge of their freely chosen path. We ask in class whether this idea of fate is true also of Tolkien's orcs. Are they doomed by the circumstances of their creation, or do they choose to do evil of their own free will? And what, then, is evil anyway? Boethius and Augustine argue that evil is the absence of good, not an entity unto itself. Is this idea true also in *The Lord of the Rings*? Or is evil for Tolkien a distinctly tangible force? As critics have remarked, one can make the case both ways.[6] Students familiar with medieval writings on the subject immediately grasp the complexity of the problem. Why does Saruman die as he does, and why are the Nazgûl wraiths? What of Ungoliant, or the Ring itself? Usually, students' dread of Latin theology week does not long survive our discussion of the problems raised by these medieval texts; indeed, these discussions are usually some of the liveliest and most contentious of the entire course.

Implicit in all these readings, Latin and vernacular, is what it means for Tolkien to be hailed as the premier mythmaker of the twentieth century. The issues Tolkien raises in his works have a lengthy history, just as the mythology he creates simultaneously derives from and builds on stories that human beings have told for centuries. His metaphor, in his short story "Leaf by Niggle," of the artist who sets himself to design a new leaf for the tree of tales is a powerful one. No leaf is entirely different from those that came before, and yet every new leaf holds something fresh, individual, and never seen before that day. What interests me most about Tolkien is how he confronts in imaginative ways some of the most difficult challenges human beings living in any era have faced: death, loss, grief, the omnipresence of evil, the seeming endlessness of war. In my class, I seek to help students understand how Tolkien's work is both rooted and individual, how this gifted writer, steeped in ancient myth and beliefs about the power of language, made use of the past to renegotiate his present.

NOTES

[1]These images of Tolkien's refusal are his, from his poem "Mythopoeia."

[2]One has to be careful in selecting the letters, especially in the beginning of a course, as students reading them sometimes disagree with Tolkien so profoundly on various personal and political issues that they have the impression they probably would not have liked him had they met him in person. This impression is rarely permanent; usually even the most hostile students develop considerable sympathy for Tolkien (the man, at least) as the class progresses. But, of course, they need not like him in order to appreciate the importance of what he wrote. In my experience, the class works better when such sentiments are postponed for later in the course, when students' views are likely to be more nuanced.

[3]A valuable anthology on the process of textual nation building and on individual works figuring in this process (including Mary-Ann Constantine's piece "The Myvyrian Archaiology of Wales") is Van Hulle and Leerssen. For Iolo Morganwg, see Jenkins.

[4]My choice of these works was originally governed by the easy availability of the now out-of-print *The Tolkien Fan's Medieval Reader*, by Turgon, although its translations were for the most part so old and unsatisfactory that I often ended up recommending alternative translations or bringing in handouts of my own. Translations of some works included in *The Tolkien Fan's Medieval Reader* are available online, such as Arthur Gilchrist Brodeur's translation of the excerpts from *The Prose Edda* (Sturluson, "Gylfaginning" and "Prologue") and John Martin Crawford's equally outdated 1888 translation of *The Kalevala* (Lönnrot, *Kalevala*). More modern online texts, often prepared for the classroom, include Jonathan Glenn's translations of *The Battle of Maldon*, "The Wanderer," and "The Seafarer."

[5]*Cad Goddeu* may be found in Ford. "The Adventures of the Sons of Eochaid Mugmedón" and "The Death of Diarmait Mac Cerbaill" are included in Koch and Carey. At the time of this writing, these works also are available online in very dated English translations (see M. Jones).

[6]For one critic's discussion of such ideas, see Shippey, *J. R. R. Tolkien* 112–60.

Teaching the Oral Tradition in *The Lord of the Rings*

Leslie Stratyner

The experience of teaching Tolkien to undergraduates has always been manifestly different from teaching them Joyce, Dickens, or Chaucer. Many, if not most, students in any course involving Tolkien's fiction arrive the first day of class knowing all about Middle-earth. What students for the most part do not know, however, is Tolkien's intellectual background, his sources, or his reliance on and incorporation of aspects from traditional texts. Although they know about his created world and its inhabitants, they are almost completely unaware of his other life as a philologist and medievalist.

The suggestions in this essay grow out of my experiences with developing classroom discussions of Tolkien's reliance on the oral tradition in his fiction—discussions that center on but are not limited to *The Lord of the Rings*. This approach is intended primarily for use in comprehensive, mixed-major, sophomore-level courses on Tolkien's work, in which an examination of the sources and analogues of his accomplishments can become pivotal and enduring aspects of discussion. I have been teaching such a stand-alone course for nearly twenty years, and my approach reflects not only the explosion of Tolkien criticism that has emerged in the past two decades but also more current developments in oral formulaic theory, which no longer view oral and literate composition as mutually exclusive. This evolving perspective "sees orality and literacy not as discrete, competing cultural forces but as subtly—and necessarily—intertwined and deeply interdependent ones" (Amodio 3–4).

When one teaches undergraduates, especially some that may be simply devotees of Tolkien but not English majors, beginning with an overview of what Tolkien himself taught and studied offers a useful method for engaging students with deeper and perhaps more esoteric aspects of his fiction. Their admiration for Tolkien, and their familiarity with his fiction, seems to authenticate his influences in reverse.

Thus, before I open up any discussion of orality or oral formulaic theory in *The Lord of the Rings*, I first emphasize to students some vital biographical information. During the time he was creating both *The Hobbit* and some of *The Lord of the Rings*, Tolkien was the Rawlinson and Bosworth Professor of Anglo-Saxon at Oxford, a position he held from 1925 to 1945. Students are impressed (but not surprised) that he was probably the single most influential Anglo-Saxon scholar of the twentieth century and that his "Beowulf: The Monsters and the Critics" is credited with single-handedly invigorating *Beowulf* scholarship. I bring to class as well my battered copy of his scholarly edition of *Sir Gawain and the Green Knight*, originally prepared (with E. V. Gordon) some eighty-five years ago, and tell them that this text still remains the standard.

These realizations prepare my students to be open to and interested in a discussion of Tolkien's influences and sources. But they may be more important when one considers the influence of oral composition, and oral tradition, on Tolkien's creation of Middle-earth. Tolkien was obviously a scholar, a literate man creating a text; he was very aware of the process in which the first stories were invented, long before writing. I quote from his influential essay "On Fairy-stories," in which he describes the preliterate storyteller creatively spooning his tale out of a "soup" that was begun long before the advent of writing (47).[1] Even though he is referring to fairy stories, what he says applies to all literature in an oral tradition.

Although students easily grasp the basic concept of oral composition and oral transmission in the modern world, through their exposure to urban legends and hip-hop music, most are not quite prepared to contemplate the process of poetic composition in preliterate societies. Telling them that Tolkien deeply admired poems created in an oral tradition, or even that he created characters that relied on such traditions, is not sufficient. Some knowledge of oral versus literate culture, and a familiarity with the basics of oral formulaic theory, is necessary for them to appreciate the value of oral literature and Tolkien's appropriation and reference to it in his fiction.

We discuss how much oral formulaic theory has changed in the last fifty years, using the theories of Walter Ong and Albert Lord as a necessary first step. Thirty or forty years ago, when these authors were doing their foundational explorations of oral versus literate culture and of oral composition, the divide perceived between the oral and literate worlds was a profound one. Since then, these realms have been rethought and reinterpreted; critics, having moved away from the purist theories that separate the cultures, now see the oral mind and the literate mind as wired differently.

The basis of oral formulaic theory is that oral poets, such as Homer, do not recite from a fixed text in their heads and do not follow, in fact, a fixed text at all. They sing their poetry not from memory or from any sort of visual or textual clues. Instead, oral composition is an improvisation utterly dependent on formulaic phrases and themes, which for many oral poets is geared to the requirements of the meter: dactylic hexameter in Homer's case and stress-based, alliterative meter in Anglo-Saxon poetry. Each instance in which the oral formulaic poet composes a song is, by definition, different and not a verbatim recitation from memory. The oral text is inherently flexible, though its essential outline remains the same. Poets in a pure oral tradition have composed masterworks without ever reading or writing. Poetic composition that has no access to writing can be a unifying social event, and an oral poem can become a repository of information about myth, culture, religion, and the practices of society. In this way, oral poets function as the social and historical memory of their cultures. Thus they are inherently traditional poets, concerned with preserving.

Students typically find this perspective alien. Most have a vision of poetic composition radically at odds with oral tradition: literate authors, sequestered and composing alone, write poetry that is published and then read by their equally sequestered readers, who also read alone. Any students who have submitted their own work to our school's literary magazine know that method. Yet for the oral poet, poetry is communal, spontaneously composed in front of an audience and centered not in reciting and singing a new and different story in a new and different way but in singing an old story in an old way but better than it was ever sung before. Tolkien attempts this approach with his fiction, and classroom discussion on oral composition focuses on how he presents his text as an old story told in an old way.

Tolkien has a fictive textual editor try to translate and edit *The Red Book of Westmarch*, an old tale whose original text was lost. That he invents the story and the editorial persona is not striking: on its own, we might consider the intrusion of a created manuscript history a bit self-conscious or twee. It is nothing of the sort, however, for the distance this persona creates between Tolkien the author and his own text puts Tolkien in close kinship with oral poets, who claim no ownership over any poem. This textual editor is not a Chaucerian attempt to inject a shadow self into the story to evade recrimination and blame; rather, it is Tolkien's effort to authenticate his work by setting it in a tradition and by portraying it as history rooted in the preliterate world of oral poets and storytellers. Even the fictive editor of *The Red Book of Westmarch* asserts that the book contains elements "probably written down from oral tradition" (Tolkien, *Adventures* 191). More important, as Maria Prozesky points out, "most of the lore and literature mentioned in the story is presented in oral form" (21). The primary point that I make to my students is that Tolkien self-consciously creates texts that reflect both oral histories and oral poetry.

One could create an entire course (or three) that focuses completely on Tolkien's use of oral composition, as well as on his incorporation of texts that are "oral-derived"—that is, "text(s) with roots in oral tradition" (Foley 60). A comprehensive examination of issues like the role of the minstrel in relation to *The Book of Lost Tales* (entirely reliant on oral transmission), the songs of Laketown, Tom Bombadil, Bilbo, and any number of other oral and oral-derived aspects of Tolkien's work would easily fill such a course. Because it is not possible to spend such a vast amount of time in a sophomore survey of Tolkien's work, I center my students on representations of primary orality in *The Lord of the Rings* and on Tolkien's reverence and appreciation for oral composition. As Verlyn Flieger asserts, Tolkien attempts "to create an authentic and convincing oral tradition, a legacy of songs and stories attributed to identifiable bards and storytellers and perpetuated by subsequent performers" (*Interrupted Music* 61). From these sources, his world achieves its depth and resonance.

Tolkien's reverence for oral history and oral poetry is best reflected in a central example of primary orality in Middle-earth, the people of Rohan, who are modeled on the Anglo-Saxons and actually speak Old English. Tolkien viewed Anglo-Saxon poetry as steeped in oral tradition, and he understood, of course, that the initial Germanic invaders to Britain possessed primary orality. That is, "the settlers lived lives in which tradition, knowledge and belief had their existence in memory and utterance rather than in writing" (Magennis 92). Much important scholarship in oral formulaic theory and Anglo-Saxon literature antedates Tolkien's creation of *The Lord of the Rings*, and Tolkien was not unaware of the process of oral composition with regard to Anglo-Saxons. He incorporates this preliterate creative process into his depiction of Rohan and its inhabitants with Aragorn's words to Gimli that describe the Riders of Rohan as "wise but unlearned, writing no books but singing many songs" (*Lord* 430; bk. 3, ch. 2).

The example of the Riders of Rohan emphasizes to students that in Tolkien's universe learning in the sense of literacy does not necessarily impart integrity or wisdom. Nor does it impart the ability to create art or poetry, as Aragorn later demonstrates when he chants a poem of Rohan, a song of Eorl the Young, that Tolkien based on the Old English poem "The Wanderer." There is "strong music" in this poetry, which Legolas states "is like to this land itself; rich and rolling in part, and else hard and stern as the mountains" (508; bk. 3, ch. 6).

The Riders of Rohan are still composing orally and still singing songs of their heroic ancestors. "So men still sing in the evening," Aragorn says after finishing his song (508; bk. 3, ch. 6). Aragorn himself, under the name Thorongil, served the previous king of Rohan, Thengel, so he was certainly in a position to hear such oral compositions, and he may have composed them himself at the hearth in Meduseld. Note that he has already composed orally, spontaneously, a lay for Boromir after his death.

Perhaps most important of all is Aragorn's assertion that the poet himself is "forgotten" and the poem made "long ago" (507; bk. 3, ch. 6). Characteristic of many, if not most, poems composed in a primary oral culture is the fusion of poet with tradition, so that the identity of the poet, and thus the originality of the poem, is of no concern. It is the communal history that is vital. The poet is forgotten, but Eorl the Young, father of Rohan, is still a living part of Rohan's memory.

These old, orally composed stories and songs are much more than ornamental for men, for elves, and certainly for hobbits, though hobbits are ironically one of the most text-oriented races in Middle-earth. Many of the hobbits with whom we are most familiar have some connection with the compilation of *The Red Book of Westmarch*. Although writers and residing in a textual environment (one thinks of the will left by Bilbo, and the required signatures in red ink) and although their culture has progressed past that of the Riders of Rohan to create and embrace literacy, the hobbits have a culture that retains a strong oral residue.

When I ask my students how we know of the oral tradition among hobbits, invariably one of them will answer, "Songs." Songs pepper both *The Hobbit* and *The Lord of the Rings* and are as important to hobbits as they are to men like Aragorn, if not more important. Indicative of the framework of oral tradition in Tolkien's work is that hobbits, though they are sequestered from the rest of Middle-earth, share with Aragorn an almost identical attitude toward song.

One of the main purposes of poems composed in an oral tradition is that they authenticate their subjects. That Greek heroes fight for *kleos* ("glory") is memorialized by the Greek singer. Beowulf's story provides the best and most student-friendly example of this authentication, especially since students will be familiar with some degree of Anglo-Saxon culture and poetics after being introduced to the Riders of Rohan. When Beowulf kills Grendel, he achieves recognition for his deed in a song from the scop (oral poet). This song is what signifies that Beowulf has reached heroic status. In the hero's world, which is a traditional world, the deeds and history of men are passed on through oral tradition, and an unsung hero is no hero at all.

Sam understands this relation between oral composition and heroic status. Although he is part of a literate culture, he never dreams that his story of trials and deeds will be recorded in a book. Instead he imagines the creation of a song that tells of "Nine-fingered Frodo and the Ring of Doom." He does not wish to read the story in a book. He says "I wish I could *hear* it!" (*Lord* 950; bk. 6, ch. 4 [emphasis mine]). After the Ring has been destroyed and that song emerges in the form of a lay sung by a minstrel of Gondor, Sam weeps with joy.

At the close of *The Lord of the Rings* lies the very dramatization of Ong's notion that oral literature is "empathetic and participatory," in that "the individual's reaction is not expressed as simply individual or 'subjective,' but rather as encased in the communal reaction, the communal 'soul'" (46). At that moment, listening to the minstrel of Gondor's song, the collective joy of the free peoples of Middle-earth becomes most real, most present, and "their hearts, wounded with sweet words, overflowed, and their joy was like swords, and they passed in thought out to regions where pain and delight flow together and tears are the very wine of blessedness" (*Lord* 954; bk. 6, ch. 4).

My suggestions only scratch the surface of the issue of the oral traditions reflected in Tolkien's work, and I encourage teachers to develop their own means of delving deeper. The posthumous publication of Tolkien's *History of Middle-earth* has opened up many possibilities for such delving.

NOTE

[1] See the discussion of Tolkien's soup metaphor in Flieger's essay in this volume.

Becoming Tolkien: Reading His Anglo-Saxon and Boethian Sources

Liam Felsen

J. R. R. Tolkien firmly believed that we should not simply mine a literary work in order to find its literary and historical sources; instead, he considered it necessary that we view the work as a whole in order to see the fundamental, universal ideas that lie beneath.[1] When I teach Tolkien, I want students to think about not only what Tolkien was influenced by and then made use of but also why. I utilize a process that I call becoming Tolkien, in which I try to put my students in Tolkien's shoes by experiencing and examining firsthand those works that so greatly influenced him and his literary works. We are, of course, limited to the confines of a fifteen-week semester (as opposed to Tolkien's lifetime of study), and a two-week reading of Anglo-Saxon poetry or Boethian literature can never substitute for the way Tolkien immersed himself in the same materials. Nevertheless, we go beyond simple source study and into a more fundamental study of the Anglo-Saxon and Boethian themes in his stories.

By reading Anglo-Saxon and Boethian materials before reading *The Lord of the Rings*, students gain insight into the texts that Tolkien was most steeped in and begin to see in them the origins of his ideas and themes. Understanding key Anglo-Saxon concepts such as *comitatus*, exile, elegy, and the set of values we term the heroic code enables students to more fully examine fellowship, courage, and loss in Tolkien's fiction. It was through reading Anglo-Saxon and Boethian texts, especially Boethius's *Consolation of Philosophy*—against the backdrop of his experiences in World War I (and World War II, in which his son Christopher fought)—that Tolkien developed his concepts of providence, chance, fate, free will, and the battle between good and evil in *The Lord of the Rings*.

I start by having students read several short Anglo-Saxon poems—*The Battle of Maldon*, "The Wanderer," and "The Seafarer" (see Glenn)—and then *Beowulf* to focus on *comitatus*, exile, elegy, and the heroic code.[2] When discussing *The Battle of Maldon*, we focus on the heroic code and the *comitatus*. The *comitatus* is the fellowship between a lord and his thanes (and among thanes); it is the reciprocal relationship within which the lord distributes gold, rings, and treasure (and with them a sense of social, economic, and emotional belonging) to his thanes, who in return will fight for and protect him, even unto death.[3] If this sense of identity is the foundation of Anglo-Saxon warrior society, the heroic code is the set of values by which these warriors live. To face your foe and fight fairly, to fight honorably beside your fellow thanes, to defend your lord (or his body, should he be slain in battle), to die in battle if need be: these are the central tenets of the "northern courage" that Tolkien found fascinating, the "theory of courage" that he called "the 'great contribution' to humanity of the old literature of the North" (Shippey, *Road* 158). In *The Battle of Maldon* the warriors fight to the death; as their numbers dwindle and hope seems lost, glory becomes all the greater, and rather than despair and give up all hope, they fight on to the finish. This type of courage offers "no reward for virtue except the somber satisfaction of having done what is right. Tolkien wanted his characters in *The Lord of the Rings* to live up to the same high standard" (156).

Examining these themes in *The Battle of Maldon* offers students a greater understanding of Tolkien's *The Lord of the Rings*. For example, when Merry and Éowyn defend the body of their fallen lord, Théoden, at the Battle of the Pelennor Fields and Merry's heart cries, "King's man! King's man! . . . You must stay by him" (*Lord* 840; bk. 5, ch. 6), we see the power of the lord-thane relationship. We also consider characters such as Denethor, who turns his back on this theory of courage and instead chooses despair and suicide, even attempting to sacrifice his son. By understanding the Anglo-Saxon heroic code and its relation to the *comitatus*, students will appreciate better the final stand of Tolkien's Fellowship against the massed forces of Sauron's army at the Black Gate. This final stand, which has no certain end but death, is undertaken in the hope that it may give Frodo more time to complete his journey. Even Pippin embodies this courage when he says, "[W]ell, now at any rate I understand poor Denethor a little better. We might die together, Merry and I, and since die we must, why not? Well, as he is not here, I hope he'll find an easier end. But now I must do my best" (892; bk. 5, ch. 10).

An example from *The Hobbit* shows how *comitatus* leads to a better understanding of fellowship in virtually all Tolkien's works. To be sure, it is fascinating to discover that Bilbo's stealing the cup from Smaug's lair derives from the account of the thief who stole the cup from the dragon's lair in *Beowulf*, that the runes on Bilbo's map are derived from the Anglo-Saxon futhark,[4] and that there are Anglo-Saxon and Old Norse analogues to the riddles Bilbo and Gollum ask each other in the cold dark beneath the Misty Mountains.[5] But with the help of the central concepts of *comitatus* and exile, students can delve deeper than such simple source finding. During one class, a student realized that when Bilbo, already under the influence of the Ring, returns to the dungeons of the Elvenking to save his dwarf comrades, he is turning his back on exile and embodying the Anglo-Saxon concept of the *comitatus*. Alone and wretched (like Gollum and Grendel), he has been "left to wander miserably in the forest, terrified of losing himself" (*Annotated* Hobbit 226). Almost embodying the figure of an exile, he

> no longer thought twice about picking up a supper uninvited if he got the chance, he had been obliged to do it for so long, and he knew now only too well what it was to be really hungry, not merely politely interested in the dainties of a well-filled larder. Also he had caught a glimpse of a fire through the trees, and that appealed to him with his dripping and ragged clothes clinging to him cold and clammy. (238–39)

But Bilbo rejects his Gollum-like existence and instead embraces the fellowship of his friends, actively seeking a way to free his dwarf comrades. By closely examining such scenes, students see how integral the Anglo-Saxon concepts are to Tolkien's works.

When discussing "The Wanderer," "The Seafarer," and *Beowulf*, my students and I focus again on exile and elegy, the loss of the *comitatus*, and the greater sense of loss that inhabits *The Lord of the Rings*. In each of the two shorter poems, the speaker is a lone thane, described as a *wraecca* ("wretched one"), who is exiled and separated from the *comitatus*, cut off from his lord and fellow warriors, all of whom have died in battle. The poems express the elegiac sense of loss Anglo-Saxon warriors experience: as their lords and comrades die around them, they begin to question the values of the heroic code itself. Tolkien, in the foreword to the second edition of *The Lord of the Rings*, recalls World War I:

> An author cannot of course remain wholly unaffected by his experience, but the ways in which a story-germ uses the soil of experience are extremely complex, and attempts to define the process are at best guesses from evidence that is inadequate and ambiguous. . . . One has indeed personally to come under the shadow of war to feel fully its oppression; but as the years go by it seems now often forgotten that to be caught in youth by 1914 was no less hideous an experience than to be involved in 1939 and the following years. By 1918 all but one of my close friends were dead. (*Lord* xxiv)

The fellowship, despair, and courage that Tolkien shared with friends who went to battle with him, the harrowing events of war itself, the death of his comrades—he found all this in the Anglo-Saxon poems. Sam knows the same emotions when he thinks Shelob has killed Frodo: "'What shall I do, what shall I do?' he said. 'Did I come all this way with him for nothing?'" (731; bk. 4, ch. 10). Sam decides, of course, to go on, but not before questioning everything that brought him to that point: "'What? Me, alone, go to the Crack of Doom and all?' He quailed still, but the resolve grew. 'What? *Me* take the Ring from *him*? The Council gave it to him. . . . Why am I left all alone to make up my mind?'" (732). The heartbreak of Sam at the apparent death of Frodo is the heartbreak of the Anglo-Saxon Wanderer and Seafarer at the deaths of their lords and fellow thanes and the heartbreak of Tolkien at the deaths of his friends in war. Students recognize that Sam's courage to go on anyway is the same courage found in *The Battle of Maldon*.

When we read *Beowulf*, I encourage students to observe that the poem's sense of loss goes beyond the death of a lord or thane: the *comitatus* fails, the heroic code fails, the glorious days of Beowulf himself come to an end in the fiery battle with the dragon, and the entire kingdom of the Geats approaches destruction. In much the same way, loss for the elves in Middle-earth is inevitable whether they win or lose the battle. Galadriel says that "through ages of the world we have fought the long defeat" (*Lord* 357; bk. 2, ch. 7). She tells Frodo that "if you fail, then we are laid bare to the Enemy. Yet if you succeed, then our power is diminished, and Lothlórien will fade, and the tides of Time will sweep it away. We must depart into the West, or dwindle to a rustic folk of dell and cave, slowly to forget and to be forgotten" (365). Tom Shippey recognizes this sense of defeat in the trilogy as well:

> The good side in *The Lord of the Rings* does win, but its casualties include, besides Théoden and Boromir, beauty, Lothlórien, Middle-earth and even Gollum. Furthermore, the characters are aware of their losses all the time, and bear a burden of regret. They just have to make the best of things and not confuse "sorrow" with "despair." (*Road* 156)

Even after the Ring is destroyed and the Shire saved, Frodo tells Sam, before they head to the Grey Havens, "I have been too deeply hurt, Sam. I tried to save the Shire, and it has been saved, but not for me. It must often be so, Sam, when things are in danger: some one has to give them up, lose them, so that others may keep them" (*Lord* 1029; bk. 6, ch. 9). At the end of *Beowulf*, the time of the heroic code has passed and Beowulf himself is laid to rest; at the end of *The Lord of the Rings*, the time of the Ring has passed and the Ring bearers must travel into the West.

Because Tolkien uses Anglo-Saxon sources so extensively, from particular plot devices (such as the stealing of the cup from Smaug's lair) to universal themes, it is easy for students to recognize his indebtedness to them. Boethius's *Consolation of Philosophy*, while not as evident an influence, is so integrated into *The Lord of the Rings* that studying it is essential for students to learn what mattered most to Tolkien. Shippey writes that he

> thought more deeply than his critics have ever recognized about just those issues he is commonly alleged to ignore: the processes of temptation, the complex nature of good and evil, the relationship between reality and our fallible perception of it. . . . [P]roper understanding . . . depends on comparing ancient things and modern ones, checking old texts against new understandings and against timeless realities. (*Road* 140)

Before launching into *The Lord of the Rings*, we take a week to read *The Consolation of Philosophy*. As my students and I explore the Boethian concepts together, we consider why they were so important to Tolkien.

When students wonder how the Ring came to Bilbo and then Frodo, it helps them to know that Tolkien is ruminating on Boethian notions of providence, fate, chance, free will, and fortune. In the *Consolation*, Boethius describes how human beings, with their limited vision, cannot perceive the larger divine plan. What may seem to us to be chance is really not, and ultimately we must have faith that the plan exists. This concept is closely related to Tolkien's notion of eucatastrophe at work: when all seems lost, we must never give up hoping that the larger plan will lead to a good ending. Gandalf himself says that "there was something else at work, beyond any design of the Ring-maker. I can put it no plainer than by saying that Bilbo was *meant* to find the Ring, and *not* by its maker. In which case you also were *meant* to have it. And that may be an encouraging thought" (*Lord* 56; bk. 1, ch. 2). Providing another illustration of the same point, Shippey writes:

> In Middle-earth, one may say, Providence or the Valar sent the dream that took Boromir to Rivendell. But they sent it first and most often to Faramir, who would no doubt have been a better choice. It was human decision, or human perversity, which led to Boromir claiming the journey, with what chain of ill-effects and casualties no one can tell. "Luck," then, is a continuous interplay of providence and free will, a blending of so many factors that the mind cannot disentangle them. (*Road* 152–53)

This interplay between fate and faith is the central point of *The Consolation of Philosophy*. Understanding it can help students "elucidate critical episodes . . . and direct us toward a clearer vision of Tolkien's providential cosmos" (Dubs 39). In class, we ask if the Ring is an external evil force or instead acts on its bearers internally, activating the evil inherent within them. These notions of good and evil do not originate with Tolkien; rather, he dramatizes Boethian and Manichaean ideas about them. Only by first grappling with the Boethian material can students come to grips with what Shippey calls "a philosophical crux in the very nature of the Ring, one that was certainly apparent and deeply interesting to Tolkien, and one which he furthermore expressed with great care and deliberation. . . . The uncertainty over evil in a way dominates the entire structure of *The Lord of the Rings*" (*Road* 145). Indeed, even the interlacing narrative structure of *The Lord of the Rings* exemplifies the way Tolkien has internalized Boethius's notions of divine providence (135–76).

By reading these Anglo-Saxon and Boethian texts and seeing how Tolkien incorporated them, students will have a better understanding of all his works, not just *The Lord of the Rings*. Students have written essays that combine Boethian philosophy with Tolkien's ideas about subcreation and examine external evil versus internal evil in regard to the Ring. One student wrote about Foucault's ideas about power and evil in relation to Sauron and the Ring. Others found connections between Tolkien's most influential works and his shorter texts. A student paper examined the corruption of objects of power, not only in connection with the Silmarils and the Ring but also as applied to the star on Smith's forehead in *Smith of Wootton Major*. Another paper explored ideas of fellowship and the *comitatus* in "Leaf by Niggle," arguing that Niggle was ultimately saved by his rejection of lonely exile as seen in his acceptance of Parish as his companion.

Reading the Anglo-Saxon and Boethian sources that influenced Tolkien encourages both students and teachers to see what he himself wanted us to understand. In "Beowulf: The Monsters and the Critics," and also in "On Fairy-stories," he urges critics (and students are critics, albeit novice ones) to move beyond mere source study. To be sure, we do read the source material—in this case, the Anglo-Saxon and Boethian sources—but we do so not simply to find the exact spot in *Beowulf* that is analogous to Bilbo's stealing a cup. We learn why these sources were so important to Tolkien, what it was about his personal experiences and thoughts that drew him so strongly to these late classical and early medieval works.

NOTES

[1] See, for example, Tolkien's famous "allegory of the tower" in "Beowulf: The Monsters and the Critics" (7–8). Martin also discusses Tolkien's tower allegory in his essay in this volume.

[2] The Anglo-Saxons themselves never used the term *heroic code*, but scholars find this term useful to describe the sociopolitical relationship.

[3] This concept is found throughout Tolkien's works. For example, Fili and Kili, the nephews of Thorin Oakenshield, fall at Thorin's side, defending their lord "with shield and body" (*Annotated* Hobbit 351).

[4] A useful discussion of the *futhark* system of runes appears in Page.

[5] Tolkien was familiar with several compendiums of Anglo-Saxon and Old Norse riddles, among them *Solomon and Saturn*, the elder or poetic Edda, and *The Saga of King Heidrek the Wise* (Shippey, *Road* 344–46).

Tolkien as Nation Builder: Teaching *The Lord of the Rings* in an Epic Literature Class

Melissa Ridley Elmes

For many years, I taught a British literature special-topics elective course on the writings of C. S. Lewis and J. R. R. Tolkien. But after a while I wanted to teach something new, something that I had not previously taught and that was not being taught on most college campuses. Simultaneously with this inkling quest for instructional innovation, epic literature came back around in my course rotation. I dearly love to teach this class, but my students generally meet the subject with ambivalence, if not outright antipathy. How does a teacher get them to read *The Iliad* or *The Aeneid* in its entirety, much less understand the importance of *The Song of Roland* or *Beowulf*? I distinctly remember the moment when, looking over my epic literature syllabus with an eye to revision, the thought flashed through my head: *I wish I could help them to love Achilles as much as they love Aragorn*. Although I did not realize it at the time, a new course was born.

Because today's students have essentially grown up with *The Lord of the Rings* thanks to the success of Peter Jackson's films, they are often eager to read these books. That Tolkien's work is the only requisite reading some of my students actually complete led me to the practice of assigning it more widely, hoping to broaden student interest in other types of literature by association. It was simple enough for me to insert *The Lord of the Rings* into courses on medieval literature and medievalism in literature, as well as into contemporary British literature courses. When I set out to revise my epic literature course to feature *The Lord of the Rings*, the first obstacle I faced was that Tolkien himself shied away from calling his story epic; he preferred "myth," "legend," "fairy story," and "romance" (*Letters of J. R. R. Tolkien* 144–45, 146, 149, 159–60 [letter 131]). The second challenge was that although *The Lord of the Rings* is widely referred to as an epic tale, the classicists, who most properly lay claim to the epic genre, do not generally claim Tolkien's text as one of their own. A third difficulty was that, as a medievalist, I had been schooled to see Tolkien's work as predominantly an amalgamation of medieval genres, with an emphasis on the literary forms of the British Isles.

Still, I determined that evidence existed in Tolkien's own words to support the idea that *The Lord of the Rings* was influenced not merely by myth, romance, and medieval folklore but also by its being envisioned as an epic text. In a 1953 letter, Tolkien writes, "I was brought up in the Classics, and first discovered the sensation of literary pleasure in Homer" (*Letters of J. R. R. Tolkien* 172). In another letter, he writes of his conception of the work in a way that sounds much like a textbook definition of an epic:

> I was from early days grieved by the poverty of my own beloved country: it had no stories of its own (bound up with its tongue and soil) . . . I had a mind to make a body of more or less connected legend . . . which I could dedicate simply to: to England; to my country. It should possess the tone and quality I desired, somewhat cool and clear, be redolent of our "air" (the clime and soil of the North West, meaning Britain and the hither parts of Europe . . .) and, while possessing (if I could achieve it) the fair elusive beauty that some call Celtic . . . it should be "high," purged of the gross, and fit for the more adult mind of a land long now steeped in poetry. (144–45)

In other words, Tolkien wanted a story that would reflect and pay homage to the traditions of the England he knew. Nevertheless, the story he wrote—featuring physical and moral conflict between good and evil, a hero who returns to claim his rightful place as king, and a focus on men and their actions—is replete with the characteristics of a classical epic. Yet, Tolkien steadfastly avoids the term. This led me to ask myself, Is *The Lord of the Rings* an epic? I decided that this specific question would serve as the backbone of my course. Instead of following a traditional classroom style, in which I delivered carefully developed lectures containing information I thought students should know, information that they, in turn, applied in their analysis of Tolkien's work, I opted to present them with only the question at the outset. Through reading, study, discussion, and reflection, my students would decide for themselves if Tolkien's work fit in among the traditional texts we define as epics.

A student-oriented course is a risky business: you never really know what caliber of students you will get, what prior knowledge they will bring with them, or how they will respond when they discover that the course will not be a spoon-feeding of facts, figures, and themes. Some students thrive on the autonomy that a more organic, free-form, do-it-yourself class grants them; they like to follow branching, thought-provoking lines of inquiry. Some are immobilized by fear: they don't know what you want or how they will be graded. Some think you have constructed the class in this way because you are too lazy or too uninformed in the subject to teach it. Because of these many possibilities, such a class needs to give students something to work toward besides a response to a question that, in the end, may or may not be "right." In my epic literature class, I resolved this need by considering the aims of the other epics I chose to teach: Homer's *Iliad*, Vergil's *Aeneid*, *The Song of Roland*, and *Beowulf*. Although these works originated in different cultures (Ancient Greece, Ancient Rome, Medieval France, and Anglo-Saxon England), they are all nation-building texts.[1] Tolkien's invented Middle-earth, with its battle against Mordor and its unification of various cultural groups supporting a common cause, also can be viewed as a nation-building text.

We therefore begin the first half of the term by discussing the four traditional epics as nation-building works, each constructed in part by propaganda and by vast fictions based in kernels of history for the purpose of defining a society. After we establish the elements specific to nation-building epics and read the older works with attention to the conventions of the epic narrative, epic language, the epic hero, and the hero's journey, we read *The Lord of the Rings* in its entirety for the second half of the term, considering the conventions of epic and whether or not, as well as to what degree, Tolkien might be said to have employed them.[2] We also discuss and analyze typical literary conventions—plot, narrative, character, tone, style, structure, and so forth.

I assign three papers, with the purpose of encouraging students to engage with the subject matter. The first paper (3–5 pages), requiring a character analysis of Achilles in *The Iliad* as an epic hero, provides students with experience analyzing a conventional epic hero and employing a set of guidelines against which to measure later the heroes of Tolkien's work. The second paper (6–8 pages), asking students to compare and contrast *The Aeneid* with another epic of their choice in terms of epic conventions, has them complete the research necessary to evaluate the presence and employment of those conventions in a work; it also pushes them to read *The Aeneid* more thoroughly than they might otherwise. Since many epic elements in *The Lord of the Rings* closely align with those in *The Aeneid*, this assignment provides students with the base knowledge they need for constructing a strong critical evaluation of Tolkien's work. For the third paper (10–15 pages), I give my students a list of epic conventions found in the four conventional epics we study, drawn from our discussions and analysis over the term, and ask them to compare how these are used in the four texts and in *The Lord of the Rings*. Their goal in this paper is to answer the question, Can *The Lord of the Rings* be classified as an epic?

In addition to these three papers, my students complete an individual presentation. These presentations cannot merely rehash what we have discussed in class; students must research aspects of the texts beyond their epic quality and aside from the basic elements of the story. Some presentation topics have been Ancient Greek culture and mythology, Roman holiday traditions, the Amazons, medieval folklore, French history, the legend of Charlemagne, the Crusades, Viking boat making, treasure hoards, migration patterns of Nordic peoples, monsters in epics, and the geography of a given epic. Students distribute a list of the works they cite, which provides every student with additional directions for research. These presentations play a key role in expanding the class's knowledge base and add depth and meaning to class discussion and textual analyses.

My epic literature students also complete a group project, which cannot be traditional in nature, incorporating *The Lord of the Rings* and addressing the idea of Tolkien as a nation builder. I usually suggest a number of possibilities to get students thinking about how they might approach this project. One project involved putting Tolkien on trial for plagiarism in terms of his appropriation of the warrior woman from *The Aeneid*. Students demonstrated, through depositions and testimony from figures like Vergil and Spenser, that Vergil's Camilla had been plagiarized by medieval and Renaissance English writers and that

Tolkien then stole the motif from these writers. The group sought to prove that in actuality Tolkien's characterization of Éowyn as a shield maiden belonged to the Romans and did not derive from Tolkien's English predecessors. This project provided a lovely twist when the English side called to the stand as a surprise witness Geoffrey of Monmouth, to testify that, because the English, through the British and Aeneas's descendant Brutus, are actually Romans by descent, Tolkien must be acquitted.[3] Another group's project presented a Travel Channel–style documentary on the geography and topography of Middle-earth, proving that the Shire was actually Wales, suggesting where in Europe the other Middle-earth cities and territories might be located, and including a talk show segment in which the minority groups of Middle-earth had the chance to confront their oppressors. In this last segment of the project, Tolkien appeared as the mediator, explaining where each represented group (Sauron included) hailed from in real-life England and Europe. In nearly every class, one group project deals with Tolkien's novel as an allegory of postwar English national identity or as a green novel wherein Tolkien's work is intended to found an ecology movement in England. For these projects, I insist only that students take the assignment seriously, that they research and document their ideas and information carefully, and that they take special care to demonstrate how they view Tolkien as a nation builder. I approve the final ideas for these projects and point out any major difficulties a group might encounter in its project's execution (Tolkien objected, for example, to having his work viewed as allegory), but the projects are ultimately the students' work.

Throughout the term, I give five timed in-class essays (one for each text) to help students continue to think about epic as a foundation for national identity. I assign these essays during the last week of instruction on each text. The question for each essay is the same, altered only in terms of which text we study during that unit:

> What is specifically Greek about *The Iliad*?
> What is specifically Roman about *The Aeneid*?
> What is specifically French about *The Song of Roland*?
> What is specifically Anglo-Saxon about *Beowulf*?
> What is specifically English about *The Lord of the Rings*?

After these essays are scored and returned to students, they serve as the basis for further class discussion in which we elaborate on points made in the essays concerning not only what is specific to each tradition but also what is not culturally specific—what is universal, what is foreign, and how such elements affect the whole text. These discussions have led to extremely good analysis from students in terms of how the epics helped shape each nation's idea of itself, historically and culturally.

Teaching Tolkien's *The Lord of the Rings* as the central focus of an epic literature class has proved to be an effective use of his work for a variety of classroom purposes. Such purposes include introducing students to the multiple interpretations and functions of a text; working with comparative analysis; applying genre conventions to evaluate texts; demonstrating the evolution of a genre from its historical, classical roots to the present day; and, most important, teaching students to use a set of criteria and prior knowledge to evaluate a text critically on multiple levels in order to construct a solid argument backed with primary and secondary evidence. Is Tolkien's *The Lord of the Rings* an epic? There is, obviously, no right answer to this question. Nevertheless, I have found that a class structured around this question opens the door to a particularly rich and ongoing dialogue.

NOTES

[1] Employment of the term *nation* is controversial but remains the most readily accessible method by which to impart to my students the nature of the work they are attempting, which is to explain how these texts helped establish the idea of Greek, of Roman, of French, and of Anglo-Saxon.

[2] I avoid showing Jackson's films in class, because students usually have seen some or all of them and because the films are too long and far too altered in scope and content to serve as appropriate auxiliary materials for a course focusing on the author's decision making and craft. I strongly advise against using the films in a course of this nature, even as a reward or on days when papers are due.

[3] This group included students who had taken my medieval British literature or Arthurian literature course. Such a degree of sophistication does not always obtain in my epic literature course; this presentation serves, however, as an excellent example of what a motivated and well-prepared group can do with this assignment.

Conceptions of the Pastoral in *The Fellowship of the Ring*

Philip Irving Mitchell

> "Lothlórien is beautiful because there the trees were loved."
>
> —J. R. R. Tolkien, letter to the editor of the *Daily Telegraph*, 30 June 1972

Although one can expect a few literature or classics majors to be familiar with the pastoral genre, most students will have only a dim awareness of its literary traditions. In my course Tolkien and the Medieval Tradition, we begin by briefly reviewing the typical conventions of this literary mode as seen in Theocritus and Vergil, as well as in Philip Sidney's *Arcadia* and Matthew Arnold's *Thyrsis*. The conventions of pastoral literature are rather formal in nature: the pastoral presents an idealized rural life of shepherds and shepherdesses, who evince rustic innocence, idleness, and do little actual shepherdlike work. Even less realistic is that they speak in courtly rather than natural language. The pastoral also stresses the loves and sorrows of the shepherds, as well as how nature or natural objects may personify their emotions. These strict, classical characteristics are not adopted by Tolkien, yet introducing students to pastoral concepts in *The Fellowship of the Ring* has much to recommend it.

As William Empson observes, the pastoral can express the complex through the medium of the simple (53), and this insight directs students' attention to how pastoral settings can move beyond the tradition's specific conventions and still preserve an idealized human condition that reflects moral and aesthetic virtues and endears them to its readers. The pastoral romance, for example, may borrow the ancient trope of country and city: the country portrayed as a garden of peace, innocence, simplicity, and community set against the corrupt, hypocritical, backstabbing urban world. Ironically, the pastoral's comic tradition of playing up the rustic bumpkin's ignorance and poor taste, ever gawking at the higher culture, can be joined with this tradition of admirable innocence. The theme of rural wisdom and skill in farming can play a similar role in the pastoral setting, as can the neo-Romantic and neopagan divinization of nature.

I end my review of the pastoral by suggesting to students that the high and the low, the holy and the comic, the perilous and the homespun all appear in the pastoral tradition and that these juxtapositions help prepare readers for the seemingly contradictory portraits of a pastoral ideal in the Shire and in Lothlórien. The two lands in *The Lord of the Rings* differ in a number of remarkable ways but share an inseparable connection of the inhabitants to the land and a kind of power resident in the land. The elves of the Golden Land and the hobbits of the Shire share a parochialism that makes them less interested in the outside world, for both realms are protected. Both are also destined to change in the coming world: the elven will fade away, and the Shire will assume more of its own defenses.

To understand why two very different realms, the Shire and Lothlórien, carry such imaginative freight for Tolkien, one needs to examine his long-standing attitudes toward nature, the village, and technology. A good start for this examination can be made by asking students what his bucolic portraits idealize. The journey of the hobbits out of the Shire, for example, reveals the importance of landscape and geography to their identity. Frodo and Sam are encompassed by their surroundings, which Tolkien lovingly describes: the "far off twinkling in the gentle valley of the Water," the "[t]hin-clad birches, swaying in a light wind above their heads," "the deep resin-scented darkness," the "icy cold" water of a little fall, and so on (*Lord* 71–73; bk. 1, ch. 3). Frodo and Sam are still home, so they take these blessings for granted. Yet we already sense that part of the hobbits' being is tied to and expressed in this bucolic world. Sam pauses before he takes the next step beyond where he has never traveled. Bilbo's walking song is similarly full of such pastoral hope, even though it looks for these hopes beyond home, and with a little encouragement students should be able to locate the song's natural imagery. It helps to introduce Tolkien's songs either by singing them oneself in a comic voice or by playing recordings, such as those by Rob Inglis or by the Tolkien Ensemble.

The parochial quality of the hobbits may still escape students. One should point out the misgivings that Shire, Buckland, and Bree folk have about one another. Shire hobbits regard Buckland hobbits as strange since Buckland hobbits use boats, and the Gaffer considers it a good thing that Frodo was brought by Bilbo from Buckland "to live among decent folk" (23; bk. 1, ch. 1). But Farmer Maggot tells Frodo that Frodo should never have gone to the Shire, since "[f]olk are queer up there" (24; bk. 1, ch. 4). Bree, too, while something of a crossroads community, has turned inward and considers the Shire folk "Outsiders." While the Shire can speak of things "*Strange as News from Bree*" (150; bk. 1, ch. 9), the people of Bree in turn proverbially note, "There's no accounting for East and West" (156; bk. 1, ch. 9). Tolkien gently mocks their myopia, but it also has social consequences. Parochialism blinds each place to more disturbing kinds of evil in the east and south, and the inhabitants find it hard to believe or act on news from beyond—and they disapprove of those who travel outside their borders.

Still, the rustic qualities of hobbits can make for great humor. Shire songs are walking songs, drinking songs, and bath songs. They are homely in the best sense of that word, concerned not with great matters and heroic deeds but with simple pleasures and creature comforts. Their loud singing imparts joy. The debates in the Green Dragon, as well as the initial response in Butterbur's Prancing Pony to Frodo's ruse of writing a book, are comic, but we are meant to laugh with the hobbits rather than at them. Even in the argument between Sam and Ted over elves, giant tree men, and dragons, there is something true to life and wryly amusing.

I draw students' attention to Tolkien's treatment of these pastoral elements with praise and gentle mockery and observe how high and low coexist in certain characters. Sam is emblematic of the strengths and weaknesses of rustic parochialism. Like his father, the Gaffer, he is more than capable on his own ground—a good gardener and a crack shot with an apple. His uneducated speech is laughable, and he is always ready for a pint at the inn. He is deeply loyal to family, to Frodo, and to the Shire. Unfortunately, he is also quick to judge, distrustful of strangers and of what he does not understand, and initially he has little concern with matters outside the Shire, excepting elves. Focusing students on his rustic, comic songs, along with a few passages that stress his unusual interest in things elven, is a helpful way to unpack this mixture. To elaborate on a textual example, I play the BBC-Caedmon recording of Tolkien's recitation of Sam's "The Stone Troll" (Tolkien, *J. R. R. Tolkien Reads*). I ask students why Tolkien laughs aloud at the end. They often note the joy in his voice. This exercise helps them see how Sam's rural language functions to both familiarize and defamiliarize readers with his character.

The figures of Butterbur and Farmer Maggot can lead students to fruitful discussions about pastoral character conventions. Butterbur is harried, full of platitudes, and comically forgetful. Yet, when Frodo is tempted to judge him as "kind and stupid," Gandalf defends him as "wise enough on his own ground," able to "see through a brick wall in time" (*Lord* 220–21; bk. 2, ch. 1). Maggot is even more respected by Tom Bombadil. The hobbits consider the old farmer shrewd and formidable, but Bombadil considers him "a person of more importance than they had imagined" (132; bk. 1, ch. 7).

If the Shire, Buckland, and Bree suffer from the danger of parochialism, they also have a great power in belonging to a place and being shaped by it. The wisdom of Maggot is agrarian, born of a loving working of the land. I continue to be surprised that my mostly urban students are mystified by Bombadil's observation of Maggot: "There's earth under his old feet, and clay on his fingers; wisdom in his bones, and both his eyes are open" (132; bk. 1, ch. 7). This quotation encourages them to question prejudices toward rural life but also to ask whether Tolkien's idealizations are fully justified.

Another interesting example of Tolkien's vision of the pastoral involves Tom Bombadil and Goldberry. As *Adventures of Tom Bombadil* suggests, Goldberry is a kind of naiad: "But one day, Tom, he went and caught the River-daughter, / in green gown, flowing hair, sitting in the rushes, / singing old water-songs to birds upon the bushes" (201). In the song, Bombadil embodies the medieval pastoral trope of the singer's catching and seducing the shepherdess. In *The Lord of the Rings*, Goldberry has a particular quality that Frodo also recognizes as worthy of the trope of medieval love, yet hers is a power different from that of the elves: "less keen and lofty was the delight, but deeper and nearer to mortal heart; marvellous and yet not strange" (123; bk. 1, ch. 7). Indeed, her power is not unlike that in the Shire itself: she can protect the hobbits from nightly noises, yet she also merges with the vegetable world about her.

Students often find Bombadil, unlike Goldberry, an intriguing, annoying, even disturbing figure. Many who have seen only the Peter Jackson movies are taken aback by the merry fellow's presence in *The Fellowship of the Ring*. Since he ia a conundrum for them, I approach him as a fuzzy set of problems to be at least clarified, if not entirely solved. First I ask the class simply to compile a list of his chief characteristics and actions. Next I read aloud selections from two 1954 letters by Tolkien that discuss Bombadil. One letter describes him as embodying "a natural pacifist view" that counters the just violence of other characters:

> [I]f you have, as it were taken "a vow of poverty," renounced control, and take your delight in things for themselves without reference to yourself, watching, observing, and to some extent knowing, then the question of the rights and wrongs of power and control might become utterly meaningless to you, and the means of power quite valueless.
>
> (*Letters of J. R. R. Tolkien* 179)

The other letter pictures Bombadil as a principle of natural science "that desires knowledge of other things, their history and nature, *because they are 'other'* and wholly independent of the enquiring mind, a spirit coeval with the rational mind, and entirely unconcerned with 'doing' anything with the knowledge" (192). I ask students to consider if Tolkien's account of Bombadil as an expression of "natural science" and "pacifism" can be another manifestation of the pastoral. Is love of knowledge for its own sake grounds for a principled rejection of power over others? How can Bombadil take a Lenten vow that refuses to use applied science? How can his power as master be both altruistic and causal?

Finally I offer a list of twelve possibilities for Bombadil's identity and ask student groups to debate them. Bombadil is:

1. Eru, that is, God (an option, I point out, that Tolkien found appalling)
2. the Vala Aulë, that is, the angelic deity of land and craft
3. another angelic deity, otherwise unnamed Vala
4. a Maia, a minor angelic deity, gone native
5. one of the Istari, or wizards, such as Radagast the Brown
6. a personification of a geographic region
7. an Earth principle
8. an archetypal trickster figure
9. an example of unaccountable anomaly in the system
10. a singular being without species

11. an unaligned spirit
12. a power in service to knowledge instead of knowledge advancing power

I try not to steer my students to any answer, but the one that most resonates with me is that Bombadil is the presence of a place, that is, a genius loci. Seen in this way, his character, life, and manner represent the pastoral. He has the appearance of the rustic clown whose spoken prose and poetry is marked by the cadence of singing. Yet he is master in the cordoned-off realm where he lives, and he can turn back Old Man Willow, as well as the Barrow-wights. In him merge the high and holy, the rural and laughable. When he tells stories in song and half song to the hobbits, they begin to learn of the natural world apart from them, "indeed to feel themselves as the strangers where all other things were at home" (*Lord* 129–30; bk. 1, ch. 7). When his stories regress through history all the way back to the dark and stars before the awakening of the first elves, he tells the hobbits that he is eldest, that he came before the ages of elves and humanity began. In the end, I do not attempt a conclusion, suspecting that even Tolkien did not have one, and let students ponder the possibilities for Bombadil.

Once students have read all of *The Fellowship of the Ring*, I ask them to consider Lothlórien, which has a literary flavor different from that of the Shire. I read aloud the description of the Mound of Amroth, beginning, "When his eyes were in turn uncovered, Frodo looked up and caught his breath," and ending with the description of the winter flowers *elanor* and *niphredil* (350; bk. 2, ch. 6). I ask students to compare this description with other pastoral elements we have discussed and to read the passage closely. Tolkien's description of the mallorn trees in a "double crown" combines the realm's pastoral and the artistic natures without sacrificing the organic to the artificial (350). The passage's stress on color and form is married to a sense of naturalness. Nature and art are not to be teased apart here, for the scene employs the language of grandeur as it ends with the simple and gentle.

The hobbits' responses to Lothlórien in the next few pages are important. Sam compares the experience with being "*inside* a song." Frodo's description is high and holy rather than rustic or comic. Frodo compares looking upon Lothlórien with looking upon a land that has long vanished, one without blight, disease, or stain and illuminated with a light for which he has no words. It is as "a timeless land that did not fade or change or fall into forgetfulness." He is amazed that when he touches the tree, he delights in the wood, in "the living tree itself," not as a thing to build with. He is stunned by the "power and light" of Lothlórien (351; bk. 2, ch. 6). I ask students to consider if this realm is like Farmer Maggot's—one formed by love, though perhaps of a much more exalted tenor. I also help them see that the elves are, in their own fashion, parochial. They, too, have cordoned themselves off. Their purity comes at the cost of refusing to concern themselves with others. It is only the larger geopolitical evil of Mordor that has forced them to look outside themselves, as Frodo is reminded by the shadow already gathering beyond.

A pastoral model by its very nature invites discussion of home, hospitality, and ecology, all of which are present throughout *The Lord of the Rings*. I leave Rivendell out of my presentation, though students inevitably bring it up. Rivendell, "the Last Homely House," has rich possibilities for exploring hospitality, a virtue often overlooked in our culture (225). Tolkien, too, was distrustful of modern industrialism, and today he would be labeled a conservationist, if not green, in his environmental views. When we reach *The Two Towers*, I sometimes invoke Matthew Dickerson and Jonathan Evans's ecological model in which the hobbits represent agriculture or the life of the soil; the elves horticulture, the life of food preparation; and the ents feraculture, the life of the wilderness. Such a model expands the categories enough to consider the pastoral in the most elastic way possible. I also draw students' attention to the pastoral conventions present in Treebeard's song of the ents and entwives, verses worth reading aloud or listening to in a musical setting (469; bk. 3, ch. 4).

The nature of love in the pastoral offers strong connections to Tolkien's work, but I find that many students need to have the definitions of love expanded beyond the erotic and romantic (as commonly understood). I find C. S. Lewis's discussion of friendship and familial love in *The Four Loves* (chapters 3–4) and Wendell Berry's discussion regarding local culture in *What Are People For?* (153–69) to be good sources to illustrate for students how love and place are twined together in Tolkien in ways that evoke earlier conventions of the pastoral. As Sam observes of the elves of Lothlórien:

> Now these folk aren't wanderers or homeless, and seem a bit nearer to the likes of us: they seem to belong here, more even than Hobbits do in the Shire. Whether they've made the land, or the land's made them, it's hard to say, if you take my meaning. . . . If there's any magic about, it's right down deep, where I can't lay my hands on it, in a manner of speaking. . . . I've never heard of a better land than this. It's like being at home and on a holiday at the same time, if you understand me. (360–61; bk. 2, ch. 7)

I hope to leave my students with the possibility that the literary gestures and mode of the pastoral, instead of simply denoting an ideal, point to the embodied and localized nature of human loyalties and affections. That Sam senses the deep connections between two pastoral visions—the deep-down magic of Lothlórien and the homely earth of the Shire—suggests that human beings, too, may yet find the wisdom and power of places that are well loved.

Teaching Tolkien in the Context of the Fantasy Tradition

Christopher Cobb

A key challenge of teaching a course on genuinely popular literature is guiding students to see the significance of what they are reading without spoiling the fun by raising topics they see as remote from the pleasures of the text. In my experience, a course on Tolkien and modern fantasy can address this challenge by leading students to think in sophisticated ways about genre theory, to practice close intertextual reading in order to grasp and experience the imaginative power of *The Lord of the Rings*, and to appreciate the work's engagement with contemporary aesthetic, social, and ethical concerns. I approach *The Lord of the Rings* through genre because one of the clearest signs of the text's power is that it has "created a genre *almost* single-handed" (Shippey, *Road* 377n7).[1] Few works in literary history can be said to have created a genre, so the development of fantasy literature around Tolkien's work provides an unusual opportunity to examine both the operation of literary influence and the significance of a literary genre for the culture from which it emerges.

Topics in genre theory relating to the influence of *The Lord of the Rings* and the significance of genre can be framed in a variety of ways to appeal to different student audiences. In an upper-level course primarily for English majors, genre theory topics can be raised directly by including selections from criticism such as T. S. Eliot's "Tradition and the Individual Talent," Northrop Frye's *Anatomy of Criticism*, Harold Bloom's *The Anxiety of Influence*, M. M. Bakhtin's *The Dialogic Imagination*, Ursula K. Le Guin's essays on the fantasy genre (*Language*), or Brian Attebery's *Strategies of Fantasy*, as well as Tolkien's own examination of tradition and influence in "On Fairy-stories." Since a few samples of this kind of criticism can enliven even an introductory course, the main question for instructors wanting to employ genre theory is how to frame it, given the many available approaches. In my course, which generally attracts a mix of majors and nonmajors, I avoid a definitional approach to genre, which leads to questions about whether a work is or is not fantasy,[2] in favor of an approach that looks at genre in terms of tradition. Such an approach favors analysis of relationships between works and between texts and readers, which helps less sophisticated readers see that genre membership is not a simple either-or matter while enabling more sophisticated readers to perceive the complexity of intertextual relationships.

This tradition-based approach to genre can be engaged without using any theoretical texts, by talking with the class about the remarkable place of *The Lord of the Rings* in the history of fantasy as a publishing category and the associated critical controversies.[3] I begin my course with this story each semester. Students are fascinated by the fact that a section of bookstores they take for granted did not exist a half century ago, and they are astonished that a work now so massively popular and increasingly respected had trouble finding a publisher. Stories of the unauthorized Ace edition and the "book of the century" controversy further heighten their awareness that *The Lord of the Rings* has had a hotly contested impact on English and American culture. From this history, students gain a new appreciation for the historicity of genre, which prompts them to explore how and why *The Lord of the Rings* made such an impact.

The rest of my course is designed to guide and further encourage this exploration, which I initiate by offering a preliminary answer to the question of how *The Lord of the Rings* established a recognized generic tradition. I suggest that Tolkien's accomplishment entailed both creative genius and a deep knowledge of literary sources unknown to most contemporary readers. A third necessary element, however, seems to me the most intriguing: Tolkien's development of strategies for making his genius and knowledge meaningful to a diverse contemporary readership. This third element becomes the primary focus of the course. Tolkien was not the first writer to create a new world in his writings, nor was he the first to adapt the aesthetics and values of medieval literature for a modern audience. But he was the first twentieth-century writer to combine these two projects in a manner that engaged a wide readership.[4] In my class, we assess how he created this appeal by comparing his approach with that of earlier writers who had similar goals and by considering how his work provided a model for later writers. By exploring the difference between Tolkien's relationship to his predecessors and the relationship of his successors to him, students can see the emergence of a tradition and the coherent set of ideas about the world with which that tradition engages.[5] To set up these comparisons, I divide my course into three parts: backgrounds to *The Lord of the Rings* (two and a half weeks), *The Lord of the Rings* itself (five weeks), and the uses of fantasy after *The Lord of the Rings* (six weeks).

Identifying this set of ideas through the study of relationships between texts is particularly important because it moves the class from formal analysis of literary techniques to the cultural question, Why fantasy? Why has engagement with this set of ideas appealed so strongly to readers since the 1950s? Does fantasy offer purely escapist artistic pleasure, or is it meeting identifiable cultural needs?[6] Questions of this kind challenge students to reflect self-consciously on their own tastes, on the purpose of their preferences and pleasures. Their pleasure in the texts becomes part of the subject matter of the course, so that the course deals with the perceived tension between intellectual seriousness and reading pleasure by making reading pleasure a topic for serious intellectual inquiry.

Exploration of backgrounds to *The Lord of the Rings* entails studying works that may look little like Tolkien's on the surface but that nevertheless contain images, incidents, attitudes, themes, or devices of narrative and style that contributed to Tolkien's development of the fantasy genre as it is now recognized.[7] In the works of William Morris, Lord Dunsany, and E. R. Eddison, Tolkien found models for building a secondary world.[8] H. Rider Haggard and, more remotely, Sir Walter Scott showed him how to develop a dynamic adventure with deep historical roots.[9] Ideas about how to use fantasy as a vehicle for religious themes came to him from the works of George MacDonald, G. K. Chesterton, and David Lindsay.[10] From among the many works of these prolific writers, instructors can select those that highlight aspects of *The Lord of the Rings* they wish to emphasize.

My usual selections from this group are novels by Morris and Dunsany, who pioneered the creation of secondary worlds set off from ordinary reality by the style in which they are rendered—the creative strategy that Tolkien would later make fundamental to the fantasy tradition.[11] Although Tolkien imitates neither author directly in *The Lord of the Rings*, he uses not only their strategies of building extraordinary worlds through style but also their selection of folkloric and premodern sources, blending the Germanic traditions emphasized in Morris with the Celtic traditions employed by Dunsany (see Burns, *Perilous Realms*). Study of Morris and Dunsany thus sets up a helpful framework for analyzing Tolkien's use of style in his creation of Middle-earth.

Among Morris's relevant works, I have found *The Glittering Plain* to be the most teachable. Short enough to be covered in a week, it unfolds with a clarity of action and of values that makes it accessible to students, even as it confronts them with an unfamiliar, highly mannered style, as in the passage in which the young hero discovers that trouble has suddenly entered his life:

> Then he looked up hastily, and saw the maidens drawing near . . . and he beheld them that their faces were pale and woe-begone, and their raiment rent, and there was no joy in them. Hallblithe stood aghast while one who had gotten off her horse (and she was the daughter of his own mother)

> ran past him into the hall, looking not at him, as if she durst not. . . . And he knew that now he was the yokefellow of sorrow. (5)

To demonstrate the relevance of this style of writing to Tolkien's works, I show passages from *The Book of Lost Tales, Part I*, that closely match Morris in syntax and vocabulary (e.g., the Noldor's preparations for departure from the Undying Lands [163]). Although Tolkien was no longer directly imitating Morris's style when he came to write *The Lord of the Rings*, Morris's example still informs Tolkien's use of archaism to convey values and shape moods remote from modern sensibility.[12] Analysis of the values implied by Morris's style prepares students to interpret similar effects in Tolkien's description of Hobbits, where the values of their community in the Shire underlie the humble but unquenchable heroism they display during the Ring quest.

Stylistic analysis of early fantasy texts like *The Glittering Plain* can open up into a broader discussion about the way the design of Tolkien's world offers the reader an implicit structure of values. Morris unfolds his created world by means of a simple quest plot. Sorrow has come to Hallblithe because his "trothplight maiden" (19) has been kidnapped by sea raiders, so he must leave home to find her, journeying first to the inhospitable land of the sea raiders and then to the Glittering Plain itself, a land of beauteous immortality. There he is offered a life of eternal bliss, if he will remain to wed the Undying King's daughter. Only after Hallblithe rejects temptation can he find his beloved and return home. Consideration of the way Morris sets homely pleasures and domestic values against the bold but brutal life of the raiders and the more deeply enticing life of idle bliss prepares students to read the moral geography of Middle-earth. When Tolkien's Hobbits encounter Elves and Ents, the Riders of Rohan and the grave Men of Gondor, and even the Orcs, the contrasts of settings and communities raise issues of value the same way Morris does. Although Tolkien's treatment of the enticements of immortal beauty differs from Morris's, reading Morris trains students to read Tolkien.

Dunsany's novel *The King of Elfland's Daughter* uses style and setting to establish values in ways that parallel Morris's. Dunsany, however, replaces Morris's rather generic Earthly Paradise with Elfland. He engages with Celtic traditions of Faërie as he depicts a timeless realm that exists in "perpetual contemplation of all the beauty there has ever been" (40), which the magic of the Elf King preserves against the ravages of time. Tolkien's depiction of the lands of the Elves (especially Lórien) responds quite directly to Dunsany's, and his consideration of the relations between Elves and Men in Middle-earth owes something to Dunsany's portrayal of the vast gap between the perspectives of mortals and immortals in the troubled relationship of the earthly prince Alveric with the princess Lirazel, the king of Elfland's daughter. Class discussion of the tension in Dunsany's novel between the human characters' desire for magic and the fear and discomfort they experience when it actually arrives readies students for the ambivalence of the mortal characters in *The Lord of the Rings* toward the Elves.

Because encounters between mortals from simple, earthy communities and immortals from lands of unchanging beauty are the chief events in both *The Glittering Plain* and *The King of Elfland's Daughter*, the plots of Morris and Dunsany anticipate *The Fellowship of the Ring*, which carries the reader from the Shire to Rivendell and Lórien. Yet neither the War of the Ring nor Frodo's wrestling with the Ring in the later stages of the quest has precedent in the works of Morris or Dunsany. Tolkien's conception of the Fellowship's quest as a struggle against a world-destroying evil, represented in the mode of high adventure, was instead inspired by MacDonald, Haggard, and Scott. Since my students tend to see the centrality to fantasy of high adventure and the battle of good versus evil more easily than they recognize the centrality of world building, mannered style, and encounters with immortal beauty, starting with Morris and Dunsany enables me to draw their attention to significant aspects of *The Lord of the Rings* that they might disregard otherwise.[13]

While my course on Tolkien and the fantasy tradition chooses precursors to Tolkien that lead directly into the opening sections of *The Lord of the Rings*, it selects successors to Tolkien that respond directly to *The Lord of the Rings*' climactic images. My own reading of the fantasy tradition suggests that Tolkien creates this tradition in *The Lord of the Rings* by establishing the idea that a profound encounter with a vision of the good is a prerequisite for true heroic action. Tolkien's complex articulation of the good links his work to diverse earlier fantasies (and the folk traditions that lie behind them), in which Tolkien perceives both the homely virtues of the Shire and the immortal beauty of the Elves. He radically transforms his sources, however, by allying homely virtue and immortal beauty, which his predecessors treat as incompatible versions of the good. This innovation enables him to extend the moral and narrative reach of fantasy to include heroic struggle against evil. This heroic narrative has seized the imagination of modern readers through its depiction of an encounter with evil that resonates deeply with concerns about fascism, totalitarianism, industrialism, and environmental destruction. This heroic aspect of *The Lord of the Rings* is both reinterpreted and reconfirmed in the works of Tolkien's successors.

The field of fantasy after Tolkien is much larger than the field of fantasy before him, so instructors can construct a unit on his successors in many different ways. In my course, I work to show the scope of fantasy after Tolkien by turning first to fantasy works in which his influence is strongly marked in imagery, plot, and theme. I follow these with texts in which his influence works indirectly through his theories about world building and the purposes of fantasy. I also mix in at least one work by a writer who rejects Tolkien's example and values.

From among the works of post-Tolkien fantasy strongly influenced by *The Lord of the Rings*, I teach Peter S. Beagle's *The Last Unicorn* and Ursula K. Le Guin's first Earthsea trilogy.[14] These books work well because they are not formulaic imitations of *The Lord of the Rings* but clearly draw inspiration directly from Tolkien, especially in their themes and climactic imagery. In *The Last Unicorn*, the unicorn's quest to find her people is quite unlike Frodo's quest, but the climactic scene, in which Schmendrick's magic and the unicorn's courage are both awakened, owes its structure to Tolkien's depiction of the awakening of Merry's courage on the fields of the Pelennor. By identifying and discussing such influences, students can refine their understanding of Tolkien's treatment of his major themes and their larger cultural significance as they discover what leads Le Guin and Beagle to follow his example. Imagery inspired by Frodo and Sam's journey through Mordor and by the fall of Barad-dûr is especially prominent in both authors' works. In *The Last Unicorn*, students can find reconfigurations of Mordor and Barad-dûr in images such as the barrenness of Haggard's country and the fall of his castle when the unicorns are released from the sea. Similar images appear in Earthsea when Ged and Tenar escape from the Tombs of Atuan, which then fall in an earthquake, and when Ged and Lebannen journey across the Dry Land of the dead in *The Farthest Shore*. Other reconfigurations of imagery from the later books of *The Lord of the Rings* emerge throughout *The Last Unicorn* and the first Earthsea trilogy, rewarding careful reading and sparking comparative discussions.

Because Beagle and Le Guin build on Tolkien's work in addition to following in his footsteps, students can consider the continuing development of the fantasy genre as well as the power of Tolkien's influence when reading them. Tolkien, as I noted earlier, significantly reconfigured a basic narrative of fantasy when he allied immortal beauty to homely values instead of treating the two qualities as antithetical. One consequence of this change was the recuperation of certain kinds of magic. Tolkien makes such magic part of the allure of fantasy, but it still holds a subsidiary position in his work, dropping away in moments when heroic courage is most essential. Beagle and Le Guin explore the potentials of rehabilitated magic in fantasy more thoroughly by making their protagonists magicians. The bumbling wizard Schmendrick may not be the hero of *The Last Unicorn*, but readers share his point of view, and his discovery of his magic plays an essential role in the regeneration of his world. Le Guin makes the wizard Ged her protagonist and hero, thereby intensifying the psychological complexity of the problem of power, which Tolkien had addressed through the One Ring: in Le Guin, power becomes an attribute of the hero himself rather than an attribute of an object that can (with great difficulty) be separated from the self and cast away.

When taken far enough, extensions of this type eventually leave behind Tolkien's direct influence to become independent explorations of the potential for fantasy that his work reveals. Discussion of Beagle's and Le Guin's extensions of Tolkien's structures and images sets up a transition to other works that connect to Tolkien mainly in their approaches to world building and views of the purpose of fantasy. Because I focus on Le Guin as a direct imitator of Tolkien, I find it useful to make the turn to indirect influence with her work as well. In her fourth Earthsea novel, *Tehanu*, she shifts from responding intuitively and directly to Tolkien's example to responding consciously and indirectly to the fantasy tradition. She documents her reconsideration of fantasy in *Earthsea Revisioned*, her essay about writing *Tehanu*. In *Tehanu*, which was written sixteen years after the Earthsea trilogy, she reworks her approach to gender and heroism in fantasy so that it does not merely reflect either prior tradition or received social stereotypes. This change entails the reimagination of her own imagery. The spider imagery in *The Farthest Shore*, for example, there associated with evil (as in Tolkien), reappears in *Tehanu* differently valued: it is associated with the inner heroism of women raising children and bridging social gaps.

Le Guin's transition from direct imitation of Tolkien to engagement with his conception of the purpose of fantasy is not uncommon among other authors as they mature.[15] Guy Gavriel Kay, for example, after his direct imitation of Tolkien in the Fionavar Tapestry trilogy, has turned to historical fantasies deliberately designed around the value of consolation (Cobb 89–90), which according to Tolkien is one of the primary uses of the fairy story ("On Fairy-stories" 79–90). In his later works, Kay picks up motifs from Fionavar in ways that resemble Le Guin's reconsideration of her earlier Earthsea novels in *Tehanu* and other later writings on Earthsea.[16] I have not myself taught the Fionavar Tapestry, but Kay's historical fantasies *Tigana* and *A Song for Arbonne* may be readily taught as works that employ Tolkien's conception of the purpose of fantasy in order to develop the potentials of the tradition in new ways. Like Kay, Patricia McKillip has created a more independent space for herself after her strongly Tolkienian Riddlemaster trilogy and extended the scope of fantasy by reaching around Tolkien to the roots of his fantasy in fairy tales. Some of her novels directly rework traditional folktales, as in *Winter Rose*'s retelling of "Tam Lin"; others capture the mysterious feel of the folktale without following a traditional source, as in *Ombria in Shadow*. Returning to folk sources enables McKillip to reengage with the ominous qualities of immortal beauty and magic that Tolkien revised. It seems, though, that some element of remoteness, of a return to the time when folktales were living stories, is necessary to restore this ominous quality: when McKillip makes a venture into a contemporary setting in *Solstice Wood*, a sequel to *Winter Rose*, its plot turns on the forging of an alliance between immortal beauty and homely values when both are threatened by industrial and commercial culture. Reading *Solstice Wood* as a companion to *Winter Rose* brings Tolkien's revisions of the fantasy tradition back into focus as a move driven by his response to industrial civilization.

Other fantasists well worth teaching as examples of writers who have used Tolkien's conception of fantasy to create worlds of their own include Charles de Lint and J. K. Rowling. De Lint, the foremost practitioner of urban fantasy, reimagines the alliance of immortal beauty and homely value by bringing fantasy into a contemporary urban setting, in which essential evil and its outgrowths of oppression, industrial waste, and despair originate in one's own neighborhood, not in the Black Land far away. De Lint's first collection of Newford stories, *Dreams Underfoot*, engages students strongly.[17] Its connections to Tolkien—a character named for Peregrin Took in the opening story and a character reminiscent of Bombadil in "The Conjure Man," right down to his blue jacket and yellow boots—enable students to follow the dialogue de Lint sets up between his approach to fantasy and Tolkien's.[18] His essay "The Tale Goes Ever On" richly recounts his experience of reading *The Lord of the Rings* and can deepen students' observation of his response to Tolkien's formation of the fantasy genre. Rowling's works currently provide an excellent point of reference for discussion of the fantasy tradition, whether they are on one's syllabus or not, since almost all the students in my fantasy classes in the last decade have read the Harry Potter books. Of these, *Harry Potter and the Prisoner of Azkaban* seems the best to teach, being manageable in length and energized in its depiction of the conflict between good and evil by means of reconfigured images from Tolkien, such as the Dementors and Wormtail. Rowling's choice to make the Dementors servants of the Ministry of Magic rather than of her own Dark Lord, Voldemort, reconfigures the nature of the conflict with evil in fantasy, much as Le Guin's making of Ged into a wizard reconfigures the problem of power.

Although de Lint and Rowling do not follow Tolkien in the design of their fantasy works, their uses of fantasy are consistent with his vision of the purpose of fantasy, summed up in "On Fairy-stories" as fantasy, recovery, escape, and consolation (67–87). To make the influence of Tolkien's vision as well as the impact of his practical example evident to students in another way, I include in my course a work by a writer who eschews or even emphatically rejects his vision. Works such as these show what fantasy outside the scope of Tolkien's influence looks like and give an idea of the diversity of contemporary fantasy. The writers who do not look to Tolkien as the founder of the tradition in which they are working tend to look instead to the related traditions of sword and sorcery and horror that developed in the American pulp magazines of the 1930s. Fritz Leiber's stories of Fafhrd and the Gray Mouser are among the best in this vein; I usually teach his 1959 satire of religion, "Lean Times in Lankhmar," as an example of a vision of the purpose of fantasy and the role of belief in its effects that is contrary to Tolkien's. Leiber articulates his differences from Tolkien and the roots of his own tradition in a brief, genial headnote to *The Swords of Lankhmar*, which I share with students. Reading Leiber's account of his project helps them appreciate his attempt to create "a couple of fantasy heroes closer to true human stature than supermen like Conan and Tarzan" and see the link to horror when Leiber describes his "stuff as at least equally fantastic as [Tolkien's], but it's an earthier sort of fantasy with a strong seasoning of 'black fantasy'—or of black humor."

Leiber's comfortable sense of being "at the opposite extreme from the heroes of Tolkien" seems to be shared by other major American writers who have developed their fantasies out of the pulp tradition, such as Roger Zelazny and

Steven Brust.[19] British fantasists who follow the pulp sword-and-sorcery tradition, on the other hand, tend to criticize Tolkien's work and reject his influence emphatically. Michael Moorcock is the most prominent of these. His Eternal Champion books provide a number of works that offer a strong counterpoint to Tolkien,[20] while his essay "Epic Pooh," which takes Tolkien and his followers to task for writing fantasy that is too comfortable, is among the more famous anti-Tolkien screeds. More recently, China Miéville and Philip Pullman have taken up Moorcock's mantle as anti-Tolkienian fantasists.[21] Miéville's work would be particularly appropriate to a course that takes a turn into urban fantasy, perhaps with de Lint, while Pullman could counterpoint Rowling, if a Harry Potter text is included. Neil Gaiman should perhaps also be mentioned as a prominent and influential British fantasist who steers clear of Tolkien. Like Miéville, his works, especially *Neverwhere* and *American Gods*, bear comparison to de Lint's. Looking at any of these writers in the context of Moorcock's or Miéville's critical remarks should help students reflect on both the limits of Tolkien's accomplishments and the cultural causes of unsympathetic readings of his work.

As the expansive list of authors in this essay suggests, one of the exciting features of a course on Tolkien and the fantasy genre is the openness of its subject. Such a course can bring *The Lord of the Rings* into direct engagement with contemporary writers and issues, revealing the ongoing, dynamic role of Tolkien's fiction in shaping this literary tradition. It can also get students to take up the challenge of writing criticism about contemporary fantasy literature. Although more good scholarship on Tolkien and fantasy exists now than fifteen years ago, when I first began developing my course, knowledge of Tolkien's connections to his predecessors and successors in the fantasy tradition is still fragmentary, and little criticism has been written on many of the major post-Tolkien fantasists. Students therefore have the opportunity to do original, foundational work on the development of the fantasy tradition after Tolkien as well as on Tolkien's relationship to his own models. I encourage my students to make their final essay a comparative analysis of Tolkien and a contemporary fantasy writer whose work is not on our syllabus. Their excitement at the discovery of unexpected intertextual connections and cultural resonances in works they have previously read is one of the many rewards of a course on this subject. Nothing convinces students more of the importance of Tolkien's writing than recognizing its traces in the work of other writers whom they admire.

NOTES

[1]On *The Lord of the Rings* as the work that created fantasy as a genre, see also Anderson, "Mainstreaming"; Attebery 13–17; Schweitzer 18–19.

[2]This is a topic Attebery handles particularly well in *Strategies* 1–17.

[3]For the standard account of the publication history of *The Lord of the Rings*, see Carpenter, *J. R. R. Tolkien* 206–63. The critical debate over Tolkien is addressed in the

essays by James McNelis and Craig Franson elsewhere in this volume, but on the book-of-the-century polls that sparked the latest round of intense debates over the merits of *The Lord of the Rings*, see Shippey, *J. R. R. Tolkien* xx–xxiv; Pearce, *Tolkien: Man* 1–10.

[4]John Hunter points out that James Macpherson's Ossianic poems, Sir Walter Scott's historical novels, the folklore project of the Brothers Grimm, and Elias Lönnrot's *Kalevala* all anticipate Tolkien's methods and popular success, while Andrew Lynch notes resemblances between Lord Alfred Tennyson's *Idylls of the King* and Tolkien's project. Among these authors, Scott shares with Tolkien the distinction of inventing a new form in the historical novel, which makes him an important contributor to the fantasy genre.

[5]A course could also emphasize the process by which coherence was achieved through focusing on the interaction of Tolkien's writings with those of his immediate contemporaries, especially the Inklings. On these interactions, see especially Carpenter, *Inklings*; Flieger, *Splintered Light* 35–107; Glyer.

[6]For thoughtfully developed and varied perspectives on the cultural significance of Tolkien's appeal, see Curry, *Defending*; Rosebury, *Tolkien* 134–92; Pearce, *Tolkien: Man*.

[7]For related perspectives, see Lobdell, *Rise*; Nelson, "Literary Influences"; Mathews 16–25. A broad sampling of the work of pre-Tolkien fantasy writers appears in Anderson, *Tales*.

[8]Among Morris's many works, his romances, frequently considered the first true examples of the fantasy genre, are of most interest. His first three romances (*The House of the Wolfings*, *The Roots of the Mountains*, and *The Glittering Plain*) present an ideal, reconstructed image of primitive Germanic society and its values. Morris's last romances (*The Wood beyond the World*, *The Well at the World's End*, *The Water of the Wondrous Isles*, and *The Sundering Flood*) had less influence on Tolkien, but the influence of the whole range of Morris's work on him has been documented (see Perry, "William Morris"; Mathews 85–95; Scoville; Burns, *Perilous Realms* 75–92; Amison). Dunsany is most renowned as a fantasist for his short stories, but his only fantasy novel, *The King of Elfland's Daughter*, is of greater interest in relation to *The Lord of the Rings*. Eddison's most accessible fantasy work is his first novel, *The Worm Ouroboros*, but his Zimiamvia trilogy is also of interest. Tolkien described Eddison as "the greatest and most convincing writer of 'invented worlds' that I have read" (*Letters of J. R. R. Tolkien* 258).

[9]Of Haggard's novels, *King Solomon's Mines* and *She* appear to have most strongly influenced Tolkien (Green, "King Thorin's Mines"; Rogers and Underwood), but recent scholarship has made it clear that images from many of Haggard's works lodged in Tolkien's imagination and found their way into *The Hobbit* and *The Lord of the Rings* (Nelson, "Literary Influences" 368–70 and "Tolkien's Further Indebtedness"). The feel of his adventure writing, though not the specifics of his influence on Tolkien, can be effectively conveyed by a shorter piece like "Black Heart and White Heart: A Zulu Idyll." For Scott, *Ivanhoe* probably provides the clearest model for fantasy, although *Minstrelsy of the Scottish Border* is also influential for both its content and Scott's attitude to his traditional materials.

[10]George MacDonald's two adult dream visions, *Phantastes* and *Lilith*, are often cited as works of significance to the fantasy tradition, and their influence on C. S. Lewis is substantial. For Tolkien, however, several of MacDonald's fairy tales for children (*The Princess and the Goblin*, *The Princess and Curdie*, and *The Golden Key*) are more relevant, as is his essay "The Fantastic Imagination" (see Kreglinger; J. Long). Chesterton is important for Tolkien's formation of fantasy more as a critical source than as a literary

one (Milbank), but of Chesterton's creative writing, the early stories collected in *The Coloured Lands* are likely the most significant. David Lindsay's *Voyage to Arcturus* was also of interest to both Lewis and Tolkien.

[11] In treating these elements of their work as foundational to the fantasy tradition, I follow Tolkien's observation that "the making or glimpsing of Other-worlds, was the heart of the desire of Faërie" ("On Fairy-stories" 64) and Le Guin's insight that "style is of . . . fundamental significance in fantasy" ("From Elfland" 95). I choose Morris and Dunsany over Eddison as examples primarily because of considerations of time—Eddison has no short novels.

[12] On the development of Tolkien's style from his early imitation of Morris to his mature style in *The Lord of the Rings*, see Rosebury, *Tolkien* 89–104. Tolkien comments on the role of archaism in his style in a letter to Hugh Brogan (*Letters of J. R. R. Tolkien* 171).

[13] A course strongly interested in the religious aspect of *The Lord of the Rings*, however, might well begin with MacDonald and Chesterton, whereas Haggard and Scott would be valuable for courses exploring the development of the adventure plot in fantasy, especially as fantasy's embedding of adventure in a complexly constructed history may link adventure to issues of race, class, gender, and (colonial) politics.

[14] The books in Le Guin's first Earthsea trilogy are *A Wizard of Earthsea*, *The Tombs of Atuan*, and *The Farthest Shore*. For a brief analysis of the widely recognized influence of Tolkien on Le Guin's Earthsea books, see Kaveney 165–66. Le Guin herself is one of Tolkien's best critics. Her essays "From Elfland to Poughkeepsie," "The Child and the Shadow" (both in Le Guin, *Language*), and "Rhythmic Pattern in *The Lord of the Rings*" (in Haber) are insightful, accessible, and suggestive of the writing strategies Le Guin learned from Tolkien.

[15] For analyses of the relations between direct and indirect imitation of Tolkien in authors' careers, see Kaveney; Ringel; Shippey, "Literature" 379–82.

[16] Each of Kay's historical fantasies is set in a world that offers an alternative version of a historical period in Earth's history. The first two of these, *Tigana* (an analogue to Renaissance Italy) and *A Song for Arbonne* (corresponding to Languedoc during the age of the troubadours and the Albigensian Crusade), are the most strongly engaged with the fantasy tradition. If the Fionavar Tapestry is used as a direct imitation of Tolkien, then *Ysabel*, which returns to some of the characters from Earth who travel to Fionavar, would be an interesting novel to include as an example of indirect influence.

[17] De Lint's short story collections, which feature interlinked stories and recurring characters, offer the instructor the advantage of flexibility as well as explicit references to Tolkien, but his early novels *Moonheart* and *Memory and Dream* seem eminently teachable and reveal de Lint's theories of fantasy more than do the short stories. His later novels and stories respond more to his own early works than to Tolkien, so they would be more difficult to link back to *The Lord of the Rings* unless some of his earlier work is included to show the intermediary steps in his development.

[18] The inclusion of characters in urban fantasy stories who are readers of Tolkien often provides a way for writers in this fantasy subgenre to work out the impact of Tolkien on their work without following his model for creating a fantasy world. For a study of several women writers employing this device, see Ringel 165. A very fine contemporary example of this kind of fantasy is Jo Walton's *Among Others*.

[19] For Zelazny, the opening novels of his first Amber series—*Nine Princes in Amber* and *The Guns of Avalon*—and his stand-alone novel *Lord of Light* would probably be

the most interesting to teach as counterpoints to Tolkien. For Brust, the opening novels of his Vlad Taltos series, *Jhereg* and *Yendi*, would probably work well, though his *Phoenix Guards* (the first of his Khaavren Romances) could be interesting in a course looking at Tolkien's connections to historical fiction, as *Guards* is an homage to Alexandre Dumas's *Three Musketeers*.

[20]Moorcock's Eternal Champion books have been published in many combinations. Because the stories of Elric of Melniboné are the most popular and influential of his works, these should be used in class. *Elric of Melniboné*, the first novel in the chronology of that world, introduces the flavor of Moorcock's work.

[21]*Perdido Street Station* is arguably Miéville's most accomplished novel. For his view of Tolkien's work, see "Tolkien—Middle-earth Meets Middle England." Pullman's most significant fantasy work is His Dark Materials trilogy: *The Golden Compass*, *The Subtle Knife*, and *The Amber Spyglass*. Its overt antichurch stance has stimulated lively critical debate. Burton Hatlen offers the most thorough scholarly account of Pullman's challenge to Tolkien, including Pullman's major statements about Tolkien's work (76–80).

Tolkien and the Modern: Reading the Canon through *The Lord of the Rings*

Sharin Schroeder

"No poet, no artist of any art, has his complete meaning alone. . . . You cannot value him alone; you must set him, for contrast and comparison, among the dead."
—T. S. Eliot, "Tradition and the Individual Talent"

"Such is modern life. Mordor in our midst."
—J. R. R. Tolkien, letter to Rayner Unwin, 24 October 1952

In the preface to his revised *The Road to Middle-earth*, Tom Shippey rejects his previously "unconsidered assumption that [Tolkien] had no literary context, that he was a 'one-off'" in his time. Instead, he links Tolkien with a group of "'traumatised [twentieth-century] authors,' writing fantasy, but voicing in that fantasy the most pressing and most immediately relevant issues of the whole monstrous twentieth century—questions of industrialised warfare, the origin of evil, the nature of humanity" (xvii). For Shippey, "it is the fantasists like Orwell or Golding or Vonnegut or Tolkien who have been confronting the fearful and horrible issues of political life, while the E. M. Forsters and John Updikes stayed within their sheltered Shires" (326). Shippey's position, both in his preface to *The Road to Middle-earth* and in his *J. R. R. Tolkien: Author of the Century*, has certainly sparked debate, but his case for the value of studying *The Lord of the Rings* in the context of twentieth-century literature convinced me to include Tolkien in my course Modern Fiction. As I taught Tolkien first in this lower-level course and later in an upper-level course, Tolkien: Medieval or Modern?, my thinking about Tolkien's relation to both modernity and modernism changed. Teaching Tolkien in his contemporary context, I discovered, gives students a better understanding of a literary period with which they are frequently unfamiliar.[1] Tolkien's work serves as a gateway to discussions of twentieth-century literary history, the study of which, in turn, illuminates students' understanding of Tolkien's work.

My goal in Tolkien: Medieval or Modern? is, by contextualizing Tolkien's work, to help students understand why certain themes, literary genres, writing styles, and methods of characterization are popular in their time periods. Who determines the quality of a literary work? Why are some types of literature better received than others in various time periods? What makes a literary work last? We investigate Tolkien's relation to medieval and twentieth-century writers by paying attention to critical judgments and reception history. In order to get students actively involved in the investigation, I assign a reviewer impersonation project, the heart of my course. By the end of the course, students understand differences between Tolkien and many of the modernists in ideology and writing style. In addition, they perceive that Tolkien shared several modernist motivations for writing. For example, his work responded to World War I; like the modernists, he questioned the purpose of literature in the twentieth century, the role of literary history in artistic creation, and the position of the artist.[2]

On the first day of Tolkien: Medieval or Modern?, I ask students to tell me what affinities Tolkien's work has with medieval literature and with modern (or modernist) literature.[3] I write my binary on the board, putting "medieval" on the left side and "modern/modernist" on the right.[4] We brainstorm similarities in the themes, genre, and writing style of Tolkien with those of other authors in each time period. Even though we have this discussion on the first day of class, when the students have not done any reading, I find they tend to know more about Tolkien's writing than about medieval or modernist literature. Some say that, although they associated Tolkien with medieval literature when they signed up for the class, they are already beginning to see commonalities between his work and those of other twentieth-century writers.[5] I end this discussion by telling the class that we are not looking for a definite answer to the medieval-or-modern question, but that studying Tolkien will help us better understand both medieval and modern literature as well as Tolkien's writing.

In the first week, while students are reading *The Fellowship of the Ring*, we spend time in class reading three essays aloud: Virginia Woolf's "Modern Fiction" (1919), C. S. Lewis's "On Science Fiction" (1955), and George Orwell's "Good Bad Books" (1945). Woolf's essay does an excellent job of setting up what modernist fiction is. While Woolf praises James Joyce for "being concerned at all costs to reveal the flickerings of that innermost flame which flashes its messages through the brain" and thereby getting closer to "life itself" than the conventional realist novel, she also recognizes that Joyce's artistic decisions, although "bringing us closer to what we were prepared to call life itself," still exclude or ignore "not only other aspects of life, but more important ones into the bargain" (151, 152). She prefers Joyce's "spiritual" qualities to works by authors she calls "materialist" but concludes that "'[t]he proper stuff of fiction' does not exist; everything is the proper stuff of fiction" (154). I ask students to contrast the literary concerns Woolf valued with those that Tolkien valued. To what extent does Woolf's essay on the "proper stuff of fiction" include *The Lord of the Rings*? Does *The Lord of the Rings* have anything to do with "life itself"? How so or how not?

Lewis's essay provides a counterpoint to Woolf's. Lewis questions the way critics judge particular kinds of literature. Considering the critical response to science fiction in the first half of the twentieth century, he points out that most negative reviews were written by critics who "clearly hated the kind [genre] they wrote about. It is very dangerous to write about a kind you hate. Hatred obscures all distinctions" (81).[6] Lewis's essay particularly engages students who dislike *The Lord of the Rings*, of whom there were many in my first modern fiction course. We try to identify reasons for their dislike: are they resistant to the genre of fantasy or to some other aspect of Tolkien's work? Are their criteria for judging aesthetic value related to genre? Do they believe that a critic who dislikes a certain genre can still be a good critic of it? These questions will provoke debate even if the entire class loves Tolkien. If a class loves *The Lord of the Rings* but dislikes *To the Lighthouse* or *The Waste Land*, bringing their attention back to Lewis's essay when modernist texts are studied has two positive effects. Requiring students to try to identify what exactly they dislike in these texts makes them more careful critics; it also usually makes them give the texts a more patient reading.

Finally we turn to Orwell's essay, which is also about assessing literary value. Orwell, who reviewed Lewis's *That Hideous Strength* but died before *The Lord of the Rings* was published, discusses "what Chesterton called the 'good bad book': . . . the kind of book that has no literary pretensions but which remains readable when more serious productions have perished" (348). According to Orwell, escape literature fits this definition, but he claims that perhaps "the supreme example of the 'good bad book' is *Uncle Tom's Cabin*. It is an unintentionally ludicrous book, full of preposterous melodramatic incidents; it is also deeply moving and essentially true; it is hard to say which quality outweighs the other" (349). Orwell ends by stating, "I would back *Uncle Tom's Cabin* to outlive the complete works of Virginia Woolf or George Moore, though I know of no strictly literary test which would show where the superiority lies" (350).

After these essays are read, I ask students to devise three distinct literary tests, one that makes good books out of works by high modernists such as Woolf and Joyce, one that makes a good book out of *The Lord of the Rings*, and one that makes a good book out of *Uncle Tom's Cabin*. I also ask them to devise literary tests for labeling each work a bad book. Do they consider any of these literary litmus tests valid? Should *The Lord of the Rings* be judged an example of a good bad book? Or is it something else?

After we discuss the various judgments a critic might make about *The Lord of the Rings*, the class is prepared for the reviewer impersonation project. For this project, my students receive a course packet that includes several reviews of each volume of *The Lord of the Rings*. They select a reviewer to impersonate after we finish each volume. A panel might comprise six reviewers for *The Fellowship of the Ring* (Lewis, Edwin Muir, Alfred Leo Duggan, Naomi Mitchison, Richard Hughes, and W. H. Auden), four for *The Two Towers* (Muir, Duggan, Maurice Richardson, and Donald Barr), and six for *The Return of the King* (Lewis, Duggan, Muir, Auden, Edmund Wilson, and Mark Roberts).[7] In a larger class, one might put together a panel of reviewers of another text in the course, such as T. S. Eliot's *The Waste Land* or Woolf's *To the Lighthouse*.[8] Another option is to create a panel of reviewers of *The Hobbit* or a panel of Tolkien's later reviewers in order to judge the changing reception history of his works. A panel of reviewers or fans from the 1960s would be a particularly interesting option for a larger class, as would a panel of reviewers who returned to Tolkien's text after the release of Jackson's films.[9]

Through the reviewer impersonation project, students uncover biographical information about reviewers such as Mitchison, Wilson, and Auden by using the online databases *Dictionary of Literary Biography*, *Oxford Dictionary of National Biography*, and *Contemporary Authors*.[10] Having students act out the critical arguments over Tolkien helps them distinguish among different schools of thought in the 1950s and alerts them to reviewers' professional and familial connections. Students learn, for instance, that Naomi Mitchison, a fiction writer who joined Lewis in giving Tolkien a laudatory review of *The Fellowship of the Ring*, was J. B. S. Haldane's sister, the same Haldane who so violently disagreed with the views on science, politics, and ethics that he saw in Lewis's space trilogy (see Haldane; Lewis, "Reply"). Students also discover that Edmund Wilson, who wrote the (in)famous 1956 review "Oo, Those Awful Orcs!,"[11] reviewed Eliot's *The Waste Land* very positively, writing in 1922, "Mr. Eliot's trivialities are more valuable than other people's epics" ("Poetry" 86).[12]

In the panel discussion, reviewers introduce themselves and explain their commitments and qualifications as literary critics. They then present their opinions on the book, debate the strengths and weaknesses of Tolkien's fiction, and answer questions from the class. Unless the student is portraying Lewis, who had read the entire *Lord of the Rings* when *The Fellowship of the Ring* was published, students may comment only on the parts of *The Lord of the Rings* that were published before the critic they are portraying wrote the review.

After we read *The Fellowship of the Ring* and hold the first reviewer panel discussion, we spend the next portion of the course reading the first half of *The Two Towers* alongside medieval texts that have affinities with Tolkien's writings. We read *Beowulf* (and Tolkien's "Beowulf: The Monsters and the Critics"), *The Battle of Maldon* (and Tolkien's "Ofermod"), "The Wife's Lament," and *The Wanderer* (and Auden's "The Wanderer").

Of all Tolkien's works, *The Two Towers* raises the question of the medieval versus the modern most strikingly. The first half introduces a culture highly influenced by the Anglo-Saxons, while the second half portrays Gollum's divided and interior-looking self, Sauron's bureaucratic Orcs, and the war-destroyed wasteland of the Dead Marshes. But as we read about Tolkien's Rohirrim, I point out that even they portray themselves as belonging to a modern age; they are pragmatic and skeptical. To both Éothain and Théoden, halflings "are only a little people in old songs and children's tales out of the North," and the industrializing Saruman seems at first a wiser ally than Gandalf (434; bk. 3, ch. 2).

Students contrast the medieval and modern elements of *The Two Towers* as they read. They become especially interested in how, by giving the Orcs a voice (however limited), Tolkien has created a different sort of monster than those depicted in *Beowulf*. I ask them to test Shippey's theory that Tolkien's treatment of evil is singularly modern.[13] In order to discuss the differences between medieval and twentieth-century monsters, I write, "Things I have learned about Orcs" on a transparency and list several (simplified) characteristics of Orcs from *The Two Towers*:

1. Orcs follow orders, even at the risk of life and limb. There appears to be some willingness to devote themselves to a higher cause (445–47; bk. 3, ch. 3).
2. Orcs may be loyal to their comrades. In addition to his desire "to see that Orders are carried out and the prisoners safe," Grishnâk claims he returned to the beleaguered Uruk-hai camp in order to help "some stout fellows . . . that are too good to lose" (451; bk. 3, ch. 3).
3. Orcs go into the decorative arts. Gimli looks in disgust at the Orc-weapon Pippin used to cut his own and Merry's bonds: "[T]he carved handle . . . had been shaped like a hideous head with squinting eyes and leering mouth" (489; bk. 3, ch. 5).
4. Orcs can get along with men. Wormtongue has the ability to fall in with Orcs and not get killed (529; bk. 3, ch. 7).
5. Orcs like to sing. Merry notes that they "were all singing with harsh voices, and laughing, making a hideous din" (566; bk. 3, ch. 9; see also Shippey, "Orcs" 185–86).

I ask students, "Is this account of Orcs' positive qualities a misreading?" I ask how Orcs are similar to or different from the monsters in *Beowulf*. Do Grendel and his mother evoke any sympathetic response from the reader?

Claiming that sympathetic readings of *Beowulf*'s monsters are done against the text, I further ask students whether giving Tolkien's monsters sympathy is reading against the text.[14] We continue the discussion by asking how Gollum, in the second half of *The Two Towers*, fits our understanding of a monster. He certainly is no Grendel. Gollum allows the class to consider the difference between a monster and an exile.[15] Grendel, the descendant of the kin-killing exile Cain, is a monster. Unferth, another kin killer, is welcome in Hrothgar's hall perhaps because the societal requirement of the wergild has been met. It is worthwhile to read passages from *The Two Towers*, *Beowulf*, and *The Wanderer* side by side in order to see how Sméagol, yet another kin-killing exile, abandons his wandering and takes Frodo as his liege lord, betraying Frodo only after Sméagol himself feels betrayed in Ithilien.[16] But the truly modern, even modernist, aspect of Tolkien's treatment of Sméagol consists in Sam's decision to turn the way the story is told upside down, examining it from Gollum's point of view: "I wonder if [Gollum] thinks he's the hero or the villain? Gollum!" he called. "Would you like to be the hero . . . ?" (713; bk. 4, ch. 13). No one ever asks Grendel if he would like to be the hero.

Before we read *The Return of the King*, we take a break from *The Lord of the Rings* to examine the theoretical and thematic affinities that Tolkien's works have with works by writers such as Woolf, Eliot, and Auden.[17] Eliot's "Tradition and the Individual Talent" is strikingly applicable to Tolkien.[18] Instead of valuing originality above all else, Eliot claims that "not only the best, but the most individual parts of [the poet's] work may be those in which the dead poets, his ancestors, assert their immortality most vigorously" (48). He insists that the best poet is one who is cognizant

> not only of the pastness of the past, but of its presence; the historical sense compels a man to write not merely with his own generation in his bones, but with a feeling that the whole of the literature of Europe from Homer and within it the whole of the literature of his own country has a simultaneous existence and composes a simultaneous order. (49)

Eliot's essay becomes important to the course not only because Tolkien's writing fits his qualifications but also because so many affinities exist between Eliot's views on the modernist poet and Tolkien's views on the *Beowulf* poet. In "Beowulf: The Monsters and the Critics," Tolkien describes the *Beowulf* poet as someone who "draws on tradition at will for his own purposes, as a poet of later times might draw upon history or the classics and expect his allusions to be understood" (21). In the poem, old legends and history have been remade into a coherent whole that allows poet and listener to see the world anew. Tolkien compares the *Beowulf* poet's use of older materials to a man who builds a tower from the stones of an ancient ruin because he wished to see the sea (8).

The artistic vision that Tolkien identifies in the *Beowulf* poet is more explicitly the theme of *To the Lighthouse* and "Leaf by Niggle," which we read next. Woolf's Lily Briscoe experiences a frustrated artistry similar to Tolkien's Niggle, and their paintings have similar fates.[19] Niggle's leaf is consigned to the corner of a museum that eventually burns down; Lily knows her work will be "hung in the servants' bedrooms . . . rolled up and stuffed under a sofa," "hung in attics," and "destroyed" (158, 208). Again, Tolkien's interpretation of the *Beowulf* poet, in whom Tolkien recognizes the same concerns, allows students to debate whether Lily's and Niggle's anxieties about the insignificance and impermanence of their work is really modernist or, alternatively, whether Tolkien's position as a twentieth-century critic made him project his views onto the *Beowulf* poet. Tolkien sees the *Beowulf* poet as an artist cognizant of his own and of his heroes' future insignificance. As Tolkien sees *Beowulf*, "Its author is . . . rehandling in a new perspective an ancient theme: that man, each man and all men, and all their works shall die. . . . As the poet looks back into the past . . . he sees that all glory (or as we might say 'culture' or 'civilization') ends in night" ("Beowulf" 23).[20]

To the Lighthouse, by addressing the death of all work from the perspective of the twentieth-century artist, ties together two of my course themes: changing views of the role of the artist and changing understandings of war.[21] Woolf's Mr. Ramsay, worried about the durability of his work as well as that of authors such as Sir Walter Scott and Shakespeare, glories in the misguided heroism of Alfred Lord Tennyson's "Charge of the Light Brigade," striding up and down the lawn "gesticulating" and shouting out Tennyson's line "Some one had blundered" (18). Mr. Ramsay's love of "The Charge of the Light Brigade," combined with Andrew Ramsay's briefly reported World War I death in the "Time Passes" section of *To the Lighthouse*, makes the novel pair extremely well with our discussions of the changing views of war evident in Tolkien's writing. For this connection, we read Tolkien's juvenilia, selected letters, and "The Homecoming of Beorhtnoth Beorhthelm's Son" and "Ofermod"—the last two works respond to the Old English poem *The Battle of Maldon*. In "Ofermod," Tolkien connects Tennyson's poem to a heroic ideal that he sees spanning portrayals of warriors from Beowulf's retainer, Wiglaf, to soldiers in the Crimean War: "Their part was to endure and die, and not to question, though a recording poet may fairly comment that someone had blundered" ("Homecoming" 25).

Some forty years after "The Charge of the Light Brigade," and in Tolkien's lifetime, another poet, Sir Henry Newbolt, wrote "Vitaï Lampada," which compares "the last heroic wicket stand in a cricket match with a soldier's last stand in some corner of a foreign field" (Macintyre). Ben Macintyre notes, "A generation of cricket-mad Englishmen marched off to the First World War reciting this exhortation to self-sacrifice." In my course, we compare "Vitaï Lampada" with Tolkien's 1911 poem about rugby, "The Battle of the Eastern Field" (written for the King Edward's School *Chronicle*).[22] We examine how these poems differ from opinions expressed in Tolkien's letters to his King Edward's friends in the Tea Club and Barrovian Society (TCBS), in "Ofermod" and "The Homecoming of Beorhtnoth Beorhthelm's Son," in *The Two Towers*, and in his World War II letters to his son Christopher. We contrast Tolkien's perspective on war with the perspectives in Woolf's *To the Lighthouse*, Eliot's *The Waste Land*, and Wilfred Owen's "Dulce et Decorum Est."

After sojourning in literary modernism, we finish *The Return of the King* and move on to our final reviewer panel. With its emphasis on the disagreement between Edmund Wilson, a reviewer who loved *The Waste Land*, and Auden, a modernist poet and reviewer who loved Tolkien, this last panel is an important capstone for our course. Auden, who hailed *The Lord of the Rings* in a November 1955 radio talk by saying, "If someone dislikes it, I shall never trust their literary judgement about anything again" (qtd. in Tolkien, *Letters of J. R. R. Tolkien* 229), stepped back from this extreme position two months later in his review of *The Return of the King*:

> I rarely remember a book about which I have had such violent arguments. Nobody *seems* to have a moderate opinion: either, like myself, people find it a masterpiece of its genre or they cannot abide it, and among the hostile there are some, I must confess, for whose literary judgment I have great respect. ("At the End")[23]

It becomes clear to students that critical opinions on modernist prose and poetry played a role in this bifurcated reception of Tolkien's work. Many of Tolkien's negative reviewers had no problem lambasting positive reviews by

Lewis, Mitchison, and Hughes, who all compared *The Fellowship of the Ring* with works by classical, medieval, and early modern writers, but they seemed to feel a stronger need to account for Auden's praise (see Richardson 836; Edmund Wilson, "Oo"). Wilson spent a portion of his review "Oo, Those Awful Orcs!" explaining why Auden, though a "master of English verse and a well-equipped critic of verse" (312–13), had, in Wilson's mind, so terribly misjudged the quality of Tolkien's work. Wilson eventually decides that what "has misled Mr. Auden is his own special preoccupation with the legendary theme of the Quest," though Wilson finds Frodo's quest "an extremely unrewarding one" (313). His reviews of Eliot and Tolkien, read alongside Auden's writing, serve as a springboard for discussion about the role of the quest and the epic in *The Lord of the Rings*, *The Waste Land*, and Auden poems such as "The Shield of Achilles" and "Musée des Beaux Arts." If *The Waste Land* offers a reward, what is it? What makes a rewarding quest in the twentieth century? Why do critics differ so much in their views on this question?

By the end of the course, students have formed a nuanced, multidimensional view of the literary culture of the first half of the twentieth century. Because I interweave the medieval texts, Tolkien's work, the modernist texts, and the reviewer impersonation projects throughout the course, students have many opportunities to refine their understanding of literary history and of Tolkien's reception history. They better comprehend the context in which *The Lord of the Rings* and modernist fiction and poetry were written, and they learn to assess astutely the distinctions and commonalities in style and substance between Tolkien's work and that of modernist writers. Students also learn how deeply mid-twentieth-century critics cared about how other readers judged Tolkien's literary merit. What the public thought about *The Lord of the Rings* mattered. Indeed, I tell students that the strong arguments over Tolkien's work remind me of the fights marking the onset of modernism: the 1913 Igor Stravinsky *Rite of Spring* riots and the fights and police presence following René Fauchois's 1910 lecture on Racine. "That is what I call a real vital interest in literature," T. E. Hulme wrote (60). In Tolkien: Medieval or Modern? the energy from the arguments over modernism and over *The Lord of the Rings* rubs off on students, and they begin to take a vital interest of their own in twentieth-century literary criticism.

NOTES

[1]The students in my course Modern Fiction were nonmajors, while Tolkien: Medieval or Modern? attracted students almost equally from the English department and other departments. In both cases, few came into the course with a knowledge of modernism. In Modern Fiction, I assigned a group project in which students researched an outside text in order to inform the class about its relation to a work we read in class. *Beowulf* was the assigned outside text for *The Two Towers*, and students in that group became fascinated by the poem. One of them said, "We should have read *Beowulf* in class." When I

responded, "It's not exactly modern fiction," her bright response was, "Oh, but it feels modern!"

[2]Clearly, Tolkien's style is different from that of the modernists, and some critics bridle at the idea of making comparisons between them. Anna Vaninskaya claims that one problem in associating Tolkien with twentieth-century writing is "the perceived Modernist associations of any such contention." Although Vaninskaya finds Tolkien representative of many aspects of the twentieth century, she hopes to "bring to an end the heroic but futile attempts to assimilate Tolkien to the Modernist mould in an effort to salvage his academic reputation: that venerable last-ditch manoeuvre of all beleaguered champions of pariah authors and movements" (4). Michael Drout, in contrast, finds the fact that Tolkien's work easily fits the abstract theories of the modernist critics who hated it to be evidence that those theories were not as strong as their authors believed: "Tolkien's work is like kryptonite for weak literary theories. A really simple test of any supposedly brilliant literary theory is to put Tolkien's work into it. If the theory breaks, then the theory wasn't that good" ("*Beowulf*" 19–20). For more information on Tolkien's relation to modernism and other twentieth-century literature, see Mortimer; Nicolay; Shippey, *J. R. R. Tolkien*, particularly 312–18; and Flieger, *Question*, especially 2–3, 6–27, 218–25.

[3]Although this essay is concerned mainly with methods of teaching modern fiction in a course devoted to Tolkien, teaching Tolkien in a course not devoted to him (as I initially did) changes the dynamics of the course. When I first taught Tolkien in the same course as *To the Lighthouse*, I expected my Modern Fiction students to thank me for a quick-moving plot and a reprieve from stream of consciousness. Surprisingly, because they had fallen in love with Woolf, when we got to Tolkien, they were extremely resistant to studying fantasy. They responded to Tolkien in much the same way Humphrey Carpenter says that many Oxford dons (including Tolkien and Lewis) responded to teaching post-1830 literature. As Carpenter wrote in *The Inklings*, "The English Faculty had always been embarrassed by those in the University—and there were many—who alleged that undergraduates could read English literature in their baths, and did not need dons to teach it to them any more than they needed nursemaids to wipe their noses" (26; see also Lewis, "Our English Syllabus" 30). "I just don't understand why we are reading this in class," said one of my students. But resistant students' responses often generate the best class discussions. Such resistance encourages all students to examine why we value literature, how our critical judgments are informed, and how these judgments compare with those of opposing camps.

[4]At this time, I allow students to define *modern* as they will. Although my students are aware of many of the problems people faced in the first half of the twentieth century (the ever-increasing importance of the machine, alienation, world wars, totalitarianism, etc.), only a few are aware of the deliberate breaks modernist writers made with literary and artistic traditions. We differentiate between *modern* and *modernist* later in this class period and throughout the course.

[5]Vaninskaya agrees that such response to Tolkien is typical: "Nobody needs convincing of the presence of Anglo-Saxon and Old Norse elements in *The Lord of the Rings*, but an assertion of a similar kind with regard to the twentieth century still meets with suspicion" (3).

[6]Lewis continues, "Many reviews are useless because, while purporting to condemn the book, they only reveal the reviewer's dislike of the kind to which it belongs. Let bad tragedies be censured by those who love tragedy, and bad detective stories by those who

love the detective story. Then we shall learn their real faults. Otherwise we shall find epics blamed for not being novels, farces for not being high comedies" ("On Science Fiction" 81).

[7]The reviews in my students' reading packet are included in the works-cited list for this volume.

[8]For a sampling of reviews of *The Waste Land*, see Brooker. For Eliot's *The Waste Land*, just as for *The Lord of the Rings*, positive reviewers praised the work effusively, while negative critics refused to take it seriously. For reviews of Woolf's *To the Lighthouse*, see McNees.

[9]In courses where we study a work by Tolkien among works by other authors, I have also had success dividing the class into small groups, giving each group a review, asking group members to read it, and then asking them to debate the quality of Tolkien's fiction with one another by espousing the ideas in the review they have read.

[10]If your library resources are limited, allowing students to find information about their reviewers from *Wikipedia* may be necessary. However, the library databases listed here provide information that *Wikipedia* lacks. While Donald Barr, Alfred Leo Duggan, and Mark Roberts (the most difficult reviewers to research) have no entries in *The Dictionary of Literary Biography* or the *Oxford Dictionary of National Biography*, Barr and Duggan appear in *Contemporary Authors*, and their obituaries appear in the *New York Times* (for Barr's, see Saxon) and the London *Times* ("Mr. Alfred Duggan"). Duggan, whose work has generated some literary criticism, comes up in an *MLA International Bibliography* search. Roberts's obituary is published in the *Independent* on 22 August 2006 (see Singh). (Roberts's 1956 review "Adventure in English" addresses Tolkien's "On Fairy-stories" alongside *The Lord of the Rings*, calling the ideas in Tolkien's essay "perverted Coleridge" [451].)

[11]For additional discussion of this review, see the essay by McNelis in this volume.

[12]Indeed, Wilson's friend Burton Rascoe describes his lunch with Wilson and Gilbert Seldes as a meeting of cohorts who "made merry over the fact that here were gathered together three critics looked upon as archconspirators in the effort to palm off on the public an unintelligible poem by an obscure scribbler as the great poetic work of the year" (91).

[13]See Shippey, *Road* 136–40, 150 and "Orcs." In *The Road*, Shippey notes the modernity of the Ring, which he claims illustrates Lord Acton's statement, "Power tends to corrupt, and absolute power corrupts absolutely" (136). Shippey also points out, "The Ring is 'addictive'" (139). The word and psychology of addiction, he claims, gave rise during Tolkien's lifetime to "entirely new ideas about the nature and limitations of human will" (139).

[14]See Tolkien, "Beowulf." Tolkien discusses the monsters' separateness from the human beings in the poem: "Most important is it to consider how and why the monsters became 'adversaries of God', and so begin to symbolize (and ultimately to become identified with) the powers of evil, even while they remain . . . mortal denizens of the material world" (20). Later in the essay, Tolkien notes that the human beings in the poem know God is on their side and not on the side of the monsters: "Man alien in a hostile world, engaged in a struggle which he cannot win while the world lasts, is assured that his foes are the foes also of Dryhten, that his courage noble in itself is also the highest loyalty" (26). Note how, without this assurance, the human beings, so described, would be like any twentieth-century existentialist.

[15]My understanding of Gollum here is informed by Kisor.

[16]See Gollum's moment of near repentance in *Lord* 714 (bk. 4, ch. 8); see the wanderer's description of his exile in lines 40–51.

[17]The Auden poems on my syllabus are "The Wanderer," "The Musée des Beaux Arts," "The Unknown Citizen," and "The Shield of Achilles," from *Collected Shorter Poems, 1927–1957*, and "Lullaby," "The Truest Poetry Is the Most Feigning," and "On the Circuit," a poem in which Tolkien's name appears, from *As I Walked Out One Evening*.

[18]Although I know of no direct link between Eliot and Tolkien, many indirect ones exist. Wilson reviewed *The Waste Land* and *The Lord of the Rings*, and Lewis wrote about and to Eliot even before Charles Williams introduced them. In 1943, Lewis wrote to Eliot the following: "I hope the fact that I find myself often contradicting you in print gives no offence: it is a kind of tribute to you—whenever I fall foul of some wide-spread contemporary view about literature I always seem to find that you have expressed it most clearly. One aims at the officers first in meeting an attack!" (*Books* 557). For Tolkien's brief remarks on Eliot, see *Letters of J. R. R. Tolkien* 350, 353.

[19]Lily Briscoe is not Woolf's only character to go through an artistic struggle similar to Niggle's. Woolf's Orlando, in her novel of the same name, works most of his-her extraordinarily long life creating and improving an imagined tree: "a roll of paper, sea-stained, blood-stained, travel-stained—the manuscript of her poem, 'The Oak Tree'. . . . She had been working on it for close on three hundred years now. It was time to make an end" (*Orlando* 226).

[20]The history of the medieval texts themselves reflects their impermanence. Niggle's fictional leaf was lost in a museum fire; a similar fire destroyed *The Battle of Maldon* manuscript and almost destroyed *Beowulf*. Twentieth-century writers often note the precariousness of art. World War I, in which Tolkien lost two friends he once considered destined for greatness, and World War II, with its destruction of so many cultural artifacts, reinforce the modernity of this problem.

[21]As is well known, World War I changed modernism's character. Michael Levenson writes, "The war . . . remained a goad to experiment. Disenchantment, revulsion, and trauma were shocks to the world-picture of modernity—individual and social—but were also incitements to create new forms" (227).

[22]The entire poem was reprinted in *Mallorn*. See Tolkien, "Battle."

[23]Auden's evolving conception of reader responses to Tolkien can be seen in his notes on the record lining of Tolkien's 1967 *Poems and Songs of Middle Earth*. After praising Tolkien's verse extensively, Auden cautions, "I presume that most people who buy this record will already have read Professor Tolkien's tetralogy, and I hope it will persuade anybody who has not, to do so at once. A prospective reader, however, should, I think, be warned: 'This is a work that will either totally enthrall you or leave you stone cold, and, whichever your response, nothing and nobody will ever change it.' As a member of the enchanted party, I have found by experience that it is quite useless to argue with the unenchanted" ("Liner Notes").

The Tower, the Sausage Maker, and the Soup: Teaching Tolkien in a Postmodern Classroom

Thomas L. Martin

How do we address the needs of all the students enrolled in a class on the literature of J. R. R. Tolkien? These students will have varying levels of interest in Tolkien and range from the unexposed to his literature to the overexposed to the movies and pop culture spin-offs, from the critically wary who have misgivings about an author with old-world values to the traditionalists who mistrust literature that deviates from the canons of realism. How do we create for them all an educational experience that brings the literature to life as well as shines on it the light of critical reflection? How do we teach them the literature while at the same time giving them a greater awareness of the aesthetic, critical, and philosophical issues involved? Tolkien, if approached with some sense of these challenges presented by the students and by the material, can be an enriching experience for both undergraduates and graduates.

I break my course into seven units or assignment blocks and lay out the responsibilities of both teacher and students over the duration of the term. While we work through these assignments, we progress through the literature. Students are responsible for manageable chunks of reading for each class, until they have completed the novels and short stories by semester's end. I prepare for them a surprise that comes in the last week, to end the course on the right note.

Each unit of my course is accompanied by several vivid metaphors Tolkien uses over the span of his career to crystallize what he thinks a literary scholar does and what a writer of fantasy does. In other words, he theorizes about the nature of his writing, in both its modes. As I feature his critical and aesthetic principles in class discussions, they add a layer of metacommentary to the course. I refer not to the commentary in Tolkien's *Letters* or *The History of Middle-earth*, which reflects on his secondary world and gives further detail on issues that naturally arise, including questions such as "What is a balrog?" and "Who is Goldberry?" Instead, I offer students insight into those signal places in his writing where Tolkien theorizes about the nature of literary meaning itself and how readers access or encounter it. My students begin to see that he is not only a scholar and writer, someone whose works ought to be subject to the latest critical interrogations, but also a theorist of culture whose critical thinking ought to be placed beside that of other theorists, even those whose critical concerns shape and direct much of what we study in a postmodern literature classroom. As Tolkien comments on the nature of literary meaning, on readerly reception, on critical institutions, even on the shape of history and human society, he does so with considerable awareness of the issues in his own day and with foresight on issues to come. I impress on my students that this author, who works out the details of his literary world arguably more than any author has before or since, does not overlook the theoretical and aesthetic principles that undergird his entire project.

I call the first assignment block in my course "Scholarly Immersion." In it, I try to immerse students in the life and times of Tolkien but avoid tying that material too closely to any particular theory of literary context. Simply put, I want students to ask who he was and how his life and times help us understand his literature. Good scholarly form requires that we leave behind, or at least bracket for the time being, our own context and interests in order to see how the world operated in the author's time.

As much as I can, I try to get the students to see, hear, smell, touch, and taste Tolkien's life. Most students will not have time to read Humphrey Carpenter's *J. R. R. Tolkien: A Biography* in addition to the other reading assignments, so I typically devote the first meeting to distilling for them his biography into a single multimedia lecture. Photographs, from books and the Web, show young Ronald, his earliest days in South Africa, a young man in school in England, Edith and their children, his fellow Tea Club and Inklings members, the author in the army, the professor at Oxford. One picture I find essential to include is of a postcard of Josef Madlener's *Der Berggeist*, which Tolkien picked up in Switzerland as a young man and on which he later wrote "Origin of Gandalf."

These images—presented along with key stories and scenes from his life and perhaps even accompanied by Tolkien's own voice, as the author reads or is interviewed—can help bring him to life for students. Many scenes from the biography ignite their imaginations and draw them into the world in which he lived: scenes from South Africa, including his last memory of his father, who was painting their name on a trunk that would travel with wife and children on their one-way passage to England; from Tolkien's education both in school and at home; of Tolkien as a boy inventing private languages; of his romance with Edith and the life they built together; of his experience with war; of his settled life on campus; and of his teaching and writing habits. The curious student will want to know more about his thoughts on modern society and technology, on the Roman Catholic Church and the Church of England, about politics and his reservations about democracy, about his thoughts on education and the role of language in it. As students come to understand more of his life and times, his thoughts and attitudes, they will begin seeing him as both a product of the world he grew up in and a modern English writer who altered that world.

The next assignment block is "Word Studies." Tolkien is a wonderful mentor to students on the importance of words. This assignment gives them an appreciation of the level of his linguistic detail even as they face the prospect of some two thousand pages of primary reading material. A self-professed "niggler" who could fuss endlessly over the creation of a single leaf, he produces dense forests of words, and one can easily miss the individual words by attending to the shape of the forest, the story. This assignment gets students to focus on a single word and how it can reveal many aspects of the entire work, how one detail in the hands of an artist can carry the weight of history and great significance. This lesson stays with students long after the Tolkien course is over. They learn how words unlock story meanings that they would miss if they read only for the sake of action and adventure.

In this unit, I ask students to select a word they want to explore. In Tolkien's work, proper nouns always yield a wealth of insight. Tolkien creates them as part of his world building. Here, the first of our critical metaphors appears: Tolkien speaks of the material from which he created his stories as a great "compost-heap" (Carpenter, *J. R. R. Tolkien* 131). He explains that he never directly adapted material from other writers, that he stitched together a tree using the leaves of other trees as those leaves fell and amassed in great quantity. Moldering for a long while, they became the fertile soil from which new seeds of imagination could sprout. This notion of a literary and linguistic compost heap—the more broken down it is, the more fertile—provides a model for understanding the influences of tradition on Tolkien. The metaphor offers two principles for scholars and critics: one, that we can trace the subtle changes of material as it morphs from one constitutional form to another; two, that we should never simply equate any one form with another.

To begin rooting around in Tolkien's vast compost heap, students may consult the *Oxford English Dictionary* for their chosen word or its close relatives. That step, however, is only the first for this assignment. To get to the core meaning or meanings of a word, students find they must consult other dictionaries, must continue with an Old English dictionary and dictionaries of other languages. In these they discover, for example, that the word *ent* means "giant," *Théoden* means "lord," *Boromir* might mean "fort" and "bury," and *Beorn* suggests both "bear" and "warrior." As they consider the etymological material available to them from real world languages, they also are encouraged to integrate what they find in the secondary world languages of Tolkien's stories. In *The Silmarillion* especially, etymological material is abundant. To take one example, the name *Ilúvatar* means "All Father" in the stories but outside them *Ilu* is the word for God in Assyrian, and in Latin the name might also suggest *vates* ("poet") and perhaps even the English *illume*, from Latin *illuminare* ("to give light").

Students can widen their search from these various linguistic sources to check names for close relatives in ancient mythological writings. Many wonderful discoveries await them, especially in the Norse, Finnish, and Celtic mythologies. To their delight and surprise, they will discover many of the names so familiar to them from Tolkien's works in the characters and places of these myths: Gandalf, Thorin, Gríma, and even Middle-earth itself.

Students bring this linguistic and literary material back into Tolkien's legendarium to see how it interacts with the semantic logic of his stories. Subtle analysis of the stories can pay rich dividends here. For example, as Peter Kreeft has noticed, the name *Denethor* is *Théoden* in reverse syllables. What does this reversal say about the relation between these two lords and their relative stories? What does the storyteller intend by this arrangement? Literary patterns become evident when students pursue such etymological, morphological, and semantic inquiries.

The next assignment, "Source, Influence, and Analog Studies," comes naturally on the heels of the previous one. It requires students to think about the influence of other stories on Tolkien's. I want students to ask, Are the similarities between Tolkien's stories and others the result of conscious influence or merely family resemblances attributable to their belonging to the same genre? Is Tolkien an allusive author, or are the materials antecedent to him so well digested in his compost pile as to leave little suggestion of their identity? I want students not to direct their investigations from any strong theoretical commitment at this point but simply to see that Tolkien's stories are similar to others in the literary tradition yet stand uniquely on their own. For example, *Hobbit* literally means "hole dweller" in Tolkien's fictional etymology, but Tolkien said that the formation of the word was also from the name Babbitt (Carpenter, *J. R. R. Tolkien* 168). What bearing do Sinclair Lewis's character and story have on *The Hobbit*? Or what does Tolkien's story have to do with Edward Wyke-Smith's *The Marvellous Land of Snergs*, likely an "unconscious source" for the stories, as Tolkien admitted to his former student W. H. Auden (168)?

Some students, enthralled by the adventure in Tolkien's stories, will miss his allusiveness; some will see many connections between them and other works of literature. Generally, I find that once students are prompted to look, they are quite good at coming up with comparisons to study further. That the sources of, influences on, and analogues to Tolkien's works sprawl widely across Western literature has been indicated by many critics. As students grapple with issues of influence, genre, and allusion, they ask whether the similarities they discover are significant or superficial. Are they the result of unconscious influences as a natural development in a literary tradition or the result of conscious allusions to individual works? Students will need to consider issues related to genre studies to decide what is a convention and what an innovation. Such determinations are not always easy, or even possible, but they are important in the maturation of any good literary reader and critic.

Another Tolkien metaphor shows its usefulness: the tower in "Beowulf: The Monsters and the Critics." In this essay, Tolkien speaks of a tower that a man builds from the stones left in a field he inherited. Others come to inspect his work, find it intriguing for different reasons, then commence to knock it down to see how it was made. Some study the curious inscriptions on the stones, some seek the quarries from which the stones were hewn, some consider what ancient buildings were constructed of the stones before the tower was erected, and still others examine the deposit of coal now exposed in the ground beneath. "But," Tolkien continues, "from the top of that tower the man had been able to look out upon the sea" (8). He refers to the "visionary height" afforded by the tower, a metaphor that turns out to be a fascinating way to think about literary source, influence, and analog (33). Students, not to mention the critics Tolkien addresses in his essay, might, in their earnestness to seek out antecedents, lose sight of the work itself and the prospects it opens onto human life and history. As important as those earlier formations may be, they can never replace the work and its uniqueness both as a thing made and as a way of seeing.

In our next assignment block, "Textual Analysis," I ask students to focus on what distinguishes a course on literature from a course in other academic disciplines, even though it may borrow insights from them. The who, what, where, when, why, and how questions we ask of any literary work prove that character, action, setting, and motive are important, as these form what Tolkien calls the secondary world. Students who tend to read him primarily for the excitement can be led to consider the complexities of narrative, the development of character, and other literary aspects of the work. Further, they can be pushed beyond action to consider theme. Students more disposed to read Tolkien for language or technique can be encouraged to consider also symbolism, vision, and moral and philosophical issues involved. They can be pushed beyond technique to consider meaning. A student should confront all features of a literary text: what the story is, how it is told, the issues and meanings it engages, the narrative and figurative strategies it deploys, and the individual and social effects it is bound to.

As students study the fine grain of literary texture, a third metaphor from Tolkien proves useful. In "On Fairy-stories," he speaks of stories as "soup": while it might be interesting to look at the ingredients that went into making the soup, the work of understanding would be incomplete (46). In this metaphor he again expresses his distrust of generic criticism and emphasizes the importance of literary analysis. Identifying original source material, where it is available, is one of the easier tasks that critics set themselves. What he finds "more interesting" and "difficult" is, for fairy stories in particular, "to consider what they are, what they have become for us, and what values the long alchemic processes of time have produced in them" (46). He calls this work of literary analysis "criticism of the soup as soup," and it is interesting that he includes in it both audience and the history of reception (47). He insists that when we turn our focus from the unchanged ingredients of the work to how the author creates from them something new and unique, we open ourselves to a greater understanding of the work.

For example, I might ask my students, Why are there so many stone statues dotting the landscape in *The Lord of the Rings*? The question, note, is not, What works before Tolkien's epic romance featured similar carved images? It presses students to consider what the author is doing with these images and "what they have become for us" (46). We see the stone Argonath on either side of the Great River, the Púkel-men statues overlooking the Dunharrow Road, the headless statue of the enthroned king on the way to the Cross-roads, and the carved statues in the Hall of the Kings in Minas Tirith. Students should consider how Tolkien the narrative artist makes this material part of the fabric of his stories. Their realization that the statues convey the weight and depth of the past as well as veneration for ancestors will lead them further into the story's meaning.

For example, are the characters the "lesser sons of greater fathers," or will they prove to be something more? The stone monuments effectively pick up a theme common to all the metaphors: using markers not unlike these stones, critics who seek to keep track of past, present, and future forms should preserve all the stories without conflating them and losing what is now to what comes before or after, across a history of changes and a tradition of great variety.

Our last assignment block, "Theory Panels," is one of the most interesting parts of the course. After the word, analog, and textual studies are well under way, I ask students to pair the literature with a dominant critical school or principal theorist in line with their own critical interests and convictions. I ask them not to arrange the theory with the literature in a hierarchical fashion, as if the theory were there merely to explain the literature, but to present both more in the manner of a side-by-side dialogue, so that each can help students think about the other more clearly and carefully. I explain that a common mistake students commit as they engage in theoretical work is to look to theory as a philosophical or other kind of agenda that the literature passively serves. To do so is to miss both the theoretical dimension of the literary text and the literariness of the theoretical text. When students surrender their readings like this—or, worse, seek in literature mere illustrations for a single theoretical term or principle—they have done little in the way of reading, thinking, or theorizing.

Tolkien is particularly helpful in this regard: the more developed a literary secondary world like his is, the more developed the social and psychological details will be as part of the created ontology. Details of critical interest cohere with other details that compose the secondary world, functioning not merely as a representation of the world the reader or theorist happens to inhabit. For example, a political theory that holds monarchy as essentially oppressive might miss the hard-won consensus and essential goodness in Aragorn's reign, or a psychological theory that locates the source of dreams in psychosexual energies might miss the surprisingly fully developed theory of dreaming at work in the dreams and nightmares of Frodo and the other hobbits. I want students to consider whether Tolkienian readings of the theorists are as possible as the theoretical readings of his literature. Certainly, "applicability," as Tolkien thought about it (*Lord* xxiv; foreword), brings together many issues within its purview, even as he manifestly addresses many issues of the modern world—language, technology, and so on. I give students a wide range of freedom in this assignment, opening it to serious and even satirical treatments, as long as they keep something like the parity of give and take intact and approximate something like a genuine intellectual conversation.

When we place the theory next to the literature, we do not assimilate one into the other but instead allow each to help us think more clearly and deeply about the other. This juxtaposition brings us to the last of Tolkien's metaphors that we use in the classroom. In "A Valedictory Address to the University of Oxford," Tolkien speaks disparagingly of the school's "B. Litt. sausage-machine" (226). The image of the sausage machine is suggestive for many reasons, but particularly for the homogenization of thinking it embodies, along with the butcher's approach it requires to render a thoroughly uniform product of knowledge. That product is in fact typical as reigning academic orthodoxies sweep across a university and various pressures are exerted in the profession and in the classroom. Tolkien's antidote for the institutionalized procrusteanism at work in this ever-grinding sausage machine is the "genuine curiosity" of the individual scholar (227). Tolkien is always urging scholars and students to credit as equal both simplicity and complexity, discovery and innovation, reception and evaluation. If we take this metaphor seriously, we might find a place in our classrooms for both cultural literacy and cultural critique, for the aesthetics of reading and the criticism of cultural forms.

In addition to these assignments, I give quizzes and assign a research paper. Because students often think they already know the story, I find that regular reading quizzes are in order, perhaps even in every class period. In their research papers, I require students to bring together insights from all their work throughout the entire semester. I impress on them that the final research paper should be nuanced, that they should examine the complex relations that the other assignments began to explore and go significantly beyond the in-class discussions and their own earlier work in the course.

The surprise I keep until the end of the course may not surprise readers of this volume, that the distinct steps students have followed in their major assignments throughout the semester are the ones scholars follow as they produce articles and books for publication. For the graduate students, I often require an additional annotated bibliography and a paper abstract, for possible presentation at an upcoming fantasy conference. As they submit their final papers, I urge those who are confident they have produced research of high quality to revise it according to my feedback and to submit their abstracts to a conference. Many of my graduate students who carefully and thoughtfully follow these steps find they have a paper worthy of an academic conference and are delighted when their proposals are accepted and their work is taken seriously by others in the field. Some students go on to develop their papers further and eventually publish research articles.

Few would disagree today that reading *The Lord of the Rings* is one of the great literary and imaginative experiences a reader can have. The large groundswell of popular interest in the stories has also created a cultural phenomenon that deserves critical study. The mounting professional interest in Tolkien gives teachers and students a growing body of scholarly material to explore. A course like this offers a rich array of ideas and challenges, if not comparable in reward to that met by the characters in the stories, then as a worthwhile educational journey in its own right.

Teaching Tolkien and Race: An Inconvenient Combination?

Dimitra Fimi

One of the main attractions of the invented world of Middle-earth is that it is inhabited by a great variety of peoples, each with its own history, language, and culture. In J. R. R. Tolkien's cosmology, Elves, Dwarves, and Men, as well as the Orcs and Men allied to Melkor or Sauron, are further divided into subcategories determined by linguistic, cultural, and historical factors. Although these cultural groups highlight fascinating aspects of Tolkien's mythology, his constructed history, and his treatment of good and evil, their very existence poses challenges for teachers. While some scholars argue positively for Tolkien's use of multiculturalism (e.g., Straubhaar; Dawson), students are more likely to be familiar with accusations of racism that have become even more entangled and confused by the cinematic adaptation of *The Lord of the Rings* by Peter Jackson. John Yatt, writing for *The Guardian*, and Stephen Shapiro, who was interviewed for *The Scotsman* (Reynolds and Stewart), made headlines with their comments concerning racial bias in *The Lord of the Rings*, and their views are still discussed in Internet forums and online fan communities. On the other hand, an outspoken defense of Tolkien against charges of racial prejudice has been voiced by Patrick Curry ("Charges"). My students typically grapple with issues of race and culture in Tolkien's works by asking such questions as these:

> Why are there evaluative rankings for people in Middle-earth, like the Elves, who are "higher" beings than Men, and the Númenóreans, who are more "noble" than other Men?
>
> Why are the Men allied to the forces of good (Rohirrim, Gondorians, etc.) generally fair-skinned, while the evil Men (Southrons, Easterlings, Haradrim, etc.) are dark-skinned?
>
> Did the Germanic mythology that informs Tolkien's mythopoeia lead to the portrayal of the heroic characters as white, "Aryan" types?

While a variety of responses to such questions are open to teachers, my view is that race and culture are central to Tolkien's legendarium and should form part of any course that focuses on his work. In both my traditional (lecture-based) and online Tolkien classes, I always include an entire session on race, a session that typically inspires lively and rich discussion with my students.

Many teachers would agree that Tolkien's medievalism is one of the most fruitful approaches to his fiction. Northern European myth, legend, and folklore root his work in medieval literature, and many university courses on Tolkien devote at least some sessions to his medieval inspiration. The evident hierarchy among the different anthropomorphic beings of Middle-earth, with the Elves at the top and the Orcs at the bottom, can be examined in class within the context of an invented world that is medieval in inspiration and setting. To explore this idea further, I introduce my students to the great chain of being, which reflects the medieval worldview of cosmic hierarchy.

The great chain of being was a powerful visual metaphor, representing a divinely planned hierarchical order that ranked all forms of life according to their proportion of spirit and matter. The more spirit and less matter a form of life contained, the higher it was placed on the chain. As would be expected, God himself was at the top, followed by the angels, men, animals, and finally plants and stones. That Tolkien conceived Middle-earth in this style is apparent from one of his early linguistic manuscripts, edited posthumously and published in the journal *Parma Eldalamberon*. Although this journal is difficult to obtain, it is worth tracing in order to present students with Tolkien's explicit "hierarchical reordering of the seven categories of beings" in his early mythology (Tolkien, "Early Qenya Fragments" 7): the Valar and their folk appear at the top, followed by the Fays (later to become the Maiar), then the Elves and Fairies (at that stage of the mythology the terms were used interchangeably), and the Children of Men, "who thus occupy the middle place in the seven orders" (10). The three last categories are the "Earthlings," which include the Dwarves, who at that point were an evil people; the "Beasts & Creatures," which point to the animal world; and finally the "Monsters," which include the creatures of Morgoth, mainly Orcs and demons (10).

As with the medieval cosmic hierarchy, Tolkien's ranking criteria are based on moral and spiritual values. Beings allied to the forces of good are higher up in his chain, while Morgoth's creatures, intrinsically evil in this early version of the mythology, are at the bottom. Students can compare this early "chain of being" with his classification of the three subdivisions of the Elves in his 1954 letters to Naomi Mitchison, in which it is evident that the "Lesser Elves" (called the Avari in *The Silmarillion*) are inferior to the Eldar in a theological sense, since they choose not to heed the summons of the Valar and follow them to the paradise island of Valinor (*Letters of J. R. R. Tolkien* 176, 198). Teachers may also ask students to compare this early chain to Treebeard's poem, "Learn now the lore of Living Creatures," when Treebeard discovers Merry and Pippin in Fangorn Forest (*Lord* 464; bk. 3, ch. 4). By recounting the "old lists," the poem offers another evaluative classification of Middle-earth beings from higher to lower. A fruitful discussion can be started by asking students to determine the criteria for Tolkien's early chain and how those criteria change in Treebeard's classification (which, interestingly, mentions Ents quite high up in the hierarchy but does not include Hobbits at all).

The same approach of contextualizing Middle-earth as a pseudo-medieval world, conflating race with spiritual qualities, has also been used to consider the dark skin of Tolkien's "evil" Men. Margaret Sinex has argued that the construction of the racial "other" in Tolkien's world is based on medieval racial stereotypes and prejudices familiar to Tolkien from a great number of medieval texts.

Such texts view any bodily traits that deviate from the white European physique as signs of inner blemishes, and the European Christian writers of these texts often saw people who were "racially" different as not dissimilar to the mythical "monstrous races" depicted on medieval maps. Tom Shippey made a similar point in a question-and-answer session with Tolkien fans, originally published on the HarperCollins Web site (sadly, no longer available). Answering a question about Tolkien's allegedly racist portrayal of Sauron's minions, he said:

> The mention in "The Battle of the Pelennor Fields" of "black men like half-trolls" certainly sounds racist. I think I would say here that Tolkien at this point is trying to write like a medieval chronicler, and when medieval Europeans first encountered sub-Saharan Africans, they were genuinely confused about them, and rather frightened. As Tolkien pointed out in his early scholarly works, the ancient English seemed to have a belief in fire-demons, who naturally enough had skin like soot—their word for them, *harwan*, is related to Latin *carbo*, "soot," or carbon. An Anglo-Saxon meeting an African for the first time might then really wonder (for a moment, from a distance) whether this was a demon from his own mythology. This doesn't mean that Tolkien shared the mythology, or the mistake. ("Interview")[1]

This approach, which focuses on medieval constructions of the other, can be outlined in class or set as a question point in a seminar environment or an online discussion forum.[2] Students with a sound background in medieval literature have responded positively to such discussions, expanding them by tying in Tolkien's medievalism in terms of sources and setting.[3]

The medieval approach may offer excellent insights into the hierarchical cosmology of Middle-earth, but Tolkien was a man who lived mostly in the twentieth century and was not detached from what was happening around him. Since *race* was a term that changed in meaning during his lifetime, it is important that students approach his construction of race also in the context of the cultural and intellectual environment in which his works were produced.

In my classes, I usually start these discussions with an overview of Victorian and Edwardian "racial" anthropology, covering its main characteristics, ideology, "scientific" basis, two of its most important trends (social Darwinism and the eugenics movement), and final discrediting around the time of World War II (Fimi 132–35). Presenting material on these issues helps students realize that dividing people into races with fixed biological characteristics, and associating these physical traits with specific mental abilities, was considered not only natural but also scientifically proved in the nineteenth and the early twentieth centuries. Social Darwinism extrapolated from Darwin's theory of evolution and reduced its findings to the simplistic motto of "the survival of the fittest." At the same time, the eugenics project, which encouraged "more-evolved races" to procreate and discouraged procreation for "less evolved" ones, was taken up enthusiastically by a number of scientists who were adamant that they were only speeding up a "natural" process. Not until World War II were disagreements brought to the forefront of discussion and the scientific community declared race a myth, a subject useful only for biology and genetics and not for anthropology and ethnology.

Tolkien's views on race changed throughout his life, reflecting contemporary ideas and intellectual trends. Students can trace this gradual change through a selection of quotations from various writings by Tolkien. A way to start what can be a lively discussion is to use the shocking (to our modern sensibilities) extract from an article in his school magazine, the *King Edward's School Chronicle*. The article presents an account of the school's Annual Open Debate, in which Tolkien, aged nineteen, is reported to have supported the (tongue-in-cheek) motion "[t]hat the works attributed to William Shakespeare were written by Francis Bacon," by pouring

> a sudden flood of unqualified abuse upon Shakespeare, upon his filthy birthplace, his squalid surroundings, and his sordid character. He declared that to believe that so great a genius arose in such circumstances commits us to the belief that a fair-haired European infant could have a woolly-haired prognathous Papuan parent. (Tolkien, "Debating Society" 43)

Compare this extract, which reproduces nearly all the stereotypes of Victorian racial anthropology, with Tolkien's declarations against Nazi Germany and its Aryan ideology in his 1938 letters to Stanley Unwin (*Letters of J. R. R. Tolkien* 37) and Rütten and Loening Verlag (37–38), his 1941 letter to Michael Tolkien (54–56), and his 1967 letter to Charlotte and Denis Plimmer (372–78). The difference between young Tolkien's lighthearted comments, which fall within what contemporary science would have supported, and his much more heated exclamations a few years later, when he was asked to take a political stance on the emerging Nazi ideology, is striking and motivates a much more informed discussion on his complex construction of race.[4]

It is also important for students to understand that Tolkien's area of expertise, philology, preserved a Romantic and somewhat confusing conflation of language with race. For Victorian scientists and philologists, language was another exciting tool to research the history of the "human races." Early ethnologists like James Cowles Prichard and Robert Gordon Latham used linguistic evidence in their classification of peoples according to blood and descent. Even Darwin, influenced by the philologist Franz Bopp, claimed that an accurate genealogical classification of the races of man would allow the best categorization of the languages they spoke (Alter 30–32). Many philologists of Tolkien's time used the term *race* loosely to refer to groups of people with a shared language and cultural identity (what we would call today national or ethnic groups), but even in these cases, *race* often retained its evaluative sense and implied a hierarchical classification of different peoples, nations, or cultures.

This relation between a philological understanding of language and an evaluative way of looking at subdivisions of Men is evident in Tolkien's mythology and can be demonstrated to students by discussing an important extract from his 1960s essay "Of Dwarves and Men," published posthumously in *The Peoples of Middle-earth* (307–08). In this extract, which deals with the pedigree of the three Houses of Men, racial physical characteristics are associated with similarities or differences in the languages spoken by the Men of Hador, Bëor, and Haleth (Fimi 145–46).

Within the context of the history of contemporary ideas, discussing Tolkien's hierarchical invented world sheds light on the perceived contradiction between his vehement comments against the Nazis and the strict racial divisions in Middle-earth. Another strand that serves as a valuable addition to a lecture or seminar discussion on Tolkien and race is the way Peter Jackson's cinematic adaptation of *The Lord of the Rings* has added a layer of complexity (and often confusion) to readers' interpretations of race in Tolkien's work. Both Yatt's and Shapiro's arguments that *The Lord of the Rings* is rooted in racism are based entirely on, or influenced by, Jackson's adaptation (Rearick).

It is important to remember that film adaptations are as much a product of their own cultural moment as the original literary works that they interpret were of theirs. The echoes of medieval cosmology and Victorian anthropology in Tolkien's work take on a very different hue in Jackson's post-9/11 film trilogy. As visual media, Jackson's films have accentuated the "racial otherness" of the "evil" Men of Middle-earth by basing their characteristics on a (sometimes haphazard) blend of non-European material cultures: North African, Maori, Pacific Island, and Japanese (Kim; Rosebury, "Race"). In a period of high tension between the Eastern and Western worlds, such cultural borrowings can be deemed purposefully offensive and ideological.

Although critical responses to the films is actually about the reception of Tolkien's works rather than about the works themselves, introducing such topics in a class or online discussion can encourage students to think about Tolkien's term "applicability" (*Lord* xxiv; foreword), a notion not dissimilar to reader-response criticism. In most such discussions, my students themselves often bring in a poignant passage from *The Two Towers*, which Jackson kept in the eponymous film, albeit giving it to a different character. When Faramir's company attack the Easterlings and then discover Frodo and Sam, Jackson's adaptation provides a shot in which Faramir stares at a dead young Easterling before saying, "His sense of duty was no less than yours, I deem. You wonder what his name is, where he came from. And if he was really evil at heart. What lies or threats led him on this long march from home. If he would not rather have stayed there . . . in peace" (Jackson, *Two Towers*; ch. 30). These words reproduce nearly verbatim Sam's inner thoughts when witnessing the same scene in *The Lord of the Rings* (661; bk. 4, ch. 4). Both extracts can be compared and contrasted in class, discussing how source and adaptation deal with this response to racial otherness in the midst of war and within the formal (written vs. visual medium) and cultural (post–World War II vs. post-9/11) context of each text.

Race is an emotionally charged word carrying ideological and political baggage that is bound to produce strong feelings among students and teachers alike. I suggest that the best way to teach race and culture in Tolkien is to open up the discussion, introduce students to different arguments, give them some solid background on the historical context of *The Lord of the Rings*, and allow them to debate a number of different points as long as it is on the basis of textual evidence.[5] I would discourage teachers from preempting a debate by condemning or defending Tolkien in the way they approach this topic. The debate itself is worth having not only for pedagogical reasons (learning to construct a complex line of argument, evaluating the use of evidence, etc.) but also for revealing the complexity of Middle-earth and bringing home the notion that Tolkien's legendarium was developed over a period of nearly sixty years, so not everything within it is consistent. From the time Tolkien began *The Book of Lost Tales* in the 1910s to his late writings in the early 1970s, the mythology was evolving, not only according to his creative vision but also as a response to his sociohistorical circumstances. If it is accurate, as I have argued elsewhere, that Tolkien's legendarium started as a Victorian work but ended as a modern literary venture, then the issue of race offers a prominent example of his changing ideas and the way these filtered into his creative writing.

NOTES

[1]The "early scholarly works" Shippey references is Tolkien's two-part essay "Sigelwara Land," in which Tolkien explores the Old English word *Sigelhearwan*, translated as "Ethiopians."

[2]Recent work on race in the Middle Ages that students can be referred to includes Strickland; J. Cohen.

[3]The medieval approach is also supported by McFadden; Chance, "Tolkien and the Other."

[4]See also Chism for a deft analysis of how Tolkien and the Nazis drew different purposes and outcomes from the same medieval sources.

[5]Other relevant discussion points are the idea of the noble savage, interracial marriages, and racial characteristics of the Orcs (see Fimi 150–57), as well as a lively recent debate on Tolkien and anti-Semitism (see Brackmann; Vink).

Women Students and *The Lord of the Rings*: Showing Them Where They Fit In

Shelley Rees

Each spring, I teach an undergraduate course called Writing about Literature, which uses science fiction and fantasy texts. Unfortunately, I find women are more likely than men to end up in this class because other sections are full or scheduled at unpopular times, and women are more often indifferent or hostile to my subject material than their male peers. One explanation for this phenomenon remains the regrettable paucity of relatable female characters in the canonical texts of speculative fiction. Anyone with peripheral familiarity with fantasy and science fiction has reason to believe that women characters in these genres are rounded but rarely round. The cover art of many such novels reveals much of what we need to know about the treatment of women in their pages: images of sexualized bodies indeed worthy of the label "fantastic." To be fair, as culture has progressed, so has its fiction. Complex, nontraditional women characters are more frequent in speculative fiction than ever before. Nevertheless, too many science fiction and fantasy heroes persist in stubborn maleness, their narratives still steeped in heteronormativity, and as a teacher I cannot be an apologist. In fact, I spend so much time making sure my students learn to recognize sexism and phallocentrism in general that if I suddenly decided to brush such criticisms aside for a favored genre, I would lose credibility.

In short, women have reason to view speculative fiction with suspicion, and teachers of this literature must acknowledge the understandable reluctance in women students—and feminist men—to trust works in these genres.[1] I never claim that sexism and heterocentrism are nonexistent in these works, but I teach students to identify not only literal femininity but also symbolic femininity in fantasy and speculative fiction. I lead them to scrutinize characters, whether male or female, who embody feminine values and characteristics. In doing so, my purpose is to excavate a narrative niche into which women can read themselves. Fortunately, J. R. R. Tolkien's *The Lord of the Rings* provides a convincing foundation from which to demonstrate feminine-friendly canonical fantasy, as the book decries the exclusion of traits and ideals that patriarchal culture tends to relegate to the feminine, and ultimately the book hails those marginalized traits as indispensable to preserving civilization.

When I posit a study of gender in *The Lord of the Rings*, students respond with confusion: "But there aren't many women in the book." There are not many women characters, yes, certainly very few who appear onstage in the narrative action for long periods, and there are no women in the Fellowship. At this point in the discussion, it becomes crucial that we establish and agree upon a definition of *gender*, as most students today—most people in general—perceive women as gendered in a way that men are not; the gendering of masculinity tends to be much less problematized and consequently less visible. Students grasp the concept of invisible masculinity quickly once I ask them why we find academic articles that analyze characters such as Grendel's mother, Shelob, and the Medusa as female characters, while similar studies of Grendel, the Balrog, or the Kraken as male characters remain absent. In part, this invisibility prevails because male and female students alike learn to accept maleness as the default human condition. Girls discover early that fictional heroes with mass appeal—the eponymous protagonists—will much more often be Harry Potter than Hermione Granger, so women readers become accomplished cross-readers, orienting their reading consciousness with opposite-sex heroes in ways rarely required of male readers.

Again, it is important that we not attempt to apologize for what is, without question, a manifestation of patriarchy. Despite notable progress, traditional heroic fantasy remains a male-dominated genre, in both authorship and readership, and some of its demographic appeal derives from an embedded lack of will to challenge essentialist archetypes of sex and gender. Indeed, underscoring the preponderance of male characters, the metaphoric landscape of *The Lord of the Rings* seethes with symbolic masculinity, featuring swords, bows, axes, staffs, towers, and mountains. Still, feminine-coded roles, ideas, and character traits may exert enormous influence over a text even in the absence of women, and *The Lord of the Rings* provides a critical gateway for young women to investigate roles the genre can offer them. Even admitting the dearth of actual female characters, a symbolic femininity drives the narrative, and the reclamation of Middle-earth for the forces of good relies on the healthy integration of masculine and feminine. Coaxing all students to recognize this dynamic makes them better readers of Tolkien and other complex narratives, and it allows women a less alienated reading experience in which they do not have to cross-dress as male heroes but can acknowledge embodied male characters as symbolically feminine.

Gender-diverse interpretations of *The Lord of the Rings* are well documented in scholarship. Some of these critiques address the female characters as such. For example, Nancy Enright claims that "Tolkien's female characters epitomize his critique of traditional, masculine and worldly power" ("Tolkien's Females" 93), and Leslie Donovan identifies Galadriel, Shelob, Éowyn, and Arwen with the mythology of the Valkyries, asserting that Tolkien "constructs them as reflective of moral good, heroic ideals, noble behavior, and responsible leadership" (109). Susan Carter calls Galadriel "lady of the lacuna," comparing her with Morgan le Fey[2] and locating her power in her lack of definition (73). Other approaches focus on functions of the feminine in the book, citing figurative or literary femininity as opposed to literal women characters. For instance, Ernelle Fife dissects the trope of the "wise warrior" figure as it applies to male and female characters in *The Lord of the Rings*, and Melanie Rawls demonstrates how male characters in the novel embody feminine values and ideals. William Green even argues for feminine influence in *The Hobbit*, a book with no major women characters at all ("Mama"). Finally, some scholars perform queer readings of Tolkien's work. Anna Smol argues, "[I]t is evident that the Frodo-Sam relationship continues to challenge categories of gender, sexuality, and male friendship" ("Oh" 950).

All these articles are accessible to college undergraduates, as their language is scholarly but not opaque. One simple exercise I find successful with students even before reviewing the scholarship is to ask them plainly if *The Lord of the Rings* is a masculine or feminine narrative and have them justify their conclusions. To facilitate their brainstorming, I divide the board into the categories "masculine" and "feminine" and ask students to call out everything they can think of that would fall under either label, including personality traits, Freudian imagery, symbols, values, actions—anything that might carry gender encoding. We typically end up with a rubric that resembles this:

Masculine	**Feminine**
war, battles, fighting, physicality, strength	home, domestication
kings	beauty
politics	nurturance
swords	empathy
staffs	emotionality, sensitivity
bows, arrows	hills, valleys, caves
mountains, volcanoes	magic, witches
towers	moon
pride	water
power, domination	virtue, purity
aggression, anger	passivity
fathers, sons	motherhood
primogeniture, patriarchy	circles
wizards	intuition, connectedness
sun	nature

Overwhelmingly, students deem the tale masculine, citing "war," "kingship," "epic battles," "politics," and the novel's impressive array of phallic symbols. The next task I give them is, "Apply the feminine and masculine codes we have identified as a rubric for understanding specific characters and their associations with ideas in *The Lord of the Rings*. Why and how do these codes matter in this text? What functions do they perform?" I like to begin this task by discussing the hobbits, as they represent the most accessible example of the complexity of gender in Tolkien's narrative as well as fiction in general and, one might argue, on into real life. I initiate this discussion with the simple question, "What is the gender of the hobbits?" Students reply that the main hobbit characters, the Fellowship hobbits, are all male. I agree with them but then ask that they support their reading of the hobbits as male using our rubric of gender characteristics. An alternative strategy is to assign the work to groups in which some students work on gendering the hobbits and others on gendering different characters.

Faramir and Boromir, for example, present intriguing material for gender investigation, as does Gandalf.

Students soon realize that the hobbits, although there are no females in the Fellowship and although the hobbits in the Fellowship are all physiologically male, function as placeholders for such stereotypical feminine qualities as limited physical strength, heightened emotionality, connection to nature, and domesticity. Every mention of the hobbits' stunted swords and stumpy ponies underscores their physical inferiority and compromised masculinity as compared with men. Further, Frodo, Sam, Merry, and Pippin love one another unabashedly, often weeping and expressing sentimental attitudes. Additionally, hobbit culture embodies passive domesticity, the Shire recalling a cushy, multiplexed womb in its verdant hills and flourishing gardens and snug holes, cultivating a sense of enclosed safety.

In this discussion, students also notice that the most overt instance of a feminized hobbit appears in Merry's empathetic conflation with Éowyn. Both characters are excluded from the march to Gondor by King Théoden because they are not men, Éowyn for being nonmale and Merry for being nonman. Thus it is no coincidence that Éowyn and Merry end up together, told by the patriarch that they are not big enough for the men's war, exposing the masculine value system that aligns physical size and prowess with competence and ability. Like Merry, Éowyn is perceived as weak because she is smaller in stature than a human male, but she is large enough to pass in armor if she avoids close scrutiny. Merry is too small to pass. Éowyn tells him that since they have no mail in the armory small enough for him, he could not even attempt such a disguise. Although in doing so she risks her own disguise, her empathy with the feminized Merry inspires her to invite him to ride with her on her horse. She tells him, "Such good will should not be denied," speaking of her own determination to ride with Théoden as well as of Merry's (*Lord* 804; bk. 5, ch. 3). Students soon recognize that Éowyn and Merry, in disobeying Théoden's command and refusing to accept being categorized as useless, represent a feminine system of ethics that emphasizes intent and sincerity over utility, exposing Théoden's paternalism, and the benevolent patriarchy he exemplifies, as unjust even if well meant.

Tellingly, our class discussion further encourages students to see that Tolkien's narrative rewards the ideals embodied by Éowyn and Merry without equivocation, as they become the battle's greatest heroes. The very smallness of Merry allows him to go unnoticed long enough to stab the Witch King; as he explains, "It's not always a misfortune being overlooked" (859; bk. 5, ch. 8). Moreover, no one on the field except Éowyn, not a man, can capitalize on the Wraith's Macbeth-like misunderstanding of his inability to be killed by a man; only she can turn his masculine hubris against him, because she functions outside it. Thus, feminine values of empathy, cooperation, and complementarity facilitate a crucial victory on the masculine battlefield that initially excludes them.

Students uncover many lessons in the Éowyn-Merry story, and paper topics asking them to explain the relation of this narrative thread to larger ideas or themes in the novel often generate insightful responses. Moreover, when I assign response essays and blog entries along with this material, students often write about personal experiences of feeling marginalized in various ways other than by sex. Every term, the demographic of my speculative fiction class attracts more men than women as students, but it also attracts more of a specific kind of man than others and has in fact been dubbed "the geek class" in some circles. It is not uncommon, then, for these students to identify and empathize with both Merry and Éowyn, regardless of sex, and to write about socially marginalized groups and the social mechanics of othering using Tolkien's novel as a springboard.

The character of Gollum invites many such explorations. Gollum has no friends, no relatives, no relationships, and no future, and he is bullied, tortured, and despised. Even Faramir, one of the book's most deliberative, even-tempered characters, almost executes him. However, as with Merry and Éowyn, the position of the narrative in relation to Gollum supports its message of inclusivity by encouraging readers to consider what would be lost if characters outside the masculine system of warfare were denied participation, if Merry and Éowyn were left behind and Gollum executed. Tolkien establishes that without Gollum and his connection to the Ring, no one would be able to hinder Frodo's claiming and using it, and all of Middle-earth would perish. Because Gollum retakes the Ring from Frodo at the Cracks of Doom, one could argue that Gollum saves the world more single-handedly than any other character. The motivations are complicated, of course—Gollum's motives are less than altruistic and even less than conscious—but in recognizing Gollum as a fellow victim of the Ring's poison, Frodo experiences not merely pity but empathy for him, especially in the light of Gollum's ambiguous identity: we do not know what Gollum is, but he is said to be related to hobbits. In the end, Tolkien makes it obvious to the reader that Frodo submits to the Ring and claims it for his own, just as Gollum has. In this way, Tolkien establishes their pathetic and empathetic kinship as another example of empowerment that appears weak and ineffectual until its context is expanded beyond traditional categories, which affords students more material for studying the function of feminized characters and ideals in the novel.

Other masculine characters inhabit and perform feminine roles. Some entire races echo the traditional feminine through their associations with nature. Although the Ring is coded feminine in its circular structure, it is also associated with the artificiality of patriarchy, an unnatural object forged by a masculine will to power; thus the characters allied most closely with the natural or feminine remain most immune to its appeal. Elves, though brilliant fighters when necessary, view Men's wars and struggles for dominance with disdain, preferring rural beauty and reclusiveness to the artifice of human politics. Similarly, the Ents, though imbued with phallic strength, are emasculated to some degree through their loss of the Entwives as well as through their patient, passive reticence and connection to the reclusive, mysterious natural forest. Aragorn and Faramir occupy complex gender positions. For all the attention paid to patriarchal power inherited through Aragorn's male line, the abilities that most unquestionably establish his kingship in Gondor involve healing, not killing. The fraught relation of Faramir to the aggressive masculine legacy of his father, and to a lesser degree of his brother, likewise marks him as a nuanced portrait of masculinity. While Éowyn chafes at being confined by the healers, Faramir bows to their expertise, though he could order his own release if he chose, demonstrating his willingness to accept a subordinate (one might say feminized) position as the situation dictates. All these characters provide stimulating examples for student contemplation.

Another strategy to help students engage sex and gender in the novel involves assignments that focus on ideas instead of characters. One example lies in the way pity appears as a virtue. A useful essay or group work option asks students to examine the conversation below and form an argument about the place of pity in the text's system of values:

> Frodo: "What a pity that Bilbo did not stab that vile creature, when he had a chance!"
>
> Gandalf: "Pity? It was Pity that stayed his hand. Pity, and Mercy: not to strike without need. And he has been well rewarded, Frodo. Be sure that he took so little hurt from the evil, and escaped in the end, because he began his ownership of the Ring so. With Pity."

When Frodo opines that Gollum deserves death, Gandalf replies that "the pity of Bilbo may rule the fate of many—yours not least" (59; bk. 1, ch. 2).

The conclusion students derive, as they consider the question in the context of gendered virtues, is that Tolkien's narrative lauds the traditionally feminized traits of pity and mercy as indispensable to moral victory. Not the strength of Bilbo or the power of Bilbo, or even the cleverness of Bilbo, but his pity may rule the fate of many, an emotion one expects to be derided as weakness in a story about war and dominated by male characters. Later, Frodo replays this conversation in his mind when faced with Gollum himself, and he makes the same decision as Bilbo, proclaiming that though he is afraid, he will not kill Gollum: "For now that I see him, I do pity him" (615; bk. 4, ch. 1). Again, pity informs a decision that changes the world more than any military strategy in the tale, upholding the importance of feminized traits within the masculinized context of war and victory.

Everyone realizes Éowyn is important in *The Lord of the Rings*, but readers could feel she is but a token, a pacifier. As a result, I make sure in my class not to rest the case for feminine power in Tolkien's text on her proud shoulders alone. Besides, the point of this lesson is not to argue that *The Lord of the Rings* represents a feminist manifesto. The lesson offers students a useful example of how fantasy, as a genre steeped in characters that symbolize archetypes and grand ideas, can dramatize gender in a way that undermines the patriarchal privileging of masculinity and invites feminine and even feminist readers to participate in the reclamation of Middle-earth for the forces of good.

I try to illustrate for students how fiction can promote feminine values and experiences through any character who exists outside patriarchal masculinity or otherwise serves as a stand-in for femininity. Ultimately, my students find that Tolkien's narrative employs a more complex system of gender markers than the literal sexes of his characters suggest. Values such as empathy, cooperation, and emotionality—identified with the feminine in our class chart—are celebrated in the text by male and female characters alike. Thus, while it may appear counterintuitive to use the traditionally masculine genre of fantasy to study symbolic femininity, studying these ideas through the text of *The Lord of the Rings* fosters an unimpeded interpretive lens for students to look not at the physical sex of characters but instead at more semiotic and textual functions of gender.

NOTES

[1]One of my most memorable experiences in teaching gender in relation to Tolkien's works involved a young man who approached me privately and confessed that, as a Tolkien fan, he worried about condoning sexism and expressed how my assertions that we need not worry lifted a burden for him.

[2]"Fey" is Carter's spelling.

Language, Culture, Environment, and Diversity in *The Lord of the Rings*

Deidre Dawson

The Residential College in the Arts and Humanities at Michigan State University has a curriculum combining interdisciplinary studies in the humanities, studio and performing arts, and civic engagement. Our courses are taught from a transcultural perspective, which emphasizes the ethical use and application of knowledge and the arts to advance the common good of society. An essential part of the curriculum is the language proficiency requirement, for which students must not only demonstrate the ability to communicate orally in a world language but also successfully complete two courses under the Language and Culture rubric. The aim of these courses is to foster critical reflection on language as it relates to historical, cultural, and social identity and to issues of class, race, and power. Such a liberal arts college, which values creative work as much as traditional research papers and views the study of language as essential to understanding the depth and breadth of human culture, offers unique opportunities for approaching the study of Tolkien's writings. So, when I was asked to help design the Language and Culture curriculum, I proposed a course entitled Linguistic, Cultural, and Biodiversity in the Work of J. R. R. Tolkien as well as another on the theme of language preservation and revitalization, Preserving the World's Endangered Languages. These are two distinct courses with entirely different readings and assignments, but they share some themes.[1] Indeed, Mark Abley begins his work *Spoken Here: Travels among Threatened Languages* with a quotation from Tolkien's essay "English and Welsh": "*O felix peccatum Babel!*" (194).

In recent years, linguists have increased their efforts to draw the public's attention to the alarming rate at which languages are becoming extinct. The National Geographic Society's Enduring Voices project, devoted to documenting and preserving languages in danger of extinction, announces in bold letters on its Web page that every fourteen days a language dies (*Disappearing Languages*). Were he alive today, Tolkien would be distressed at this phenomenon, which has reached such dramatic proportions that some linguists use terms such as "language murder" or "linguicide" to describe the role external forces play in the rapid decline of the world's languages (Nettle and Romaine 4–6; Hagège 119–20). Although Tolkien was self-avowedly proud of his English (in particular, Mercian) heritage, he delighted in the sounds and structure of other languages and expressed disapproval of the idea that English should become what we would call today a global language. In a letter written to his son Christopher in 1943, he grumbled, "Col. Knox says 1/8 of the world's population speaks 'English', and that is the biggest language group. If true, damn shame—say I. May the curse of Babel strike all their tongues till they can only say 'baa

baa'. . . . I think I shall have to refuse to speak anything but Old Mercian" (*Letters of J. R. R. Tolkien* 65).

Most students, even those who have already read *The Hobbit*, *The Lord of the Rings*, and parts of *The Silmarillion*, are unaware, before taking my course, of the primacy of linguistic matters in Tolkien's life and work. Some know that Quenya and Sindarin are languages created by Tolkien, but like many readers in the public at large, they are under the impression that he invented them as he was writing *The Lord of the Rings*. They are unaware that the study of language was a lifelong occupation and passion for the professor. Students are amazed when they read, in another letter to Christopher in 1958, Tolkien's assertion, "Nobody believes me when I say that my long book is an attempt to create a world in which a form of language agreeable to my personal aesthetic might seem real. . . . [I]t was an effort to create a situation in which a common greeting would be *elen síla lúmenn' omentielmo*, and . . . the phrase long antedated the book" (*Letters of J. R. R. Tolkien* 264–65).[2] I hasten to point out to them that one does not have to be a renowned scholar of Anglo-Saxon language and literature like Tolkien or hold an advanced degree in a world language (my own background is in French) to delight in the beauty, the complexity, and the creative potential of language: we are all philologists, in the literal etymological sense of the word, if we are lovers of language. Again, drawing from Tolkien's correspondence, I read aloud the passage from a letter to W. H. Auden in which Tolkien compares his stumbling upon a Finnish grammar in the Exeter College library to "discovering a complete wine-cellar filled with bottles of an amazing wine of a kind and flavour never tasted before. It quite intoxicated me" (214).

One of our first class discussions, therefore, entails a brief introduction of what language meant to Tolkien and moves rapidly to the broader subject of what language means to us all as human beings. I ask students to think about the importance of languages in their own lives and whether they have experienced the thrill of discovery that Tolkien describes. Some students talk about the excitement they felt when they were first able to make themselves understood in another language;[3] others tell of grandparents or other relatives whose mother tongue was not English and relate memories of hearing them speak or sing lullabies in this language. Next we turn to Tolkien's essay "English and Welsh," which says that "language—and more so as expression than as communication—is a natural product of our humanity" (190). I ask students to imagine themselves in a situation in which they are prohibited from speaking their mother tongue or have no one with whom to speak it. How would this linguistic isolation make them feel about who they are? Even if they were proficient in a second language, would they be able to convey all their thoughts and emotions in exactly the same way that they could in their first language? How does the idiom of American English, which most of us use in day-to-day interactions with friends, family, colleagues, and fellow students, reflect American culture in the early twenty-first century?

After these preliminary discussions about the importance of language to identity and culture, I distribute a handout containing the following questions to serve as a springboard for discussion throughout the course and as preparation for student assignments and presentations:

How are the various peoples of Middle-earth represented in the story, and by whom are they represented?
How do these peoples view themselves, and how are they viewed by others; that is, what do Elves think of Hobbits, Dwarves of Elves, Elves of Men, and so on?
What historical, environmental, geographic, or cultural elements have shaped these perceptions?
Do any characters change their perceptions of other peoples throughout the narrative? If so, what leads to this change?
How does the language of each people reflect its history, culture, and worldview?
What kind of tales, songs, and legends does each people have?
Finally, for each people that we focus on, choose a song or poem that you think best represents it.

At the beginning of the semester, I ask students what works of Tolkien they have already read and how recently. Most have read *The Hobbit*, about a third have read *The Lord of the Rings*, and few are familiar with *The Silmarillion*. We start with *The Silmarillion*, then proceed book by book through *The Lord of the Rings*, focusing our discussions on the above-mentioned themes. We do not read *The Silmarillion* in its entirety but concentrate on the "Quenta Silmarillion," to gain an understanding of how Tolkien, as a philologist, could not create languages without also envisioning a history behind them.

When we study the fictional origins of Tolkien's languages, we spend some time examining the genealogies of the races (in particular, that of the Quendi). We explore how conflict, migration, and exile led to the Sundering of the Elves and, consequently, to the sundering of the elvish tongues into various dialects, which eventually diverged until their speakers could no longer fully understand one another, much as a speaker of French and a speaker of Romanian might find it difficult to carry on a fluent conversation, even though both languages derive from Latin. We examine passages from "The Quenta Silmarillion" that refer specifically to language, such as the description of the meeting of the Grey-Elves of Beleriand and the Noldor in chapter 13, "Of the Return of the Noldor": "[B]ut speech at first was not easy between them, for in their long severance the tongues of the Calequendi in Valinor and of the Moriquendi in Beleriand had drawn far apart" (*Silmarillion* 108). This description allows me to introduce the broader subject of historical linguistics (philology) and how languages evolve over time.

Next, we examine the "Tree of Tongues" portion of "The Llhammas" chapter in *"The Lost Road" and Other Writings* (170). Even though it shows a different stage in the evolution of Tolkien's languages and thus could lead to student confusion, I find it useful to compare the Tree of Tongues with some examples of Indo-European language trees to illustrate how Tolkien used a historical model in constructing his languages. Students note that Tolkien's languages have a common linguistic ancestor, Valarin, and that Tolkien avoids the terms *living* and *dead* when referring to them—in his language tree, he distinguishes instead between languages "that are yet spoken" and languages "that are yet held in mind and preserved in writing" (170), open to the possibility of keeping a language alive not only through writing but also through collective memory. As we discuss the language trees, I point out how events such as the Roman conquest of Gaul in the first century BCE and the Norman invasion of Britain in 1066 dramatically altered the linguistic landscapes of those areas. As most students have not been exposed to Anglo-Saxon or Middle English, I show examples of two texts in their original languages that Tolkien studied and translated, *Beowulf* and *Sir Gawain and the Green Knight*, to further illustrate the many changes that English has undergone. Students can see for themselves how the introduction of Latinate words into English from 1066 onward has influenced the evolution of the language.

Our discussion of the languages of the Elves from the perspective of philology provides insights into the relevance of history and cultural memory to the language and lore of a people. Students note that many of the songs and stories of the Elves deal with the past and are about loss—the story of the separation of Nimrodel from Amroth as sung by Legolas is a good example and gives me an opportunity to describe the poetic genre of the elegy and introduce students to etymological research, using the *OED Online*.[4] We study how the modern English word *elegy*, "a song of lamentation, *esp*. a funeral lament or song for the dead," derives from the French word *élégie*, which derives from the Latin *elegīa*, which in turn evolved from the Greek ἐλεγεία and ἔλεγος 'a mournful poem' ("Elegy"). We note that while elegiac verses can be quite literally songs for the dead, such as the "Lament for Boromir," sung by Legolas, Gimli, and Aragorn in "The Departure of Boromir" (*Lord* 417–18; bk. 3, ch. 1), others, such as "The Fall of Gil-galad,"[5] evoke events that stretch far back into the past of the Elves. Language death can also be a cause for lament, as expressed by Jeanne McCarthy, a student, in the opening lines of her original Quenya poem "Lámatyáveo Mauya," an elegy for lost language, which was accompanied by an English translation: "Do you come upon the paths of forgotten words? Do you see the words left behind, like leaves of the old willow, by languages of old?"

That the eventual departure of the Elves from Middle-earth is evoked several times in the narrative of *The Lord of the Rings* leads us to consider the fate of elvish languages. What will become of them? Will they be "held in mind" after the coming of the Fourth Age, the Age of Men, and if so, by whom? We know that Aragorn, the last descendant of the Númenóreans, is rare among men in his knowledge of elvish tongues and lore. Since his queen, Arwen, is an elf, the couple could naturally speak Sindarin to each other, and possibly to Eldarion, their son and heir to the kingdoms of Gondor and Arnor, and to their daughters. But will the language survive the passing of Arwen and Aragorn? As linguists have noted, "When a language is no longer being passed on at home, efforts to promote it outside that domain . . . usually end up being symbolic and ceremonial" (Nettle and Romaine 178). Will the Common Speech become the global English of Middle-earth, eventually supplanting Sindarin as a language for daily use among the few elves remaining? Will Sindarin be reserved only for "ceremony, and for high matters of lore and song" (*Lord* 1127; app. F) as Quenya has been?

These questions address the issue of whether preserving language is essential to preserving culture.[6] In their newfound role as linguistic anthropologists, my students find the Hobbits to be an interesting case. In the section on Hobbits in appendix F of *The Lord of the Rings*, "The Languages and Peoples of the Third Age," we read that the Hobbits have been using the Common Speech for over a thousand years and that, furthermore, "[t]here is no record of any language peculiar to Hobbits." On the contrary, they have been linguistic sponges throughout their history, because "[i]n ancient days they seem always to have used the languages of Men near whom, or among whom, they lived" (1130). Yet, despite their lack of a language distinct from the languages of Men, the Hobbits do not lack a distinctive *use* of language. My students usually find the Hobbits' approach to language unique in its combination of pragmatism and playfulness, an upbeat counterpoint to the sadness-tinged beauty of the poetry of the Elves or the warrior songs of the Riders of Rohan. Whereas the Elves use language to recapture something of their past, the Hobbits use language to celebrate the simple pleasures of the present. When asked to choose a poem or song that best characterizes the Hobbits, students often choose "The Bath Song," "A Drinking Song," or Bilbo's "Walking Song" for their joyous evocation of creature comforts. The Hobbits also use songs to boost their morale or to fend off fear and despair, as in Sam's spontaneous composition of "The Troll Song" when the hobbits and Strider pause to rest on their way to Rivendell (206–08; bk. 1, ch. 12). Reading aloud the songs not only adds variety to the format of class meetings but also enhances students' appreciation of shared oral traditions. In the foreword to her illustrated anthology of Hobbit songs, Mira Spaulding, a student, notes, "Songs are embedded in the themes of language and culture. . . . By including these songs and rhymes in his work, Tolkien grounds the languages he has created in reality. . . . [H]e is adding substance to the mythological history and tradition of his work, making the languages and culture of Middle-earth more believable and real to the reader."

The songs performed by Frodo, Merry, Pippin, and Sam, composed in a borrowed rather than ancestral language, reflect the adaptability and resilience of Hobbit culture. As we study the various peoples of Middle-earth and their languages, we also note through an exercise in lexical work how environment can shape language and culture. In this assignment, students list elvish words for elements of the natural world in *The Lord of the Rings*. These lists reveal that Elves have many words for trees and plants in general, which students relate to the fact that the Elves often dwell among trees. Their knowledge of the medicinal properties of plants (shared by Aragorn, who was raised by the Elves of Rivendell) makes them unparalleled healers. From our discussion of *The Silmarillion* students learn that as the Firstborn, the Elves have a special relation to both language and nature: they have communicated with the rest of the natural world from the beginning of its creation. As Treebeard states, "They always wished to talk to everything, the old Elves did" (468; bk. 3, ch. 4).

By contrast, the Dwarves, who were made in secret by the Vala Aulë, have a secretive approach to their language, as Tolkien notes in appendix F: "Yet in secret (a secret which unlike the Elves, they did not willingly unlock, even to their friends) they used their own strange tongue. . . . Few of other race have succeeded in learning it" (1132). Students often note that the isolated and hidden environment in which the Dwarves live and work, mines and caves dug deep into the earth, is not conducive to communicating with other peoples. Yet the Dwarves, though they seem to be polar opposites of the loquacious and tree-dwelling Elves, share with them a reverence for environment. Gimli's description of the Glittering Caves of Aglarond is so rhapsodic, it moves even Legolas, who dislikes being underground, and he agrees to return to Helm's Deep to visit these caves with Gimli on the condition that the dwarf visit Fangorn Forest with him. The class discusses how Legolas and Gimli's willingness to explore each other's home indicates a desire to more fully understand the other and solidifies their new friendship. Like learning the language of another people, immersing oneself in and learning to respect another ecosystem, where different customs and practices must be followed, is a gateway to understanding a people's history and culture. When asked to identify other episodes in *The Lord of the Rings* in which intercultural understanding occurs, students often refer to the scene in "The Mirror of Galadriel," in which the powerful elf queen speaks in the dwarvish language to Gimli, who has been subjected to the humiliation of being blindfolded during the walk through Lothlórien because of his race: "And the Dwarf, hearing the names given in his own ancient tongue, looked up and met her eyes; and it seemed to him that he looked suddenly into the heart of an enemy and saw there love and understanding" (356; bk. 2, ch. 7). Gimli is not the only member of the company transformed by Galadriel's words. From this moment on, Legolas, who previously shares all the elvish prejudices against Dwarves, hardly leaves Gimli's side. Galadriel's uttering of dwarvish words illustrates the healing power of language for Legolas no less than for Gimli.

Treebeard and Tom Bombadil both have a unique relation with language and the environment. Bombadil's speech, with its distinctive metrical and rhyming qualities, resembles song, and his songs have the ability to command beings in his realm—the incidents involving Old Man Willow and the Barrow-wights are examples. When Frodo asks Goldberry who Bombadil is, her first response is to say simply, "He is." We talk about the significance of Goldberry's use of *to be* as opposed to a verb of action. A few lines later, she calls Bombadil "Master of wood, water and hill," but when Frodo asks if this means that the land belongs to him, she replies, "The trees and the grasses and all things growing or living in the land belong each to themselves" (124; bk. 1, ch. 7). We discuss the various meanings of the word *master* and generally conclude that if Tom Bombadil is the master, it is in the sense of one who teaches, not one who commands; he teaches us the value of being and letting others be. Treebeard shares with Bombadil the distinction of being among the oldest of Middle-earth's inhabitants. However, whereas Bombadil's use of language is largely performative—he sings to amuse himself or to keep unruly creatures like Old Man Willow in line—Treebeard is not only a shepherd of the trees but also a custodian of the languages and lore of Middle-earth. Students sometimes compare Treebeard with a Celtic bard or African griot, in that he is able to hold all the names and languages of the inhabitants of Middle-earth in memory. Just as an oral historian updates and modifies his narrative to include recent events, such as births and deaths, in the history of his people, Treebeard is quite willing to include a verse about Hobbits in the lists of living creatures: "Half-grown Hobbits, the hole-dwellers" (465; bk. 3, ch. 4). When the Hobbits, who "always seem to have got left out of the old lists, and the old stories," are added to Treebeard's list, they become part of the recorded history of Middle-earth.

Through their study of the diverse languages and cultures of Tolkien's world, students come to a deeper understanding of the importance of preserving linguistic diversity, cultural diversity, and biodiversity in our own world. Middle-earth would be less rich if any of the peoples or their languages—even the Orcs and their speech "full of hate and anger" (445; bk. 3, ch. 3)—were omitted from Tolkien's text. For her final student project, Jessica Newby imagined she was an anthropologist, Vaeoryn Eorl, whose mission was to study the orcs taken as prisoners, in order to determine if they could be reformed and somehow reintegrated into Middle-earth. This passage from Vaeoryn Eorl's journal provides a fitting conclusion to my essay:

> They are forced to spend their new existence in states of complete silence, as the Lords of the Holding Posts are wary of even having the Black Speech uttered aloud. . . . And yet, language is how we may come to understand one another. King Elessar charged me with the mission of attempting to reform these creatures—how am I to accomplish such a thing if I am forbidden to even communicate with them in their own language, as broken and twisted as it may be? How are we to understand them without hearing and understanding their language?

NOTES

[1]Throughout this essay, I refer to ideas from my language preservation course that are relevant to a discussion of language and culture in Tolkien's work.

[2]Dimitra Fimi demonstrates that Tolkien began work on the first elements of his mythology in poems written between 1910 and 1915 and that he did not begin work on the first of his invented languages, Qenya (which later evolved into Quenya), until 1915. According to Fimi, Tolkien invented the "myth" that he wrote his stories later, as a vehicle for his languages, in order to justify his "secret vice," his obsession with language (63–67, 99–100).

[3]For Verlyn Flieger, Tolkien's theory of subcreation, as developed in his essay "On Fairy-stories," can be applied to the learning and use of language: "To hear or speak a new language is to be, for the moment, in a new and strange world created by unfamiliar words expressing different perceptions and a different imaginative vision—in effect a Secondary World whose colors are refracted through the prism of language. We may say then, that any world in which human beings live and speak is sub-created by their words and is thus a Secondary World" (*Splintered Light* 95).

[4]Etymological research was of course an essential part of Tolkien's work as a scholar and as an inventor of languages. I refer students who wish to learn more about his participation in the *OED* to Gilliver, Marshall, and Weiner. As a way of bringing etymology alive for the students, I ask them to do etymological research on their given names or family names, which they then share with the class.

[5]Sam recites some verses from the lay "The Fall of Gil-galad" in response to Merry's question "Who was Gil-galad?" as the hobbits and Strider are making their way toward Weathertop. Sam is under the impression that Bilbo, who taught him the poem, also composed it, but Strider notes that it was composed "in an ancient tongue" and surmises that Bilbo must have translated it into the Common Tongue before teaching it to Sam (*Lord* 185–86; bk. 1, ch. 11). This scene is a good illustration of how history can be transmitted orally over many generations through poetic language, thanks to mnemonic devices such as rhyme, meter, and alliteration. I use this scene to introduce a discussion of other epic poems, such as *The Iliad* and *The Odyssey*, and various theories regarding their composition.

[6]The role of language in preserving culture is of particular importance and urgency to indigenous peoples. Some American Indian tribes whose languages were classified as extinct began efforts to reconstruct them on the basis of writings of nonnative people who recorded parts of these languages centuries ago (P. Cohen).

Starting with the Film: Jackson as a Way Back to Tolkien on Heroism and Evil

Christopher Crane

Peter Jackson's film trilogy *The Lord of the Rings* offers an interpretation of J. R. R. Tolkien's story that for many new readers of the book is the primary one. In 2009, I surveyed students in my Tolkien unit about their exposure to Jackson's films. Of the thirty-seven who responded, only two said they had not seen the films before reading the text in my course, and fifteen had seen them before their first reading of the text. Only five had read the text more than once, but thirty-two had seen the films more than once—and thirteen said they had seen the films five times or more. Teachers who love Tolkien's original may find themselves up against misconceptions about the story created by this dominant and vivid cinematic interpretation. Rather than fighting this trend, however, I use Jackson to benefit my goals as a teacher. Studying the relationship between an original text and its adaptation can deepen the understanding of both. In particular, I find that Jackson's revisions to Tolkien's portrayal of heroism and the nature of evil provide an invaluable means of more clearly teaching students the same themes in Tolkien's original.

The need for such an approach becomes clear early on through a reading quiz over book 1 of *The Fellowship of the Ring*. I often ask, "How does Frodo escape from the Black Riders across the river?" A few responses along the lines of "Arwen takes him to safety on her horse" reveal that some students have relied on their knowledge of the film in lieu of reading the day's assignment. More importantly, however, this question leads into a discussion of heroism and evil in Tolkien's text at the climax of book 1. After the quiz, we read aloud the last few pages of "Flight to the Ford," in which Frodo rides (alone) on the horse of the elf lord Glorfindel to escape the Ringwraiths. He defies them even with his weakened will and despite the strong pull of the Ring in their combined presence, a pull magnified by the Nazgûl-blade wound in his shoulder. The primary suspense in this passage lies in whether, under these extreme conditions, Frodo will choose to give in to the deadly call of the Riders. He feels a powerful compulsion to surrender, to let the Ringwraiths take him away to Mordor, to stop fighting. Instead of giving in, however,

> Frodo sat upright and brandished his sword. . . .
>
> "The Ring! The Ring!" they cried. . . .
>
> "By Elbereth and Lúthien the Fair," said Frodo with a last effort, lifting up his sword, "you shall have neither the Ring nor me!"
>
> (*Lord* 214; ch. 12)

Although he collapses soon after, Frodo wins the battle of wills, defeating the evil within and evading the evil without.

To help the class better appreciate Tolkien's depiction of Frodo's struggle and victory in this passage, I have my students watch Jackson's revision of the scene: Arwen fearlessly outrides the nine Nazgûl across the river ford, holding a semiconscious, nearly dead Frodo with one hand and the reins of her white horse in the other. "Give us the Halfling!" comes a deep-throated, hissing voice. "If you want him, come and claim him," the elf princess taunts, casting a spell to flood the river and sweep the wraiths away—a victory achieved by Elrond's power in Tolkien's original.

This suspenseful, well-crafted scene is one of several places in the film where Jackson's screenplay departs significantly from Tolkien's text for reasons other than the need to simplify the plot for the sake of time. I point out to my class that Jackson could have easily stayed with the text here without making the film longer. Why then, I ask my students, does he alter Frodo's state and role so significantly? What effect does this revision have on the tale as a whole? Another way to put this question might be, Why didn't Tolkien have Arwen (or Glorfindel or Aragorn) rescue Frodo in this way?

Examining Tolkien's and Jackson's versions side by side helps students consider different ways to relate Frodo's will to the combined influences of the Ring, the evil poison of the Morgul blade tip in Frodo, and the Nazgûl. Because Jackson keeps Frodo semiconscious throughout the scene, the suspense centers on whether the physical, externally imposed evils will overcome him before Arwen can take him to safety. Furthermore, by removing Frodo's inner battle, his freedom to choose, Jackson simplifies the threat to that of the Ringwraiths and the poison they have embedded in Frodo. This scene is one of several in the film trilogy in which Jackson depicts both an evil and a heroism that differ significantly from Tolkien's. Because Jackson's memorable interpretation will be the primary, if not the only, version many students know, such revisions make Tolkien's original stand out more clearly in comparison. The flight to the ford scene and a few others from the films offer teachers a useful starting point—a way in—for helping students appreciate Tolkien's more complex portrayal of evil and of Frodo as a modern hero and appreciate as well Tolkien's characterization of Aragorn and Faramir as epic medieval heroes.

As a modern hero, Tolkien's Frodo struggles with many doubts and fears. He often feels small and weak compared with the warriors and the wise with whom he travels. He is the hero with whom readers most closely identify, the hero who "evokes the identification and empathy which the modern reader has come to expect from fiction" (Flieger, "Frodo" 135). Although the beneficiary of much guidance and protection from wise and powerful figures like Gandalf, Galadriel, Aragorn, and Faramir, Frodo chooses his own path and his own fate, perhaps more freely and with greater consequences and personal cost than any character in the tale. Yet in Jackson's film he is portrayed as far more helpless and less heroic than in Tolkien's text, where he evades the riders and resists them by choice. Students more clearly see the battle for Frodo's will in the text if they are shown how readily Jackson has him succumb to the influence of the Ring in the presence of Sauron's power—conveyed through proximity to the Nazgûl and the Morgul blade wound in his shoulder. Some of the film's revision in this scene is due clearly to the desire to enhance Arwen's role, but changing Frodo's characterization from Tolkien's modern, common-man hero into a victim is not an isolated occurrence in the films.[1]

Jackson not only offers an "infantilization" of Frodo (Chance, "Tolkien's Women" 179) but also subtly shifts the depiction of evil and its influence: his evil is more concrete, more visible, than Tolkien's. Comparing the text and films on this point can help students better grasp Tolkien's more traditional, subtle, and sophisticated depiction of evil and its intersection with human choice.

Tom Shippey has eloquently demonstrated that Tolkien characterizes evil in *The Lord of the Rings* as both the absence of good and a force in its own right. In Tolkien's text, evil manifests as a temptation within a character, as a shadow that has no substance of its own, only the appearance of a good, real thing. It can also be a separate power that opposes good by asserting its own will distinct from a person's will. As Shippey summarizes, "One can never tell for sure, in *The Lord of the Rings*, whether the danger of the Ring comes from inside, and is sinful, or from outside, and is merely hostile" (*J. R. R. Tolkien* 142). By discussing this theme in conjunction with Jackson's films, students can more easily recognize the internal depiction of evil in the fact that the Ring affects characters in varying degrees and in different ways, magnifying and corrupting their own inner impulses. Boromir desires intensely to use it to save Minas Tirith, but Sam is only slightly tempted to use it to overthrow Barad-dûr and turn Mordor into a garden. Because of their nature, Hobbits are generally more (but not entirely) resistant to the Ring's corruption. However, the Ring—or perhaps Sauron's will operating through the Ring—also exerts its own will to corrupt characters from without, providing impulses they would not otherwise have.

Jackson preserves some of the tension between these views of evil in his cinematic version, but he generally emphasizes the external, more objective manifestations of evil over the shadowy, internal aspect, which is equally vital in Tolkien's text. To demonstrate further both Jackson's revised portrayal of evil and his lessening of Frodo's modern, common-man heroism, I next take students to book 4 in *The Two Towers*, where Frodo, Sam, and Gollum pass the entrance to Minas Morgul on their way to the stairs of Cirith Ungol. Feeling a strong pull toward the dark city, "as if some force were at work other than his own will" (704; ch. 8), Frodo begins to move toward it until Sam physically catches him and urges him not to go that way. Frodo feels the Ring pulling him in the opposite direction but resists it. When we watch Jackson's version of this scene in class, students see Frodo drawn magnetically toward the great bridge, helpless, showing no sign of inner struggle or resistance. Only by physical force (versus Tolkien's combination of physical restraint and verbal appeal) does Sam return him to the correct path. In the film, Frodo and Sam lie still, Frodo clutching the ring at his breast as the lord of the Nazgûl exits the city and utters a piercing cry (Jackson, *Return*, sc. 11 ["Minas Morgul"]). In contrast, Tolkien emphasizes Frodo's inner struggle at this point. As the Nazgûl lord approaches, riding (not yet flying, as Jackson has him) in front of his army, Tolkien's Frodo feels a powerful call to his will, "more urgent than ever before," to put the Ring on. However, just as in the scene by the river ford, his will asserts itself: "But great as the pressure was, he felt no inclination now to yield to it. He knew that the Ring would only betray him, and that he had not, even if he put it on, the power to face the Morgul-king—not yet. There was no longer any answer to that command in his own will" (*Lord* 706; bk. 4, ch. 8). The external evil actually moves Frodo's hand toward the Ring, but "then his own will stirred," forcing his hand instead toward the phial of Galadriel, the grasping of which frees his mind from the Ring's power (707). No such exertion of will occurs in Jackson's film.

Jackson's treatment of King Théoden's release from Saruman's influence offers a third contrast that can illuminate how Tolkien depicts the battle of the heart against evil. In *The Two Towers* (both text and film), King Théoden of Rohan has become apathetic about defending his land and has lost hope for his people, having succumbed to lies from his adviser, Wormtongue, who is an agent of the corrupted wizard, Saruman. Tolkien's Gandalf sings a song of light and hope to revive Théoden's courage and will: "Take courage. . . . No counsel have I to give to those that despair. . . . Too long have you sat in shadows" (514; bk. 3, ch. 6). Jackson's Gandalf, on the other hand, performs a kind of exorcism, pointing his staff at Théoden as Saruman, leagues away in Isengard, speaks through Théoden's mouth much as a demon might in a horror film (sc. 16 ["The King of the Golden Hall"]). Jackson thus pits Gandalf and Saruman directly against each other through the king, who has little to say, choose, or do until the wizards' conflict over his mind is resolved. Tolkien emphasizes Théoden's despair, fed by Saruman's lies administered through Gríma Wormtongue. "[T]wisted tales and crooked promptings" (514; bk. 3, ch. 6)—not outright sorcery and possession—are the source of his darkness. Wormtongue's physical presence has exerted Saruman's will externally, but Tolkien leaves the primary responsibility and choice on Théoden himself to remain in darkness or to return to his former strength at Gandalf's prompting.

Frodo is not the only hero whom Jackson revises. Jackson's portrayal of Aragorn can help students see Tolkien's original character as a medieval hero whose great deeds flow from his inner character, which does not change fundamentally during the tale. Many of Tolkien's choices about Aragorn's identity, ancestry, and attitude toward his destiny echo those of heroes from medieval British and other northern European legends (Flieger, "Frodo" 126–27). This epic heroism may be less detectable to many students than it is to their literature professors, but Jackson's portrayal of Aragorn as an existential hero calls attention to it in Tolkien's text. In *The Fellowship of the Ring*, though brave and willing to sacrifice, Jackson's Aragorn must wage an inner battle with self-doubt and the fear that he, like his ancestor Isildur, will be corrupted by power before he can successfully wage war against Sauron's forces. In Rivendell, Arwen approaches him and says, "Why do you fear the past? You are Isildur's heir, not Isildur himself." "The same blood flows in my veins," Aragorn replies. "The same weakness" (sc. 25 ["The Sword That Was Broken"]). Shortly after, he tells Elrond, "I do not want that power. I have never wanted it" (sc. 28 ["Gilraen's Memorial"]).[2] The Aragorn of Tolkien's text, in contrast, demonstrates no doubt or fear about his destiny. From the first time we meet him, in book 1, he is portrayed as the hidden king, an unknown warrior who is by blood the long-lost heir to the throne of Gondor. In token of his status, Aragorn carries the broken blade of Isildur from his first appearance in Bree. Tolkien characterizes him, disguised as Strider, as biding his time to take up his birthright until Sauron is defeated. Jackson's scene in which Aragorn expresses doubt has no counterpart in Tolkien. Arwen and Elrond never urge him to fulfill his destiny. At the Council of Elrond, when Boromir challenges Aragorn's identity, Aragorn responds, "For my part I forgive your doubt," followed by the words Jackson borrows for Arwen: "I am but the heir of Isildur, not Isildur himself" (248; bk. 2, ch. 2). He speaks with humility but also with confidence in his identity. He takes up the reforged sword before the Fellowship leaves Rivendell in the hope that the quest will end not only with the destruction of Sauron but also with the coronation of Aragorn as the king of Gondor. Jackson's Aragorn remains in self-doubt, reluctant to see himself as more than a ranger and warrior until midway through *The Return of the King* film, when Elrond himself journeys all the way to Rohan to present him with the sword. "Behold Andúril—Flame of the West . . . reforged from the shards of Narsil," Elrond says, urging Aragorn to claim the sword as his inheritance. "Put aside the Ranger. Become who you were born to be!" (sc. 30, "Andúril—Flame of the West"). Aragorn's personal journey in the film culminates with this moment as he finally chooses to forge his own destiny, embracing his right to the throne of Gondor. From this moment, having won an internal battle and defined himself, Aragorn moves forward confidently toward the final external conflict. Though well done, this sequence gives us a different Aragorn, a different heroism.

As with Aragorn, Jackson's revisions to Faramir make him more existential; in the classroom he can therefore serve to highlight the medieval, epic qualities of Tolkien's original hero. In both book and film, Faramir first appears in *The Two Towers*, encountering Frodo and Sam on their quiet, plodding journey to Mordor with the Ring. He has the opportunity to take the Ring from Frodo and return to Gondor with it, just as his fallen brother Boromir sought to do in *The Fellowship of the Ring*. Students more familiar with Jackson's film will likely perceive Faramir as torn between a conscience that urges him to let Frodo continue on his journey and the desire to earn his father's withheld love by bringing his father the Ring. Jackson provides us with a more pragmatic, emotionally conflicted Faramir, who eventually makes the right choice but whose moral character differs from his brother's in degree, not in kind. I show my class "The Window on the West" scene, which shows Faramir in turmoil after he discovers what Frodo carries. The Ring's power is working upon him. He threatens Frodo with his sword, using it to lift the Ring as it hangs from Frodo's neck on its chain. When he learns of their mission, Faramir keeps the hobbits in custody in order to take them to Minas Tirith (Jackson, *Two Towers*, sc. 40). Not until a much later scene in Osgiliath, with no direct parallel in Tolkien's text, does Faramir finally recognize the Ring's corrupting power and agree to let Frodo and Sam continue on their journey, risking his father's wrath (sc. 57 ["The Nazgûl Attack"]).[3] Jackson's Faramir, like his Aragorn, is presented as existentially good rather than essentially so.

Moving from this familiar twenty-first-century heroism to the less familiar medieval heroism of the text will show students Tolkien's Faramir as a character whose noble actions, like those of his returning king, are rooted in virtues tied to his essential nature. In Tolkien, Faramir indicates his deep understanding of lore, history, and good and evil when discussing the as yet unrevealed burden Frodo carries: "I would not take this thing, if it lay by the highway," he tells Frodo and Sam (*Lord* 671; bk. 4, ch. 5). Later, after discovering that Frodo carries the One Ring, he shows no temptation to take it, though like Gandalf he acknowledges that it could tempt him, and he wisely keeps his distance from it. Recounting his earlier words, he tells Frodo, "Even if I were such a man as to desire this thing, and even though I knew not clearly what this thing was when I spoke, still I should take those words as a vow, and be held by them" (681). Unlike Boromir, he is essentially not such a man. He chooses good actions out of his good nature.

Jackson's Faramir and Aragorn are more like us—more like Tolkien's Frodo, in fact: modern heroes in a medieval-like tale, confused by conflicting desires and lacking the wisdom to know what is best or sometimes the courage to do it. Without examining the films closely, students may miss the fact that Tolkien's

Faramir and Aragorn possess such wisdom and courage long before we meet them.

Although many if not most students will know the films better than the original text, the teacher of Tolkien can use that familiarity to enrich their understanding of it. Heroism and evil work well with this approach because a few scenes from the film offer ample material for discussion of these themes in the text and of the contrast between Tolkien's modern medievalism and Jackson's appeal to postmodern popular culture. Jackson's films hold many other points for comparison, and they have many merits in their own right. They are excellent examples of adaptation. Instead of lamenting students' unfamiliarity with the text, we can use their love and knowledge of Jackson as a way in—or a way back—to Tolkien.

NOTES

[1] Daniel Timmons provides a detailed catalog and critical interpretation of Jackson's changes to Frodo's character through all three films. In addition to Flieger's essay on Frodo and Aragorn as heroes, I recommend Wiggins; Grindley for film and book comparisons; and Petty for teaching heroism in Tolkien in general.

[2] This scene appears only in the extended DVD version.

[3] This scene also reinforces for students Jackson's pattern of making Frodo almost completely without free will when the external evil of the Ring's power is exerted on him.

Tolkien and Faith: An Interdisciplinary Approach

Nancy Enright

> It is presumptuous of me to touch upon such a theme; but if by grace what I say has in any respect any validity, it is, of course, only one facet of a truth incalculably rich: finite only because the capacity of Man for whom this was done is finite. (Tolkien, "On Fairy-stories")

The hint of humility, almost shyness, with which J. R. R. Tolkien spoke of conveying religious themes in his creative work offers a partial explanation for the subtlety with which religion is handled in *The Lord of the Rings*. Because of this subtlety, many students reading his works in a classroom setting, familiar with only the books themselves or the movie versions of them, are often unaware of any religious resonance in *The Lord of the Rings*. Yet scholars have produced a large number of articles and books about Tolkien's deeply held Christian, specifically Roman Catholic, beliefs and how they inform his epic fantasy. These analyses range from Stratford Caldecott's examination of Tolkien's use of imagery of the Virgin Mary to Thomas Howard's discussion of the narrative and sacramental qualities of Tolkien's work as characteristically Catholic.[1]

Since most students entering one of the two courses in which I teach *The Lord of the Rings* know nothing of this scholarship, it devolves on me to introduce them to the crucial role of religion in this work. The first course, Foundations of Christian Culture, is sponsored by Seton Hall University's Catholic Studies Program; cotaught by faculty members from the departments of English, religion, and history; and held at Oxford University. The second, Signature III / Engaging the World: Religion and Fantasy: Lewis, Tolkien, and Their Precursors (called hereafter simply Religion and Fantasy), is the third in a series of many core courses required of all Seton Hall students and deals with questions of meaning and values in a variety of disciplines. Teaching *The Lord of the Rings*, I link Tolkien's work to some of the religious fantasy of C. S. Lewis and explore the thematic symbolism of both. I use visual stimuli and active participation to enhance students' experience of the texts.

Because I teach Tolkien and Lewis together, I begin with a discussion of their friendship, a topic interesting to most undergraduates. Some know about the Inklings, but most do not know that *The Lord of the Rings* and *The Chronicles of Narnia* developed while being read aloud to a group of friends and writers who met regularly, typically either in Lewis's rooms in Magdalen College, Oxford, or in the group's favorite Oxford pub, the Eagle and the Child. In the Oxford class, we actually take students to Magdalen College, show them (from the outside) Lewis's former rooms, and tell them about the pub, whose walls are now lined with photographs of the Inklings. In my Religion and Fantasy class, taught on Seton Hall's campus, I show students slides of these locations in Oxford and explain the importance of the friendship between Lewis and Tolkien. Many students are unaware that Lewis, much more widely known as a Christian writer than Tolkien, came to Oxford as an atheist, then was an agnostic.[2] He was converted to Christianity in large part, as he himself attests, through a late night conversation with Tolkien and another Inkling, Hugo Dyson, as all three walked along a path called Addison's Walk, beside a stream on the grounds of Magdalen College. The subject of their conversation involved the concept of myth as a vehicle for divine truth. Tolkien's argument, expressed also in his poem "Mythopoeia" and his essay "On Fairy-stories," that pagan mythology (and by extension fantasy literature) can serve as a way of conveying the Christian gospel, was so convincing to Lewis that he wrote in a letter to a friend shortly afterward, "I have just passed on from believing in God to definitely believing in Christ—in Christianity. My long night talk with Dyson and Tolkien had a good deal to do with it" (Carpenter, *Inklings* 45).

Discussing the friendship between Tolkien and Lewis with my students leads naturally to a comparison of the two writers' works of fantasy. Although Lewis did not write pure allegory (Gresham), his Narnia books tend much more in the direction of allegory than do the works of Tolkien, who uses only symbolism to convey religious themes. In my courses, I teach Lewis's *The Lion, the Witch, and the Wardrobe* and sometimes *The Last Battle* and *That Hideous Strength*. As we approach the many and complex symbols conveyed in *The Lord of the Rings*, we compare Lewis's Aslan, as a single representative of Christ, with Tolkien's many Christlike characters, no single one of whom serves as a complete Christ figure (see Enright, "Images" 554–56). I encourage students to point out the Christlike attributes of various characters in *The Lord of the Rings*, noting also that none perfectly fills the role of Savior. For example, Aragorn is a king in exile, living humbly and unrecognized, who, with hidden power and healing hands, comes eventually to victory and fulfillment of his destiny as king in *The Return of the King*. He is Christlike, but he is not the one who sacrifices himself to overthrow evil. That role falls to Frodo, who, also like Christ, willingly bears a burden in order to save others and lays down his life in the process. But Frodo is not a perfect Christ figure either, as he falters in his attempts to throw the Ring into the fire, and only Gollum, ironically trying to seize the Ring for himself, makes its destruction possible. A third Christlike figure is Gandalf, who apparently dies on behalf of his companions in *The Fellowship of the Ring* and rises from the dead to return in *The Two Towers*. But he also is not a complete Christ figure—Tolkien has compared him with an angel in the way he intervenes in the affairs of the peoples of Middle-earth (*Letters of J. R. R. Tolkien* 202). My students and I explore how Christ figures, Christlikeness, good and evil, sacrifice, and redemption are depicted in the precursors, those earlier works that may have been an influence on Lewis, Tolkien, or both: *Beowulf*, some Arthurian legends, and George MacDonald's *The Princess and the Goblin*. They deal with issues relevant to *The Lord of the Rings*, including the central problem of good and evil.

When examining Tolkien's view of evil, I remind my students of the Augustinian view, in which evil has no entity of its own but is only a diminishment of the good. In *Confessions*, Augustine writes, addressing God, "I saw, then, for it was made clear to me, that you have made all good things, and that there are absolutely no substances that you have not made. . . . For you evil has no being at all" (18–19; bk. 7, secs. 12–13). Most students at Seton Hall are familiar with Augustine, many having read excerpts from *The Confessions* and *The City of God* in their first- and second-year core courses. As a result, they have encountered the idea of evil as a mere taking away of the good. Looking at *The Lord of the Rings* in the light of the Augustinian view of evil lends coherence to the entire text, for all Tolkien's evil characters exist only as diminished versions of initially good creations, and the battle between good and evil in *The Lord of the Rings* is never really a battle between equals. Evil is parasitical in relation to good, in both Augustine's and Tolkien's theologies. As Elrond says at the council held at Rivendell, "[N]othing is evil in the beginning. Even Sauron was not so" (*Lord* 267; bk. 2, ch. 2). Therefore, since good, unlike evil, is rooted in its nature to the source of all, it is destined to triumph over evil, even though the possibility for failures of will always exists.

The goodness of creation, specifically of nature, is a key theme of *The Lord of the Rings*. My students and I explore the ways in which all Tolkien's good characters value nature, while his evil characters are marked by their lack of appreciation of it. Hobbits love the land, Elves love the trees and starlight, Dwarves love caves and jewels and metals—all value the beauties of nature, which the evil characters disparage. Sauron's Mordor is characterized by the blight on the natural world surrounding it, and a clear sign of the fall of the wizard Saruman is his lack of reverence for creation, as when he allows the orcs to chop down trees for no reason. Through discussions on examples such as these, my students come to understand that a deep and sacramental respect for nature is a cornerstone of the morality of Tolkien's world.

I encourage students to look carefully at Tolkien's female characters in the light of religion (see Enright, "Tolkien's Females"). Tolkien has been criticized for a lack of female characters and for what is assumed to be patriarchal and stereotypical depictions of females in general. Students should review such arguments with regard to the text itself and the insights afforded by a religious and specifically Catholic Christian understanding of his admittedly few female characters. Clyde S. Kilby writes that he remembers Tolkien's expressing special appreciation for the Gospel of Luke "because that writer included so much about women" (54). This insight into the spirituality of the author and the value he places on women in a religious context might prompt students to analyze his text with an eye on both religion and gender. Caldecott argues that the Virgin Mary's humility paradoxically renders her powerful and that this virtue "occupies a central place in Tolkien's cosmos" (6). He connects Mary with Galadriel, referencing Tolkien's own affirmation of this connection in a letter: "I think it is true that I owe much of this character to Christian and Catholic teaching and imagination about Mary" (*Letters of J. R. R. Tolkien* 407). Similarly, Caldecott links Elbereth, the almost divine being honored by all Elves and especially by

Galadriel, to Mary: Elbereth is a bearer of light and queen of the stars, phrases that echo a special Catholic prayer to Mary (7).

Other female characters in *The Lord of the Rings* have a religious resonance. Students may be surprised by some of the radical inversions of traditional and stereotypical uses of power that occur through them. Arwen, for example, is the only character in *The Lord of the Rings* to give up an immortal nature for a mortal one, enacting a Christlike kenosis, a self-emptying out of love, as experienced by Jesus, who, according to Saint Paul,

> although He existed in the form of God, did not regard equality with God a thing to be grasped, but emptied Himself, taking the form of a bond-servant, and being made in the likeness of men. Being found in appearance as a man, He humbled Himself by becoming obedient to the point of death, even death on a cross.
>
> (*New American Standard Bible* [Phil. 2.5–8])

Arwen gives spiritual and supernatural comfort to Frodo in his suffering after the destruction of the Ring by offering him a white gem and also her place on the elven ship that will eventually leave for the immortal West (*Lord* 974–75; bk. 6, ch. 6). Éowyn too embodies the triumph of good over evil in her vanquishing of the chief Nazgûl, showing that "born in the body of a maid, [she] had a spirit and courage at least the match of yours," as Gandalf points out to Éomer (867; bk. 5, ch. 8). However, Tolkien shows the masculine and traditional version of power, at which Éowyn excels, to be limited, as she must also learn the power of gentleness and healing in the Houses of Healing. By no means regressing into a passive female stereotype, the healed Éowyn embodies instead a new (and deeply Christian) definition of power, in which gentleness and nonviolence are far stronger than military strength and prowess. Perhaps most of all in his female characters, Tolkien undercuts the expectation that strength must always be physical and involve domination. After studying these gender issues, many students, particularly females, select as a topic for their research paper some aspect of Tolkien's depiction of females in connection with religion.

Finally, I introduce my students to the concept of eucatastrophe, a term coined by Tolkien meaning "good catastrophe" and defined by him in some length in "On Fairy-stories." We consider how he defines this word as "the sudden joyous turn" from imminent evil to great good. The prototype of all eucatastrophes is the gospel, the "evangelium," as Tolkien always refers to it in that essay. He writes, "The Birth of Christ is the eucastastrophe of Man's history. The Resurrection is the eucatastrophe of the story of the Incarnation. This story begins and ends in joy" (88–89). I ask my students to find the moments of eucatastrophe not only in *The Lord of the Rings* but in other texts also—the works of Lewis as well as other precursor texts we study. Students might look for eucatastrophe even in some well-known fairy tales.

Students come into my courses about *The Lord of the Rings* with a feeling that they know and like the work but with little sense of its religious dimension. As they uncover that dimension, they can experience a kind of epiphany. As Michael Bolin, one of the students in my class, wrote:

> I feel that the Engaging the World class as a whole helped me see common novels and stories that I have read previously on a whole new level. . . . I did not expect to learn what I . . . in fact learned . . . but I do know that next time I look at movies like *The Lord of the Rings*, *The Chronicles of Narnia*, etc., I will not only look at the film itself, but I will delve deeper into the ideas behind the movie, the themes prevalent within the story which in turn correlate with the Signature Core courses at Seton Hall.

Michael's comments, sent to me in an e-mail message a year after he took the course, are representative of what I most hope to achieve when teaching *The Lord of the Rings* in connection with religion. I particularly encourage my students to deal with the attack of escapism often leveled at fantasy literature by asking them to consider how texts like Tolkien's, in a religious context, can serve as models and perhaps even as catalysts for engaging the world morally and spiritually. In Tracy Kidder's *Mountains beyond Mountains* (about Paul Farmer, founder of Partners-in-Health), an interesting comment about *The Lord of the Rings* is made by Farmer, a person most definitely engaging the world and as far from escapism as it is possible to imagine. Referring to two of his favorite books, he says, "I mean, what could be more religious than *Lord of the Rings* or *War and Peace*?" (49). Kidder goes on to explain how Tolkien's book links with Farmer's work: "To Farmer, Haiti's history seemed, indeed, like *The Lord of the Rings*, an ongoing story of a great and terrible struggle between the rich and the poor, between good and evil" (63). My hope is that my students will begin to make some of the same connections between text and life, in the light of a religious interpretation of *The Lord of the Rings*.

NOTES

Some of the material in this essay makes use of my "Tolkien's Females and the Defining of Power."

[1]Books on this subject have been published for decades, such as Purtill; Milbank; Kreeft. Articles by Caldecott; Maher; Kilby; Howard are only a few of the many analyses of Tolkien's faith and its influence on his fantasy. Important analyses of the religious nature of his works also appear in Bloom, *J. R. R. Tolkien's* The Lord of the Rings; Chance, *Tolkien*. Additional collections focus only or mainly on the religious themes in Tolkien's works: for example, Boyd and Caldecott.

[2]For the story of Lewis's conversion, see Enright, "Images" 548–49.

Melkor, Moon Letters, and Menelmacar: Middle-earth in the Science Classroom

Kristine Larsen

Science fiction and fantasy literature and films have long been used in the interdisciplinary teaching of science (Larsen and Bednarski). J. R. R. Tolkien's works are no exception to this. While some scientists and Tolkien aficionados may express initial surprise at the claim that science is central to the construction of Middle-earth, a careful reading of his legendarium will convince even the most stubborn skeptic. From elven genetics to the metallurgy of meteoritic iron, from constellations to plate tectonics, and from solar eclipses to lunar calendars, Tolkien incorporates numerous scientific references into the pages of *The Hobbit*, *The Lord of the Rings*, and *The Silmarillion*. His attention to such scientific details should surprise no one, for Tolkien himself listed "history, astronomy, botany, grammar, and etymology" among his childhood interests ("On Fairy-stories" 64). As an adult, he considered himself a "scientific philologist" (*Letters of J. R. R. Tolkien* 345) and brought his detail-oriented and methodical eye to all aspects of his writing, including his letters, philology, and fantasy fiction. His personal letters contain many weather observations and a working knowledge of weather patterns, and both his letters and his fiction prove that he was well versed in botany. In the light of such a wealth of science in his writings, pedagogical strategies that highlight science concepts in his legendarium may be used effectively in courses for nonscience majors.

General education courses in science are often the bane of students and professors alike. Students majoring in disciplines outside science too often enter such courses with equal parts science phobia and science disinterest. When I teach such courses, I try to engage my students in the material before even attempting to impart knowledge of science content and the scientific method. Because of the widespread popularity and common knowledge of Tolkien's works (and related films), the science of Middle-earth provides an obvious hook that instructors can use to reel in their students to appreciate science topics from the real world. When exposed to this approach, students in general education science courses are surprised to learn that Tolkien, who was an author and English professor but no scientist, integrated much authentic astronomy, geology, botany, and genetics into his works to make his subcreated world as self-consistent and realistic as possible.

When introducing scientific topics to students not majoring in science, examples from Tolkien's works, such as the following vivid yet scientifically descriptive passage from *The Return of the King*, can be used to break the ice when discussing volcanic activity:

> Sam was looking at Orodruin, the Mountain of Fire. Ever and anon the furnaces far below its ashen cone would grow hot and with a great surging and throbbing pour forth rivers of molten rock from the chasms in its sides. Some would flow blazing towards Barad-dûr down great channels; some would wind their way into the stony plain, until they cooled and lay like twisted dragon-shapes vomited from the tormented earth.
>
> (899; bk. 6, ch. 1)

In another example, Tolkien implies that Hobbits evolved from an ancestor common to humans (2; prologue), which offers a natural springboard for discussions of human evolution, including the current debate as to whether the so-called hobbits of Indonesia (*Homo floresiensis*) are truly a separate species from modern human beings (Wong).

Even when Tolkien's works themselves are not covered in a general science education course, exam questions referencing Tolkien and other science fiction or fantasy works can be crafted to get students to consider course material from other perspectives. For example, I have used the following exam question to encourage students to synthesize ideas discussed in class:

> The authors J. R. R. Tolkien and C. S. Lewis used singing as the method of creation in their imaginary universes (Middle-earth and Narnia, resp.). Discuss this observation in terms of its parallels to and connections with the ancient Greek and medieval concepts of the music of the spheres and modern cosmological models (specifically, the cosmic microwave background radiation of the big bang).

Discussions of Middle-earth can also serve as a useful preface to covering issues of science and society (such as technology and ethics), the relevance of observations of the natural world to human culture (such as the phases of the moon), and pretechnological views about the universe (mythological explanations for observed phenomena). Relevant topics for introducing such concepts are Tolkien's well-documented love for the environment and distrust of technology, his use of the phases of the moon to time and coordinate the movements of the Fellowship throughout *The Lord of the Rings*, and his mythological descriptions of eclipses as reflecting the ongoing strife among Melkor, Arien, and Tilion (the latter two drive the heavenly lights of the sun and moon in Tolkien's cosmology) (*Silmarillion* 99–102).

Science teachers can develop hands-on activities and lab exercises from science references in Tolkien's work. For example, Tolkien correctly notes that "Elves and Men are evidently in biological terms one race [species], or they could not breed and produce fertile offspring—even as a rare event: there are 2 cases only in my legends of such unions" (*Letters of J. R. R. Tolkien* 189). One such case is Eärendil, who becomes the Evening and Morning Star (the planet

Venus) of Middle-earth. Both the human-elven genetics and the heavenly motions of Eärendil (*Silmarillion* 250, 260) may be explored by students in an exercise I call "The Line of the Evening Star." In a related exercise entitled "The Stars of Middle-earth," students identify the elven stars and constellations of Menelvagor, Remmirath, and Borgil (*Lord* 81; bk. 1, ch. 3) by comparing them with the constellations of our own world. This exercise ends with the attempt of students to solve a lingering mystery in Tolkien scholarship—namely, the identification of the "crown of stars" constellation that Durin sees when he looks into the Mirrormere. Students are excited to work on a problem that has no widely accepted solution. As a follow-up activity, I ask them to explore the astronomical observations of the Eldar, who first awoke at the rising of Menelmacar (Orion) and Helluin (Sirius), for astronomical accuracy (*Silmarillion* 48). Shorter exercises are "What Day Is It, Mr. Frodo?,"[1] which explores the lunar chronology of *The Lord of the Rings*, and "It Mirrors Only Starlight and Moonlight," from which is developed the science of ithildin and the moon letters of Thorin's map (*Annotated* Hobbit 95).[2]

While using bits and pieces of Tolkien's legendarium to spice up units in introductory-level science courses is certainly a successful pedagogical strategy, complete immersion of students in the science of Middle-earth will enhance their appreciation of the relevance of both Tolkien and science to modern life. I first began teaching a topics course for nonscience majors entitled The Science of Middle-earth in the fall 2007 semester. As a freshman learning community centered on Tolkien's works, students in this course were simultaneously enrolled in a special section of freshman composition taught by a colleague in the English department. Having the same cohort of students in both courses allowed instructors to assign *The Silmarillion*, *The Hobbit*, and *The Lord of the Rings* in a single semester (along with selections from the *Letters of J. R. R. Tolkien* and *History of Middle-earth* volumes) and provided students with the opportunity to read these texts through the lenses of multiple disciplines.[3] Topics covered in the science portion of these courses included the night sky, cosmology, creation of the earth and moon, conserving natural resources, earthquakes and volcanoes, the origin of life, genetic engineering, and the Atlantis myth.

In this interdisciplinary learning community, one of the hooks we used to link the two classes was the topic of geomythology, the concept that some myths contain a verifiable geological basis or truth (Vitaliano 272). Some geomyths, also called euhemeristic myths, are based on actual events (usually catastrophes), such as the scientifically accurate description (couched in the language of myth) of the explosion that created Crater Lake, which has been passed down through the Klamath people of Oregon. In contrast, etiological myths attempt to explain generally the causes of natural events (for example, that earthquakes are caused by underground demons). Both kinds of geomyths (and corresponding astromyths) appear in Tolkien's works. Examples are the earthquakes and floods witnessed by the Eldar at Cuiviénen, explained as the result of a distant battle between Melkor and the Valar (*Silmarillion* 51), and eclipses, explained as the result of strife in the heavens involving Melkor, Arien, and Tilion (Larsen, "Shadow").

In my freshman learning community course, I used Tolkien's works to provide examples of geomythology in literature. As the course's capstone activity, students created their own geomyth based on an actual historical earthquake or tsunami. They wrote about the science of the event, then crafted a myth about it. They also did a poster of their work, which they presented at an end-of-the-semester event in our university's science building. Student comments on an anonymous course evaluation were highly positive, as these examples show:

> The ability to relate science and things around the world to literature is pretty important. . . . This course was one of my favorites because it taught me so much in a semester and I'm really fascinated to learn about the place where we live and how it functions.
>
> You can never learn enough from a book. Just when I thought I had learned everything about the trilogy and *The Silmarillion*, another new and fascinating concept would be revealed. It is amazing how much science went into the writing of these books.
>
> I realized how beautiful and complex our world is through the eyes of Tolkien's works.

An important concept covered in most of my nonmajor and interdisciplinary science courses is the development of creation myths. As Barbara Sproul explains, "The most profound human questions are the ones that give rise to creation myths: Who are we? Why are we here? What is the purpose of our lives and deaths? How should we understand our place in the world?" (1–2). One might wonder why creation myths should be taught in a science course. One answer is that they teach us about the origins of science: the primal need to know the universe. As cultural constructs, creation myths bring the universe closer to us and make it more personal. This approach can make the modern study of the natural world less abstract and foreign to many students in general education courses. Science, through its relation to creation mythology, becomes a human activity that has gone on for millennia. Another answer is that creation myths teach respect for other cultures by emphasizing our commonalities over our differences. Yet another answer is that class assignments on the topic of creation myths enable students to integrate writing, analysis, science, and creativity.

An article by Dorothy Matthews, "Effect of a Curriculum Containing Creation Stories on Attitudes about Evolution," provides a good argument for including creation myths in science courses. Her study demonstrates that the myths make students more receptive to the theory of evolution. Students tend to retain nonscientific conceptions about the origin of life and species when taught a traditional biology curriculum, which does not address their private universe. In order for conceptual change to occur, Matthews shows, they must weigh their preexisting ideas against the material being taught. Otherwise, they are most likely to reject the new information. The analysis by students of creation myths as part of a biology course led to significant gains in their scores on Matthews's "Attitudes toward Evolution" survey.

R. J. Stewart notes that creation myths "fused myth, astronomy, cosmology and poetic or mystical intuition in a synthesis that is often unacceptable to the modern intellect. . . . [However,] the viewpoint of the ancients was coherent, organic, and holistic" (32). Tolkien's creation myth (as laid out in the first third of *The Silmarillion*) can help teachers bridge the gap between ancient and modern viewpoints of the universe and lead to a greater appreciation of both perspectives. His works therefore serve as valuable companions to traditional texts in the science classroom.

Studying a culture's creation myth in a science-based course teaches students not only about the culture's perceptions of the natural world but also a great deal about the values of that culture. Pointing to commonalities among creation myths, moreover, emphasizes the fundamental humanity of their creators, regardless of geography or century. Most myths draw from a small number of themes. They explain how the universe began (including often the roles of chaos and sexuality), explain the process responsible for creation (such as song, dance, war, or the separation of parts), and describe the origin of specific aspects of the cosmos—the sun, moon, stars, humans, plants, and animals. They show how a culture's ethics and politics derive from its fundamental worldview, including gender roles and the relation between human beings and nature; reveal the source of evil and death (including a fall from an initial state of perfection); deal with the relationship between human beings and their god or gods (including the price of disobedience); and, finally, depict the end of days and the destruction of the world or universe.

When I use *The Silmarillion* to help students connect creation myths and science, I typically ask them first to identify those parts of *The Silmarillion* that correspond to these common themes. Then I have them choose and research a primary world creation myth and repeat the same analysis. As a capstone project, students write their own creation myth for a secondary world culture (a culture on an alien planet) and then anonymously analyze a classmate's myth.[4]

Robert Carneiro of the National Center for Science Education notes that "in the eyes of anthropology, no culture holds a privileged position. None is thought to be the unique recipient of divine knowledge or benevolence." However, as individuals we are attached to our own culture and give it primacy. To treat the book of Genesis, which describes perhaps the most widely known creation myth in Western culture, as "just another creation myth" may be "puzzling, disorientating, or even objectionable" to students (W. Jones). In my experience, teaching the creation myth of an imaginary culture as the subject of a dispassionate analysis can lead them to a more successful analysis of real world cultures and a deeper understanding of the importance (and inherent beauty) of creation myths.

Tolkien's grand creation myth of Middle-earth at the core of *The Silmarillion* serves such a purpose beautifully. In addition, comparing different versions of the same myths in *The Silmarillion* and *The History of Middle-earth* provides students with a valuable lesson in the complexities of oral tradition, especially because those versions can contradict one another. Tolkien sought to create a consistent and coherent body of mythology for Middle-earth but never achieved this goal, partially because in his frequent tinkering with and rewriting of his text he sometimes pulled a strand of his story loose in a way that unraveled another tale elsewhere. A late compromise—his so-called Númenórean solution—pictures the legendarium as the product of continual oral (and later written) traditions (with errors and mistranslations). To account for internal narrative inconsistencies, he constructs the dissemination of his mythology in his texts as passed from the Eldar to the Númenóreans and then later to Bilbo and Frodo, in that way explaining why the stories were changed in such a way that they no longer represent a scientific picture of the world as it was known to be.[5] Such changes do not make the tales less valuable, just as they do not make the myths and legends of our primary world less valuable.

Students often dismiss myths as being irrelevant to modern life. Tolkien knew otherwise. Incorporating his grand mythology into classes across the curriculum allows us to demonstrate the interconnectedness of all aspects of human knowledge and to encourage students to think broadly and critically. In this way, Tolkien's works can help students appreciate the importance and relevance of the liberal arts and sciences portion of their graduation requirements.

NOTES

[1] All three exercises are described in my "Astronomy of Middle-earth" (available online at http://www.physics.ccsu.edu/larsen/teachingthrutolkien.pdf). The entire second and third exercises appear there, but the first exercise is available only at http://web.ccsu.edu/astronomy/eveningstar.html.

[2] Available online at http://www.ccsu.edu/astronomy/moonletters.html.

[3] Materials related to this course are available online at http://www.physics.ccsu.edu/larsen/courses_fall_2007.htm.

[4] I have used such an exercise in a number of different courses. Examples of this exercise can be found online at http://www.physics.ccsu.edu/larsen/paper_1.htm.

[5] For many discussions of this aspect of Tolkien's later writings, see the "Myths Transformed" essays in Tolkien, *Morgoth's Ring* 369–431.

Tolkien and Environmental Sustainability in the Science Curriculum

Justin Edward Everett

In his 1959 essay *The Two Cultures*, C. P. Snow brings to the forefront the widening divide between the sciences and the humanities. The tension between these disciplines results from scientists' belief that knowledge is best derived from objective data rather than subjective experience. Even Edward O. Wilson's later 1998 attempt in *Consilience* to unify the two cultures results in a hierarchy favoring empirical knowledge over felt experience. The debate continues in the twenty-first century, when Jonah Lehrer reveals in his 2007 book, *Proust Was a Neuroscientist*, the many contributions humanists have made to scientific thought. Despite these discussions, we are no closer to finding a bridge between the sciences and humanities than we were fifty years ago.

This hierarchy becomes evident when nonempirical texts are taught in a science curriculum, in which quantitative data are viewed as real and valuable by students, qualitative data are suspect, and knowledge gained from interpretation (especially in the humanities) is considered irrelevant. Privileging practical knowledge over the humanistic tradition has long been a part of student culture at the University of the Sciences and grows out of the university's strong focus on the professional health sciences. All the same, our university's general education curriculum emphasizes developing writing skills, critical thinking, citizenship, and ethics. My success teaching J. R. R. Tolkien in our general education program led me to consider ways to make nontraditional literature courses more relevant to the science curriculum.

When our first-year writing curriculum was restructured to include a new science-themed course in argumentative writing, one topic offered was environmental sustainability: an opportunity to bring together Charles Darwin's theory of natural selection with Wilson's arguments in *The Future of Life* concerning the threat of mass extinction. Scientific and social in its basis, *The Future of Life* is particularly suitable for our general education curriculum. But the course, instead of examining contemporary threats of mass extinction, unfortunately resulted in the clichés used in the mass media. Needed was a context that would require students to rethink the issues and develop original arguments founded in ethics, cultural values, and responsible citizenship. While other works certainly could have provided this perspective, I found *The Lord of the Rings* appropriate because Tolkien's moral universe provides a counterpoint to Darwin's amoral view of nature. This contextualization is further enriched by the mythopoesis of *The Lord of the Rings*, which creates not only a broader arena for discussing the ethics of stewardship but also helps students see the relevance of the arts to science in ways that are not constrained by the scientific method.

My first-year unit on environmental sustainability begins with a discussion of Wilson's chapter "The Bottleneck" in *The Future of Life*, which I follow with selections from *The Lord of the Rings* that emphasize the contrasting realities of Isengard and Fangorn, and I show how these selections relate to the idea of sustainability in the postindustrial world. Students interpret Wilson's two viewpoints of "the environmentalist" and "the economist" in relation to the contrast between Fangorn and Isengard, between the viewpoints of Treebeard and Saruman. After students read the "Scouring of the Shire," chapter 8 of *The Return of the King*, I ask them to engage in a fictional town meeting in the Shire, employing empirical arguments from Wilson's text with exegesis of *The Lord of the Rings*. They must attempt to develop a plan for a sustainable Shire that establishes a compromise between the environmentalism of Fangorn and the industrialization of Isengard. This assignment focuses on the differences between fact and interpretation and how each can play a role in making effective arguments. Students defend one side or the other, employing a balance of logos (factual knowledge) and pathos (felt knowledge) in making their proposals. By contextualizing the debate in this way, they can discuss the differences between factual, scientific, and statistical knowledge presented by Wilson and interpretive, felt, and mythic knowledge actualized by Tolkien. This application of interpretation develops their critical thinking skills while building the additional general education skill areas of responsible citizenship and writing.

As a complement to Wilson's text, Darwin's *The Voyage of the Beagle*, as well as cross-references in Darwin's published letters and notebooks, compares favorably with *The Lord of the Rings* not only for its artistic value but also as a narrative of a deep personal struggle. Both Darwin and Frodo are naive at the outset of their journey, but as they travel, they uncover a reality deeper than the one they knew before. As Frodo struggles against the Ring, he learns uncomfortable truths about the world from which the Shire has been long insulated—a mythos that teaches him about the created nature of the universe and the tangible struggle between the forces of good and evil. In Middle-earth, nature has not been constructed accidentally but plays an active role on the side of either creation or destruction.

Darwin's journey works somewhat in the reverse. Before Darwin published his works, nature was believed to be the product of a creator, and fossils offered evidence of the biblical flood. When he read Charles Lyell's *Principles of Geology*, his doubt gradually unfolded as evidence accumulated, causing him to question the biblical story of creation. Although that doubt would take many years to gestate into the theory of evolution we know today, his narrative in *The Voyage of the Beagle* relates a personal struggle, analogous to Frodo's, that led to the dismantling of a mythos, which shook the foundations of the Western world.

Taken together, *The Lord of the Rings* and *The Voyage of the Beagle* provide teachers with an excellent context for highlighting the value in these two very different views of reality. Darwin's view is based on the accumulation of evidence and drawing conclusions through the application of reason, while Tolkien's view is based largely on felt experience and belief.

I help students recognize that Tolkien's created universe has a moral foundation that is caught up in a struggle between the creative forces of good and the destructive forces of evil. For Tolkien, nature is aligned either with one side or the other. It is important that students understand that in this struggle one has a choice. The Ents choose to align themselves with the Hobbits and their companions in the War of the Ring; Old Man Willow chooses to become a malignant spirit. Both the Ents and Old Man Willow have grievances, yet they respond quite differently to their enemies.

The Voyage of the Beagle describes a world that is neither locked in the struggle between good and evil nor a part of the design of a grand intelligence. Students will see this difference as Darwin's story unfolds. In the first chapter, Darwin spots a white line on a cliff, which he discovers to be composed of bits of shell, evidence that the earth's age is much greater than that believed by his contemporaries. Later, he anticipates natural selection when, reflecting on the fossils he has found, he wonders if they will "throw more light on the appearance of organic beings on our earth, and their disappearance from it" (165). His voyage reveals a world without a designer and without universal good or evil, a world instead with only advantage and disadvantage, variation and adaptation.[1]

Contrasting these two works gives students the opportunity to discuss not only the different representations of nature in them—an exercise valuable enough in itself—but also the role of stewardship as represented differently in them. Although often considered a distinctly biblical concept, stewardship can be discussed in the classroom in reference to the modern conservation movement of the early twentieth century, which gave rise to today's environmentalism. In the context of environmentalism, stewardship is grounded not in the predetermined place of human beings in the universe (as stewards of the earth by God's decree) but in an awareness of the causal relation of human beings to their environment. With that relation comes the possibility that abuse of the environment, taken to the extreme, may lead to the extinction of our species. When Darwin contemplates the extinction of *Macrauchenia patachonica* in chapter 8 of *The Voyage of the Beagle*, students might wonder if humanity faces the same fate. In such a scenario, creating a sustainable environment becomes a matter of survival.

Other points of comparison between Darwin and Tolkien expand students' awareness of topics such as environmental sustainability. I find it helpful to summarize the two different worldviews and approaches to evidence by using the table in the following figure:

	The Lord of the Rings	***The Voyage of the Beagle***
Character	Frodo. His gradual discovery of his role. His internal struggle against external forces of evil threatening to destroy the world he knows.	Darwin. His gradual discovery of the theory of evolution. His internal struggle against the realization that his theory could change the view of nature and the world.
Purpose of the narrative (of the secondary world)	Imaginary. The narrative, leaving the shelter of the Shire, reveals the cosmic struggle between good and evil.	Real. Darwin discovers a complexity and interrelatedness of life not explained by the Bible.
View of nature	Moral. Nature is active, conscious, and things in nature are oriented toward good or evil.	Amoral. Nature operates without intention, through variation and adaptation.
Stewardship	People have the responsibility, given by cosmic design, to live in harmony and balance with nature (as in the Shire, Lothlórien).	Implication is that the lack of sustainable environment may lead to the extinction of many or all species.
Types of knowledge	Appeal is made to the unseen world. The empirical world is secondary to a deeper spiritual reality.	Appeal is made to material evidence. Mythos is absent, except in the implication of struggle against unfounded belief.

Karl Popper notes in *The Logic of Scientific Discovery* that imagination plays an important role in science, though it is prior to, and outside of, the formal logic of science. Similarly, in *Consilience*, Wilson addresses the divide between the "two cultures" by arguing that the humanities can provide the value of human interpretation to the underlying reality revealed by the sciences. In his second chapter, he states that linking the two cultures can move us toward a more sustainable world. But in *The Future of Life*, he outlines the threat modern civilization poses to the human race: current trends are leading to an environmental bottleneck that will result in mass extinction. The overarching problem is best taught by applying excerpts from Darwin's works and Wilson's principles from *Consilience* to the personified nature represented in *The Lord of the Rings*. Students not only enjoy this approach more but also benefit from having the debate moved to the secondary reality of Middle-earth. When arguments regarding environmental issues are put in the context of a world that operates by rules different from our own, students are more able to reassess their positions critically and to develop their own notions of sustainability, ethics, and responsible action.

In Tolkien's epic, nature must take sides in the struggle between good and evil. Because it therefore plays an active role, students must reevaluate their view of the green debate: their typically prepackaged views are ineffective in dealing with Fangorn and Isengard. *The Future of Life* is particularly appropriate for classroom discussion of the choices made by Old Man Willow, the Hobbits, Treebeard, and Saruman, because Wilson illustrates the choice between living in harmony with nature as a part of a broader, sustainable world and combating nature with the machines of civilization and industry. His characterization, in "The Bottleneck," the second chapter of *The Future of Life*, of these two positions as those of the economist and the environmentalist resonates well with sections of *The Lord of the Rings* dealing with the encroachment of civilization on nature as well as nature's ability to fight back. Episodes that work particularly well with Wilson's arguments are those featuring Old Man Willow and Tom Bombadil, those set in Lothlórien, Treebeard and the attack on Isengard, and the scouring of the Shire. Discussing them has the additional advantage of exposing Tolkien's writing to students who might not be aware of these scenes, since many of them are omitted in the Peter Jackson films.

The last chapter in *The Future of Life*, "The Solution," usefully frames a discussion of a sustainable future in relation to Tolkien's works. Wilson discusses the economic sense of creating sustainable environments through partnerships among industry, government, and technology. He brings together the two extreme positions he introduced in the second chapter, suggesting a compromise that serves the interests of economics and industry without consuming renewable resources more quickly than they can be replenished. His attempts to practice consilience by unifying the sciences, social sciences, and humanities help students combine the Darwin's evolutionary worldview with Tolkien's moral worldview. The Darwinian position, echoed by Wilson, views stewardship of the environment as a matter of survival: if we do not sustain our environment, in a world ruled only by the law of natural selection, a drastic environmental change could lead to the extinction of *Homo sapiens*. In *The Lord of the Rings*, stewardship becomes a matter of moral responsibility linked to the cosmic order: the destruction of nature is a tangible evil that must be combated by the forces of good.

When Wilson emphasizes the dual themes of practical survival and moral responsibility, he quotes a passage from the poet Janisse Ray, which I discuss with students before teaching *The Lord of the Rings*:

> If you clear a forest, you'd better pray continuously. While you're pushing a road through and rigging the cables and moving between trees on a dozer, you'd better be talking to God. While you're cruising timber and marking trees with a blue slash, be praying; and pray while you're peddling

> the chips and logs and writing Friday's checks and paying the bill—even if it's under your breath, a rustling at the lips. If you're manning the saw head or the scissors, snipping the trees off at the ground, going from one to another, approaching them brusquely and laying them down, I'd say, pray extra hard; and pray hard when you're hauling them away.
>
> God doesn't like a clearcut. It makes his heart turn cold, makes him wince and wonder what went wrong with his creation, and sets him thinking about what spoils the child. (*Future* 158–59)

In Tolkien's text, whether we view God here literally (as Ilúvatar) or figuratively (as Tom Bombadil, the personification of nature or even of the process of natural selection itself), the dual emphasis on the threat of (biblical) extinction implied by the last line combined with the moral imperative of stewardship makes this statement a powerful lead-in to a discussion of Fangorn, Treebeard, and the attack on Isengard. It compares well with Treebeard's description of Saruman as having "a mind of metal and wheels [that] . . . does not care for growing things" (*Lord* 473; bk. 3, ch. 4).

Tolkien's description of Isengard parallels Ray's description of the destruction of nature by machines. Industrial progress has come at the expense of nature: "Once [Isengard] had been green and filled with avenues, and groves of fruitful trees, watered by streams that flowed from the mountains to a lake. But no green thing grew there in the latter days of Saruman" (554; bk. 3, ch. 8). A description of Saruman's industrial complex follows, where "[i]ron wheels revolved . . . endlessly, and hammers thudded. At night plumes of vapour steamed from the vents, lit from beneath with red light, or blue, or venomous green" (554–55). In Ray's prose poem and Tolkien's novel, nature is presented as a healthy, sustainable system, whereas the machines are manufactured destroyers of that system. Ray points to God's disapproval; though Tolkien never mentions God and creation directly, his emphasis on the former Edenic beauty of Isengard, along with Treebeard's narrative, makes the moral order clear.

Teaching environmental sustainability through examples from Tolkien's text may be done in stand-alone units or in sequences that prepare students to debate the core issues. Tolkien's essay "On Fairy-stories" enables students to remove themselves from the immediate frame of their primary reality in order to see the issues more clearly against the backdrop of an imagined secondary world. Comparing *The Voyage of the Beagle* and *The Lord of the Rings* shows them how the paradigm shift of natural selection changed the way we look at the world and at the role of the human race within it. Discussing the arguments in *The Future of Life* in relation to the problems of industrialization illustrated by Tolkien lets them combine Wilson's interpretation of stewardship with Tolkien's moral view of nature. They can then see what stewardship means in reference to Darwinism, social responsibility, and morality.

Students can also develop argumentative and critical thinking skills by role-playing a solution to the scouring of the Shire.[2] I generally devote two class periods to this activity. Previous comparing and discussing has given them a knowledge base, familiarized them with the scenario, and increased their argumentation skills. In the first session, I divide students into groups representing different positions. Like the positions of the environmentalist and the economist that Wilson attempts to bring together at the end of *The Future of Life*, the positions I design are extreme. One position represents what might be considered a conservative Hobbit view, in which those who embrace rural life reject the use of all but the simplest technology—one thinks of those hobbits who considered the adventuresome Bagginses odd. The other position represents the views of those who, in league with Saruman, wish to modernize the Shire. For the purpose of this exercise, assumptions of good and evil are put aside. Student groups formulate arguments following the Toulmin system of argumentation[3] and prepare development plans for the Shire, matching their versions of a community that would benefit all. The only constraint is that students stick to their group's underlying bias, favoring either a primitive or industrialized environment.

For the second day, I pair the opposing groups with individual students selected to mediate between them and facilitate discussion of a workable compromise. Each mediator helps the groups define and try to agree on a plan for a sustainable community for the Shire. (An average class would consist of three pairs of groups, each pair with a mediator, in separate corners of the room for the discussion.) At the end of the debate (and often during the following class), the mediators report what was discussed, what strategies of critical thinking and argument were employed, and what plan, if any, was agreed on. Differences between the groups' views of morality and stewardship are discussed. This assignment can take the form of a group presentation and lead to an individual or group argumentative essay as well. The Middle-earth setting helps students evaluate their positions critically rather than simply repeat canned arguments.

In a university that emphasizes memorization, data, and empirical knowledge, subject matter associated with culture, the arts, and felt experience is often seen as irrelevant. Engaging social and scientific topics in the rich contexts provided by *The Lord of the Rings* permits students to envision the problem of environmental sustainability in new ways and discourages them from merely parroting the environmentalist or economist views summarized by Wilson and promoted by the popular media. Further, introducing two distinct approaches to environmental sustainability, based either in science or textual interpretation, allows them to develop their own views and articulate their own definitions of socially responsible action. Breaking free of scripted views, they develop perspectives that appeal both to evidence and to systems of morality, ethics, and cultural value. *The Lord of the Rings* makes this possible in its journey through a secondary world, where the strangeness of the setting allows students to see their own world more clearly.

NOTES

[1]Darwin believes in good and evil but in the social sense only. His abhorrence for slavery, amply illustrated throughout *The Voyage of the Beagle*, demonstrates this stance. He does rank human beings from a state of savagery (the Fuegians) to civilization (the Tahitians) but avoids commenting on variation and adaptation among them. He did not dare approach this topic until he published *The Descent of Man*, where he presented his argument on sexual selection in an attempt to undercut the application of natural selection to justify racial superiority.

[2]I have used Old Man Willow and Tom Bombadil as well as the Ents' attack on Isengard to illustrate this scenario, but the more realistic and practical problems of the Shire make this exercise even more productive and effective.

[3]The philosopher Stephen Toulmin introduced his system of informal logic in *The Uses of Argument*. Commonly used in writing classrooms to teach argumentative writing, this model was introduced in the 1970s through his textbook *An Introduction to Reasoning*, coauthored with Richard Rieke and Allan Janik. Toulmin's system replaces classical terminology with the more accessible terms *claim*, *data*, *warrant*, *qualifier*, *grounds*, *backing*, *objection*, and *rebuttal*.

Tolkien in the First-Year Literature Survey Course

Anna Smol

Including *The Fellowship of the Ring* in a first-year survey of major authors not only claims a place for J. R. R. Tolkien in the English literary canon but also provides a wealth of material for introducing new university students to the study of literature. As an author writing about his experiences in the twentieth century, Tolkien produced work that is especially conducive to discussions of literary traditions, genres, and their historical contexts in introductory literature courses such as my Introduction to Literature: Historical Perspectives. This course is required for English majors and honors students, although many students take it as an elective or before they know what their major subject of study is going to be. The course, then, has to provide an introduction to concepts and terms that English majors and honors students will need as they specialize. It also must serve students who may never take another English course, furnishing them with skills to read literature more attentively and analytically and with the understanding that literary texts respond to our world in different ways. Requiring all these students to read only the first volume of *The Lord of the Rings* also encourages them to read beyond the classroom and course requirements.

More specifically, my course aims to get students thinking about how we read texts from the past and how authors recreate the past to understand the present. It introduces students to the idea of historical change in language and in modes of producing literature. It discusses how historical events can be interpreted by different authors. It introduces students to concepts of genre, tradition, literary conventions, influence, and adaptation, including a brief introduction to film criticism as well. I incorporate a broad range of texts that comment on one another and deepen students' understanding of the ways literary traditions inform authors' works. One of my goals is to create a syllabus that culminates in an examination of *The Fellowship of the Ring* that draws on students' previous reading in pastoral poetry, sonnets, and heroic poetry, as well as on class discussions of themes of war, heroism, gender and sexuality, and exile and quest.

To begin the course, I present a time line stretching from the present back to the early Middle Ages, noting different literary periods and locating in time the texts and authors we will study. I emphasize that although periodization is a construct that works by critical consensus, is subject to changes in labeling, and uses artificial boundaries for every period, it offers a convenient way to see texts in a historical perspective. One of my modest goals is to prevent first-year students from calling everything written before the twentieth century Old English. With this time line in hand—which we refer to often because we do not always proceed chronologically—we first read early modern and twentieth-century pastoral poetry: Christopher Marlowe's "The Passionate Shepherd to his Love," Walter Ralegh's "The Nymph's Reply," and William Carlos Williams's "Raleigh Was Right." Beginning with short, seemingly simple poems allows me to introduce basic literary terms, the concept of a genre and its conventions, and the idea of authors working in a literary tradition.

We move on to sonnets selected from the early modern and contemporary periods. A study of sonnets further develops students' understanding of literary techniques, conventions, and themes and of how representations of masculinity and femininity differ in various authors and times. After analyzing these short poems, my students read the longer Wife of Bath's Prologue and Wife of Bath's Tale. Since Chaucer is a required part of the course at my university, I use his Wife of Bath's Tale to introduce the Arthurian adventure story. The Wife of Bath's Prologue leads into discussions about the value of manuscripts, the authority of books, and the Wife's oral challenge to a literary canon.

From this point, I make a transition to the study of orally derived poetry such as *Beowulf*. This discussion begins with an exercise that students find amusing and somewhat perplexing at first but that sets the stage for *Beowulf* and, later in the semester, *The Fellowship of the Ring*. For this exercise, students write down as many childhood songs and rhymes as they can remember: skipping rhymes, game rhymes, jokes, counting rhymes, charms, taunts, or any other song or rhyme that groups of children sing or chant in the schoolyard or at home. Working in small groups, they jog one another's memories. To get them started, I suggest a few lines: "Bob and Mary sitting in a tree" and "Rain, rain, go away." In no time, they are eagerly completing lines and remembering other scraps of oral tradition from their childhoods. Before collecting their samples, I have them note where they spent their childhoods and in what decade (we have a diverse student body). I return to the next class prepared to point out some interesting examples and pose some challenging questions, such as why one person growing up hundreds of miles from another (or possibly thousands of miles, in a different country) would know the same counting rhyme when neither of them learned it from a book. I point out slight variations in the same rhymes, variations that may result from region or date. I then add historical information, which students usually find fascinating. For instance, I tell them that while they might have chanted "Rain, rain, go away / Come again another day," a similar version was recorded in England in 1659: "Raine, raine, goe to Spain: faire weather come againe" (Opie and Opie 218). This exercise illustrates more effectively than direct lecturing that oral traditions can be transmitted over vast distances and through long periods of time, can exist simultaneously with written ones (and sometimes overlap with them), and may be regarded as the same story even with variations in wording. We then discuss the oral backgrounds of the *Beowulf* story, its manuscript version, and its retellings in later times in various media.

Of course, class discussion on *Beowulf* ranges beyond the poem's oral background to points such as the culture's view of heroism; the ideal of loyalty between a lord and his retainers; the status of women, represented primarily in the stories of Hildeburh, Wealhtheow, and Grendel's mother; the nature of the monstrous represented in the poem; and the poem's elegiac tone as well as its linked theme of exile. I next have students read *The Rape of the Lock* as a mock-heroic narrative. Most important, however, is that they read a Victorian text that introduces the concept of medievalism (the re-creation of an aspect of the Middle Ages in later times). For this purpose, I use Tennyson's "The Passing of Arthur," from the *Idylls of the King*. Showing Pre-Raphaelite paintings of Arthurian legends in this discussion illustrates the nineteenth- and early-twentieth-century interest in medievalism, while Tennyson's poem prompts students to think about how the idea of the medieval can be used to comment on an author's contemporary world.

Victorian medievalism leads into the final section of my syllabus, which covers literary responses to a historical event, specifically World War I. As background, we discuss how medievalism fostered beliefs in chivalry and heroism that prevailed before and during the war and examine related war posters from Britain, Canada, and the United States. In his classic study of World War I literature, Paul Fussell identified the pastoral as a recurrent theme; with our work on pastoral poems behind them, students can easily recognize such conventions—or their ironic inversions—in various war poems. With some prompting, they can also recognize sonnet experiments in several poems. Similarly, their previous readings in *Beowulf* and other texts provide points of comparison for discussing the World War I poets' representations of heroism, war, camaraderie, women's roles, and physical and psychological wounding. To encourage a variety of perspectives, I make sure to include poems both by men and by women, patriotic and cynical, written and oral.[1]

Placing *The Fellowship of the Ring* in this section of literary responses to World War I provides an angle from which to view Tolkien's story, though I emphasize that the work is not just about the war. Even before we engage in any discussion of *The Fellowship of the Ring*, I expect my students to question what the realism of World War I poetry has to do with a fantasy like *The Lord of the Rings*. Many of them, reading fantasy for pleasure and finding that pleasure in bookstores that shelve fantasy separately from literature, might wonder how Tolkien's text makes it onto the reading list of a university literature class. I tackle this issue by opening with the conversation between Sam Gamgee and Ted Sandyman in the Green Dragon. Ted scoffs at Sam's reports of Elves and other fantastical creatures, thinking that these stories are simply "fireside-tales and children's stories" (44; bk. 1, ch. 2). This devaluing of oral tradition is consistent with Tolkien's remark that "Fairy-stories have in the modern lettered world been relegated to the 'nursery,' as shabby or old-fashioned furniture is relegated to the play-room, primarily because the adults do not want it, and do not mind if it is misused" ("On Fairy-stories" 58). Ted boisterously proclaims a belief only in what he can see with his own eyes: "There's only one Dragon in Bywater, and that's Green" (*Lord* 44). In contrast, Sam puts his faith in, and is moved deeply by, old legends; he enacts the enchantment of these stories when, "half chanting the words," he says, "They are sailing, sailing, sailing over the Sea, they are going into the West and leaving us" (45). The narrative proves Sam right, of course: Elves and other strange creatures do exist in his world, and what seems like fantasy becomes reality in this narrative. The old stories prove repeatedly in Tolkien's work that they convey valuable truths. Having previously discussed *Beowulf*, The Wife of Bath's Tale, and Tennyson's "The Passing of Arthur," students are equipped now to consider how stories with fantastical elements can represent real concerns in our own world. This recognition lays the groundwork for the possibility that Tolkien's fantasy story contains truths about the Western world's twentieth century.

To further complicate the issue of genre, we read the foreword to the second edition of *The Fellowship of the Ring*, in which Tolkien expresses his preference for "history, true or feigned" (xxiv). Questioning what he means by "feigned" history, we discuss the ways he makes his story seem like a work of history, such as his inclusion of "Note on the Shire Records" in the prologue and various allusions to his legendarium throughout the book. Having studied oral and manuscript cultures through *Beowulf* and Chaucer, students understand the literary and historical elements of the secondary world Tolkien is trying to create. His foreword also raises the question of what *The Lord of the Rings* owes to the author's experiences in World War I. Keeping in mind Tolkien's caution that determining how an author's biography is reflected in a text is a complex exercise, we proceed to highlight World War I as one strand to be woven together with several others.

As a result of their previous readings, students have been primed to recognize the description of the Shire as drawing on the conventions of pastoral poetry. As is so often the case with Tolkien's work, he presents a more complex view than might be expected, as in his depiction of the pastora. The Shire, for example, is not a perfectly idyllic retreat. Some of its inhabitants are greedy, narrow-minded, ignorant, or proud. Still, it functions as a nostalgic ideal for which Frodo is willing to sacrifice his life. Two images, the British propaganda poster *Your Country's Call* (Imperial War Museum PST 0320) and Tolkien's drawing *The Hill: Hobbiton-across-the Water* (Hammond and Scull, *J. R. R. Tolkien* 106), can be juxtaposed to illustrate a striking parallel in the use of pastoral conventions. Our discussion of the pastoral includes the Tom Bombadil episode as well as the stays in Rivendell and Lothlórien. Each of these resting places can be measured against students' earlier readings of the idealism of Marlowe or the realism of Ralegh and Williams. Note that discussions of pastoral elements lead easily into the issue of environmentalism in Tolkien's work.

By this point in the course, students have read war poetry that depicts landscapes as utterly destroyed or as treacherously harboring deadly enemies, a strong background for considering several scenes in *The Fellowship of the Ring*. For example, in chapter 8, "Fog on the Barrow-Downs," the landscape turns from a pleasant rural scene to an ominous, foggy trap, leading to the hobbits' capture and near death in the barrow, a scene that John Garth likens to a World War I gas attack ("Frodo" 46–47). Later, readers glimpse the devastation of war in Frodo's vision from Amon Hen.

While discussion of the pastoral most readily connects to the World War I poems, the quest motif in *The Fellowship of the Ring* can be compared with *Beowulf* and The Wife of Bath's Tale. Although to some extent Tolkien followed the paradigm of the Arthurian adventure in *The Hobbit*—the hero returns home enriched literally and figuratively by his experiences—Frodo continually reminds us that his quest follows a different pattern. Contrasting his journey with Beowulf's further highlights the unique nature of the hobbit's heroism: Frodo is reluctant to leave, uncertain about what to do, and unsure of his abilities. Their differences are most keenly visible in the feasting scenes in Rivendell and Heorot. Frodo is modest and retiring, while Beowulf, in typical medieval style, boasts of his past exploits and vows to perform future ones. Furthermore, a theme common to both *Beowulf* and *The Fellowship of the Ring* is the workings of fate. By examining Frodo's choice to take the Ring first to Rivendell and then onward, as well as Sam's dawning recognition of the nature of Frodo's quest after the first meeting with the Elves in Woody End, teachers can lead students into a discussion of fate and free will, a central aspect of the quest as represented by Tolkien.

My course considers not only how Tolkien creates a twentieth-century everyman as his hero but also how he represents a medieval "theory of courage," which he identifies with northern European literatures that celebrate an unyielding will even in the face of inevitable defeat ("Beowulf" 20). When describing how Frodo demonstrates such courage, students tend to single out moments such as his announcing he will take the Ring at the Council of Elrond or deciding to go into Mordor alone. I also find it essential to draw their attention to the chapter "Flight to the Ford," in which Frodo, despite his wound and weakened condition, resists the overwhelming command of the Riders that he give in to Mordor—with only the power of his will. But each member of the Fellowship can become the subject of a discussion of heroism. When rushing to defend

Gandalf at the Bridge of Khazad-dûm, Aragorn and Boromir, for example, appear much like medieval warriors to students who see similarities to the way Beowulf's retainers attempt to back up their leader in his fight with Grendel.

Medieval texts like *Beowulf* clearly describe violence (and Beowulf's death scene details his wounds), but World War I poetry focuses on wounds, physical and psychological, more acutely and with a fuller sense of their horror. The anxiety of Frodo's companions, their efforts to bring Frodo to medical attention as quickly as possible, and his drifting in and out of consciousness are reminiscent of a number of well-known World War I poems, such as Siegfried Sassoon's "The Death-Bed" or Wilfred Owen's "Dulce et Decorum Est." Similarly, Frodo's liminal position between the world of Mordor and that of his friends, the pull of one or the other on his mind, and the later recurrence of pain form the basis for a discussion of the psychological trauma of war represented in poems such as Owen's "Mental Cases" or Ivor Gurney's "To His Love" (Smol, "Frodo's Body").

Sam's role further connects both medieval and modern accounts of warfare. Since Fussell's discussion of the relationships between officers and batmen, much has been written on the topic of Sam's relationship to Frodo. Mark T. Hooker's "Frodo's Batman" provides specific comparisons between the literary relationship and the historical. Seeing Frodo and Sam in this light raises the issue of the divisions between social classes evident in Tolkien's descriptions of Shire society and the language styles of master and gardener. Although I prefer not to give my students excerpts from *The Return of the King* in the hope that they will read it on their own later, I comment on how, by the end of the story, Sam steps into Frodo's place and rises on the social ladder. By calling Sam the "chief hero" of the tale (*Letters of J. R. R. Tolkien* 161), Tolkien elevates the common man. In this respect, he is closer to his twentieth-century peers than to his medieval predecessors. But *The Fellowship of the Ring* features warriors from noble ranks as well, allowing students to trace bonds between noble warriors such as Arthur and Bedevere in Tennyson's "Passing of Arthur" and Beowulf and Wiglaf in *Beowulf*, as well as in a pair like Frodo and Sam, thus demonstrating the continuity of such male friendships throughout centuries (Smol, "Male Friendship").

Whether discussing elite warriors or common soldiers, students tend to examine ideals of masculinity, including homosocial relationships, possibly as their own gender assumptions are challenged or as they consider gender roles in the past and the present (Smol, "Oh"). The focus on a fellowship of males in Tolkien's work should not blind readers to the fact that several women play important roles in the story. In *The Fellowship of the Ring*, the most developed example is Galadriel, best compared with the queen Wealhtheow in *Beowulf*. In *Beowulf*, the queen, concerned with family and dynasty, reminds people of their duties, urges the king to remember his sons' inheritance, and claims that her words have power over the men in the hall. Galadriel, even more than her Anglo-Saxon counterpart, wields power over her kingdom as an independent agent. Although Tolkien's noble representation of Galadriel is far from that of the comedic Wife of Bath, an interesting comparison might be made in reference to stereotypical representations of women and power.

On the other hand, Arwen, although far from a passive figure, may be approached through the paradigm of the courtly love sonnet. Her beauty and virtue, as well as Aragorn's love and willingness to take on impossible tasks to win her hand, places her in the tradition of romance. Aragorn's poem about Beren and Lúthien, Tolkien's model of romantic love, prepares readers for Arwen's first appearance in *The Fellowship of the Ring*. Like the so-called digressions in *Beowulf*, Aragorn's poem and his prose summary in chapter 11, "A Knife in the Dark," comment on characters and actions to be seen later. Since my students have been exposed to sonnets by various authors from different eras, not all of which portray conventional male-female relationships, they are able to assess the narratives of the two lovers in relation to a tradition of love stories.

Because many readers skim over the poetry in *The Fellowship of the Ring*, I consider it a challenge to interest students in Tolkien's verse. The earlier exercise introducing oral traditions becomes the foundation for how I approach Tolkien's poetry. Reminding students of their nursery rhyme examples, I turn to the chapter "At the Sign of the Prancing Pony," in which Frodo sings his version of Tolkien's "Man in the Moon" song. Because I insist throughout the semester that poetry be read aloud, I play Tolkien's recording of the poem, available in the *J. R. R. Tolkien Audio Collection* (Tolkien and Tolkien). Of course, students recognize the germ of the nursery rhyme "Hey Diddle Diddle" in the poem, but the poem also serves as an excellent example of what Tom Shippey calls an "asterisk-poem" (*Road* 34)—a reconstruction, analogous to the way philologists mark the reconstructed origins of a word with an asterisk. Students understand that the Prancing Pony song illustrates some characteristics of Hobbits and that styles of other verses represent other cultures or characters and other purposes—for example, committing lore and wisdom to memory, recording historical and mythical information, providing walking aids, giving clues to identity. Working in groups, they select one poem for a formal analysis, taking turns reading it aloud as expressively as possible. After they have recited their versions, I sometimes play Tolkien's recording of those poems from the *J. R. R. Tolkien Audio Collection*. To emphasize the nature of many verses as songs, I also play a few musical versions, such as Donald Swann's "Upon the Hearth the Fire Is Red" or the Tolkien Ensemble rendition of "I Sang of Leaves, of Leaves of Gold" (Tolkien, *J. R. R. Tolkien*: The Lord of the Rings). As a reminder that oral traditions are adapted and passed down in variants, I end this class with a contemporary example from *The Lord of the Rings* musical's 2007–08 London staging, called "The Cat and the Moon" (Warchus).[2] Although most of the wording has been changed from the Prancing Pony song, the intent and mood are the same, and it makes a rousing finish to what is usually a lively class filled with the sounds of poetry.

Since it is impossible today to teach *The Lord of the Rings* without someone's mentioning the Peter Jackson movies, I use this film version to introduce students to basic principles of film criticism and literature-film adaptations, such as mise-en-scène analysis, including lighting, camera angle, sound, actors' movements, and expressions. Although most of the special features in the extended edition DVDs of Jackson's films provide an excellent introduction to the processes of filmmaking, I play only one in class: "Editorial Demonstration: The Council of Elrond" in the "Post Production: Putting It All Together" (Jackson, *Fellowship*; "Appendices," pt. 2: "From Vision to Reality"). Within a few minutes, this feature demonstrates the basic point I want students to take away: that a film is a constructed work of art in which every second viewed on screen is the result of editorial and directorial choices. To prepare for viewing a scene from the film, I take students through Tolkien's "Bridge of Khazad-dûm" chapter, discussing the creation of tension, action, and mood in this dramatic and crucial part of the story. We then view the film version (Jackson, *Fellowship* [spec. extended ed.], pt. 2, sc. 36), pausing frequently to notice changes in musical themes, sounds, lighting, camera angles—how such elements either represent the book through means other than words or how and for what purpose the filmmakers insert new actions or revise the events of the book. Students generally undertake this kind of analysis eagerly. Consideration of a film adaptation of literature is yet another way to illustrate intertextuality, one of the main themes of the course.

Positioning *The Fellowship of the Ring* in the comparative context of my course affords numerous possibilities for essay and exam questions. To help students learn to research, I ask them to bring to class one excerpt from Tolkien's letters relevant to our class discussions. This practice makes them familiar with a useful source and allows me to demonstrate how to incorporate such excerpts into an essay and document them correctly.[3] To give them experience reading academic prose, I have them read one essay in common, such as Garth's "Frodo and the Great War." By examining Garth's organization of the argument, illustration of points, and use of other sources, students gain an awareness of how to improve their own essays.

By the end of my course, I hope that students who have previously read *The Fellowship of the Ring* will gain a broader context for understanding the book and that those new to the text will be inspired to continue a more informed reading on their own. I want all my students to gain an understanding of intertextuality, genre, and the historical contexts of literature. English majors and honors students can go on to study these basic concepts in more depth, while other first-year students can better understand how literature shapes our culture. The key to achieving these aims is a carefully constructed syllabus that allows students to build knowledge and skills and then exercise what they have learned by applying it to *The Fellowship of the Ring*. Students in my course experience Tolkien's story as a rich source of ideas, questions, and problems that would not have been evident to them without their previous readings from the medieval to the modern periods. Thus Tolkien's text becomes the ideal culmination to their semester-long examination of English literature.

NOTES

[1]Examples of soldiers' songs appear in anthologies like *The Penguin Book of First World War Poetry* (G. Walter). Other excellent resources for studying the British experience of the war—poems, photographs, videos, and more—are available at *The First World War Poetry Digital Archive*.

[2]This performance was originally available in a video clip on the play's site, lotr.com, but is now on *YouTube*.

[3]The same exercise can be repeated with other resources, such as Carpenter, *J. R. R. Tolkien*; Scull and Hammond; or Drout, *J. R. R. Tolkien Encyclopedia*.

Team-Teaching Tolkien in a Large Lecture Class: Challenges and Opportunities

Julia Simms Holderness

In January 2004, three colleagues in a department of French, classics, and Italian (a classicist, a medievalist, and an Enlightenment scholar turned Tolkien specialist) launched a new course entitled Myth and Legend in the Works of J. R. R Tolkien in the undergraduate curriculum at Michigan State University. This course did not count toward any major—students took it as a free elective—and yet we had to cap it at three hundred students, because that was the number of seats in the auditorium we had reserved. None of us had ever taught to such a large audience; we were all more comfortable leading seminar-style discussions of Greek, Latin, or French (modern and medieval) texts. We were accustomed to teaching primarily majors in our respective fields, who already had some exposure to the study of literature at the university level. How, then, could we begin to do justice to the richness of Tolkien's work, when we had a student audience with majors literally from A to Z (from astronomy to zoology, with chemistry, engineering, kinesiology, marketing, math, music, and physics in between, and English majors a small minority) and when the size of the class seemed an obstacle to meaningful class discussion or individual student work?

To address these pedagogical challenges, the three of us worked together to develop a dynamic and flexible team-lecture style; a comparative approach to teaching Tolkien, grounded in the pan-European mythological tradition; meaningful integration of audiovisual and digital materials; effective use of *PowerPoint* as a tool for teaching close reading and comparative textual analysis; Web-based resources to enhance student participation and learning; and useful assessments of student learning. From our intellectual framework to its expression in the daily running of the class, we worked hard to be both eclectic and adaptive.

Fellowship is a central force in Tolkien's world, and it was vital for us professors, too, as we structured our course. It lay behind our lecture format, for which we often divided class sessions into minilectures by each professor, who drew on her or his area of expertise to explore the same or related topics. Sometimes we spontaneously amended our syllabus, so that one colleague could follow up on another's lecture during the next session. Early in the semester, for instance, a lecture on the question of genre sparked such a response. After outlining different ideas of genre, each professor moved on to the question of how one might characterize *The Lord of the Rings*. Should one draw on, as Tom Shippey does in *J. R. R. Tolkien: Author of the Century*, the categories established in Northrop Frye's classic *Anatomy of Criticism*? The result is a gallimaufry, a vibrant jumble. And what about the distinction between epic and romance so important to late-nineteenth-century medievalism, the tradition in which Tolkien cut his intellectual teeth? As a corollary, we discussed the problem of classifying the medieval French masterpiece, the *Song of Roland*. This narrative poem exists in nine different manuscript versions, but until recently most scholarly attention focused on the copy now housed at Oxford's Bodleian Library. This is the oldest manuscript but also the one that most strictly adheres to a classic notion of epic, including its focus on the deeds of male heroes. Rather than draw a single conclusion about the question of genre, we preferred to expose our students to diverse critical approaches.

We developed our comparative approach in response to the diverse intellectual backgrounds of our students as well as to our own varied areas of expertise.[1] Our goals were to give students a better informed and more analytic understanding of Tolkien and, more broadly, to introduce them to ways of thinking about myth, mythmaking, and the fundamental human questions at stake in myths. Our assigned readings ranged from the Tolkienian canon (*The Silmarillion*, *The Hobbit*, *The Lord of the Rings*, the essays "On Fairy-stories" and "Beowulf: The Monsters and the Critics") to a broad swath of Western literature, mostly from the ancient and medieval worlds that provided the basis for Tolkien's literary universe. We also considered Tolkien's contemporary milieu. Our course reading pack included selections from Hesiod's *Theogony*; the Bible's Book of Samuel; Norse myths in *The Poetic Edda* and *The Prose Edda*; and Arthurian traditions in Geoffrey of Monmouth's *History of the Kings of Britain*, Wace's *Roman de Brut* and Layamon's *Brut*, Thomas Malory's *Le Morte d'Arthur*, and Marie de France's "Lay of Lanval." We also assigned *Beowulf* and Aldous Huxley's *Brave New World* in full.

These sources offered us a rich base for exploring both Tolkien and the European mythological tradition that inspired him. Our lectures and discussion addressed key humanistic concerns, most notably the creation of man and man's desire to create, the meaning of dreams, the power of music and the oral tradition, the nature of heroes and heroines, the ties between love and friendship, and the relationship between self and other. We also tackled more modern topics such as the multicultural nature of Middle-earth and Tolkien's preoccupation with the destruction of the natural world.

Although all these topics proved valuable in our efforts to link Tolkien's works to European mythological traditions, the relationship between self and other allowed us to explore specific myths as well as the broader notion of myth itself. Under the rubric of self and other, we addressed Tolkien's depiction of the conflicts between Men (or their peers, Hobbits, Dwarves, and Elves) and monsters, as well as the often more affectionate relationship between mortals and immortals (the Elves, in a different guise). We explored his likely sources of inspiration, such as *Beowulf* and Arthurian literature, in tandem with his own writings, including his critical articles "Beowulf: The Monsters and the Critics" and "On Fairy-stories," along with *The Hobbit* and *The Lord of the Rings*. Ultimately, this examination turned into a discussion about the good and evil that lie within all of us, as well as in Tolkien's characters, and the possible similarities between self and other.

"Beowulf: The Monsters and the Critics" was key to our examination of Tolkien's vision of the relationship between self and other. In lecture, we showed how Tolkien elevates *Beowulf* and stories like it to the level of myth, which he presents as itself a peculiar and delicate sort of life-form. As we worked through not only his essay but also *Beowulf* with our students, we focused on the ways in which his works, myths, and other monster stories in general dramatize the primal conflict between good and evil. While the proportions offered in such narratives may be magnificent, we argued that this is a human struggle, rooted in the here and now. As the son of Cain, Grendel is man's primitive and distant relation, but a relation nonetheless. He and his mother look human, even if their size and strength are unusual. The hero, Beowulf, has a similarly outlandish strength, which he employs against his adversaries in extended underwater battles. By comparing these two figures, the enemy and the hero, the other and the self, evil and good, we showed students how these opposing forces both tangle and tango together.

We turned the same type of comparison to Tolkien's monsters, illustrating for students that they are both emblems of this world and faces of what the good may devolve into. Like the usually virtuous Hobbits, Dwarves, Men, and Elves, the vicious Spiders, Wargs, Orcs, and Balrogs are divided into tribes. We reminded students that, like their adversaries, the more distinguished among Tolkien's monsters also have famous lineages: the Dragons trace their history back to Glaurung, the first of their kind, and the Spider Shelob traces hers back to the mighty and horrible Ungoliant. In class, we discussed how Sméagol-Gollum best incarnates the monstrous duality of Grendel and his clan. Gollum, too, is fallen, a counterfeit of seemlier creatures, and possessed of a hideous strength. He has been corrupted by the Ring but was once a hobbit-like creature, and this history brings him close to the current Ring bearer, Frodo.

Each professor gave a lecture on Tolkien's Elves. My own point was how the Elves embody Man's nobler side. In a letter, Tolkien wrote, "[I]f I were pressed to rationalize, I should say they [Elves] represent really Men with greatly enhanced aesthetic and creative faculties, greater beauty and longer life, and nobility" (*Letters of J. R. R. Tolkien* 176). Through such quotations, I demonstrated that, like monsters, Elves are likewise the objects of Man's desire. I also discussed how "On Fairy-stories" gives additional information about his intentions in creating the Elves when he states that the magic of "the real folk of Faërie . . . play[s] on the desires of [Man's] body and his heart" (37). Taking these ideas further, my lecture reflected on how these themes in Tolkien's tales of the love affairs between Beren and Lúthien, and between Aragorn and Arwen, hark back to similar medieval tales, such as Marie de France's "Lay of Lanval." Although Tolkien does not reference it explicitly, the "Lay of Lanval" illustrates his notion of a long-simmering "cauldron of stories" (52): its author lived in twelfth-century England, but she wrote in the French of its Norman conquerors and found inspiration in the ancient Breton oral tradition. I also showed how Tolkien frames Aragorn and Arwen's story as a continuation and renewal of Beren and Lúthien's; when Aragorn first meets his beloved, he actually takes her for the long-lost Lúthien. In "On Fairy-stories," Tolkien ascribes a particular power to the Elves, which he calls "Enchantment" and which "produces a Secondary World into which both designer and spectator can enter, to the satisfaction of their senses while they are inside; but in its purity it is artistic in desire and purpose." And yet, in Tolkien's works, it is the heroes Beren and Aragorn who master "this elvish craft" (73). Beren casts "a spell" on his beloved by using her elvish name, Tinúviel; the ephemerally "shimmering," "glistening" beauty instantly gives up flight and falls into his arms (*Lord* 204). Aragorn captures Arwen's heart (and loses his own) by singing the "Lay of Lúthien": "[H]e halted amazed, thinking that he had strayed into a dream, or else that he had received the gift of the Elf-minstrels, who can make the things of which they sing appear before the eyes of those that listen" (*Lord* 1058; appendix A). The gift of words becomes a sign of virtue.

What about more modern forms of magic? As professors devoted more to inquiry than enchantment, we found ourselves not as endowed with words as Tolkien's Elves, but we recognized the importance of drawing in students with little background in the humanities as well as those with only superficial interest in the course material. At the same time, we sought to teach some fundamental techniques for critical analysis. To this end, we followed our introductory lecture on Tolkien's life and works with a lecture on his songs, which are so formative for Middle-earth—Middle-earth is literally created through the music of the Ainur in *The Silmarillion*. Our students were surprised and charmed by audio recordings of Tolkien declaiming his verse. These recordings brought home the power of song and the oral tradition for Tolkien. They also demonstrated the power of language, especially the sung or spoken word, to inspire unique images in each listener's mind; this was no small thing for young people who might take for granted the blend of words and songs with digital imagery on *YouTube* or elsewhere.

Once we had captured our students' attention with these recordings, we moved on to discuss the idea of song as power, as in Bombadil's ability to sing Old Man Willow into submission, the musical ethnography of the various peoples of Middle-earth, and how song unites these peoples, most notably in the sense of loss they all share. The many laments for lost comrades, places, and wives (the Entwives, in particular) point to the author's own nostalgia for a lost time and place, Britain before the Great War.

When exploring Tolkien's language and that of his influences in more detail, we found *PowerPoint* to be invaluable. To many students' dismay, we avoided outline-style *PowerPoint* presentations, encouraging them to listen carefully and decide for themselves what to include in their notes. Instead, by projecting specific passages of text, we engaged in the old-fashioned, but still illuminating, practice of explication de texte. This close reading technique was unfamiliar to most of our students, who were used to reading for information rather than for style. We emphasized ways in which style could actually create content, such as the naturalness implied by Bombadil's vernacular. To illustrate this point, one slide reproduced several key quotations from Bombadil's encounter with Old Man Willow. We showed how by eschewing modern grammatical convention ("I'll freeze his marrow cold, if he don't behave himself," "What be you a-thinking of?" [131]) Bombadil demonstrates his independence from the norms of polite society.

PowerPoint enriched our lectures in other ways. For example, images of familiar cinematic monsters set the scene for my lecture on Tolkienian monstrosity. *King Kong* (1933), *The Invasion of the Body Snatchers* (1956), and *Alien* (1979), which have collectively spawned numerous imitations, remakes, and sequels, helped me illustrate Tolkien's self-professed "profound desire" for monsters ("On Fairy-stories" 64) as well as his contention that monsters are "mortal denizens of the material world, in it and of it" ("Beowulf" 20). In this lecture, I discussed how King Kong embodies the fear of our bestial nature, magnified and dressed in the unselfconsciously racist trappings of the 1930s. Although they come from other worlds, the body snatchers and eponymous aliens are also uncomfortably close to home. The former lurk among us, almost impossible to distinguish from our closest friends—the only question is, when will we, too, succumb and become one of them? The aliens hide within our very bodies, destroying our semblance of humanity when they emerge in a hideous parody of birth, which leads us to ask, are we all monsters at heart? Tolkien's defense of *Beowulf* against charges by academics that its monstrous subject matter makes it not a "well-conducted epic" ("Beowulf" 13) applies equally well to these twentieth-century monster movies.

We also occasionally screened clips from the Jackson films as visual cues for discussing both specific moments in Tolkien's work and larger issues. One such discussion revolved around Jackson's interpolation of the story of Aragorn and Arwen into his larger narrative, a tale that Tolkien relegated to an appendix. By highlighting this scene, we were able to differentiate between Jackson's interest in telling a story with a bit of something for everyone, including what we might today call romance, and Tolkien's desire to separate more formal generic notions of epic, which he espoused, from romance, which he did not.

For budgetary reasons, our large lecture course did not benefit from discussion sections, but as much as possible we encouraged independent, critical thought in our students. One way we accomplished this was by example: in our collegial discussions at the podium, we eagerly interrupted one another with questions, observations, and occasional objections, and we also responded to one another also in follow-up lectures. We made a point to set aside class time for questions and answers between students and professors. At these times, we circulated through the hall, Oprah-style, with a mobile microphone, which brought us closer to the students and allowed them to hear one another's thoughts and queries.

Given the vast size of the hall, it was more challenging to establish student-to-student discussion, even with the help of the microphone. We had greater success outside class, in the strangely more intimate realm of cyberspace. We encouraged student exchanges by setting up a message board and weekly chat room through our university's course management system. This form of participation was purely voluntary, but students who chose to engage in it were enthusiastic. The chat room stimulated lively, though disjointed, conversation. More successful was the message board, which allowed students to post questions, ideas, and responses in a more deliberate way. Some students' posts were arcane (e.g., involving convoluted Dwarf genealogy), others more targeted (thoughts about Tolkien's background and ideas, as well as suggestions to classmates for further reading). Because of our large lecture format, the message board was the only official venue, aside from the moments before and after class, for students to engage in peer-to-peer conversation. We professors read and posted on the message board regularly, but the discussion there was student-led. Our only rule was that all exchanges remain respectful, and they all were.

Individual assessment was a challenge, given our student-professor ratio[2] as well as the fact that this was an overload or extra course for each professor. We offered the most motivated students the chance to complete an independent project to meet requirements for an honors option, which would appear on their transcripts. The project could be either academic or artistic. While several dozen students took this opportunity each semester, we still needed an effective way to evaluate the class as a whole. For the first time in our careers as literature professors, we devised multiple-choice midterm and final exams that could be graded electronically by our university's testing service—not an ideal solution, but the most realistic in our situation. I cannot imagine it working in a higher-level course (200-level or above), but it worked at an introductory level for nonmajors.

In creating the exams, we sought to evaluate students' knowledge of Tolkien and his sources, as well as their understanding of our lectures. We avoided gotcha-type questions on obscure details, focusing instead on key ideas covered in class, information from Tolkien's books not found in Jackson's movies, and information from our background readings. In the absence of *PowerPoint* lecture outlines, students had had to read, listen, think, and prioritize at home and during lectures.

The questions ranged from straightforward to complex. A basic informational question might read, "Which of these unpleasant residents of Middle-earth *do* sing? (a) the Balrogs, (b) the Wargs, (c) the Goblins, (d) the Trolls." The answer, choice C, indicates solid knowledge of *The Hobbit*; it also touches on an element from our early lecture on Tolkien's songs. Multiple-choice format allows little expression of independent thought, but as much as possible we encouraged complex responses. For example, we broadened questions away from the "a, b, c, d" format—"*Beowulf* Christianizes pre-Christian sources in much the same way as (a) Hesiod's *Theogony*, (b) the *Prose Edda*, (c) C. S. Lewis's Narnia

Chronicles, (d) both b and c." The correct answer, D, reflects an understanding of multiple sources. We also used analogy questions to evaluate students' mastery of the basics and their ability to draw connections between different sources and ideas. For example, "Odysseus is to Polyphemus as (a) Bilbo is to Smaug, (b) Frodo is to Aragorn, (c) Legolas is to Gimli, (d) Beren is to Túrin." The answer, A, reflects an appreciation of the relationship between a crafty wandering hero and the fearsome monster he defeats.

We built flexibility into the exam process, aware that designing multiple-choice exams was a new exercise for us and that multiple-choice exams had limits. Each exam was followed by a detailed discussion of the questions and answers during the next class meeting. Our goal was to encourage understanding and conversation about the content of the exam. Occasionally, students discovered a bug—for example, a place where more than one correct answer was possible but no choice allowed for this possibility. In such cases, we gave students credit for either answer and recalculated their scores accordingly. We welcomed such criticism, because challenging an exam set a great example for the class to think independently.

This practice was emblematic of our collaborative and adaptive approach to the course as a whole. We recognized the limits set by a disproportionate student-faculty ratio, but we also capitalized on our strengths. The combination of our knowledge bases made possible an unusually broad yet well-informed exploration. Our students regularly saw us professors learning from one another, even as we respectfully contested one another's arguments. Our conversation was theatrical, but also a real and intimate example of what intellectual exchange can be, even in the context of a large lecture class.

NOTES

[1]This essay could not have been written without the intellectual support of the two colleagues who made the course it describes possible. I thank Deidre Dawson, with whom I had the pleasure of teaching twice, and John Rauk, whose inspiration led to the creation of the original course. I refer often to our shared methodology but generally restrict discussions of content to my own lectures.

[2]The student-teacher ratio was roughly 100:1 in the 2004 class, 150:1 in later offerings of the class.

England's Mythmaker?
A Tolkien Learning Community

James R. Vitullo and Keith W. Jensen

A learning community at William Rainey Harper College combines two or more courses in different disciplines and is organized around a common theme; instructors usually attend and participate in one another's courses.[1] Our learning community incorporating J. R. R. Tolkien's works combined the courses Introduction to Fiction and Classical Mythology. Each course had different goals, but our work together for this team-taught approach centered on an exploration of Tolkien from two perspectives: the elements of fiction and the conventions of classical and Norse mythology. For Introduction to Fiction, the class read Josip Novakovich's *Writing Fiction Step by Step*, selections from Douglas Anderson's edited collection *Tales before Tolkien*, and Martin Greenberg's edited collection *After the King*. For Classical Mythology, we read Hesiod's *Theogony*, Homer's *The Odyssey*, Ovid's "Pyramus and Thisbe" and "Orpheus and Eurydice," *The Saga of the Volsungs*, and *Beowulf*.

The fiction component's aim was to train students to analyze the structure, plot, characters, and themes of Tolkien's works and selections of other authors to examine their modes of production and places in the literary canon. We used Novakovich's text to provide a process-based approach to writing fiction, because Novakovich combines a discussion of the elements of fiction with a variety of exercises, allowing students to implement the elements in their own writing. Imagining Tolkien's process of writing gives students tools for analyzing his work.

For the mythology component of the course, we studied Tolkien's works as myths that reflect the values and belief systems of the culture in which they were written. We examined how other scholars have defined *myth* in order to inform and supplement Tolkien's definition, and we framed our discussion of topics through a series of classical motifs found in Greek myths. These motifs which include the giving (and breaking) of hospitality, appearance versus reality, testing (of individuals and groups), and the home lost and/or regained—gave structure and flexibility to our exploration of Tolkien's texts, the work of his literary predecessors and successors, his critical essays, and other scholarly essays.

Each of these motifs is found in both classical myths and Tolkien's texts. The first motif, the giving and breaking of hospitality, was important to the Greeks because they tended to be wanderers and often had to seek shelter in foreign lands. If a wanderer found himself in an unfamiliar country at a stranger's house, the host of that house was expected to provide shelter, food, and clothing without asking questions about the visitor's origins. The host and guest became guest-friends and exchanged gifts. If the act of hospitality was broken, as with Odysseus in book 9 of *The Odyssey*, then Zeus, king of the gods, punished the violator in some way. Odysseus ate food and drink from the Cyclops's cave without being invited into the cave, and the Cyclops asked questions before offering hospitality. Both Odysseus and the Cyclops were punished for breaking the bond of hospitality, Odysseus through continued wearisome wandering and the Cyclops through his blinding.

We discuss the use of this motif in *The Odyssey* and then apply it to *The Lord of the Rings*, where hospitality is equally important. For example, Tom Bombadil offers shelter to Frodo and his companions before asking them questions about themselves or the outside world. This hospitality provides a much needed rest for the hobbits and prepares them for the next stage of their journey. The Bombadil episode allows the students to connect Tolkien's novels to their classical mythical heritage, but it also provides a point of departure, because Tolkien does not always follow the old conventions. For example, the hobbits and Tom do not exchange gifts as such; although eventually Tom gives them swords to use, they do not come from his home. We use the differences to explore Tolkien's purposes in using the motif.

The title of our combined course was England's Mythmaker? The Fantasy and Mythology of J. R. R. Tolkien. We began and ended the course with this question: Does Tolkien deserve the title of England's mythmaker? At the beginning, many students had opinions on the matter, but few of these were textually grounded. At the end of the semester, they were better informed about Tolkien's place in England's literary and mythological landscape. Most saw him as instrumental in the reenvisioning of English and American fantasy and as the literary grandfather of fantasy as an adult genre today. Most students saw Tolkien the mythographer either as a Don Quixote figure, a questing soul who desires something long gone into the mists of time, or as a man with an incomplete and unfinished vision. By framing our course with this question, we highlighted for students how Tolkien's power to speak to his audience stems from his ability to see the significance, largely ignored by critics, of what connects myth, fairy tale, legend, and literature.

In our Tolkien learning community, students earned six credit hours either toward an associate's degree or for transfer (we met twice a week for nearly three hours each class). This structure provided a unique opportunity to spend quality time with the texts, allowed us to assign a healthy amount of reading, sometimes as much as 150 pages per meeting. Understanding that this was a lot of reading, we decided that quizzes and tests would add undue stress and were unnecessary anyway, as we could monitor student involvement in reading because the classes were small. We required only a few formal assignments, emphasizing class participation and oral presentations.

For our class discussions, the short story collections provided useful reference materials for issues related to fiction, allowing students to gain a sense of Tolkien's place in the literary canon of fantasy authors in early and contemporary eras. Anderson's *Tales before Tolkien* contains writers who may have influenced Tolkien or were the forerunners of contemporary fantasy, while Greenberg's *After the King* contains authors whom Tolkien influenced. We used these stories, as well as Novakovich's work, to help us answer such questions about fiction, Tolkien, and fantasy as, Why do we still read these works? How are we affected by stories of people and places so removed from our own culture? What can we learn from them? It became obvious that students responded to some of these stories but not all. We tried to determine what qualities made these stories resonate or not. Students found that Terry Pratchett's "Troll Bridge" in *After the King* dealt, humorously, with celebrity culture, tensions between rural and urban societies, a traditional versus a modern way of life, and progress as represented by industrialization. Most of the discussion was about Pratchett's idea that old things are worth remembering (43), which students recognized as agreeing with Tolkien's sentiment.

In *Tales before Tolkien*, John Buchan's "The Far Islands" contains elements evocative of Tolkien: the resemblance of the protagonist to Aragorn; the idea of the story's gift giving, similar to gift giving among the Elves; and the protagonist's departure for the Far Islands, similar to the Elves' departure from Middle-earth. This reading linked well with the last three chapters of *The Return of the King*, where Frodo discovers he cannot feel at home again and must depart to the Grey Havens. But students considered the ending of "The Far Islands" abrupt and unsatisfying. Other tales in the same collection, such as George MacDonald's "The Golden Key" and James Branch Cabell's "The Thin Queen of Elfhame," disappointed many, who saw these texts as too esoteric, complicated, or unfinished.

Our discussions of mythology began with an examination of definitions drawn from classical scholars. Walter Burkert, a noted expert on Greek religion, defines myth as "a traditional tale with secondary, partial reference to something of collective importance" for the community that preserved it and passed it down to future generations (23). We used Burkert's notions to contrast with Tolkien's "On Fairy-stories" and Michaela Baltasar's "J. R. R. Tolkien: A Rediscovery of Myth," which frames Tolkien's concept of mythology as subcreation in opposition to the theories of the noted folklorists Max Müller and Andrew Lang.

According to Baltasar, Muller's theory was philological; Müller believed that "myth was used to explain the phrases and proverbs resulting from the splintering of a parent language. In other words, myth came from 'a disease of language,' and stories existed merely as explanatory, or allegorical, devices used to alleviate anomalies" (20). Lang's theories "emphasized myth's relationship to anthropology" (24). Lang thought the study of myth assisted in "reconstructing the earliest stages of human life and culture, much as the fossil bones of a prehistorical creature could conjure up an extinct species" (Dorson 208). With regard to Müller, Tolkien felt that variances in language indicated the ability of myth "to create anew, not merely to retell or represent another story" (Baltasar 20). Tolkien himself says, "It is precisely the colouring, the atmosphere, the unclassifiable individual details of a story, and above all the general purport that informs with life the undissected bones of the plot, that really count"

("On Fairy-stories" 46). He disagreed with Lang's theories and "felt Lang's practice of reading mythology was incorrect and misleading because it turned the focus away from the story and centered instead on its potential role as a historical document" (Baltasar 26).

The four-motif approach to analyzing myth in Tolkien's texts proved productive. Hospitality was relevant to our discussion of book 2 of *The Fellowship of the Ring*. Unlike Odysseus from *The Odyssey*, who is granted hospitality in book 7 by Alkinoos, leader of the Phaiakians, without question, the Fellowship receives comfort and aid from the Elves of Lothlórien only after a period of suspicion. The differences between the texts allowed for interesting comparisons of this motif. That Tolkien did not give the Fellowship instant hospitality while Homer granted it to Odysseus suggested to our students the problems resulting from the sundering of races and the loss of trust in Tolkien's world.

Students found this four-motif approach a useful means of connecting classical myths and Tolkien's texts with northern European myths, such as *The Prose Edda*, *The Kalevala*, *Beowulf*, and *The Saga of the Volsungs*. They also established some clear links between Joseph Campbell, Carl Jung, and the four motifs, particularly in their ideas regarding the hero's journey and archetypal analysis. Brief lectures introduced these two authors, exploring Campbell's theory of the hero as expounded in *The Hero with a Thousand Faces* and Jung's theory of the unconscious mind and, with modification of his archetypes, its relation to literature. Since some students had read Campbell before, we added our own perspectives through lectures and asked students to apply Campbell's theories to Tolkien.

For both Campbell and Jung, Gandalf is a prime example of a mythical hero. He enacts Campbell's monomyth as the bringer of supernatural aid and as mentor to both Bilbo and Frodo in their respective tales. He also fits Jung's archetypes of threshold guardian, trickster, and herald. Gandalf is known to trick his foes into making mistakes, such as his use of voices to trick the trolls from *The Hobbit* into remaining outside in the sunlight. As teachers, we were aware that if this methodology had a weakness, it was that it overemphasized universality. But it helped students see connections by demonstrating an overarching unity in the depth and breadth of the works we read.

To supplement these discussions, both students and instructors reviewed a number of essays in Jane Chance's edited collection *Tolkien and the Invention of Myth*.[2] The essays compare Tolkien's writing with the mythologies that influenced it. Jen Stevens, for example, focuses on Ovid's "Pyramus and Thisbe" to explore the idea of eucatastrophe or the "joyous 'turn'" (Tolkien, "On Fairy-stories" 86), in Tolkien's story "Of Beren and Lúthien," from *The Silmarillion*. We used her method to analyze Ovid's "Orpheus and Eurydice," which is similar to Tolkien's tale. Lúthien's song parallels Orpheus's song in that each attempts to persuade Mandos or Hades, respectively, to release the singer's loved one. Instead of introducing these essays ourselves, we asked students to prepare oral presentations of them in connection with other assigned fiction.

The oral presentation assignment required each student to lead class discussion on one of the short stories from *Tales before Tolkien* or *After the King*, one of the selections from *Tolkien and the Invention of Myth*, Tolkien's "On Fairy-stories," or Tolkien's "Beowulf: The Monsters and the Critics." The student leader summarized the text, applied it to Tolkien, and prepared two questions for class discussion that allowed students to bring out their own ideas and knowledge. During these presentations, we acted as students ourselves and participated in the discussions with the rest of the class, while the student leader acted as teacher for the hour. Some presentations led to particularly meaningful discussions. The student who presented "On Fairy-stories" had read and analyzed Tolkien's essay before taking our class and provided insights that helped the other students make strong comparisons with other definitions of myth. We were fortunate: "On Fairy-stories" usually requires intensive explanation and summarizing for introductory students to understand it.

But some essays were difficult for students to understand well enough to discuss. Many had trouble with "Beowulf: The Monsters and the Critics," and we spent more time explaining the essay than analyzing it. Although this assignment required students to read select essays more carefully than they might have done otherwise, we both agree it might be more advisable to ask students to lead discussions on the works of short fiction, while instructors lead discussions on the criticism. Alternatively, we might first model an appropriate approach to reading, summarizing, and analyzing critical essays.

We also required students to keep a journal, write two formal papers, and complete a final project. The journal allowed students to test their ideas before writing their formal papers. The first formal paper required that students use "On Fairy-stories" and Baltasar's essay as guides for their analysis of Tolkien's use of myth in one of the tales of *The Silmarillion*; they were expected to use one definition of myth to explore the chosen story—Tolkien's definition[3] or a more traditional one as proposed by Burkert, Campbell, or others in Stephen Harris and Gloria Platzner's *Classical Mythology: Images and Insights*. Students needed to address a number of topics, including how well Tolkien followed the definition of myth and whether he expanded or narrowed it.

Our second paper had students work with *The Hobbit* and at least one short story from *Tales before Tolkien* or *After the King*. Students analyzed various elements of the stories (character, plot, description, structure, symbolism, etc.) and wrote on how these elements interacted with one another in *The Hobbit* and in the other story. Students either examined how the concepts of story or fairy story in their texts offered a useful medium for making a political statement or examined the relation of *The Hobbit* and the short story to one or more of our four classical motifs. They chose their element or elements of fiction to use as a lens through which to view the text. For instance, symbolism might be a lens to study Tolkien's love of nature, his use of animals such as the thrush and animal-related characters (e.g., Beorn) to further his conservational agenda. The students might contrast this symbolism with A. Merritt's "Woman of the

Wood," where the trees influence the protagonist, McKay, to kill human beings in order to preserve the woods. Tolkien had deep respect for nature, whereas Merritt, in this story, treats it with ambivalence and mistrust. To our great satisfaction, most students did well in both papers.

The final project combined the goals of both courses and allowed students to be creative: we asked them to pursue what interested them and not what they thought would interest us. Tolkien had to be included in the project, but they could make connections to other myths or pieces of fiction not discussed in class. They needed to make some arguable point, and it had to use at least seven sources, excluding the works of Tolkien, the myths, or other fiction. The project could take one of several forms: a formal paper (ten to fifteen pages); a multimedia oral presentation (twenty to thirty minutes); a Web site; or a creative project, such as a game, painting, or piece of fiction. In the case of a creative project, students were required to submit a rationale of at least five pages, defending the pertinence of their project to the spirit and intent of both courses.

During the semesters we taught the England's Mythmaker?, few students chose a traditional research paper for their final project, and the variety of creative projects was astounding.[4] Two projects that stood out were the creation of a Middle-earth cookbook and a detailed lesson plan for a unit called "Fantasy, Story, and Desire: Examining the Longing of the Heart for Another World," in which Tolkien figured heavily. The cookbook contained recipes for a variety of Shire delicacies—for example, seed cakes and beef stew—Beorn's honey cakes, and the Elves' lembas bread. This student prepared two or three of the recipes for the class to taste, including the lembas, which matched the film version in appearance if not the book version's description. The other student's lesson plan included lectures, handouts, reading assignments, exercises, and the rationale for each assignment. Other projects were board games, paintings, and film trailers and episodes.

Two criteria for assessing students' work in this learning community course were the ability to understand Tolkien's creative process and the ability to demonstrate how myths and other forms of fantasy fiction influenced Tolkien. The papers and project were the most important assessment tools, as each of these assignments required students to examine Tolkien's role as a mythographer and a fantasy writer and to use our course texts in a comparative framework. We encouraged students to develop close working relationships with their peers; the double class period, the small size of the class, and our emphasis on participation and collaborative work helped foster these relationships.[5] Our experiences taught us that a learning community is an invigorating and insightful vehicle for academic sharing and inquiry. The collaborative elements of the course allowed enthusiasm to spread among the students and instructors alike. By changing the standard classroom dynamic from a single instructor as the class's focal point to a cooperative community, responsibility shifted from the instructor to the community. We found this sort of collaborative teaching to be more organic and elastic as well. The organic side was seen in discussions but also in our recognizing the growth and needs of our students to take joint responsibility and in our freedom to direct the course in day-by-day, often moment-by-moment ways.

Collaboration in teaching is not without challenges. It may give each instructor a momentary rest now and then from writing, discussion, or other means of inquiry, but if the teachers are not in sync with one another, they may feel cheated when class time they think is theirs is used by a teaching partner. Although we each occasionally experienced this frustration, our students did not usually care about how much or little time each teacher spent on a subject, as long as to the teaching served the learning community.

One difficulty we experienced was fitting all the works of fantasy and myth needed into the constraints of a sixteen-week course. In addition, we had some transferability and enrollment issues that resulted from appealing to an audience too narrow for the combined courses' requirements. On the other hand, we knew the joys of running a collaborative teaching methodology: the camaraderie between student and faculty member, the chance to delve into certain works more deeply because of the concentrated focus, and the seminar-like qualities of the teaching. We later broadened our context to encompass a larger secondary world of subcreation ("On Fairy-stories" 37), by looking also at other authors who created new worlds—C. S. Lewis, Terry Pratchett, and J. K. Rowling. To that end, we still use "On Fairy-stories" and at least one major work of fiction by Tolkien as a foundation for exploring how myth helps authors create their fantasy worlds.

NOTES

[1]This definition is based on that of Gabelnick et al.: "A learning community is any one of a variety of curricular structures that link together several existing courses—or actually restructure the curricular material entirely—so that students have opportunities for deeper understanding of and integration of the material they are learning, and more interaction with one another and their teachers as fellow participants in the learning enterprise" (qtd. in Kilpatrick, Barrett, and Jones 3–4).

[2]These included essays by Stevens; Burns, "Norse and Christian Gods"; Dimond; Flieger, "Mythology"; West; Gay.

[3]Tolkien's definition of myth appears in Baltasar's essay and Tolkien's "On Fairy-stories," and it is hinted at Tolkien's "Beowulf: The Monsters and the Critics."

[4]While we both had taught courses providing creative options for final projects, our experience had been that only truly motivated students opt for creative pieces. Most students find a research paper structure easier to follow.

[5]Out of practicality, we assigned one grade to both classes. Each instructor graded one paper and allowed responsibility for the grading of the journal to alternate but collaborated on grades for all other assignments. This arrangement freed up one instructor's time to focus on teaching and less on grading, which improved the course experience.

"[T]hings That Were, and Things That Are, and Things That Yet May Be": Teaching Tolkien's *The Lord of the Rings* Online

Judy Ann Ford and Robin Anne Reid

In fall 2008, we offered an online graduate-level course at Texas A&M University, Commerce, titled simply Tolkien. The class was a team-taught interdisciplinary exploration of *The Lord of the Rings* offered by the History Department and the Department of Literature and Languages. We embarked on the somewhat daunting project of an interdisciplinary, team-taught, online graduate class because we had a variety of relevant background experiences. Judy Ann Ford is a history professor specializing in the Middle Ages, especially religious and social history with a particular focus on England, while Robin Anne Reid, in literature and languages, has expertise in critical theory and creative writing. Before designing this course, we had team-taught offline courses on J. R. R. Tolkien at both the undergraduate and graduate levels. Moreover, we codirected the first National Endowment for the Humanities Summer Institute for School Teachers ever funded on *The Lord of the Rings*. Students for our online Tolkien course earned graduate credit in either history or English; assignments and expectations for the history students and the literature students were identical. We used the paradigm of adaptation to structure the material, examining how Tolkien adapted medieval and modern material for his novel and how adaptations of his work subsequently formed the basis of the modern genre of fantasy in books and film. We also chose to develop the course through three overlapping frameworks: history, popular culture, and gender studies.

The course's interdisciplinary nature was challenging to the students. In our previous offline Tolkien courses, we noticed that students tended to sit grouped together by department. History majors wondered why we included so much discussion of plot and structure, while literature majors questioned the need for so much discussion of dates and chronology; both views showed the extent to which even undergraduates internalize and naturalize the conventions of their disciplines. In the online graduate course, our solution to the tendency of students to take a disciplinary perspective was to foreground the class as interdisciplinary from the start: we explained that the material would not be taught as it would be in a graduate course in a single discipline. Unable to assume common knowledge in this approach, we provided glossaries and background lectures on methodologies, as well as lectures reflecting our collaborative work, which incorporated information about disciplinary differences and assumptions and how these affect scholarship. Audio lectures accompanied by slides were an important element of instruction, as were threaded online discussions among students. We tried to make visible the invisible assumptions that can lead to confusion in interdisciplinary settings and encouraged students to talk with one another across disciplines.

The interdisciplinary nature of our students influenced the major writing assignment, which was a thesis-driven paper analyzing some element adapted by Tolkien into *The Lord of the Rings* or some element used in an adaptation of the novel into another work, such as Peter Jackson's film version. For this paper, students were given the choice to work in their own disciplinary perspective. We expected them to apply the methods we modeled during the course and to focus on analysis rather than evaluation. Because we both believe in a process method of writing, students kept a journal throughout the term. They also submitted drafts of a formal proposal as well as drafts of the paper for instructor feedback. As with all other aspects of the course, our grading was collaborative.

Some might find it counterintuitive that a class focused on *The Lord of the Rings* would earn college credit in the discipline of history, the study of "things that were." After all, the central text is not only fictional but also set in a time and place not easily identifiable as belonging to the past of our planet. Yet the reluctance of some instructors to use *The Lord of the Rings* in history courses is founded on two misconceptions. First, because Tolkien's best-known academic works, such as his studies of *Beowulf* and his translation of *Sir Gawain and the Green Knight*, are usually found in literature courses, Tolkien is remembered as having been engaged solely with medieval literature. That impression is inaccurate, because he was a historical philologist who studied a wide variety of documents from medieval history, such as chronicles, political treatises, lists, and religious texts. He produced an edition of the *Ancrene Wisse*, a book of advice for anchorites typically studied by scholars of religious history (*English Text*). Because of his familiarity with the kinds of texts used by historians, he had the knowledge needed to infuse his fiction with diverse aspects of medieval culture. Second, the field of history is often envisaged as being exclusively rooted in specific events. In actuality, the field includes the history of ideas, institutions, religious beliefs, and cultural practices. Historians look to *mentalité*—that is, to a shared understanding of the world held by people of a specific time and place—to explain how people in the past behaved. In other words, they decipher historically contingent motivations. Tolkien embedded in *The Lord of the Rings* aspects of medieval *mentalités* concerning power, government, virtue, gender, and other issues. As well as being a novel, *The Lord of the Rings* is an interpretation of medieval cultural constructs propounded by one of the leading medievalists of the mid–twentieth century; essentially, it is a secondary source on medieval Europe.

The idea that *The Lord of the Rings* can serve as a secondary source about the Middle Ages motivated a number of our course assignments throughout the semester. In order to communicate the breadth of Tolkien's background as a historical philologist, we assigned Peter Gilliver, Jeremy Marshall, and Edmund Weiner's *The Ring of Words*, which explores his two years of work on the W section of the *Oxford English Dictionary*. Additionally, Tolkien's training and influence as a medievalist was conveyed, in part, by assigning the section on Tolkien in "The Oxford Fantasists" chapter of Norman Cantor's *Inventing the*

Middle Ages. Later in the course, in conjunction with our reading of book 6 in *The Return of the King*, we shared with the class a paper we coauthored, titled "Councils and Kings: Aragorn's Journey towards Kingship in J. R. R. Tolkien's *The Lord of the Rings* and Peter Jackson's *The Lord of the Rings*," which investigates how Tolkien incorporated medieval ideas of kingship into Aragorn's narrative arc (Ford and Reid).

The Lord of the Rings fits the study of history not only as a secondary source on medieval Europe but also as a primary source for the historical context in which Tolkien developed and wrote the novel—that is, England during the early twentieth century. He composed elements of the history of Middle-earth as early as his service in World War I. The idea that his novel can serve as a primary source for early-twentieth-century Britain was communicated to our students through a combination of materials related to the war. We assigned John Garth's *Tolkien and the Great War*, which analyzes Tolkien's construction of Middle-earth as a reflection of his time as a soldier in the war. During the two weeks in which students read Garth's study, they heard an audio lecture on the war that was accompanied by photographs of trench warfare. They also participated in threaded discussions on Tolkien, war, fairy stories, and Garth's description of Tolkien as "the most dissident of twentieth-century writers" (40).

As a capstone for using *The Lord of the Rings* as both a primary and secondary source for history, we gave a lecture near the close of the semester using war as a case study. We contrasted the experiences of Aragorn and his companions in books 3 and 5 with those of Frodo and his companions in book 4, presenting the former as more reflective of medieval armies and the latter as more representative of soldier's lives during World War I. Our students had little difficulty recognizing the contrasting presentation of the medieval and the modern in Tolkien's depiction of war.

The integration of Tolkien's popular novel into the canon of traditional literary studies has been the subject of contention. Since the middle of the twentieth century, the notion of a literary canon has been transformed considerably to reflect cultural changes, such as the civil rights movements, and intellectual changes, including the developments of postcolonial, queer, and critical race theories. In our course, we made no attempt to convince the students that *The Lord of the Rings* was good literature. Instead, we focused on problematizing the notion of a literary canon. Many literature students, having internalized the view that a merit-based hierarchy of fiction was natural, were resistant to calling that hierarchy into question, while most of the history students had never thought to consider any one source as intrinsically more valuable than another and so found the idea of a literary canon perplexing. To deal with the complicated issues of canonization, we assigned Tom Shippey's *J. R. R. Tolkien: Author of the Century* along with three reviews of it from academic and general periodicals. We included an audio lecture on how canons of literature have changed over time in response to what academics decide is worth researching and teaching. Foregrounding the hostility to Tolkien's work expressed by some modernist critics, we asked the students, many of whom were training to become teachers in high school or college, to consider the ways in which a text becomes canonized—that is, comes to be considered good literature that people should study. Our exploration of literary canonization formed part of our second overlapping framework, that of popular culture.

The framework of popular culture, as the "things that are," extended the paradigm of adaptation beyond Tolkien's incorporation of medieval and modern materials into his fiction to consider how others adapted that fiction—the film adaptations, the adaptations by other authors into the modern genre of fantasy, and the adaptations into visual and creative media. In an audio lecture on adaptation terminology and methods, we stressed that most film adaptation theorists currently argue that asking how well a film adapts a novel is less useful than asking what of the novel was adapted, how it was adapted, and for what purpose. The theorists contend it is necessary to understand that both a novel and a film are affected by a variety of historical and social factors. We provided examples of how this approach might be used to analyze Jackson's *Lord of the Rings*. Jackson decided to present, through narrative action and Galadriel's voice-over in the film's prologue, events that Tolkien embedded as part of Gandalf's exposition to the Council of Elrond. Where Tolkien chose to withhold knowledge of early events until later in the narrative, Jackson used chronological order. We compared the film's lighting-of-the-beacons scene with the short description of the same event described through Pippin's eyes in the novel. A second audio lecture drew on a collaborative essay we were writing, titled "Into the West: Far Green Country or Shadow on the Waters?," which compares the endings of the book and film, paying special attention to cinematographic elements often downplayed in analysis focused on literary elements.

In the adaptation discussion, students analyzed how one of their favorite characters and scenes was adapted from the novel into the film. They were asked to focus on what was changed in the adaptation and what was not, and why the changes may have been made. Additionally, we asked them to ignore external explanations, such as cost, in their arguments about how a specific adaptation shaped the narrative, theme, characterization, or some other element of the story. In another discussion, students were asked to consider how Shippey's phrase "two roads to Middle-earth" (qtd. in Jackson, *Fellowship*) may be used to describe the existence of both Tolkien's novel and Jackson's film version of *The Lord of the Rings*, implying that there are two ways to get to the same place. Such a conceit raises Tolkien's creation of Middle-earth beyond the level of a novel to that of a common cultural property (Santa Claus, for example) that may be employed by any number of storytellers in a great number of variations. For this discussion, students were asked to speculate on what it takes to make a fictional character, location, or narrative a common cultural property; whether the qualities are more intrinsic to the work or are the result of external circumstances (such as distribution); and finally, whether or not Tolkien's Middle-earth has reached the status of cultural property.

Our final framework, gender studies, a hint at "thing that yet may be," introduced a school of literary analysis that emerged after the novel was produced. Feminist literary criticism gave us the opportunity to examine Tolkien's female characters and his portrayals of masculinity and femininity, especially in *The Lord of the Rings*. The arguments relating to Tolkien and gender that we evaluated with our students ranged from accusations of the author's personal sexism and misogyny in relegating the women to such minor roles to arguments that, in the context of the spiritual themes of the novel, women's power is greater than many readers realize. Another argument that we discussed suggests that since Tolkien's work does not describe sexual relationships, it can be dismissed as a children's book.

We provided an audio lecture on gender issues in Tolkien's work that summarized the existing scholarship by feminist and gender scholars. As background for this lecture, our students read Edith Crowe's "Power in Arda: Sources, Uses and Misuses," which argues that the themes of Tolkien's work, especially in *The Silmarillion*, actually accord with some feminist values. Students also read David Craig's "'Queer Lodgings': Gender and Sexuality in *The Lord of the Rings*," which explores how masculinity is portrayed by focusing on the changes in the construction of masculinity in postwar Britain. The class discussed the favorable response of many women fans and scholars to how the film enlarged the roles of the women characters, attributed in part to the influence of Fran Walsh and Philippa Boyens, who cowrote the script with Jackson. Finally, we offered a stylistic analysis of descriptions of Tolkien's women characters, along with a handout analyzing how the text constructs agency as ascribed to female characters through making their names or pronouns the subjects of sentences.

Since the lecture and preparatory course materials focused on constructions of women and femininities in the work, students were asked to discuss masculinity in discussion threads about book 3, practicing methodologies presented in the assigned lectures and readings. They could also consider the influence of heroic ideas from medieval epic, which had been discussed earlier in the course. We asked that students include discussion of characters from at least two races of peoples from Middle-earth. They also had to draw on a combination of historical and linguistic methodologies to reflect the interdisciplinary nature of the course.

The graduate online version of our Tolkien course might be considered a type of thick description in that it introduced students to different analytic perspectives, including gender, popular culture, and history. Few courses focus on so small a subject as one novel by one author, but this focus allowed us the luxury to teach many critical approaches. That the object of analysis, *The Lord of the Rings*, was already familiar and, in many cases, already loved, eased but did not eliminate the cognitive dissonance of students being led to question the assumptions of an academic discipline they were in the process of mastering. Instead of simply applying approaches already mastered to new objects, students in this course enriched and deepened their graduate experience by learning ways of thinking they had not studied before.

Morals and Malice in Middle-earth

James Gould and Ted Hazelgrove

Students often perceive college courses as disconnected both from other disciplines and from their lives outside college. To address this perception, interdisciplinary learning communities at McHenry County College (a public community college in Crystal Lake, Illinois) seek to integrate the content of different subjects and relate theoretical perspectives to personal experiences.[1] For several years, we have taught a learning community course, Morals and Malice in Middle-earth, that combines two courses, Philosophical Ethics and English Composition. This codesigned and team-taught class, which typically enrolls thirty-five baccalaureate transfer students taking general education courses, is scheduled in two three-hour blocks per week. We have developed the entire experience collaboratively—readings, classroom activities, and assignments—and both of us are present during all classes. This interdisciplinary collaboration allows for a more penetrating and well-rounded unpacking of J. R. R. Tolkien's *The Lord of the Rings*.

In keeping with Tolkien's stated reason for writing *The Lord of the Rings*—"the elucidation of truth, and the encouragement of good morals in this real world" (*Letters of J. R. R. Tolkien* 194)—our course centers on the dominant themes of virtue and vice, good and evil. We read the work sequentially (about forty pages per class session), also assigning complementary philosophical readings. Our course stresses close textual interpretation, logical analysis, and personal application. In-class work consists of guided discussion and minilectures interspersed with short writing activities. Students prepare a set of papers, developed jointly to meet the objectives of both the composition and philosophy courses, and all writing assignments earn credit in both. In our two-step integration model of lesson planning, we first create a holistic content by blending the insights of philosophy and literature, then relate this content to students' lives through personal writing.

The first integration connects our two disciplines: philosophical concepts and theories are used as tools to examine and understand character and conduct in Tolkien's world. Plato's moral psychology, about how desire can come to dominate reason, clarifies Gollum's duality and Frodo's moral disintegration. We also apply Jeremy Bentham's utilitarian calculus for decision making, identifying alternative courses of action and weighing the consequences of each, to the Council of Elrond's deliberation about what to do with the Ring. David Ross's ethic of prima facie duty (especially in chapter 2 of *The Right and the Good*) helps class discussions explore Beregond's conflicting obligations and decisions to disobey Denethor, leave his post, and use violence to save Faramir's life.

In this essay, we illustrate our teaching practice with an account of how we consider, through the lens of moral failure, Boromir's treacherous attempt to seize the Ring from Frodo at Amon Hen. We begin by challenging the idea that people act immorally simply for the sake of doing wrong. Most believe they are doing good, or they yield to a powerful temptation. Our students read excerpts from Plato's dialogue *Protagoras* (351b–358d) and Aristotle's *Nicomachean Ethics* (book 7) that illustrate these points.

We discuss with our students a concept proposed by Socrates, that all practical decisions are determined by beliefs about what is good. For Socrates, if expected benefit outweighs possible cost, then we choose the action; if not, we avoid it. A person who concludes that a particular action is best will pursue it. Moral failure involves a mistaken perspective (an incorrect weighing of expected consequences) and insincerity (paying lip service to a principle without holding it as a personal conviction). Socrates' view, then, is that no one chooses to do evil knowing it to be evil.

We go on to show students that Aristotle partly agrees with Socrates that mistaken perspectives are the cause of evil. Aristotle writes that powerful temptation can make people unable to think clearly and may even drive moral convictions from conscious awareness. At the moment of temptation, the knowledge that a person doing wrong—like a sleeper's knowledge of a mathematical truth—is not actively in the mind. Nevertheless, Aristotle argues that, besides ignorance, another cause of wrongdoing can be weakness of will. Even though people can know right from wrong, strong passions may defeat their better judgment and willpower. Passions can interfere with both intellect (moral judgment about what is right) and will (motivation to do what is known to be right), making people unable to resist temptation.

We highlight these two main reasons for wrongdoing. First, moral failure can be caused by ignorance and faulty beliefs (people do not think their actions are truly wrong). Second, moral failure can be caused by weakness and faulty desires (people know that what they are doing is wrong but lack the control to act properly). We apply both reasons to Boromir's attempt to take the Ring from Frodo: we have students write a short in-class essay explaining Boromir's failure at Amon Hen by using either the ignorance or weakness theory and citing evidence from Tolkien's text to support their analysis. We give them twenty-five to thirty minutes to write, then invite several students to read their work aloud. In the following discussion, we move back and forth between issues of writing technique, philosophical content, and literary interpretation.

Students who argue for Boromir's ignorance point out that his attention is focused on the Ring's good uses rather than its evil uses. They frequently cite the fact that Boromir ignores Frodo's reminder of the council's conclusion: while the short-run outcome might indeed be beneficial, the long-term result of the Ring's use would be disastrous, since "what is done with it turns to evil." Boromir, these students note, proclaims his own moral strength: "True-hearted Men, they will not be corrupted. We of Minas Tirith have been staunch through long years of trial." He proudly imagines himself a distinguished warrior—blind to his own corruption. He asserts this vision of himself when he says:

> "The Ring would give me power of Command. How I would drive the hosts of Mordor, and all men would flock to my banner!" . . . [Boromir's] talk dwelt on walls and weapons, and the mustering of men; and he drew plans for great alliances and glorious victories to be; and he cast down Mordor, and became himself a mighty king, benevolent and wise.

Students observe that this mental rehearsal of the social and personal benefits of using the Ring hides its risks and makes him want it more. Desiring military strength in a just cause, he reframes the Ring as blessing rather than curse: "[I]t is a gift, I say: a gift to the foes of Mordor" (*Lord* 398; bk. 2, ch. 10). We linger on the term "gift," which implies something that is useful and good, that fate has providentially given, that must not be rejected but used dutifully and gratefully. "I *need* your Ring," Boromir says, stressing its use as urgent and necessary rather than merely desirable (399; emphasis added).

Frustrated at Frodo's resistance, he proclaims it unfair that Frodo possesses the Ring by accident rather than deserves it by merit, whereas he, Boromir, is justly entitled to it. Students conclude that his vision is clouded, perhaps by his responsibility as a warrior to save Gondor, so that he misjudges the situation. The belief that his good-sense plan offers victory while Frodo's "folly" ensures defeat makes him unable to see beyond the immediate benefit of using the Ring. Boromir, students argue, made the same argument at the council. Although not convinced by Elrond's correction, he submits to his authority (267; bk. 2, ch. 2). As the Fellowship prepares to leave Lórien, Boromir says it is "folly to throw away" the Ring (369; bk. 2, ch. 8). He has never been convinced the Ring is bad, has not recognized its danger.

Students not convinced by this argument explain Boromir's action as weakness. They argue that deep down Boromir knows the Ring is bad, but his desires to save Gondor and gain personal fame deactivate his knowledge. His lust is evident, these students point out, in the physical descriptions of him. On mention of the Ring at Amon Hen, he says, "Ah! The Ring!," which is followed by a description of "his eyes lighting" (397; bk. 2, ch. 10). Frodo catches a "strange gleam in Boromir's eyes" (398). Boromir's body language reveals increasing agitation as the Ring's very presence—its immediate availability—increases its attractiveness. He walks about "impatiently"; he strides up and down, speaking ever more loudly, the volume of his voice a barometer of his desire; he waves his arms; he imagines battle and victory, until "his eyes were shining and his face eager" with anticipation (398–99). When he touches the hobbit's shoulder, "Frodo felt the hand trembling with suppressed excitement" (399).

When Boromir realizes that Frodo will neither lend him the Ring nor accompany him to Minas Tirith, his frustration peaks: "How it angers me," he cries; his "face was hideously changed; a raging fire was in his eyes" (399). Finally, unable to control himself, he lunges at Frodo, intent on seizing the Ring by force. Frodo escapes, and Boromir returns to his senses, crying, "Come back! A madness took me" (400).

Students note that Boromir seems drawn to the Ring from the time he arrives in Rivendell. He is intrigued to learn it did not perish but survived Sauron's defeat. When Frodo first shows the Ring, "Boromir's eyes glinted as he gazed at the golden thing" (247; bk. 2, ch. 2). Thus begins "the dreadful change that the lure of the Ring had worked in him" (672; bk. 4, ch. 5). Indeed, students argue that those who know Boromir understand he has powerful desires. The Ring, Gandalf says, "was a sore trial for such a man: a warrior, and a lord of men"; Faramir concurs that it was too strong a temptation (496; bk. 3, ch. 5; 681; bk. 4, ch. 5). In addition, students note that we cannot forget the influence of the Ring itself, its ability to control individuals. As Gandalf warns Frodo, the Ring has "an unwholesome power that set to work . . . at once" (48; bk. 1, ch. 2). Perhaps "[i]t was . . . the Ring itself that decided things" when it came to Boromir, working on him until, like Gollum, "[h]e had no will left in the matter" (55). Boromir loses control when an external force, an impulse he is helpless to resist, defeats his knowledge that the Ring is evil and best destroyed.

Although all of us agree that Boromir acts without evil intent, in class one professor promotes the ignorance explanation and the other the weakness explanation. Students benefit by hearing our opposing points of view and different ways of exploring questions—the literary-interpretive and the philosophical-conceptual—to analyze a text.

As this example shows, our course integrates learning by pairing philosophical texts with specific passages from Tolkien's epic. In other classes, we examine the virtue of conscientiousness, the feeling that one must act in a certain way, by having students read selections on obedience to duty from Immanuel Kant (*Foundations of the Metaphysics of Morals*, ch. 1). We discuss Frodo's firm determination to do what is required—first to remove the Ring from the Shire to Rivendell and then to bear it to Mordor. We also study the virtue of integrity by reading excerpts from Stephen Carter and Lynne McFall, who propose that integrity involves having principles one will uphold even at great personal cost. Because these principles are identity-conferring, to violate them is to change who one is. We discuss how integrity relates to Tolkien's characterization of Faramir, who "would not snare even an orc with a falsehood" and "would not take this thing, if it lay by the highway" (644, 671; bk. 4, ch. 5). Faramir, a paradigm of integrity, offers a significant moral contrast to the pragmatism of his brother. We discuss the vice of despair and the virtue of hope, using analyses offered by Thomas Aquinas (*Summa Theologica* 2b q17, q22) and David Hume (*A Treatise of Human Nature*, chs. 2, 3, and 9). We consider Denethor's despair—his pessimistic, hopeless despondence and its fruit: apathy and neglect of duty—and contrast it with the hope exhibited by Gandalf, Aragorn, and Sam. Such philosophical resources illuminate and expand our understanding of the moral character and choice that permeates Tolkien's literary world.

Class grades are determined by three sets of papers. In the first set, students write four two-page papers, one of which follows our discussion of moral failure. They build on their in-class writing by creating a letter of confession in which

Saruman explains his moral failure to Gandalf as either ignorant or weak. The paper must quote from Plato or Aristotle and refer to what Saruman has said, thought, or done as recorded in the text. The other three papers are an analysis of Gollum's disintegration using Plato's moral psychology, an exploration of Théoden's transformation from submissive servant to self-respecting king, and a paper that argues whether or not Frodo failed in his mission to destroy the Ring. For the next set, students write two ten-to-twelve-page research papers. The first studies virtue or vice by tracing a quality such as courage, wisdom, or hospitality through the epic; the second analyzes the traits and choices of a character in Middle-earth. For the third set of writing assignments, students write two one-page journal entries each week. One entry each week must examine a passage from *The Lord of the Rings*; the topic for the other entry is open but must relate to a topic discussed in class. All student writings are expected to integrate insights from both philosophy and literature as these relate to Tolkien's work and to demonstrate basic academic skills of analysis, synthesis, interpretation, critical thinking, and effective writing.

The second level of integration in our course connects knowledge to life. One premise of our educational philosophy is that we are all in the process of personal character construction through the numerous decisions that both reveal and create who we are. Personal change requires moral knowledge, which we find in the exemplars of Middle-earth, as well as in an awareness of our own strengths and weaknesses.

In many class periods, we move beyond textual examinations of *The Lord of the Rings* to consider our own lives. We reflect on how the virtues and vices we encounter in the story's characters encourage good moral behaviors in us. For example, after dissecting Boromir's moral failure, we ask students to think of a time when they failed morally—examining it in the light of insights from Socrates, Aristotle, and Boromir. They write, often in a disarmingly honest way, about driving drunk, shoplifting, plagiarism, and vandalism. When discussing hospitality, we have them consider a time they went out of their way to help someone—ideally a stranger. One student bought household supplies for a new neighbor whose house burned down; another invited a lonely work colleague home for Thanksgiving. Sometimes we begin a class with one of these personal compositions. When examining trust, students write about a time they trusted or distrusted someone. After fifteen minutes of writing, we direct them to analyze what trust is, using their story to identify its elements. In discussion, they share memoirs and definitions as together we build a theory of trust, supplementing it with points from philosophy. We then examine the scene at Bree in which the hobbits consider whether to trust Strider. Personal writing reinforces and extends points from readings and discussions and connects theoretical knowledge to students' personal lives.

Tolkien's epic illuminates the dichotomy between good and evil inherent in the human condition and examines how individuals negotiate moral choice. In the analysis of the epic's lessons, philosophy and literature are natural allies.

Philosophy's role is to make ideas clear by sorting out concepts, examining arguments, and generating theories. Literature's role is to make ideas real by placing them in a specific context, such as showing vice and virtue in rich detail. *The Lord of the Rings* is thus an ideal foundational text, especially when joined with philosophical ethics, for—as was Tolkien's intent—elucidating truth and encouraging good morals in the real world.

NOTE

[1] Overviews of learning community rationale, structures, and outcomes can be found in B. Smith et al. and on the National Resource Center for Learning Communities pages on the Washington Center for Improving the Quality of Undergraduate Education Web site at Evergreen College (*Washington*).

Tolkien Immersion: Why a Three-Week Intensive Course Works

Cami D. Agan

The schedule of an intensive three-week summer course might seem to militate against quality discussion and, particularly, quality student writing, but my experience developing and teaching such a course actually results both in students' gaining a greater depth of knowledge about the works of J. R. R. Tolkien and in strong discussion that leads to effective writing as well as research. In Studies in Tolkien, a course that meets a three-hour literature requirement for our university, Oklahoma Christian University, students read, discuss, research, and write each day for five days a week about *The Hobbit*, *The Lord of the Rings*, and a large portion of *The Silmarillion*. After an introductory lecture on the author and the major social, cultural, and artistic shifts of his period, my seminar-style course uses student discussion and close reading to move ideas forward. As a result, the combination of longer class periods with more time for in-depth consideration of the texts, the summer schedule when students are often taking only one course, and the ensuing sense of community developed through daily contact combine to make possible more focused, energized, and effective study and thinking.

In my course the discussion and writing assignments will have the same aims as any upper-level English literature course. As the syllabus outlines, students are challenged to explore the ramifications of Tolkien's cosmology and to examine how his historical milieu, academic experience, and personal faith shaped his creation of Middle-earth. Students are encouraged to connect literary and theoretical terminology to the texts and to account for the cult-like popularity of Tolkien's work. A clear organization of the course into three week-long units, as well as specific assignments for discussion, writing, and research, are key to the course's success. Students read, in week 1, *The Hobbit* and *The Fellowship of the Ring*; in week 2, *The Two Towers*; in week 3, *The Return of the King*; and in each week, they read selections from *The Silmarillion*. As the weeks pass, students build on themes and ideas from earlier classes and thus develop an ever-expanding understanding of Tolkien's created world.

To motivate dynamic class discussions for each three-hour class, I organize each session into manageable sections based on directed discussion topics, which I e-mail to students the evening before to preview. For example, on the first day of class, students must arrive having completed *The Hobbit*. I have already sent them a greeting with discussion ideas they must be prepared to explore. Typically, these ideas or questions include both overarching concerns with the text—thematic, structural, narrative—and specific issues, which might ask students to read closely the "Riddles in the Dark" chapter, list symbolic objects in the novel, or point to character development throughout the novel.[1] Directing students to find passages to support their claims about such topics as Bilbo's growth from reluctant Baggins to adventuresome Took typically results in a discussion that is grounded in Tolkien's text. Advance preparation has several benefits: students are aware of the general focus of ideas for the day, they can prepare for those ideas as they read or reread, the sense of coverage of the novel increases with an organized mapping of its elements, and the process of my developing ideas for discussion models how I expect students to think as they approach research and writing.

This preview of discussion does not rule out the magic of digressions, spontaneous questions from the class, and intense focus on poetic or otherwise crucial passages. In contrast to a traditional fifty- or seventy-five-minute class, the three-hour period gives students and professor alike the chance to explore a digression in detail, to return to the previewed discussion ideas, and often to develop an idea on the spur of the moment. Even if students end up not covering every question they receive before the day's discussion (which often happens), the process itself signals essential moments, elements, and questions about the text that we build on as the class progresses. As a result, students truly feel they have spent an entire week discussing Tolkien's work when one three-hour class concludes.

Of the major writing assignments in the course, the mini research project most clearly connects the research that students complete outside class with the discussions we develop in class. The topics for this assignment cover a spectrum of concerns related to *The Lord of the Rings* or to Middle-earth in general, with the goal of offering a window into scholarly research related to Tolkien's world. Once students choose a topic from a list provided on the first day of class, they must write a three-to-four-page paper that provides their peers with an overview of scholarship about the subject and concludes with three to four discussion-oriented prompts for in-class exploration. I schedule these mini research projects throughout the course. At least two hours before meeting time, students must post their completed paper to an online *Blackboard* site for their peers to read before arriving in class. Such a practice enables students to come to class well prepared to examine the topic through the researcher's questions.

Topics for the mini research project have included Tolkien and World War I, Tolkien and modernism, race in Middle-earth, magic and immortality, Tolkien as eco-author, the Inklings and homosocial interaction, the nature of evil, and women in Tolkien.[2] On days mini research projects are scheduled, students know that for the first hour of class we will focus on what their fellow students have researched. Typically, students who prepared the research function as discussion leaders, answering questions about their topic, adding information not included in the short paper, and generally serving as the experts for the day. The project begins the process of research for students, allows them to explore the ongoing scholarly conversation about Tolkien's works, and makes them responsible for fueling discussion through that research.[3] As one student developed his mini research paper into his larger assignment, he was able to provide historical context for his assertion that "Tolkien rejected the promises of modernism and chose instead to highlight alternative values . . . increasingly difficult to find in his culture" (Norton 2). This assignment thus introduces scholars, claims, critical methodologies, and potential problems into our more textually focused exploration.

My students also complete a traditional research paper, which is organized into two stages. For the first stage, students write a short thesis paper (five to seven pages) that proves a specific claim about Tolkien's texts, using only his work, fiction and nonfiction, to support it. Because students cannot rely on scholars to flesh out ideas for them, these papers often reveal their organizational abilities and critical thinking skills. Ideas for topics emerge from in-class discussion, student reading for discussion, or from students' mini research topics. As we explore ideas in class, I point to connections, questions, and structures that are strong candidates for paper topics. Particularly at the undergraduate level, it is vital to signal students overtly about these possibilities (e.g., "Exploring the functions of weaponry and history would be a great paper topic"). To encourage early focus on the paper and to develop a communal sense of the writing process, I have students informally present their theses to the class and then comment on the ideas of their peers. Grading turnaround time is a challenge for the professor, as it is crucial to return thesis papers quickly to give students enough time to develop ideas into full-blown research papers.

The short thesis paper will eventually expand into an eight-to-ten-page research paper (it must contain a minimum of ten scholarly sources). Of the writing assignments for my course, this project is the most difficult: the availability of quality online peer-reviewed source material has improved, but students must still locate, read, analyze, and integrate research into their writing in a little over a week's time. However, they are aware of this time crunch from the moment they begin their short paper and thus even at that point should be working steadily to gather and organize scholarly material.[4] The pressure does not render impossible the critical thinking and research that semester-long courses nurture and that we literature teachers find invaluable. Because students so often produce much of their work at the last minute, a three-week course at least shortens the time for such procrastination after the actual discussion in which the ideas emerged. Note too that literature majors in particular often see such an intensive summer commitment as less demanding than a typical semester's deadlines, which may include four upper-level research projects all due in the same week.

The research my students have completed for Studies in Tolkien has been some of the finest I have read for upper-level literature courses. Whether it is due to the intensity and focus of the course, the enthusiasm students have for the subject matter, or the lack of other social and university activities to distract from the writing, my students tend to produce effective, scholarly, and original research on various aspects of Tolkien's texts. Moreover, past students have also built on their work for the intensive course to submit for graduate applications, conference proposals, senior capstone presentations, and student colloquium presentations.

To provide additional context to discussion and research, I assign Tolkien's letter to his publisher Milton Waldman, printed in the second edition of *The Silmarillion*, as a passage into the mythological text. This letter, detailing the scope, thematics, purposes, and peoples of the entire legendarium, gives students a greater conception of Tolkien's creative process. Most significant, the letter introduces the notion of subcreation, which is so crucial to Tolkien's worldview and which students then recognize in the opening passages of *The Silmarillion*. In addition, Tolkien's letter reveals the purposes for the creation of Middle-earth and other central concerns for *The Lord of the Rings*, such as his distaste for allegory (xiii), his initial desire to write an epic for England (xii), his claim that "[t]here cannot be any 'story' without a fall" (xv), and his admission that his creation grew out of love of language and myth (xi). In many ways, the letter to Waldman raises the big questions we explore throughout the course, such as, Why is a fall central to story making? What is the nature of choice and freedom? How can good overcome seemingly insurmountable evil? Why is Tolkien so attentive to landscape? Why and how do Third Age characters make allusions to past times and places? What is the role of the divine in the workings of the Free Peoples?

As students begin to consider ideas for writing and research, they move from reading Tolkien's letter to his publisher to reading, each Thursday and Friday, portions of *The Silmarillion*, roughly forty-to-fifty-page segments per day, including the "Ainulindalë," "Valaquenta," and "Quenta Silmarillion." Breaking up Tolkien's cosmological and specifically Elven material adds to the course in several ways. The segments from *The Silmarillion* mitigate students' complaints that the text is dry or boring. Reading the legendarium in this way allows them to make direct connections between the Elven mythical and historical material and the more familiar episodes, characters, and details in *The Lord of the Rings* and *The Hobbit*. Thus, while Roy Rhodes sees that "Bilbo resolves his journey by contemplating the changes within himself and articulating them through art" (8), he must also note that such a process has been ongoing since the "Ainulindalë." Likewise, Angela Bebb's exploration of the Ring's destruction recognizes Gollum's ultimate role as part of a larger cycle, calling it "the greatest eucatastrophe since Eru Ilúvatar's revelation of snowflakes to the Valar and an abashed Melkor" (11). Reading *The Silmarillion* elevates students' understanding of Third Age characters, episodes, and themes, which results in broader treatments of Middle-earth in discussion and writing.

With its genealogies, vast scope, apocalyptic battles, layers of language, song, and elegiac tone, *The Silmarillion* gives students a more complete window into what Tom Shippey and others call the "depth" and authenticity of Tolkien's secondary world (*Road* 308). Students, despite their initial confusion with Elven names—"Why do they all begin with F?!"—soon grow convinced that Tolkien's world as embodied in *The Lord of the Rings* remains only partially constructed for readers unfamiliar with *The Silmarillion*. They note the interconnectedness of the texts—for example, Beren and Lúthien's tale parallels that of Aragorn and Arwen—but they also recognize the sacred, historical, and mythic nature of the Elf-centric texts for the inhabitants of Tolkien's secondary world. As a result, the chapter "Of Beleriand and Its Realms" grows from a ponderous listing of names and places long gone and dissociated from *The Lord of the Rings* into an Exodus-like document, read, memorized, cited, and sourced as wisdom for the Peoples of the Third Age. "Through characters' exposure to legends and stories," Julia Kaissling argues after reading these First Age accounts, "they become aware of their own participation in a legend that is parallel . . . to those that have thus far shaped Middle-earth" (11). On the integration of First Age accounts from *The Silmarillion*, elements in *The Lord of the Rings*—the natural world, languages, song and story, and magical objects—rise to the level of divine creation and cosmogony. Students thus read the Third Age text back through the lens of *The Silmarillion* and recognize any moment of song as potentially resonant with divine power. As one student wrote, "Understanding that the creation of Middle-earth occurred through song elevates [songs in *The Lord of the Rings*] from a means of expression to a form of worship of the Valar and their accomplishments" (K. Long, "Language" 3–4).

By reading Tolkien's letter to Waldman and much of *The Silmarillion*, students experience the broader vision of Middle-earth so necessary to understanding the cosmological implications of the work. While adding yet more reading to a short course may appear daunting, each class consistently agrees that reading *The Silmarillion* makes for a better reading of *The Lord of the Rings*. For example, because students have read and discussed *The Two Towers*, their reading in *The Silmarillion* of Yavanna's creation of plants and animals, particularly her discussion of "the Shepherds of the Trees" with Aulë, can further illuminate Treebeard and the Ents' response to Saruman, can offer more potential readings of the ever mysterious Tom Bombadil, and can better inform Tolkien's general concerns with trees and the natural world in *The Lord of the Rings*. Such realizations lead to more fruitful and nuanced discussions in class, as well as better crafted written claims about the complexity of Middle-earth.

As they read, think, discuss, write, and revise their insights into Tolkien's world in the confines of a summer course, my students immerse themselves fully in the secondary world of Middle-earth. For those three weeks, as one former student put it, "we eat, think, and dream Tolkien" (K. Long, "*Blackboard*"). The immersion metaphor functions well to align the student experience of developing a comprehensive feeling for a new world with the process of language creation and acquisition so vital to Tolkien's initial conception and construction of Middle-earth. If Tolkien's Middle-earth is "a nexus of languages" (*Silmarillion* xi), students' appreciation for and aptitude in speaking Tolkien begins with their total immersion in his texts. As with immersion in a new language, immersion in Middle-earth results in a kind of Tolkien fluency for students, who by the final days of the course are able to converse in the language of his world as native speakers.

NOTES

[1]Other fruitful prompts for discussions on *The Lord of the Rings* include lists of central themes and image patterns, Tolkien's maps and geography, examinations of rest locations such as Rivendell, passages that flesh out the history of Middle-earth (e.g., the chapters "Shadow of the Past" and "The Council of Elrond"), studies of minor characters and their functions, links to literary genres and techniques such as the epic, and questions on the ways Anglo-Saxon or Norse details emerge in the story.

[2]Additional topics students have researched are languages and their function, Tolkien's creation myth, Tolkien and pop culture, Tolkien's medieval roots, and links between *The Lord of the Rings* and *The Silmarillion*. Topics no student chooses remain excellent options for discussion ideas.

[3]Because of time constraints, I allow students to use Web-based and more general sources for the mini research project. However, I remind them that scholarly peer-reviewed sources are usually available through databases and Web searches and that only peer-reviewed sources are acceptable for the larger research paper.

[4]I make available to my students folders of articles and chapters gleaned from my own research. I usually place all library holdings related to Tolkien on reserve. Putting material on reserve guards against students' hoarding books for themselves. The growing accessibility of online, full-text articles from journals such as *Mythlore* and *Tolkien Studies* also provide students with ample sources for research.

The Council of Elrond, All Those Poems, and the Famous F-ing Elves: Teaching the Hard Parts of Tolkien

Michael D. C. Drout

In the midst of the hype surrounding the 2002 release of Peter Jackson's *The Two Towers* film, I was a guest on NPR. One caller, the owner of a bookstore, said that for decades he had been telling people to skip "The Council of Elrond" in *The Fellowship of the Ring*: with that boring and confusing chapter out of the way, readers would enjoy the rest of the novel. I reacted with some shock. How would a reader understand the War of the Ring without the background laid out in this chapter? The later actions of Boromir, Denethor, Faramir, Théoden, Saruman, and others would make little sense, and the major plot device of the entire novel would become mostly incomprehensible.

But the bookstore owner's advice was not unique. Every time I teach my Tolkien course, I ask students if they have been told to skip "The Council of Elrond," and invariably a few say that a teacher, friend, or bookstore owner (I wish I knew if it was the same one) gave them this advice. Many students also have been advised—or chosen on their own—to skip the poems in *The Lord of the Rings*, and not many have read *The Silmarillion* because they have been advised to skip this "telephone directory in Elvish," where all the characters' names begin with the letter *f*. I sympathize with the plight of dealing with difficult and unfamiliar material in a course that from the subject matter seems like it will be fun and easy, but it is important that students understand "The Council of Elrond" chapter and the poems and that they know not only the reason why so many major characters in *The Silmarillion* have names starting with *f* but also how to keep these characters straight. I have, therefore, developed a few techniques for teaching these hard parts of Tolkien's work.

In "The Council of Elrond," Tolkien lays out the geopolitics of Middle-earth in the Third Age, explains that the Ring cannot be used as a weapon against Sauron because it will invariably turn the user and his deeds to evil, and develops the plan of sending the Ring to Mordor to be destroyed. As Tom Shippey notes, the chapter is extremely complex, with an interlacing of major voices (Elrond, Glóin, Boromir, Gandalf, Aragorn, Legolas), minor voices (Bilbo, Aragorn, Galdor of the Havens, Erestor, Glorfindel), and reported voices (Dáin, Sauron's messenger, Radagast, Denethor, Saruman, Gwaihir, Gaffer Gamgee, Butterbur) establishing the novel's historical background (*Road* 90–93). Simply following the changes in speaker and discursive style can be difficult; extracting the important information is a greater challenge.

My solution is to connect geopolitics and history to personalities in order to allow students to focus on the "who wants what and why" problems they are familiar with from more ordinary literary analysis. I assign students roles representing the characters present at the Council and also other "stakeholders" of Middle-earth. Sauron and Saruman are included, as are kings Bard and Dain and Steward Denethor. Gollum also makes an appearance, as does Tom Bombadil.[1] Students are not allowed to memorize lines for their parts, and we do not act out the Council as it is written. Instead, I assemble all the players at the front of the room with large name cards set in front of them and then take on the role of moderator (my students nicknamed this enterprise "Jerry Springer Goes to Middle-earth") and proceed through an agenda:[2]

1) Is Frodo's ring the One Ring?
   a) How do we know?
   b) Who has a legitimate claim on this Ring?
2) If it is the One Ring, what should be done?
   a) Wield it as a weapon against Sauron.
   b) Send it over the sea.
   c) Send it to Tom Bombadil for protection.
   d) Keep it at Rivendell, Minas Tirith, or some other strong place.
   e) Try to destroy it in the Fire where it was made.
3) Who should do this, and how?

Working through this agenda, I call on individual characters ("Denethor, why do you think the Ring must come to Minas Tirith?," "Saruman, what's your reply to Elrond?"). As you can imagine, having Sauron and Saruman take part in these discussions strongly clarifies the geopolitics and history of Middle-earth. Sauron can put forth his claim to the Ring: it was made with his own technology and taken from him without trial or other legal proceeding, the Last Alliance was actually the aggressor in the conflict, and so forth. I have been fortunate over the years to have strong, knowledgeable students represent the evil characters. A good Saruman does not adopt Christopher Lee's generic evil wizard persona from the Jackson films but instead tries to make a reasonable case for why he could best serve Middle-earth, which usually amounts to providing "Knowledge, Rule, Order" (*Lord* 259; bk. 2, ch. 2).[3] Sauron can argue that the Elves and Númenóreans are doing a terrible job managing Middle-earth and that he will improve roads, bridges, and communication.

This exercise on "The Council of Elrond" clarifies the rules of Tolkien's secondary world, the details of the plot, and the motivations of many characters. Students often refer back to the individuals who played each role as if they still speak for Saruman, Denethor, or Gandalf: they now have faces to go with names and motivations. And students simply cannot complete the assignment if they skip "The Council of Elrond."

The case can be made that Tolkien's poems in *The Lord of the Rings* are the most widely read poems in twentieth-century English literature,[4] but such a claim must be tempered by the large number of readers who skip them. This tendency is unfortunate, because the "vast backcloths" (*Letters of J. R. R. Tolkien* 144) and depth so often praised in *The Lord of the Rings* are more evident in the poems than anywhere else in the text. A simple solution might be to give quizzes about the poems, but this approach rarely helps students understand the poetic material. So to give students some guidance, I have them treat the poems as evidence for literary forensics. Students must figure out where the poems have come from and why they appear where they do.

For this exercise to make sense, students need to understand the frame narrative of *The Lord of the Rings* and the ways the poems fit into this narrative. It is useful early in the course to direct students to the "Note on the Shire Records" at the end of the prologue (14–16), where Tolkien sets up the conceit that he is translating a copy of the *Red Book of Westmarch*. Although some readers are inclined to think of this Red Book as the big book with plain leather covers that Frodo gives Sam at the end of the novel (1026; bk. 6, ch. 9), that book was in fact Bilbo and Frodo's private diary, supplemented by three volumes of lore translated by Bilbo. One hundred years after the events described in *The Lord of the Rings*, however, several libraries with important historical books and records existed in the Shire, and these contained various copies of the Red Book, augmented with a volume of genealogies and other information about Hobbits. Some copies were further annotated and emended, the most important being the copy written in Gondor by the scribe Findegil and kept at the Great Smials in Tookland. Tolkien's "translation" of the Red Book is therefore not a translation of a unitary, single-authored volume but of a heavily annotated and varied compilation of sources. The inclusion of the many poems in the text of *The Lord of the Rings*, then, is not a strange failure in a realistic novel (how, one student asked, could anyone compose perfectly scanning and rhyming or alliterating poetry on the spot in the middle of a battle or recite poems in a language he does not speak?). Instead, the poems are much like the interlinear Old English version of Cædmon's Hymn that appears in various Latin manuscripts of the Venerable Bede's *Ecclesiastical History*, additions for the expansion or clarification made by writers different from the original author.

Keeping this frame narrative in mind, I ask students to prepare short forensic reports on each poem they encounter in their reading. For these reports, they are to list:

Title (or first line).
In-text speaker.
"Author" (if known and not the speaker).
Narrator's comments (for example, "The Mounds of Mundburg" was composed "long afterward" in Rohan [849; bk. 5, ch. 6]).
Original language (Common Speech, Sindarin, Quenya, Rohirric, etc.).
Formal characteristics, both rhyme scheme and meter (e.g., octosyllabic rhyming couplets or alliterative long lines)

Genre.
Provenance.

This last item in particular allows students some freedom of interpretation and moves the assignment beyond a simple report. I ask students to try to determine if any given poem was written (in Middle-earth) by a Hobbit, Dwarf, Elf, Man, or Ent; where it was likely written (the Shire, Bree, Rohan, Gondor, Lothlórien, Rivendell, etc.); and if it was written in the Common Speech or in another language and later translated. I encourage students to make cross-poem comparisons to justify their conclusions, pointing out, for example, that some similarity in form appears among Hobbit poems at the beginning of the narrative, so that when we encounter these forms later, we may want to attribute the poem to a Hobbit tradition. This discussion, which we continue as we encounter new poems, helps students link observations about form and genre with their reading of the narrative as a whole. Seeing the poems not only as compositions by Tolkien but also as elements in the complex textuality of Tolkien's work helps students better understand how what Gergely Nagy calls "the Great Chain of Reading" creates the characteristic impression of depth.

Teaching *The Silmarillion* is difficult for a number of reasons, most significant among them the prose style of the work and its lack of mediating figures (like the Hobbits in *The Lord of the Rings*). Since *The Silmarillion* is quite different from most literature with which students are familiar, a teacher needs to move slowly and carefully through the text, explaining Tolkien's purposes, pointing out intra- and intertextual relationships, and encouraging students to adapt their reading practices to the text. A quick fix to help students understand a work this distinct and unusual is unlikely, but at least one sticking point in *The Silmarillion*, keeping track of the confusing group of Elves whose names all begin with *f*, has a fairly simple solution. If students cannot keep these characters straight, important parts of *The Silmarillion* become incomprehensible, so clarifying the relationships among them is a valuable exercise. The problem of the f-ing Elves is a confusion that results from an unfamiliar system of nomenclature. A parallel with *Beowulf* is useful here, not only because it helps students see that the system is not capricious[5] but also because it highlights Tolkien's use of old traditions from the north and west of Europe. In *Beowulf*, a number of important characters have names beginning with *h*. Among the Danes, these are the descendants of Healfdane,[6] and among a different people, the Geats, the descendants of Hrethel.[7] Alliteration marks a family linguistically, just as last names mark a family today. Explaining this principle and asking students how they would indicate family relationships in their names if we did not use a binomial system shows them the underlying logic of the *f*-names in the House of Finwë.

But even if they understand that underlying logic, students still struggle to keep track of the various *f*-named Elves. As Shippey notes, although the audiences of Icelandic sagas were able to keep straight complex family relationships and understand the significance of pedigrees, past quarrels, and overlapping statuses (*J. R. R. Tolkien* 244), contemporary readers generally lack this cultural training. Thus the simplest way to help students keep these names straight is to explain the logic behind the naming system. (Note that I am here presenting a practical teaching method rather than going into detail of the meanings of the names within Tolkien's invented languages. Knowledge of the languages can make understanding the names easier, but the practicality of teaching Elvish morphology in a college course is not immediately obvious.)

We begin with the first king of the Noldor, Finwë. If we compare him with the kings of the other houses of the Elves (Yngwë of the Vanyar and both Olwë and Elwë of the Teleri), we note that having *-wë* at the end of a name correlates with a person's being a king. Each major house then combines that *-wë* with a key letter: *y* (and *i*) for the Vanyar, *f* for the Noldor, and *e* (and *o*) for the Teleri.[8] So the *-wë* indicates "first king," and the *Fin-* indicates Noldor, so the most significant of the Noldor, in King Finwë's family, will have *Fin-* at the beginning of their names. Therefore to make a name in the house of Finwë, you take *Fin-* and add syllables (Fingolfin, Finarfin, Fingon, Finrod, Finduilas).

Fëanor does not appear to fit this schema, but Fëanor's original name is "Curu-*fin*–wë," which both includes his father's name and keeps the suffix indicating that, as the firstborn son, Fëanor is supposed to become king in his turn. (Some of my students find the diaeresis in both Fëanor's and Finwë's names to be a useful mnemonic device.) Finwë's other sons, because they are not from the first marriage, are not supposed to become kings and so do not get the *-wë* suffix. Instead, Fëanor's half brothers have three-syllable names in the form Fin-x-fin: Fingolfin, Finarfin. Between the two *fin* syllables is a seemingly arbitrary syllable, *-gol-* or *–ar-*. Elements of these syllables, however, are carried over to the next generation, when the terminal *-fin* is dropped. The child of Fingolfin is Fingon, the child of Finarfin Finrod. Although the name of the last *f*-named character in *The Silmarillion*, the Elf-maiden Finduilas, does not fit this schema, she does have the "Fin" element in her name, and as she is the only female *f*-named Elf, readers may be less inclined to confuse her with other members of the house of Finwë.

Pointing out these naming conventions helps students keep track of which Elves are fathers, sons, uncles, and nephews of which other Elves, important information because these relationships are a driving force in the complex plot of *The Silmarillion*. The strife within the House of Finwë, for instance, is in part a result of Finwë's second marriage to Indis of the Vanyar, creating sons, Fingolfin and Finarfin, who by one set of criteria (as younger sons of the king) are inferior to their half brother Fëanor but by another are superior (they are half Vanyar, a higher-ranking Elf kindred than the Noldor). The dispossession of Fëanor's lineage—when the high kingship passes to Fingolfin (as oldest living son of Finwë after Fëanor's death) but then not back to Maedhros, the eldest son of Fëanor, but instead to Fingolfin's oldest son, Fingon[9]—is comprehensible only if we keep straight the relationships between characters and their context in a larger kinship system. Understanding this system begins with knowing all six of the *f*-ing Elves; their names and relationships are not trivial. To read *The Silmarillion* well, students need to approach characters and motivations differently than they are used to, and getting names straight is an essential first step.

Studying Tolkien is intrinsically valuable and rewarding, but it is also useful in building in students a new set of skills for interpretation and analysis. The three approaches to difficult problems outlined here are tailored to Tolkien's work, but they achieve what all good general literary pedagogy does: involve the students in the details of the text, make them active interpreters, take seriously the work being studied, and compare it to others. "The Council of Elrond" chapter, the poems, and the *f*-ing Elves may not seem the most significant elements of Tolkien's work, but if they are taught well, much else falls into place.

NOTES

[1]To best represent characters who only appear later in the *The Lord of the Rings*, I assign these roles to students who have previously read the novel.

[2]Shippey suggests that the Council can be read as a well-organized committee meeting (*J. R. R. Tolkien* 77).

[3]When, in my role as moderator, I asked a student playing Saruman in 2008 what he could offer to Middle-earth, he paused and then said, with a smile, "Hope and Change." I'm relatively certain that more than 90% of my class voted for Mr. Obama in that election, but it was still the single biggest laugh of the year—and insightful too, in a disturbing way.

[4]The claim is based on the number of copies of *The Lord of the Rings* that have been sold and the number of poems in the book.

[5]As is the confusion generated by having both villains' names in *The Lord of the Rings* begin with *s*.

[6]Healfdane's sons are Hrothgar and his brothers Halga and Heorogar. Hrothgar's sons are Hrethric and Hrothmund; his nephews are Heoroweard and Hrothulf.

[7]Beowulf's uncle, King Hygelac, is the son of Hrethel, the brother of Herebald and Hathcyn, the husband of Hygd, and the father of Heardred.

[8]Only a few Vanyar or Teleri are listed in the family trees at the end of *The Silmarillion*. Yngwë and Indis give me the *y* and *i* for the Vanyar, and Elwë, Olwë, and Eärwen the *e* and *o* for the Teleri. This is obviously a simplification, but sufficient for the purposes of this essay.

[9]This naming is paralleled by the naming conventions of the Danish ruling house in *Beowulf*.

Fellowship and the Rings: Intellectual Sociability and Collaborative Learning among Tolkien and the Inklings

Michael Tomko

Numerous biographical elements might suggest that J. R. R. Tolkien was a twentieth-century version of the lone Romantic genius, a Blakean creator who built his myth in isolation, working as much for himself as for England. From this perspective, Tolkien might be envisioned as the convalescing veteran starting the mythography of *The Silmarillion* in a hospital bed, or the exhausted scholar scribbling Bilbo into life amid a pile of exam papers, or even the strained professor and family man diverting his lucubrations to the making of Middle-earth (Carpenter, *J. R. R. Tolkien* 100, 175, 192–93). It is not without reason that W. H. Auden found *The Lord of the Rings* a quest focused primarily on "the subjective life of the individual person" ("Quest Hero" 51). Such subjective individualism, however, must be weighed against the pervasive collaboration that characterized Tolkien's life and art. In Middle-earth, isolation tends to be a necessary evil at best, even when endured for a heroic cause. Both the "ruin" of the Fellowship (*Lord* 414; bk. 3, ch. 1) and the traumatized psychological distance of Frodo of the Nine Fingers are regrettable. Worse, the separated self is often synonymous with a malignant will to power—as in Boromir's solipsistic lecture (398; bk. 2, ch. 10) or Sauron's representation as an elevated single eye. Tolkien's own dedication to fellowship was manifest in the Tea Club and Barrovian Society or TCBS, the youthful club of creative friends whom he would lose in World War I; the Coalbiters' donnish gatherings to revel in Icelandic legend and language; and the philosophical, theological, and literary discussions in Oxford's Eagle and Child pub among the Inklings, the group of friends that included C. S. Lewis and Charles Williams (Carpenter, *J. R. R. Tolkien* 53–55,125–26; Glyer 9–12, 16–20).[1] Scholarship such as Colin Duriez's *Tolkien and C. S. Lewis: The Gift of Friendship* and Diana Pavlac Glyer's *The Company They Keep: C. S. Lewis and J. R. R. Tolkien as Writers in Community* emphasizes the integral role of sociability in Tolkien's formation, intellect, and literature. Indeed, Tom Shippey has labeled the convivial debate of topics that passed into fictional form as "Inklings conversation" and identified this collaboration as one of the major critical categories to which Tolkien scholars must attend (*Roots* iii).

Yet such a vital and collective category is difficult to bring into both research and teaching. Our scholarship often abstracts an author, reducing a thinking, smoking, developing, drinking, arguing person into a discrete set of ideas, patterned stylistic tendencies, and stabilized historical contexts. Our pedagogical approaches tend to reinforce this view through quantifiable essay assignments that atomize students who had enrolled in the same course to pursue a common interest and a common set of questions. While the exigencies of introducing material and evaluating students cannot be ignored, teaching Tolkien presents a unique opportunity for extending intellectual sociability to the classroom. In my classes, I attempt to restore Tolkien to his company and, in so doing, to create intellectual fellowship among my students through what I call pub groups, collaborative small groups that not only present on but also engage in "Inklings conversation."

Teaching Tolkien in a course on the otherworldly fantasy literature of the Inklings naturally foregrounds his intellectual and creative interactions. Constructing such a syllabus is not an easy task, however, as the epic scale of *The Lord of the Rings* results in Tolkien's dominating the second half of the semester. Yet the ostensibly self-enclosed secondary world of Middle-earth seems more permeable when preceded by units on Tolkien's steadfast friend Lewis and his sometimes adversarial interlocutor Williams. In my class, Lewis's fiction is represented by *The Great Divorce*, *Till We Have Faces*, and either *Perelandra* or *The Silver Chair*, while for Williams we read *Descent into Hell* or *All Hallows' Eve*. These works raise questions about the status and purpose of their fictional worlds and explore the spiritual and moral dramas of characters inhabiting them. An introductory unit on the Inklings' forebears and influences provides a theoretical framework for addressing these issues as we read G. K. Chesterton's chapter on the "ethics of elfland" from *Orthodoxy*, Dorothy L. Sayers's discussion of analogy in *The Mind of the Maker*, and George MacDonald's essay on the dignity of the "fantastic imagination." As a result of this curriculum, the first pages of *The Lord of the Rings* open in medias res not only of the Third Age but also of the recurring questions that formed "Inklings conversation." Do fantasy worlds merely indulge an escapism that dodges the hard realities of politics and history? Or do these otherworlds seek a higher reality, which is spiritual, transcendent, and perhaps more real? Even if so, how should religion and art's common project of going beyond what Tolkien rejected as "the domination of observed 'fact'" ("On Fairy-stories" 69) and what Lewis dismissed as a world of "all fact and no meaning" ("Transposition" 19) be viewed in the light of the critique of their otherworldly evasiveness?

These interdisciplinary questions involve literary criticism with aesthetics, moral and political philosophy, and theology in a way that the Inklings often practiced within the walls of the Eagle and Child. My course, first taught in the religion and literature program at the University of Notre Dame, has continued to flourish in Villanova University's interdisciplinary humanities department, which offers a major designed to guide students through the great questions about God, nature, society, and the human person. To enable humanities majors to see how the Inklings approached these topics and how their fiction was inflected by their responses to these questions, my syllabus pairs their fictional work with shorter, related theoretical essays. For Lewis, I include pieces such as "Myth Became Fact," "Weight of Glory," selections from *Preface to* Paradise Lost, "Transposition," "On the Reading of Old Books," and "Meditations in a Toolshed"; for Williams, I include the chapter on substituted love from *He Came Down from Heaven*. The essay "On Fairy-stories" (subdivided into three installments assigned over the second half of the semester) is the essential work from Tolkien, but we also look at "Mythopoeia" as well as *The Adventures of Tom Bombadil*, which I pair with selected letters by Tolkien on that enigmatic character. Designed to illuminate the Inklings' thinking, these essays also re-create the spirit of their intellectual sociability, since presenting on one of these essays is the primary responsibility of my course's pub groups.

The pub groups consist of small groups of five or six students formed in the first or second week. Typically, my class has five or six, and their composition remains the same throughout the semester. Each group has an assignment—for example, to examine one character's contribution to the Council of Elrond or analyze a character's relationship with Orual in the opening chapters of *Till We Have Faces*—but the main task is to give a ten-to-fifteen-minute presentation on one of the theoretical essays. This presentation transitions to a discussion of the fiction that has been paired with the essay (e.g., "Weight of Glory" with *The Great Divorce*; the section on consolation, from "On Fairy-stories," with the chapters following "Mount Doom" in *The Lord of the Rings*), which enables students to make connections between the thought and the literature of the Inklings. Students sign up for their groups and choose the essay on which they will present. In my syllabus, I tell them that these groups are meant "to encourage intellectual exchange and camaraderie among members of the class" and to mirror the "literary, philosophic, and theological" discussions at the "center of the Inklings' friendship, intellectual energy, and productivity." Being explicit about the collegial purpose and proper atmosphere for the pub group is important. Group presentations and cooperative learning are becoming more common in the college classroom, but too often these result in a subdivided task (e.g., an essay might be broken into four sections so that each section can be given to a different person) that produces a disjointed, uncoordinated presentation. Social networking technology exacerbates this tendency further by making it easier for a group presentation to materialize without students ever meeting face to face.

The image of a pub—intriguingly foreign and attractively intimate to most students—helps counteract this stale simulacrum of intellectual sociability. My syllabus emphasizes that students are to meet in a convivial atmosphere, preferably over food or drink:

> "Pub Group" is a metaphor to reflect the Inklings' practice of discussion. Meetings should not be conducted in actual pubs or bars by those who are underage. They are meant to be fun and informal. I would encourage you to meet over dinner at the Dining Hall, coffee at Holy Grounds, or dessert at the Connelly Student Center.

Most groups embrace the idea in one form or another. For many students, meeting in this way is one of the rare occasions when the barrier between their school life and social life has been challenged. They are often pleasantly surprised to find that their interest in a topic is shared.

Invoking a pub atmosphere may generate enthusiasm, but to be effective this energy needs to be channeled through a structured assignment. Pub groups are therefore charged with meeting and discussing the meaning and potential significance of their essays. I tell them that there is no neutral ground in a good pub discussion and that it is not merely a task to be completed. The syllabus directs them to take a stand on their essay's argument:

> A presentation should not just summarize the main points of the essay, but should also locate arguments and counterarguments about the topic of the essay. What objections could be raised? Do you agree with those objections? How would you respond? Are there ways to misinterpret the essay? Better ways to interpret or apply it? Are there elements you don't understand? What are the various positions possible on this idea? Adopt (either sincerely or as a "devil's advocate") different positions among the members of the group and discuss. Your delineation of these "conflicts" and issues will be vital as they will set the agenda of class discussion on the day of the presentation as we tie the essay into the day's reading.

For the in-class presentation, two students in the group must support the argument of Tolkien, Lewis, or Williams; another pair must argue against; and the remaining student acts as a moderator. The group also provides a one-page handout highlighting key passages and the group's central questions and arguments. Beyond this structure, the presentation is open to creative interpretation. Students, for example, have dramatized their arguments by assuming the roles of the various Inklings in the Eagle and Child; they have provided illustrations of Tom Bombadil to make his role in the book clearer; and they have presented a rather complicated reenactment, in two and three dimensions, of Lewis's central argument in "Transposition." Not knowing how such a class will begin and what course it will take means that I must have sufficient command of the material to adjust and improvise. Yet the creative contributions of the pub group lend a quickening conversational spontaneity to the day's class.

Accountability is also a necessary part in the creation of successful pub groups. Even the most motivated students contribute more effectively when they understand that their group work factors into class participation assessment, which is worth thirty percent of the final grade. In addition, a section of the final exam is dedicated to material covered exclusively by the pub groups in the form of key terms from the essays (e.g., Tolkien's "Faërie" or Lewis's "true myth"). The result is that pub groups must conscientiously probe the essays, but the rest of the class must also engage with the readings and presentations to prepare for the final exam. This fosters an interdependence among the members of the class that strengthens the sense of intellectual community. Further, pub groups naturally form study groups when the final draws closer.

What aspects of Tolkien emerge in a class that emphasizes his place among the Inklings and attempts to recreate their exchange among students? *The Lord of the Rings* comes into focus as a philosophically and theologically nuanced text. Its depth arises not from the foisted allegorical mishandlings that Tolkien disavowed but rather from the complex conceptual framework formed by his learning, his beliefs, and his friends' influence.[2] Student papers reflect this complexity. Students understand Tolkien's writing and thought better through engagement with the essays of the other Inklings. One student, exploring why Tolkien's representation of nature was so effective, looked at the Ents through the critical lens of Sayers's conception of analogy. Another student argued persuasively for the psychological effects of an Augustinian conception of evil in *The Lord of the Rings* by comparing the wraiths to the degradation of the narcissistic Wentworth in Williams's *Descent into Hell*. Students who first broach a topic in a pub group presentation often return to it in their papers. The result of this continuation yields a more considered connection of Tolkien's thought to *The Lord of the Rings*. One student first encountered the concept of eucatastrophe in a pub group presentation. The experience helped him write an essay not on the ending of the book, as may be expected, but on the return of Gandalf in book 3 as a possible eucatastrophe. His examination of a happy ending that occurs midway through the work raised provocative questions about Tolkien's understanding of history and transcendence.

While this type of student work results from placing Tolkien in context among the Inklings, my experience further suggests that a great benefit occurs from having students consider the model of the Inklings. Pub groups are an example of collaborative learning, or "team-based" or "cooperative" learning. This pedagogical approach promotes devolution of authority in the classroom, student engagement that is active rather than passive, learning that is deep rather than surface, and a learning community that is diverse and inclusive.[3] These are all worthy ends, but my particular goal in introducing pub groups is to provide a venue for friendships centered on the intellectual life. Many students come to college seeking to enter into the life of the mind with others but are disappointed to find their companionship dictated primarily by dormitories, sports, or extracurricular activities. The pub groups give access to what A. G. Sertillanges describes as the role of fellowship and association in the intellectual life: "Friendship is an obstetric art; it draws out our richest and deepest resources, it unfolds the wings of our dreams and hidden indeterminate thoughts; it serves as a check on our judgments, tries out our new ideas, keeps up our ardor, and inflames our enthusiasm" (56).

Although Sertillanges emphasizes the benefits of cooperation for our work, Lewis outlines the human benefits when "companions discover that they have in common some insight or interest" that "others do not share, and which, till that moment, each believed to be his own unique treasure (or burden)" (*Four Loves* 65). For Lewis, this realization of shared concern does not entail univocal agreement, which the Inklings themselves did not seek, but only a shared sense of significance. I have been grateful to see such friendships grow in my classes, to hear that pub groups have continued to meet even after the semester ends, and to get reports of their development from former students years later. As Legolas says to a yielding Gimli, "You shall come with me and keep your word; and thus we will journey on together to our own lands" (981; bk. 6, ch. 6). This forging of an unlikely friendship generates a promise of mutual education at the end of *The Lord of the Rings*, and this parting collaboration serves as a closing example of what may be one of the most intriguing lessons to learn about, and from, the Inklings.

NOTES

[1]For a biographical treatment of the group, see Carpenter, *Inklings*. For their shared theological concerns, see Reilly.

[2]For an argument outlining this approach to Tolkien's religion and thought, see T. Smith 73–76.

[3]For overviews of collaborative learning practices and the varying terms to describe them, see Barkley, Cross, and Major 3–26; Millis and Cottell 3–34; Michaelsen, Sweet, and Parmelee 27–50.

NOTES ON CONTRIBUTORS

Cami D. Agan is professor of English and chair of Language and Literature at Oklahoma Christian University. She teaches British and world literature. She is the author of articles on Tolkien, medieval drama, and the eighteenth-century actress Kitty Clive, and her essay "Frances Sheridan as Case Study for Mid-Eighteenth-Century Comedy" appears in the MLA's *Approaches to Teaching British Women Playwrights of the Restoration and Eighteenth Century*

Jane Chance, Andrew W. Mellon Distinguished Professor Emerita of English at Rice and recipient of a D.Litt., Purdue, 2013, has published twenty-five books on medieval literature, mythography, and medievalism, including a coedited *Approaches to Teaching* Sir Gawain and the Green Knight. Her most recent is *The Emergence of Italian Humanism, 1321–1475* (2014), volume 3 of her *Medieval Mythography*. In progress is a book on postmodern Tolkien.

Christopher Cobb is associate professor of English at Saint Mary's College in Notre Dame, Indiana, where he teaches Renaissance literature, modern drama, fantasy literature, literary theory, and environmental studies. He is the author of *The Staging of Romance in Late Shakespeare* and several articles on Renaissance drama. His scholarly interests in fantasy include the theory of fantasy and Tolkien's influence on the genre. He has published and presented essays on Tolkien's influence on Guy Gavriel Kay and Ursula K. Le Guin.

Christopher "Chip" Crane is a lecturer at the University of Maryland, where he teaches Tolkien, medieval and Renaissance literature, and professional writing. He taught English, including Tolkien, for several years at the United States Naval Academy. He is the author of essays on medieval comedy and rhetoric. His other research interests lie in medieval (Old and Middle English) biblical literature, Renaissance devotional literature, comedy, contemporary medievalism, and young adult fantasy.

Deidre Dawson has written reviews for *Tolkien Studies* and is the author of an essay on the role of language in cultural loss and recovery in *Tolkien's Modern Middle Ages*, a monograph on Voltaire's correspondence, and several essays and coedited volumes on the Enlightenment in France and Scotland. She has taught at Georgetown and Michigan State and is currently exploring the relation among language, ethics, and otherness in Tolkien's works from the perspective of Emmanuel Lévinas.

Leslie A. Donovan is professor of the Honors College at the University of New Mexico. In addition to Tolkien courses, she teaches interdisciplinary undergraduate courses in the humanities as well as writing and communications. She is the author of essays on the mythology of Middle-earth, valkyries in *The Lord of the Rings*, women saints in Old English prose, *Beowulf*, and various topics in pedagogy. She also coedited *Perilous and Fair: Women in the Works and Life of J. R. R. Tolkien*.

Michael D. C. Drout is professor of English and director of the Center for the Study of the Medieval at Wheaton College, Norton, Massachusetts, where he teaches Old and

Middle English, Old Norse, and fantasy literature. He is the author of *How Tradition Works* and *Tradition and Influence*, editor of J. R. R. Tolkien's Beowulf *and the Critics* and the *J. R. R. Tolkien Encyclopedia*, and coeditor of the journal *Tolkien Studies*.

Melissa Ridley Elmes is a doctoral student in English at the University of North Carolina, Greensboro. Her primary field of study is post-Conquest through fifteenth-century British literatures, with particular emphasis on feasts and feasting, Arthuriana, magic and monstrosity, and gender. She is the author of essays on Chaucer's *Parliament of Fowles*, teaching Chaucer, and Arthurian tarot decks.

Nancy Enright is associate professor of English and Catholic studies at Seton Hall University. She has been involved in planning and teaching courses in Seton Hall's core curriculum, which includes classic texts explored in connection with questions about the meaning of life, death, service, and community. She is the author of essays on Dante, Augustine, C. S. Lewis, J. R. R. Tolkien, Julian of Norwich, and William Hazlitt.

Justin Edward Everett is associate professor of English and directs the writing program at the University of the Sciences in Philadelphia. His specialties include writing pedagogy, writing program administration, popular culture, science fiction, fantasy, and horror. He is the author of essays on literary theory, writing program administration, vampires, Philip K. Dick, and *Star Trek*. He recently coedited a collection of essays on the pulp magazine *Weird Tales*.

Liam Felsen retired from teaching in 2013 as associate professor of medieval English literature at Indiana University Southeast in New Albany, Indiana. He is the author of essays on Anglo-Saxon and medieval Latin literature. He is currently an associate attorney with the law firm of Frost Brown Todd LLC, working in the products liability and mass tort litigation practice groups.

Dimitra Fimi is a lecturer in English at Cardiff Metropolitan University, Wales. She is the author of *Tolkien, Race and Cultural History: From Fairies to Hobbits* (2008), which won the Mythopoeic Scholarship Award in Inklings Studies. She has also published articles and essays in journals (including *Folklore* and *Tolkien Studies*), edited collections, and reference works. She lectures on Tolkien and fantasy literature at the undergraduate and postgraduate levels.

Verlyn Flieger is professor emerita in the Department of English at the University of Maryland. She is the author of *Splintered Light: Logos and Language in Tolkien's World*, *A Question of Time*, *Interrupted Music*, and *Green Suns and Faërie: Essays on J. R. R. Tolkien*. She is the coeditor of *Tolkien Studies*. She has also published two fantasy novels, *Pig Tale* and *The Inn at Corbies' Caww*, and an Arthurian novella, *Avilion*.

Judy Ann Ford is a medieval historian whose interests include popular religion, hagiography, and sermons. She is professor at Texas A&M University, Commerce. With Robin Reid, she codirected two National Endowment for the Humanities Summer Institutes for School Teachers on J. R. R. Tolkien.

Craig Franson is associate professor of English at La Salle University in Philadelphia. His research and teaching center on British Romanticism and its nineteenth- and twentieth-century legacies. He has publications and ongoing projects about Lord Byron and his circle, Adam Smith and Scottish medical discourse, J. R. R. Tolkien, Joss Whedon, and other contemporary writers of the fantastic.

James Gould is philosophy instructor at McHenry County College in Crystal Lake, Illinois. He is the author of essays on ethics, theology, learning community design, and innovative instructional strategies. With Ted Hazelgrove, he codesigned and team-taught courses that integrate philosophy and ethics with English literature and composition.

Ted Hazelgrove is English instructor at McHenry County College in Crystal Lake, Illinois. He is a published poet and active in curriculum design and fine arts programming. With James Gould, he codesigned and team-taught courses that integrate philosophy and ethics with English literature and composition.

Julia Simms Holderness is the author of essays on politics, gender, and literary theory in medieval and Renaissance literature. She has a strong interest in the Middle Ages' legacy for later eras. She has researched and taught at Harvard, Wellesley, and Michigan State. Currently based in Cambridge, Massachusetts, she is beginning a foray into the Enlightenment, with a project on the Abbé Raynal's *Histoire des deux Indes*.

Keith W. Jensen is assistant professor of humanities at William Rainey Harper College in Palatine, Illinois. In addition to Tolkien studies subjects, his research interests include controversies in archaeology; the human body and sexuality in Western culture; theories of myth; and medieval Middle Eastern literature, particularly Sufi poetry and *The Arabian Nights*. He is the author of "Dissonance in the Divine Theme: The Issue of Free Will in Tolkien's *Silmarillion*" in *Middle-earth Minstrel: Essays on Music in Tolkien*.

Yvette Kisor is professor of literature at Ramapo College of New Jersey, where she teaches medieval literature and Tolkien. Her essays on Tolkien have appeared in *Tolkien Studies* and *Mythlore* as well as various edited collections. Her essays on medieval literature, particularly Anglo-Saxon, have appeared in *Anglo-Saxon England*, *The Chaucer Review*, and *ANQ*.

Kristine Larsen is professor of astronomy at Central Connecticut State University. Her research and teaching focus on issues of science and society, including the preparation of science educators, science outreach, and science and literature. She is the author of *Stephen Hawking: A Biography* and *Cosmology 101* and two coedited volumes, *The Mythological Dimensions of Doctor Who* and *The Mythological Dimensions of Neil Gaiman*.

Thomas L. Martin is associate professor of English at Florida Atlantic University. He is the author of *Poiesis and Possible Worlds* and essays on literary theory, Renaissance, and fantasy literature. He is the editor of *Reading the Classics with C. S. Lewis*.

James McNelis is professor of English at Wilmington College, Ohio. He is the author of "'The tree took me up from the ground and carried me off': A Source for Tolkien's Ents in Ludvig Holberg's *Journey of Niels Klim to the World Underground*" in *Tolkien Studies*. He teaches Old and Middle English, Old Norse literature, Shakespeare, fantasy and science fiction, Japanese popular culture, and the literature of the atomic bombings of Japan.

Philip Irving Mitchell is associate professor of English at Dallas Baptist University, where he teaches early modern and modern humanities and directs the University

Honors Program. He is a contributor to *Mythlore*, *Seven*, *Tolkien Studies*, *Logos*, and *The Journal of Education and Christian Belief* and is at work on monographs about G. K. Chesterton's practice of history and biography and C. S. Lewis's practice as a literary historian.

Shelley Rees is associate professor of English at the University of Science and Arts of Oklahoma. She does research on Thomas Lovell Beddoes, studies popular culture texts, and is the author of essays on Joss Whedon's *Dollhouse* and AMC's *The Walking Dead* and the editor of a collection of essays on cult television icon *Mystery Science Theater 3000*.

Robin Anne Reid is professor in the Department of Literature and Languages at Texas A&M University, Commerce. She has collaborated with Judy Ford to team-teach courses on Tolkien, publish essays, and direct two National Endowment for the Humanities Summer Institutes for School Teachers on J. R. R. Tolkien. She teaches creative writing, critical theory, and marginalized literatures in addition to Tolkien.

Sharin Schroeder has taught Tolkien's works at Taipei Tech, where she is an assistant professor of English, and at the University of Minnesota. She has published two book chapters on Tolkien: "'It's Alive!': Tolkien's Monster on the Screen" (*Picturing Tolkien*) and "She-who-must-not-be-ignored: Gender and Genre in *The Lord of the Rings* and the Victorian Boys' Book" (*Perilous and Fair*).

Anna Smol is professor in the English Department at Mount Saint Vincent University in Halifax, Nova Scotia, where she teaches courses on Tolkien, Old and Middle English literature, and Old Norse literature. She is the author of essays on Tolkien in *Modern Fiction Studies*, *Mythlore*, the *J. R. R. Tolkien Encyclopedia*, and *The Body in Tolkien's Legendarium*. She has also written essays on medievalism, children's literature, and pedagogy.

Robin Chapman Stacey is professor of history and Joff Hanauer Honors Professor in Western Civilization at the University of Washington. She is the author of essays on medieval Irish and Welsh law and the recent *Dark Speech: The Performance of Law in Early Ireland*. She teaches courses on Tolkien, Celtic civilizations, medieval women's history, medieval legal history, medieval sanctity, and medieval heresy.

Leslie Stratyner is professor of English at Mississippi University for Women, where she teaches courses in early British literature, medieval literature, and popular culture. With James Keller, she coedited four volumes of essays on topics from fantasy film to Shakespeare to *South Park*.

Michael Tomko is associate professor in the interdisciplinary department of humanities at Villanova University and book review editor for the journal *Religion and Literature*. He is the author of *British Romanticism and the Catholic Question: Religion, History, and National Identity, 1778–1829* and coeditor of *Firmly I Believe and Truly: The Spiritual Tradition of Catholic England, 1483–1999*.

James R. Vitullo is adjunct instructor of English and humanities and writing center specialist at William Rainey Harper College in Palatine, Illinois. His research interests include Roman, Greek, medieval, and Norse cultures; fantasy; and science fiction. He has taught courses on classical mythology, Tolkien, Western culture from the Stone Age through the twentieth century, English composition, and genre fiction.

Brian Walter is associate professor of English and director of Convocations at the St. Louis College of Pharmacy. His scholarly and professional work has appeared in *Boulevard*, *The Southern Quarterly*, *Nabokov Studies*, *Essays in Literature*, *Music, Sound, and the Moving Image*, *CineAction*, and *Post Script*.

SURVEY RESPONDENTS

Along with the contributors to this volume, the following teachers responded thoughtfully and carefully to a lengthy questionnaire on teaching J. R. R. Tolkien's *The Lord of the Rings* and other works. Their contributions to this volume have been invaluable.

C. N. Sue Abromaitis, *Loyola University Maryland*
Mark Adderley, *Missouri Valley College*
Rebecca G. Addy, *University of Nebraska, Kearney*
Amy Amendt-Raduege, *independent scholar*
C. Riley Augé, *Flathead Valley Community College (Montana)*
Bruce A. Beatie, *Cleveland State University*
Elisa E. Beshero-Bondar, *University of Pittsburgh, Greensburg*
Janice M. Bogstad, *University of Wisconsin, Eau Claire*
Karen Bollermann, *Arizona State University*
Troy Boone, *University of Pittsburgh*
Frank Bramlett, *University of Nebraska, Omaha*
Elizabeth Bridges, *Hendrix College*
Devin Brown, *Asbury College*
David Cappella, *Central Connecticut State University*
Sandra E. Capps, *University of Tennessee, Knoxville*
Stephen Mark Carey, *Georgia State University*
Paul Dyck, *Canadian Mennonite University*
Mary Agnes Edsall, *Bowdoin College*
Langdon Elsbree, *Claremont McKenna*
Jonathan Evans, *University of Georgia*
Rachel Fulton, *University of Chicago*
Peter H. Goodrich, *Northern Michigan University*
James Gould, *McHenry County College*
Curtis Gruenler, *Hope College*
Susan A. Hagedorn, *Virginia Tech*
Darren Harris-Fain, *Shawnee State University*
Janis Haswell, *Texas A&M University, Corpus Christi*
Edward R. Haymes, *Cleveland State University*
John R. Holmes, *Franciscan University of Steubenville*
Vickie Holtz-Wodzak, *Viterbo University*
Jackie C. Horne, *Simmons College*
Rebecca Housel, *Rochester Institute of Technology*
Suzanne Keen, *Washington and Lee University*

A. Samuel Kimball, *University of North Florida*
Romuald I. Lakowski, *Grant MacEwan College*
Stuart Lee, *University of Oxford*
Carol A. Leibiger, *University of South Dakota*
Michael M. Logan, *Northampton Community College (Pennsylvania)*
Shirley Lua, *De La Salle University*
Jeffrey MacLeod, *Mount Saint Vincent University*
Jonathan Mulrooney, *College of the Holy Cross*
Charles W. Nelson, *Michigan Technological University*
Janice Witherspoon Neuleib, *Illinois State University*
Jennifer Neville, *Royal Holloway, University of London*
Kelly A. O'Connor-Salomon, *The Sage Colleges*
Warren Olin-Ammentorp, *Cazenovia College*
Corey Olsen, *Washington College*
Gail Orgelfinger, *University of Maryland Baltimore County*
Nicholas Ozment, *Winona State University*
Susan Palwick, *University of Nevada, Reno*
Kevin Porter, *University of Texas, Arlington*
Russell Potter, *Rhode Island College*
Anne Lake Prescott, *Barnard College*
Don Riggs, *Drexel University*
Edward Risden, *St. Norbert College*
Christopher M. Roman, *Kent State University, Tuscarawas*
Amelia A. Rutledge, *George Mason University*
Joe Sutliff Sanders, *California State University, San Bernardino*
Suzanne V. Shepard, *Broome Community College (New York)*
Ted Sherman, *Middle Tennessee State University*
Charlee Sterling, *Goucher College*
Joseph Tadie, *Saint Mary's University of Minnesota*
K. Vivian Taylor, *University of South Florida, Tampa*
Christopher T. Vaccaro, *University of Vermont*
Raymond M. Vince, *University of Tampa*
Steven C. Walker, *Brigham Young University, Provo*
John Paul Walter, *Creighton University*
Stella Wang, *University of Rochester*
Cliff Wheeler, *Lincoln Christian College*
K. S. Whetter, *Acadia University*
Christopher Wielgos, *Lewis University*
S. Russell Wood, *Hampden-Sydney College*
Matthew Woodcock, *University of East Anglia*

Jed Wyrick, *California State University, Chico*
Michael W. Young, *La Roche College*
Kim Zarins, *Cornell University*
Joseph Zornado, *Rhode Island College*

WORKS CITED

Abley, Mark. *Spoken Here: Travels among Threatened Languages*. New York: Houghton, 2003. Print.

Adorno, Theodor, Walter Benjamin, Ernst Bloch, Bertolt Brecht, and Georg Lukács. *Aesthetics and Politics*. London: Verso, 1980. Print.

Alter, Stephen G. *Darwinism and the Linguistic Image: Language, Race, and Natural Theology in the Nineteenth Century*. Baltimore: Johns Hopkins UP, 1999. Print.

Amison, Anne. "An Unexpected Guest." *Mythlore* 25.1–2 (2006): 127–36. Print.

Amodio, Mark C., ed. *New Directions in Oral Theory: Essays on Ancient and Medieval Literatures*. Tempe: Arizona Center for Medieval and Renaissance Studies, 2005. Print. Medieval and Renaissance Texts and Studies 287.

Anderson, Douglas A. Introduction. Tolkien, *Annotated* Hobbit 1–28.

———. "The Mainstreaming of Fantasy and the Legacy of *The Lord of the Rings*." Hammond and Scull, Lord of the Rings, *1954–2004* 301–15.

———. "Note on the Text." Tolkien, *Lord* xi–xvii.

———, ed. *Tales before Tolkien: The Roots of Modern Fantasy*. New York: Ballantine, 2003. Print.

Ardalambion. Helge Kåre Fauskanger, n.d. Web. 11 Sept. 2013.

Aristotle. *Nicomachean Ethics*. Trans. D. Ross. Oxford: Oxford UP, 1980. Print.

Arul, Melissa Ruth. "Elvish Identity: A Journey." Festival in the Shire Conference. Aberystwyth, Wales. 13 Aug. 2010. Presentation.

Attebery, Brian. *Strategies of Fantasy*. Bloomington: Indiana UP, 1992. Print.

Auden, W. H. *As I Walked Out One Evening: Songs, Ballads, Lullabies, Limericks, and Other Light Verse*. New York: Vintage, 1995. Print.

———. "At the End of the Quest, Victory." Rev. of *The Return of the King*, by J. R. R. Tolkien. *New York Times* 22 Jan. 1956, Books sec.: 5. *ProQuest Historical Newspapers*. Web. 21 Apr. 2008.

———. *Collected Shorter Poems, 1927–1957*. London: Faber, 1966. Print.

———. "The Hero Is a Hobbit." Rev. of *The Fellowship of the Ring*, by J. R. R. Tolkien. *New York Times* 31 Oct. 1954: BR37. *ProQuest Historical Newspapers*. Web. 21 Apr. 2008.

———. Liner notes. *J. R. R. Tolkien: Poems and Songs of Middle Earth*. By J. R. R. Tolkien, William Elvin, and Donald Swann. Dir. Howard Sackler. Caedmon Records, 1967. LP.

———. "The Quest Hero." Zimbardo and Isaacs 31–51.

Augustine. *City of God*. Trans. Henry Bettenson. London: Penguin, 2003. Print.

———. *The Confessions*. Trans. Maria Boulding. New York: Vintage, 1998. Print.

Bakhtin, M. M. *The Dialogic Imagination: Four Essays*. Ed. Michael Holquist. Trans. Caryl Emerson and Holquist. Austin: U of Texas P, 1981. Print.

Bakshi, Ralph, dir. *J. R. R. Tolkien's* The Lord of the Rings. Warner Home Video, 1978. DVD.

Ballinger, Lucy. "Welsh Star in Race Row." *Wales News Online*. Media Wales, 18 Jan. 2004. Web. 9 July 2012.

Baltasar, Michaela. "J. R. R. Tolkien: A Rediscovery of Myth." Chance, *Tolkien and the Invention* 19–34.

Barkley, Elizabeth F., Patricia K. Cross, and Claire Howell Major, eds. *Collaborative Learning Techniques: A Handbook for College Faculty*. San Francisco: Jossey-Bass, 2005. Print.

Barr, Donald. "Shadowy World of Men and Hobbits." Rev. of *The Two Towers*, by J. R. R. Tolkien. *New York Times* 1 May 1955: BR4. *ProQuest Historical Newspapers*. Web. 21 Apr. 2008.

Barthes, Roland. *Mythologies*. Trans. Annette Lavers. New York: Hill, 1972. Print.

"BBC Reveals a Hundred Great British Heroes." *BBC News*. BBC Online Network, 22 Aug. 2002. Web. 8 Sept. 2013.

Beagle, Peter S. *The Last Unicorn*. New York: Roc, 1968. Print.

Beahm, George W. *The Essential J. R. R. Tolkien Sourcebook: A Fan's Guide to Middle-earth*. Illus. Colleen Doran. Franklin Lakes: New Page, 2003. Print.

Bebb, Angela. "Pity, Mercy, and Empathy: Emotional Weapons for Internal Battle in *The Lord of the Rings*." 2008. TS.

Benjamin, Walter. "The Task of the Translator." *Illuminations*. Ed. Hannah Arendt. Trans. Harry Zohn. New York: Schocken, 1968. 69–82. Print.

Bentham, Jeremy. *An Introduction to the Principles of Morals and Legislation*. Oxford: Clarendon, 2007. Print.

Berry, Wendell. *What Are People For?* London: Rider, 1991. Print.

Bertenstam, Åke. *A Chronological Bibliography of the Writings of J. R. R. Tolkien*. Bertenstam, 2003. Web. 26 Aug. 2012.

"The Big Read." *BBC*. BBC Online Network, Apr. 2003. Web. 16 Nov. 2012.

Blackham, Robert S. *The Roots of Tolkien's Middle Earth*. Stroud: Tempus, 2006. Print.

———. *Tolkien's Oxford*. Stroud: History, 2008. Print.

Bloom, Harold. *The Anxiety of Influence: A Theory of Poetry*. New York: Oxford UP, 1973. Print.

———, ed. *J. R. R. Tolkien's* The Lord of the Rings*: Modern Critical Interpretations*. New York: Chelsea, 2008. Print.

Bogstad, Janice M., and Philip E. Kaveny, eds. *Picturing Tolkien: Essays on Peter Jackson's* The Lord of the Rings *Film Trilogy*. Jefferson: McFarland, 2011. Print.

Bolin, Michael. Message to Nancy Enright. 6 Dec. 2010. E-mail.

Boyd, Ian, and Stratford Caldecott, eds. *A Hidden Presence: The Catholic Imagination of J. R. R. Tolkien*. South Orange: Chesterton, 2003. Print.

Brackmann, Rebecca. "Dwarves Are Not Heroes: Antisemitism and the Dwarves in J. R. R. Tolkien's Writing." *Mythlore* 28.3–4 (2010): 85–106. Print.

Bratman, David. "History of Middle-earth: Overview." Drout, *J. R. R. Tolkien Encyclopedia* 273–74.

———. "Summa Jacksonia: A Reply to Defenses of Peter Jackson's *The Lord of the Rings* Films, after St. Thomas Aquinas." Croft, *Tolkien on Film* 27–62.

Brooker, Jewel Spears, ed. *T. S. Eliot: The Contemporary Reviews*. Cambridge: Cambridge UP, 2004. Print.

Buchan, John. "The Far Islands." 1899. Anderson, *Tales* 245–67.

Burkert, Walter. *Structure and History in Greek Mythology and Ritual*. Berkeley: U of California P, 1979. Print.

Burns, Marjorie J. "Norse and Christian Gods: The Integrative Theology of J. R .R. Tolkien." Chance, *Tolkien and the Invention* 163–78.

———. *Perilous Realms: Celtic and Norse in Tolkien's Middle-earth*. Toronto: U of Toronto P, 2005. Print.

Caldecott, Stratford. "The Lord and Lady of the Rings: The Hidden Presence of Tolkien's Catholicism in *The Lord of the Rings*." *Touchstone* 15.1 (2002): n. pag. Web. 27 May 2012.

Cantor, Norman. *Inventing the Middle Ages: The Lives, Works, and Ideas of the Great Medievalists of the Twentieth Century*. New York: Harper, 1993. Print.

Carneiro, Robert. "Origin Myths." *National Center for Science Education*. NCSE, 3 Nov. 2008. Web. 10 July 2010.

Carpenter, Humphrey. *The Inklings: C. S. Lewis, J. R. R. Tolkien, Charles Williams, and Their Friends*. Boston: Houghton, 1979. Print.

———. *J. R. R. Tolkien: A Biography*. Boston: Houghton, 1987. Print.

Carroll, Lewis. *The Annotated Alice*. Ed. Martin Gardner. New York: Norton, 2000. Print.

Carter, Stephen L. *Integrity*. New York: Harper, 1996. Print.

Carter, Susan. "Galadriel and Morgan le Fey: Tolkien's Redemption of the Lady of the Lacuna." *Mythlore* 25.3–4 (2007): 71–89. Print.

Chance, Jane. The Lord of the Rings*: The Mythology of Power*. Lexington: UP of Kentucky, 2001. Print.

———, ed. *Tolkien and the Invention of Myth: A Reader*. Lexington: UP of Kentucky, 2004. Print.

———. "Tolkien and the Other: Race and Gender in Middle-earth." Chance and Siewers 171–86.

———. "Tolkien's Women (and Men): The Films and the Book." Croft, *Tolkien on Film* 175–93.

———, ed. *Tolkien the Medievalist*. New York: Routledge, 2002. Print.

Chance, Jane, and Alfred K. Siewers, eds. *Tolkien's Modern Middle Ages*. New York: Palgrave, 2005. Print.

Chism, Christine. "Middle-earth, the Middle Ages, and the Aryan Nation: Myth and History in World War II." Chance, *Tolkien the Medievalist* 63–92.

Clark, George, and Daniel Timmons, eds. *J. R. R. Tolkien and His Literary Resonances: Views of Middle-earth*. Westport: Greenwood, 2000. Print.

Cobb, Christopher. "Guy Gavriel Kay and the Psychology of History." *Foundation: The International Review of Science Fiction* 34 (2005): 87–99. Print.

Cohen, Jeffrey Jerome, ed. *The Postcolonial Middle Ages*. New York: Palgrave, 2000. Print.

Cohen, Patricia. "Indian Tribes Go in Search of Their Lost Languages." *New York Times* 6 Apr. 2010, natl. ed: C1. Print.

Constantine, Mary-Ann. "Welsh Literary History and the Making of 'The Myvyrian Archaiology of Wales.'" Van Hulle and Leerssen 109–28.

Craig, David M. "'Queer Lodgings': Gender and Sexuality in *The Lord of the Rings*." *Mallorn* 38 (2001): 11–18. Print.

Croft, Janet Brennan, ed. *Tolkien and Shakespeare: Essays on Shared Themes and Language*. Jefferson: McFarland, 2007. Print.

———, ed. *Tolkien on Film: Essays on Peter Jackson's* The Lord of the Rings. Altadena: Mythopoeic, 2004. Print.

———. *War and the Works of J. R. R. Tolkien*. Westport: Praeger, 2004. Print.

Crossley, Robert. "Education and Fantasy." *College English* 37.3 (1975): 281–93. Print.

Crowe, Edith L. "Power in Arda: Sources, Uses and Misuses." *Mythlore* 21.2 (1996): 272–77. Print.

Curry, Patrick. "Charges of Racism in *The Lord of the Rings* Are Mistaken." *Readings on J. R. R. Tolkien*. Ed. Katie de Koster. San Diego: Greenhaven, 2000. 104–14. Print.

———. *Defending Middle-earth: Tolkien: Myth and Modernity*. Boston: Houghton, 2004. Print.

———. "Tolkien and His Critics: A Critique." *Root and Branch: Approaches towards Understanding Tolkien*. Ed. Thomas Honegger. Zurich: Walking Tree, 2005. 75–139. Print.

Darwin, Charles. *The Voyage of the Beagle*. 1839. Ware: Wordsworth, 1997. Print.

Dawson, Deidre. "English, Welsh, and Elvish: Language, Loss, and Cultural Recovery in J. R. R. Tolkien's *The Lord of the Rings*." Chance and Siewers 105–20.

De Lint, Charles. "The Tale Goes Ever On." Haber 175–84.

Dickerson, Matthew T., and Jonathan Evans. *Ents, Elves, and Eriador: The Environmental Vision of J. R. R. Tolkien*. Lexington: UP of Kentucky, 2006. Print.

Dimond, Andy. "The Twilight of the Elves: Ragnarök and the End of the Third Age." Chance, *Tolkien and the Invention* 179–90.

Disappearing Languages, Enduring Voices: Documenting the World's Endangered Languages. Natl. Geographic Mission Program and Living Tongues Inst. for Endangered Langs., n.d. Web. 10 July 2010.

Donovan, Leslie A. "The Valkyrie Reflex in J. R. R. Tolkien's *The Lord of the Rings*: Galadriel, Shelob, Éowyn, and Arwen." Chance, *Tolkien the Medievalist* 106–32.

Dorson, Richard M. *The British Folklorists: A History*. Chicago: U of Chicago P, 1968. Print.

Drout, Michael D. C., ed. *J. R. R. Tolkien Encyclopedia: Scholarship and Critical Assessment*. New York: Routledge, 2006. Print.

———. "A Mythology for Anglo-Saxon England." Chance, *Tolkien and the Invention* 229–47.

———. "Towards a Better Tolkien Criticism." Eaglestone 15–28.

Drout, Michael D. C., and Hilary Wynne. "Tom Shippey's *J. R. R. Tolkien: Author of the Century* and a Look Back at Tolkien Criticism since 1982." *Envoi* 9.2 (2000): 101–67. Print.

Dubs, Kathleen E. "Providence, Fate, and Chance: Boethian Philosophy in *The Lord of the Rings*." *Twentieth Century Literature* 27.1 (1981): 34–42. Print.

[Duggan, Alfred Leo]. "The Epic of Westernesse." Rev. of *The Two Towers*, by J. R. R. Tolkien. *Times Literary Supplement* 17 Dec. 1954: 817. *Times Literary Supplement Centenary Archive*. Web. 23 May 2008.

———. "Heroic Endeavour." Rev. of *The Fellowship of the Ring*, by J. R. R. Tolkien. *Times Literary Supplement* 27 Aug. 1954: 541. *Times Literary Supplement Centenary Archive*. Web. 23 May 2008.

———. "The Saga of Middle Earth." Rev. of *The Return of the King*, by J. R. R. Tolkien. *Times Literary Supplement* 25 Nov. 1955: 704. *Times Literary Supplement Centenary Archive*. Web. 23 May 2008.

Dunsany, Lord. *See* Plunkett, Edward

Duriez, Colin. *J. R. R. Tolkien: The Making of a Legend*. Oxford: Lion Hudson, 2012. Print.

———. *Tolkien and C. S. Lewis: The Gift of Friendship*. Mahwah: Hidden Spring, 2003. Print.

Eaglestone, Robert, ed. *Reading* The Lord of the Rings*: New Writings on Tolkien's Classic*. New York: Continuum, 2005. Print.

"Elegy." *Oxford English Dictionary*. Oxford UP, n.d. Web. 16 July 2014.

Eliot, T. S. "Tradition and the Individual Talent." 1920. *The Sacred Wood: Essays on Poetry and Criticism by T. S. Eliot*. 3rd ed. London: Methuen, 1932. 47–59. Print.

Empson, William. *Some Versions of the Pastoral*. New York: New Directions, 1974. Print.

The Encyclopedia of Arda. Mark Fisher, 2012. Web. 26 Aug. 2012.

Enright, Nancy. "Images of the Messiah and of Salvation in Lewis, Tolkien, and Williams." *Chesterton Review* 33.3–4 (2007): 547–62. Print.

———. "Tolkien's Females and the Defining of Power." *Renascence* 59.2 (2007): 93–108. Print.

"Entertainment Star Wars: George Lucas Strikes Back." *BBC News*. BBC Online Network, 14 July 1999. Web. 9 July 2012.

Feist, Raymond E. "Our Grandfather: Meditations on J. R. R. Tolkien." Haber 7–20.

Fife, Ernelle. "Wise Warriors in Tolkien, Lewis, and Rowling." *Mythlore* 25.1–2 (2006): 147–62. Print.

Fifield, Merle. "Fantasy in and for the Sixties." *English Journal* 55.7 (1966): 841–44. Print.

Fimi, Dimitra. *Tolkien, Race and Cultural History: From Fairies to Hobbits*. Basingstoke: Palgrave, 2008. Print.

Fisher, Jason, ed. *Tolkien and the Study of His Sources: Critical Essays*. Jefferson: McFarland, 2011. Print.

Flieger, Verlyn. "The Footsteps of Ælfwine." *Tolkien's* Legendarium*: Essays on* The History of Middle-earth. Ed. Flieger and Carl F. Hostetter. Westport: Greenwood, 2000. 186–97. Print.

———. "Frodo and Aragorn: The Concept of the Hero." Zimbardo and Isaacs 122–45.

———. *Interrupted Music: The Making of Tolkien's Mythology*. Kent: Kent State UP, 2005. Print.

———. "A Mythology for Finland: Tolkien and Lönnrot as Mythmakers." Chance, *Tolkien and the Invention* 277–84.

———. *A Question of Time: J. R. R. Tolkien's Road to Faërie*. Kent: Kent State UP, 1997. Print.

———. *Splintered Light: Logos and Language in Tolkien's World*. 2nd ed. Kent: Kent State UP, 2002. Print.

———. "Tolkien and the Idea of the Book." Hammond and Scull, Lord of the Rings, *1954–2004* 283–99.

———. "What Good Is Fantasy?" *Chesterton Review* 31.3–4 (2005): 217–21. Print.

Foley, John Miles. *The Singer of Tales in Performance*. Bloomington: Indiana UP, 1995. Print.

Fonstad, Karen Wynn. *The Atlas of Middle-earth*. Rev. ed. Boston: Houghton, 1991. Print.

Ford, Judy Ann, and Robin Anne Reid. "Councils and Kings: Aragorn's Journey towards Kingship in J. R. R. Tolkien's *The Lord of the Rings* and Peter Jackson's *The Lord of the Rings*." *Tolkien Studies* 6 (2009): 71–90. Print.

———. "Into the West: Far Green Country or Shadow on the Waters?" Bogstad and Kaveny 169–82.

Ford, Patrick K., trans. and ed. "*Cad Goddeu*." *The Mabinogi and Other Medieval Welsh Tales*. Berkeley: U of California P, 1977. 183–87. Print.

Foster, Robert. *Tolkien's World from A to Z: The Complete Guide to Middle-earth*. New York: Del Rey, 2001. Print.

Frye, Northrop. *Anatomy of Criticism: Four Essays*. Princeton: Princeton UP, 1957. Print.

Fussell, Paul. *The Great War and Modern Memory*. Oxford: Oxford UP, 2013. Print.

Garth, John. "Frodo and the Great War." Hammond and Scull, Lord of the Rings, *1954–2004* 41–56.

———. *Tolkien and the Great War: The Threshold of Middle-earth*. Boston: Houghton, 2003. Print.

Gay, David Elton. "J. R. R. Tolkien and the *Kalevala*: Some Thoughts on the Finnish Origins of Tom Bombadil and Treebeard." Chance, *Tolkien and the Invention* 295–304.

Gianluca, Mezzofiore. "The Far Right Link between Norwegian Killer Breivik and Florence Gunman Casseri." *International Business Times*. Intl. Business Times, 14 Dec. 2011. Web. 9 July 2012.

Giddings, Robert, ed. *J. R. R. Tolkien: This Far Land*. London: Vision, 1983. Print.

Gilliver, Peter, Jeremy Marshall, and Edmund Weiner. *The Ring of Words: Tolkien and the* Oxford English Dictionary. Oxford: Oxford UP, 2006. Print.

Glenn, Jonathan A., trans. "The Battle of Maldon." *Lightspill Poetry from the Old English*. Jonathan Glenn and Teresa Glenn, 21 Sept. 2014. Web. 10 Feb. 2015.

———, trans. "The Seafarer." *Lightspill Poetry from the Old English*. Jonathan Glenn and Teresa Glenn, 24 Dec. 2014. Web. 10 Feb. 2015.

———, trans. "The Wanderer." *Lightspill Poetry from the Old English*. Jonathan Glenn and Teresa Glenn, 24 Dec. 2014. Web. 10 Feb. 2015.

Glyer, Diana Pavlac. *The Company They Keep: C. S. Lewis and J. R. R. Tolkien as Writers in Community*. Kent: Kent State UP, 2007. Print.

Gordon, E. V., trans. *The Battle of Maldon*. Turgon 69–76.

Green, William H. "King Thorin's Mines: *The Hobbit* as Victorian Adventure Novel." *Extrapolation: A Journal of Science Fiction and Fantasy* 42.1 (2001): 53–64. *Expanded Academic ASAP*. Web. 29 June 2010.

———. "'Where's Mama?': The Construction of the Feminine in *The Hobbit*." *The Lion and the Unicorn* 22.2 (1998): 188–95. Print.

Greenberg, Martin H., ed. *After the King: Stories in Honor of J. R. R. Tolkien*. New York: Tor, 1992. Print.

Gresham, Douglas. "Past Watchful Dragons: Fantasy and Faith in the World of C. S. Lewis." Belmont U, Nashville. 3 Nov. 2005. Lecture.

Grindley, Carl James. "The Hagiography of Steel: The Hero's Weapon and Its Place in Pop Culture." *The Medieval Hero on Screen: Representations from Beowulf to Buffy*. Ed. Martha W. Driver and Sid Ray. Jefferson: McFarland, 2004. 151–66. Print.

Gysin, Christian, Neil Sears, and Sam Greenhill. "Anders Behring Breivik Played *Lord of the Rings* on His iPod to Drown Out Screams." *Daily Mail Online*. Assoc. Newspapers, 26 July 2011. Web. 9 July 2012.

Haber, Karen, ed. *Meditations on Middle-earth*. New York: St. Martin's, 2001. Print.

Hagège, Claude. *On the Death and Life of Languages*. Trans. Jody Gladding. New Haven: Yale UP, 2009. Print.

Haldane, J. B. S. "Auld Hornie, F. R. S." *Modern Quarterly* ns 1.4 (1946): 32–40. Print.

Hammond, Wayne G. *J. R. R. Tolkien: A Descriptive Bibliography*. Winchester: St. Paul's Bibliographies, 1993. Print.

Hammond, Wayne G., and Christina Scull. *The Art of* The Hobbit *by J. R. R. Tolkien*. Boston: Houghton, 2012. Print.

———. *J. R. R. Tolkien: Artist and Illustrator*. New York: Houghton, 2004. Print.

———, eds. The Lord of the Rings, *1954–2004: Scholarship in Honor of Richard E. Blackwelder*. Milwaukee: Marquette UP, 2006. Print.

———. The Lord of the Rings*: A Reader's Companion*. Boston: Houghton, 2005. Print.

———. "Note on the Fiftieth Anniversary Edition." Tolkien, *Lord* xviii–xxi.

Hargrove, Gene. "Music in Middle-Earth." *Beyond Bree* Jan. 1995: 1–2. Web. 29 Aug. 2012.

Harris, Stephen L., and Gloria Platzner. *Classical Mythology: Images and Insights*. 5th ed. Boston: McGraw, 2008. Print.

Hatlen, Burton. "Pullman's *His Dark Materials*, a Challenge to the Fantasies of J. R. R. Tolkien and C. S. Lewis, with an Epilogue on Pullman's Neo-Romantic Reading of *Paradise Lost*." His Dark Materials *Illuminated: Critical Essays on Philip Pullman's Trilogy*. Ed. Millicent Lenz with Carole Scott. Detroit: Wayne State UP, 2005. 75–94. Print.

Hobb, Robin. "A Bar and a Quest." Haber 85–100.

Hooker, Mark T. "Frodo's Batman." *Tolkien Studies* 1 (2004): 125–36. Print.

Hostetter, Carl F., ed. *The Elvish Linguistic Fellowship*. Elvish Linguistic Fellowship, 2013. Web. 10 Sept. 2013.

———. "Tolkienian Linguistics: The First Fifty Years." *Tolkien Studies* 4 (2007): 1–46. Print.

Howard, Thomas. "Sacramental Imagination." *Christian History* 22.2 (2003): 23–25. Print.

Hughes, Richard. "The Lord of the Rings." Rev. of *The Fellowship of the Ring*, by J. R. R. Tolkien. *The Spectator* 1 Oct. 1954: 408–09. Print.

Hughes, Shaun F. D. "Postmodern Tolkien." *Modern Fiction Studies* 50.4 (2004): 807–13. Print.

Hulme, T. E. "Romanticism and Classicism." *The Collected Writings of T. E. Hulme*. Ed. Karen Csengeri. Oxford: Clarendon, 1994. 59–73. Print.

Hume, David. *A Treatise of Human Nature*. Oxford: Oxford UP, 1978. Print.

Hunter, John. "The Reanimation of Antiquity and the Resistance to History: Macpherson-Scott-Tolkien." Chance and Siewers 61–75.

Hurst, Roy. "Stepin Fetchit, Hollywood's First Black Film Star." *NPR Books*. NPR, 6 Mar. 2006. Web. 9 July 2012.

Iser, Wolfgang. *The Act of Reading: A Theory of Aesthetic Response*. Baltimore: Johns Hopkins UP, 1978. Print.

Jackson, Peter, dir. *The Fellowship of the Ring*. New Line Cinema, 2001. DVD.

———, dir. *The Fellowship of the Ring*. New Line Cinema, 2002. Spec. extended ed. DVD.

———, dir. *The Return of the King*. New Line Cinema, 2003. DVD.

———, dir. *The Two Towers*. New Line Cinema, 2002. DVD.

Jauss, Hans Robert. *Toward an Aesthetic of Reception*. Trans. Timothy Bahti. Minneapolis: U of Minnesota P, 1982. Print. Theory and History of Lit. 2.

Jenkins, Geraint. *A Rattleskull Genius: The Many Faces of Iolo Morganwg*. Rev. ed. Cardiff: U of Wales P, 2009. Print.

Johansson, Emil. *LOTR Project*. LotrProject, 2013. Web. 10 Sept. 2013.

Johnson, Judith A. *J. R. R. Tolkien: Six Decades of Criticism*. Westport: Greenwood, 1986. Print. Bibliogs. and Indexes in World Lit. 6.

Jones, Mary. "The Celtic Literature Collective." *Mary Jones*. Jones, 2012. Web. 21 Jan. 2012.

Jones, William. "Creation Stories and Epics—Introduction." *AHA Teaching and Learning in the Digital Age*. American Historical Assn., n.d. Web. 10 July 2010.

"JRR Tolkien's Oxford." *Virtual Tour of Oxford*. U of Oxford, 2002. Web. 10 Sept. 2013.

Kaissling, Julia. "The Purpose of Self-Conscious Participation of Story-Making in *The Two Towers*." 2006. TS.

Kane, Douglas Charles. *Arda Reconstructed: The Creation of the Published* Silmarillion. Bethlehem: Lehigh UP, 2009. Print.

Kant, Immanuel. *Foundations of the Metaphysics of Morals*. Trans. L. Beck. Indianapolis: Bobbs, 1969. Print.

Kaveney, Roz. "In the Tradition. . . ." Eaglestone 162–75.

Kidder, Tracy. *Mountains beyond Mountains: The Quest of Dr. Paul Farmer, a Man Who Would Cure the World*. New York: Random, 2004. Print.

Kilby, Clyde S. *Tolkien and* The Silmarillion. Wheaton: Shaw, 1976. Print.

Kilpatrick, Sue, Margaret Barrett, and Tammy Jones. "Defining Learning Communities." *Australian Association for Research in Education*. AARE, 2003. Web. 12 June 2010.

Kim, Sue. "Beyond Black and White: Race and Postmodernism in *The Lord of the Rings* Films." *Modern Fiction Studies* 50.4 (2004): 875–905. Print.

Kirby, W. F., trans. *Kalevala: The Land of the Heroes*. Comp. Elias Lönnrot. J. M. Dent and Sons, 1907. 2 vols. New York: Dutton, 1951. Print.

Kisor, Yvette. "Gollum as Exile." Forty-Second Intl. Congress on Medieval Studies. Western Michigan U, Kalamazoo. 10 May 2007. Presentation.

Koch, John T., and John Carey, eds. *The Celtic Heroic Age: Literary Sources for Ancient Celtic Europe and Early Ireland and Wales*. 4th ed. Aberystwyth: Celtic Studies, 2003. Print.

Kreeft, Peter. *The Philosophy of Tolkien: The Worldview behind* The Lord of the Rings. San Francisco: Ignatius, 2005. Print.

Kreglinger, Gisela. "George MacDonald." Drout, *J. R. R. Tolkien Encyclopedia* 399–400.

Larsen, Kristine. "The Astronomy of Middle-earth: Teaching Astronomy through Tolkien." *Cosmos in the Classroom 2004*. Ed. Andrew Fraknoi and William Waller. San Francisco: Astronomical Soc. of the Pacific, 2004. 237–45. Print.

———. "Shadow and Flame: Myth, Monsters, and Mother Nature in Middle-earth." *The Mirror Crack'd: Fear and Horror in J. R. R. Tolkien's* The Lord of the Rings *and Its Sources*. Ed. Lynn Forest-Hill. Newcastle upon Tyne: Cambridge Scholars, 2008. 169–96. Print.

Larsen, Kristine, and Marsha Bednarski. "Muggles, Meteoritic Armor, and Menelmacar: Using Fantasy Series in Astronomy Education and Outreach." *Preparing for the 2009 International Year of Astronomy*. Ed. Michael G. Gibbs et al. San Francisco: ASP, 2008. 82–90. Print.

Led Zeppelin. "The Battle of Evermore." *Led Zeppelin IV*. Atlantic Records, 1971. LP.

———. "Ramble On." *Led Zeppelin II*. Atlantic Records, 1969. LP.

Lee, Stuart D., and Elizabeth Solopova. *The Keys of Middle-earth: Discovering Medieval Literature through the Fiction of J. R. R. Tolkien*. New York: Palgrave, 2005. Print.

Le Guin, Ursula K. *Earthsea Revisioned*. Cambridge: Children's Lit. New England, 1993. Print.

———. "From Elfland to Poughkeepsie." Le Guin, *Language* 83–96.

———. *Language of the Night: Essays on Fantasy and Science Fiction*. Ed. Susan Wood. New York: Putnam's, 1979. Print.

Lehrer, Jonah. *Proust Was a Neuroscientist*. New York: Houghton, 2007. Print.

Leiber, Fritz. "Author's Note." *The Swords of Lankhmar: The Fifth Book of Fafhrd and the Gray Mouser*. New York: Ace, 1968. N. pag. Print.

Lesnik-Oberstein, Karin. "Defining Children's Literature and Childhood." *International Companion Encyclopedia of Children's Literature*. Ed. Peter Hunt. London: Routledge, 1996. 15–29. Print.

Levenson, Michael. *Modernism*. New Haven: Yale UP, 2011. Print.

Lewis, C. S. *Books, Broadcasts, and the War, 1931–1949*. Ed. Walter Hooper. New York: Harper, 2004. Print. Vol. 2 of *The Collected Letters of C. S. Lewis*.

———. "The Dethronement of Power." Zimbardo and Isaacs 11–15.

———. *The Four Loves*. New York: Harcourt, 1960. Print.

———. "The Gods Return to Earth." Rev. of *The Fellowship of the Ring*, by J. R. R. Tolkien. *Time and Tide* 35 (1954): 1082–83. Print.

———. *Of This and Other Worlds*. Ed. Walter Hooper. London: Fount, 1994. Print.

———. "On Science Fiction." Lewis, *Of This* 80–96.

———. "Our English Syllabus." *Image and Imagination*. Ed. Walter Hooper. Cambridge: Cambridge UP, 2013. 21–33. Print.

———. "A Reply to Professor Haldane." Lewis, *Of This* 81–94.

———. "Transposition." *"Transposition" and Other Essays*. London: G. Bles, 1949. 9–20. Print.

Lindsay, David. *A Voyage to Arcturus*. 1920. Radford: Wilder, 2007. Print.

Lobdell, Jared. *The Rise of Tolkienian Fantasy*. Peru: Open Court, 2005. Print.

———, ed. *A Tolkien Compass*. Peru: Open Court, 2003. Print.

Long, Josh. "Clinamen, Tessera, and the Anxiety of Influence: Swerving from and Completing George MacDonald." *Tolkien Studies* 6 (2009): 127–50. *Project Muse*. Web. 29 June 2010.

Long, Kate. "*Blackboard* Survey." Oklahoma Christian U, Dec. 2007. Assessment report.

———. "Language: Functions and Necessity in Tolkien's Literature." 2006. TS.

Lönnrot, Elias. *The Kalevala*. Trans. John Martin Crawford. *Internet Sacred Text Archive*. John Bruno Hare, n.d. Web. 16 Mar. 2010.

Lynch, Andrew. "Archaism, Nostalgia, and Tennysonian War in *The Lord of the Rings*." Chance and Siewers 77–92.

MacDonald, George. "The Fantastic Imagination." 1890. *Fantastic Literature: A Critical Reader*. Ed. David Sandner. Westport: Praeger, 2004. 64–69. Print.

Macintyre, Ben. "Play Up! Play Up! And Rhyme the Game. The Sublime Poetry of Cricket." *Times* [London] 9 Sept. 2005: n. pag. *The Times and Sunday Times Archive*. Web. 17 July 2010.

Magennis, Hugh. "Audience(s), Reception, Literacy." *A Companion to Anglo-Saxon Literature*. Ed. Phillip Pulsiano and Elaine Treharne. Oxford: Blackwell, 2001. 84–101. Print.

Maher, Michael W. "'A Land without Stain': Medieval Images of Mary and Their Use in the Characterization of Galadriel." Chance, *Tolkien the Medievalist* 225–36.

Mathews, Richard. *Fantasy: The Liberation of Imagination*. New York: Twayne, 1997. Print.

Mathijs, Ernest, ed. The Lord of the Rings*: Popular Culture in Global Contexts*. New York: Wallflower, 2006. Print.

Matthews, Dorothy. "Effect of a Curriculum Containing Creation Stories on Attitudes about Evolution." *American Biology Teacher* 63.6 (2001): 404–09. Print.

McCarthy, Jeanne Meehan. "Lámatyáveo Mauya." 2009. TS.

McFadden, Brian. "Fear of Difference, Fear of Death: The Sigelwara, Tolkien's Swertings, and Racial Difference." Chance and Siewers 155–69.

McFall, Lynne. "Integrity." *Ethics* 98.1 (1987): 5–20. Print.

McNees, Eleanor Jane. *Virginia Woolf: Critical Assessments*. Mountfield: Helm Information, 1994. Print.

Merritt, A. "The Woman of the Wood." 1926. Anderson, *Tales* 417–49.

Michaelsen, Larry K., Michael Sweet, and Dean X. Parmelee, eds. *Team-Based Learning: Small-Group Learning's Next Big Step*. San Francisco: Jossey-Bass, 2008. Print.

Miéville, China. "Tolkien—Middle-earth Meets Middle England." *Socialist Review* Jan. 2002: n. pag. Web. 29 July 2010.

Milbank, Alison. *Chesterton and Tolkien as Theologians: The Fantasy of the Real*. London: Clark, 2007. Print.

Millis, Barbara J., and Philip G. Cottell, Jr. *Cooperative Learning for Higher Education Faculty*. Phoenix: Amer. Council on Educ.; Oryx, 1998. Print.

Mitchison, Naomi. "One Ring to Bind Them." Rev. of *The Fellowship of the Ring*, by J. R. R. Tolkien. *New Statesman and Nation* 18 Sept. 1954: 331. Print.

Moorcock, Michael. "Epic Pooh." 1978. *Revolution: Science Fiction*. Rev. ed. N.p., n.d. Web. 29 July 2010.

Morris, William. *The Glittering Plain*. 1891. Rockville: Wildside, 2001. Print.

Mortimer, Patchen. "Tolkien and Modernism." *Tolkien Studies* 2 (2005): 113–29. *Project Muse*. Web. 23 May 2010.

"Mr. Alfred Duggan." *Times* [London] 6 Apr. 1964: 19. *Times Digital Archive*. Web. 7 July 2010.

Muir, Edwin. "A Boy's World." Rev. of *The Return of the King*, by J. R. R. Tolkien. *Observer* 27 Nov. 1955: 11. Print.

———. "The Ring." Rev. of *The Two Towers*, by J. R. R. Tolkien. *Observer* 21 Nov. 1954: 9. Print.

———. "Strange Epic." Rev. of *The Fellowship of the Ring*, by J. R. R. Tolkien. *Observer* 22 Aug. 1954: 7. Print.

Nagy, Gergely. "The Great Chain of Reading: (Inter)Textual Relations and the Technique of Mythopoesis in the Túrin Story." Chance, *Tolkien the Medievalist* 236–58.

———. "The Medievalist('s) Fiction: Textuality and Historicity as Aspects of Tolkien's Medievalist Cultural Theory in a Postmodernist Context." Chance and Siewers 29–41.

Nelson, Dale. "Literary Influences, Nineteenth and Twentieth Centuries." Drout, *J. R. R. Tolkien Encyclopedia* 366–78.

———. "Tolkien's Further Indebtedness to Haggard." *Mallorn* 47 (2009): 38–40. Print.

Nettle, Daniel, and Suzanne Romaine. *Vanishing Voices: The Extinction of the World's Languages*. New York: Oxford UP, 2002. Print.

New American Standard Bible. La Habra: Lockman, 1975. Print.

Newby, Jessica. "Charge of the Orcs." 2009. TS.

Nicolay, Theresa Freda. *Tolkien and the Modernists: Literary Responses to the Dark New Days of the Twentieth Century*. Jefferson: McFarland, 2014. Print.

Nimoy, Leonard. "The Ballad of Bilbo Baggins." Perf. Ricky Nelson. *Malibu U*. ABC, 21 July 1967. Television.

Noel, Ruth S. *The Languages of Tolkien's Middle-earth*. Boston: Houghton, 1980. Print.

Norman, Philip. "'More Than a Campus Craze, It's Like a Drug Dream': The Prevalence of Hobbits." *New York Times Magazine*. New York Times, 15 Jan. 1967: 31+. Web. 29 Aug. 2012.

Norton, Wil. "'The Escape of the Prisoner': Tolkien's Response to Modernism." 2010. TS.

Novakovich, Josip. *Writing Fiction Step by Step*. Cincinnati: Story, 1998. Print.

Oberhelman, David. "Textual History: Errors and Emendations." Drout, *J. R. R. Tolkien Encyclopedia* 640–41.

O'Hehir, Andrew. "The Book of the Century." *Salon*. Salon Media Group, 4 June 2001. Web. 3 Dec. 2012.

Ong, Walter. *Orality and Literacy*. 2nd ed. London: Routledge, 2002. Print.

Opie, Iona, and Peter Opie. *The Lore and Language of Schoolchildren*. Oxford: Clarendon, 1959. Print.

Orwell, George. "Good Bad Books." *The Complete Works of George Orwell*. Vol. 17. Ed. Peter Davison. London: Secker, 1998. 347–50. Print.

Page, R. I. *An Introduction to English Runes*. 2nd ed. Rochester: Boydell, 2000. Print.

Partridge, Brenda. "No Sex Please—We're Hobbits: The Construction of Female Sexuality in *The Lord of the Rings*." Giddings 179–97.

Pauli, Michelle. "Harper Lee Tops Librarians' Must-Read List." *Guardian*. Guardian News and Media, 2 Mar. 2006. Web. 3 Dec. 2012.

Pearce, Joseph, ed. *Tolkien: A Celebration*. San Francisco: Ignatius, 2001. Print.

———. *Tolkien: Man and Myth*. San Francisco: Ignatius, 1998. Print.

Perry, Michael W. *Untangling Tolkien: A Chronology and Commentary for* The Lord of the Rings. Seattle: Inkling, 2003. Print.

———. "William Morris." Drout, *J. R. R. Tolkien Encyclopedia* 439–41.

Pettersson, Ninni M. "What's in the History of Middle-earth? A Detailed List of the Contents of the Twelve HoMe-volumes and Unfinished Tales." *Mellonath Daeron—The Language Guild of the Forodrim*. N.p., 8 Apr. 2000. Web. 2 Oct. 2013.

Petty, Anne. *Tolkien in the Land of Heroes*. Cold Spring Harbor: Cold Spring, 2003. Print.

Plato. Protagoras *and* Meno. Trans. A. Beresford. London: Penguin, 2005. Print.

Plunkett, Edward. *The King of Elfland's Daughter*. 1924. New York: Ballantine, 1969. Print.

Popper, Karl. *The Logic of Scientific Discovery*. 1959. New York: Routledge, 2002. Print.

Pratchett, Terry. "Troll Bridge." Greenberg 34–43.

Prozesky, Maria. "The Text Tale of Frodo Nine-Fingered: Residual Oral Patterning in *The Lord of the Rings*." *Tolkien Studies* 3 (2006): 21–43. Print.

Purtill, Richard. *Lord of the Elves and Eldils: Fantasy and Philosophy in C. S. Lewis and J. R. R. Tolkien*. Grand Rapids: Zondervan, 1974. Print.

Rankin, Arthur, Jr., and Jules Bass. *The Hobbit*. Warner Home Video, 1977. DVD.

———. *The Return of the King*. Warner Home Video, 1980. DVD.

Rascoe, Burton. "In Defense of T. S. Eliot." Brooker 91–93.

Rateliff, John. *The History of* The Hobbit. 2 vols. Boston: Houghton, 2007. Print.

Rawls, Melanie. "The Feminine Principle in Tolkien." *Mythlore* 10.4 (1984): 5–13. Print.

Realms of Tolkien: Images of Middle-earth. London: Harper, 1996. Print.

Rearick, Anderson. "Why Is the Only Good Orc a Dead Orc? The Dark Face of Racism Examined in Tolkien's World." *Modern Fiction Studies* 50.4 (2004): 861–74. Print.

Reid, Robin Anne, and Judy Ann Ford. "From *Beowulf* to Post-modernism: Interdisciplinary Team-Teaching of J. R. R. Tolkien's *The Lord of the Rings*." *The Ring Goes Ever On: Proceedings of the Tolkien 2005 Conference: Fifty Years of* The Lord of the Rings. Ed. Sarah Wells. Vol. 1. Coventry: Tolkien Soc., 2008. 105–10. Print.

Reilly, Robert James. *Romantic Religion: A Study of Barfield, Lewis, Williams, and Tolkien*. Athens: U of Georgia P, 1971. Print.

Reynolds, James, and Fiona Stewart. "*Lord of the Rings* Labelled Racist." *Scotsman* 14 Dec. 2002: n. pag. Web. 31 July 2010.

Rhodes, Roy. "'The Way to Talk to Dragons': The Rhetoric of Bilbo Baggins." 2008. TS.

Richardson, Maurice. "New Novels." Rev. of *The Two Towers*, by J. R. R. Tolkien. *New Statesman and Nation* 48 (1954): 835–36. Print.

Ringel, Faye. "Women Fantasists: In the Shadow of the Ring." Clark and Timmons 159–71.

Ripp, Joseph. "Middle America Meets Middle-earth: American Discussion and Readership of J. R. R. Tolkien's *Lord of the Rings*, 1965–1969." *Book History* 8 (2005): 245–86. Print.

Roberts, Mark. "Adventure in English." Rev. of *The Lord of the Rings*, by J. R. R. Tolkien. *Essays in Criticism* 6 (1956): 450–59. Print.

Rogers, William N., II, and Michael R. Underwood. "Gagool and Gollum: Exemplars of Degeneration in *King Solomon's Mines* and *The Hobbit*." Clark and Timmons 121–31.

Roos, Richard. "Middle Earth in the Classroom: Studying J. R. R. Tolkien." *English Journal* 58.8 (1969): 1175–80. Print.

Rosebury, Brian. "Race in Tolkien Films." Drout, *J. R. R. Tolkien Encyclopedia* 557.

———. *Tolkien: A Cultural Phenomenon*. 2nd ed. Basingstoke: Palgrave, 2003. Print.

Ross, David. *The Right and the Good*. 1930. Oxford: Oxford UP, 2002. Print.

Russell, Gary. *The Art of* The Lord of the Rings. Boston: Houghton, 2004. Print.

Salo, David. *A Gateway to Sindarin: A Grammar of an Elvish Language from J. R. R. Tolkien's* Lord of the Rings. Salt Lake City: U of Utah P, 2007. Print.

Saxon, Wolfgang. "Donald Barr, 82, Headmaster and Science Educator." *New York Times* 10 Feb. 2004, late ed.: B8. *ProQuest Historical Newspapers*. Web. 6 July 2010.

Schweitzer, Darrell. *The Fantastic Horizon: Essays and Reviews*. Rockville: Wildside, 2009. Print.

Scoville, Chester N. "Pastoralia and Perfectibility in William Morris and J. R. R. Tolkien." Chance and Siewers 93–103.

Scull, Christina, and Wayne G. Hammond, eds. *The J. R. R. Tolkien Companion and Guide*. 2 vols. Boston: Houghton, 2006. Print.

Sertillanges, A. G. *The Intellectual Life: Its Spirit, Conditions, Methods*. Washington: Catholic U of America P, 1998. Print.

Shippey, Tom. "An Interview with Tom Shippey." *HarperCollins*. Harper, 2001. Web. 15 Jan. 2004.

———. *J. R. R. Tolkien: Author of the Century*. Boston: Houghton, 2002. Print.

———. "Literature, Twentieth Century: Influence of Tolkien." Drout, *J. R. R. Tolkien Encyclopedia* 378–82.

———. "Orcs, Wraiths, Wights: Tolkien's Images of Evil." Clark and Timmons 183–98.

———. *The Road to Middle-earth*. Rev. ed. Boston: Houghton, 2003. Print.

———. *Roots and Branches: Selected Papers on Tolkien*. Zurich: Walking Tree, 2007. Print.

Sinex, Margaret. "'Monsterized Saracens,' Tolkien's Haradrim, and Other Medieval 'Fantasy Products.'" *Tolkien Studies* 7 (2010): 175–96. Print.

Singh, G. "Professor Mark Roberts: Distinguished Literary Critic." *Independent* 22 Aug. 2006: n. pag. Web. 2 Apr. 2012.

"Slaughter." *The Great War and the Shaping of the Twentieth Century*. PBS Home Video, 1998. VHS.

Smith, Barbara Leigh, et al. *Learning Communities: Reforming Undergraduate Education*. San Francisco: Jossey-Bass, 2004. Print.

Smith, Thomas W. "Tolkien's Catholic Imagination: Mediation and Tradition." *Religion and Literature* 38.2 (2006): 73–100. Print.

Smol, Anna. "Frodo's Body: Liminality and the Experience of War." *The Body in Tolkien's Legendarium: Essays on Middle-earth Corporeality*. Ed. Christopher Vaccaro. Jefferson: McFarland, 2013. 39–62. Print.

———. "Male Friendship in *The Lord of the Rings*: Medievalism, the First World War, and Contemporary Rewritings." *Mount Saint Vincent University E-commons*.

Mount E-commons, 12 Aug. 2010. Web. 4 Feb. 2014. <http://dc.msvu.ca:8080/xmlui/handle/10587/629>.

———. "'Oh . . . *Oh . . . Frodo!*': Readings of Male Intimacy in *The Lord of the Rings*." *Modern Fiction Studies* 50.4 (2004): 949–79. Print.

Snow, C. P. *The Two Cultures*. 1959. Cambridge: Cambridge UP, 1998. Print.

Spaulding, Mira. "Songs of the Hobbits from *The Lord of the Rings*." 2009. TS.

Sproul, Barbara. *Primal Myths*. San Francisco: Harper, 1991. Print.

"Stand, Men of the West." *British National Party*. British Natl. Party, 9 Aug. 2007. *Internet Archive*. Web. 3 June 2012.

Stanton, Michael N. "Teaching Tolkien." *Exercise Exchange* 18.1 (1973): 2–5. Print.

Stevens, Jen. "From Catastrophe to Eucatastrophe: J. R .R. Tolkien's Transformation of Ovid's Mythic Pyramus and Thisbe into Beren and Lúthien." Chance, *Tolkien and the Invention* 119–32.

Stewart, R. J. *The Elements of Creation Myth*. Dorset: Element, 1989. Print.

Straubhaar, Sandra Ballif. "Myth, Late Roman History and Multiculturalism in Tolkien's Middle-earth." Chance, *Tolkien and the Invention* 101–18.

Strickland, Debra Higgs. *Saracens, Demons, and Jews: Making Monsters in Medieval Art*. Princeton: Princeton UP, 2003. Print.

Sturluson, Snorri. "Gylfaginning." *The Prose Edda*. Trans. Arthur Gilchrist Brodeur. Internet Sacred Text Archive, n.d. Web. 16 Mar. 2010.

———. "Prologue." *The Prose Edda*. Trans. Arthur Gilchrist Brodeur. Internet Sacred Text Archive, n.d. Web. 16 Mar. 2010.

Swann, Donald, comp., and J. R. R. Tolkien. *The Road Goes Ever On: A Song Cycle*. 2nd ed. London: Harper, 2002. CD, print.

Taylor, William L. "Frodo Lives." *English Journal* 56.6 (1967): 818–21. Print.

Thomas, Melissa. "Teaching Fantasy: Overcoming the Stigma of Fluff." *The English Journal* 92.5 (2003): 60–64. Print.

Thomas Aquinas. *Summa Theologica*. Internet Sacred Text Archive, n.d. Web. 4 Feb. 2015.

Timmons, Daniel. "Frodo on Film: Peter Jackson's Problematic Portrayal." Croft, *Tolkien on Film* 123–48.

Tolkien Ensemble. The Lord of the Rings*: Complete Songs and Poems*. Niederrohrdorf: Membrane, 2006. CD.

Tolkien, J. R. R. *The Adventures of Tom Bombadil*. Tolkien, *Tolkien Reader* 189–231.

———. *The Annotated* Hobbit. Ed. Douglas A. Anderson. Rev. 2nd ed. Boston: Houghton, 2002. Print.

———. "The Battle of the Eastern Field." *King Edward's School Chronicle* 26.186 (1911): 22–26. Rpt. in *Mallorn* 12 (1978): 24–28. Print.

———. Beowulf*: A Translation and Commentary*. Ed. Christopher Tolkien. Boston: Houghton, 2014. Print.

———. Beowulf *and the Critics*. Ed. Michael D. C. Drout. Tempe: Arizona Medieval and Renaissance Texts and Studies, 2002. Print. Medieval and Renaissance Texts and Studies 248.

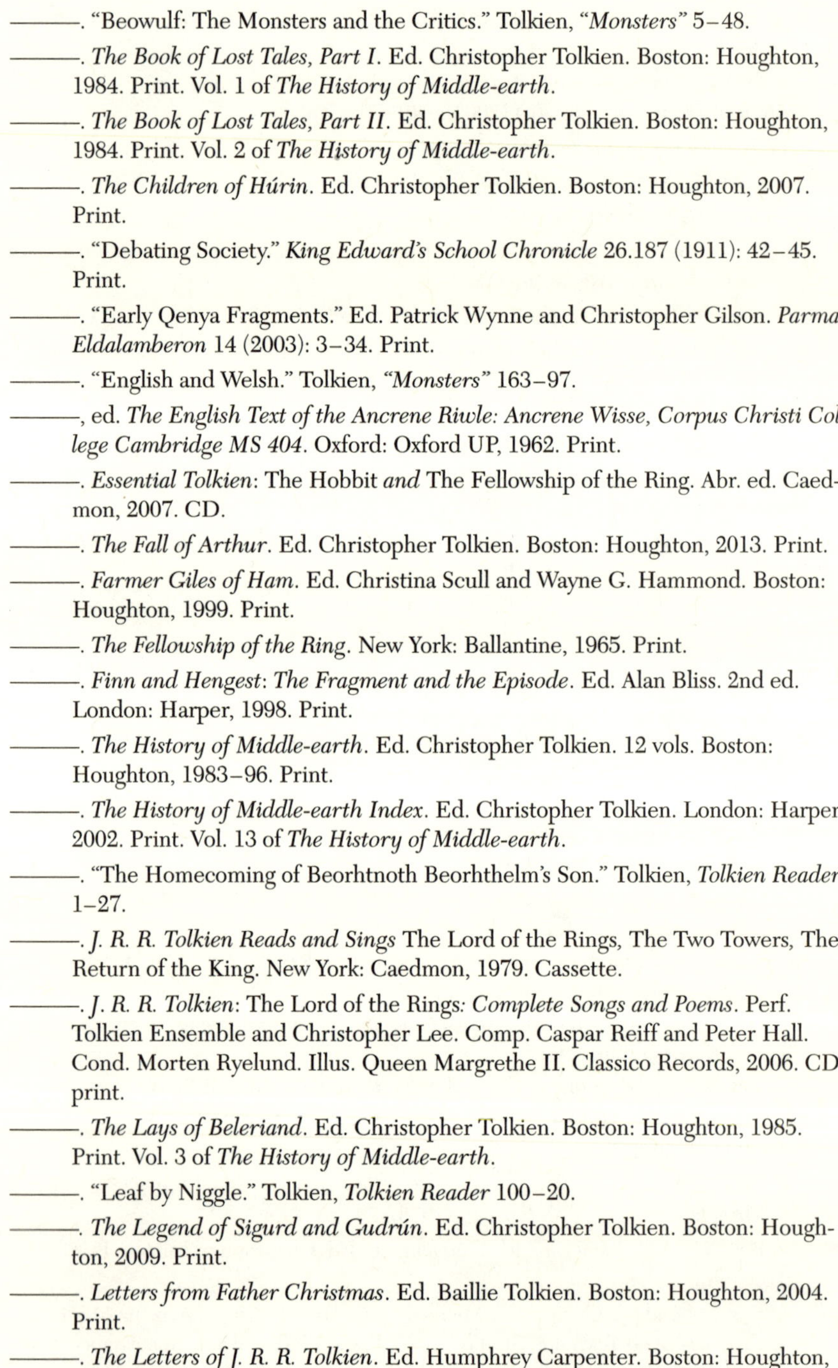

———. "Beowulf: The Monsters and the Critics." Tolkien, *"Monsters"* 5–48.

———. *The Book of Lost Tales, Part I*. Ed. Christopher Tolkien. Boston: Houghton, 1984. Print. Vol. 1 of *The History of Middle-earth*.

———. *The Book of Lost Tales, Part II*. Ed. Christopher Tolkien. Boston: Houghton, 1984. Print. Vol. 2 of *The History of Middle-earth*.

———. *The Children of Húrin*. Ed. Christopher Tolkien. Boston: Houghton, 2007. Print.

———. "Debating Society." *King Edward's School Chronicle* 26.187 (1911): 42–45. Print.

———. "Early Qenya Fragments." Ed. Patrick Wynne and Christopher Gilson. *Parma Eldalamberon* 14 (2003): 3–34. Print.

———. "English and Welsh." Tolkien, *"Monsters"* 163–97.

———, ed. *The English Text of the Ancrene Riwle: Ancrene Wisse, Corpus Christi College Cambridge MS 404*. Oxford: Oxford UP, 1962. Print.

———. *Essential Tolkien*: The Hobbit *and* The Fellowship of the Ring. Abr. ed. Caedmon, 2007. CD.

———. *The Fall of Arthur*. Ed. Christopher Tolkien. Boston: Houghton, 2013. Print.

———. *Farmer Giles of Ham*. Ed. Christina Scull and Wayne G. Hammond. Boston: Houghton, 1999. Print.

———. *The Fellowship of the Ring*. New York: Ballantine, 1965. Print.

———. *Finn and Hengest: The Fragment and the Episode*. Ed. Alan Bliss. 2nd ed. London: Harper, 1998. Print.

———. *The History of Middle-earth*. Ed. Christopher Tolkien. 12 vols. Boston: Houghton, 1983–96. Print.

———. *The History of Middle-earth Index*. Ed. Christopher Tolkien. London: Harper, 2002. Print. Vol. 13 of *The History of Middle-earth*.

———. "The Homecoming of Beorhtnoth Beorhthelm's Son." Tolkien, *Tolkien Reader* 1–27.

———. *J. R. R. Tolkien Reads and Sings* The Lord of the Rings, The Two Towers, The Return of the King. New York: Caedmon, 1979. Cassette.

———. *J. R. R. Tolkien*: The Lord of the Rings*: Complete Songs and Poems*. Perf. Tolkien Ensemble and Christopher Lee. Comp. Caspar Reiff and Peter Hall. Cond. Morten Ryelund. Illus. Queen Margrethe II. Classico Records, 2006. CD, print.

———. *The Lays of Beleriand*. Ed. Christopher Tolkien. Boston: Houghton, 1985. Print. Vol. 3 of *The History of Middle-earth*.

———. "Leaf by Niggle." Tolkien, *Tolkien Reader* 100–20.

———. *The Legend of Sigurd and Gudrún*. Ed. Christopher Tolkien. Boston: Houghton, 2009. Print.

———. *Letters from Father Christmas*. Ed. Baillie Tolkien. Boston: Houghton, 2004. Print.

———. *The Letters of J. R. R. Tolkien*. Ed. Humphrey Carpenter. Boston: Houghton, 1981. Print.

———. *The Lord of the Rings*. 50th anniversary ed. Boston: Houghton, 2005. Print.

———. *"The Lost Road" and Other Writings*. Ed. Christopher Tolkien. Boston: Houghton, 1987. Print. Vol. 5 of *The History of Middle-earth*.

———. *"The Monsters and the Critics" and Other Essays*. Ed. Christopher Tolkien. Boston: Houghton, 1984. Print.

———. *Morgoth's Ring*. Ed. Christopher Tolkien. Boston: Houghton, 1993. Print. Vol. 10 of *The History of Middle-earth*.

———. *Mr. Bliss*. London: Harper, 2011. Print.

———. "Mythopoeia." Tolkien, *Tree* 83–90.

———. "On Fairy-stories." Tolkien, *Tolkien Reader* 33–99.

———. "On Translating Beowulf." Tolkien, *"Monsters"* 49–71.

———. *The Peoples of Middle-earth*. Ed. Christopher Tolkien. Boston: Houghton, 1996. Print. Vol. 12 of *The History of Middle-earth*.

———. *The Return of the King*. 2nd ed., rev. impression. Boston: Houghton, 1987. Print.

———. *The Return of the Shadow*. Ed. Christopher Tolkien. Boston: Houghton, 1988. Print. Vol. 6 of *The History of Middle-earth*.

———. *Roverandom*. Ed. Christina Scull and Wayne G. Hammond. New York: Houghton, 1999. Print.

———. *Sauron Defeated*. Ed. Christopher Tolkien. Boston: Houghton, 1992. Print. Vol. 9 of *The History of Middle-earth*.

———. "A Secret Vice." Tolkien, *"Monsters"* 198–223.

———. *The Shaping of Middle-earth*. Ed. Christopher Tolkien. Boston: Houghton, 1986. Print. Vol. 4 of *The History of Middle-earth*.

———. "Sigelwara Land." *Medium Aevum* 1.3 (1932): 183–96; 3.2 (1934): 95–111. Print.

———. *The Silmarillion*. Ed. Christopher Tolkien. 2nd ed. Boston: Houghton, 2001. Print.

———. "Sir Gawain and the Green Knight." Tolkien, *"Monsters"* 72–108.

———, trans. Sir Gawain and the Green Knight, Pearl, *and* Sir Orfeo. London: Allen, 1975. Print.

———. *Smith of Wootton Major*. Ed. Verlyn Flieger. Extended ed. London: Harper, 2005. Print.

———. *Tales from the Perilous Realm*. Boston: Houghton, 2008. Print.

———. *Tolkien: "On Fairy-stories."* Ed. Verlyn Flieger and Douglas A. Anderson. London: Harper, 2008. Print.

———. *The Tolkien Reader*. 2nd ed. New York: Ballantine, 1989. Print.

———. *The Treason of Isengard*. Ed. Christopher Tolkien. Boston: Houghton, 1989. Print. Vol. 7 of *The History of Middle-earth*.

———. *Tree and Leaf, Including the Poem "Mythopoeia" [and] "The Homecoming of Beorhtnoth Beorhthelm's Son."* London: Harper, 2001. Print.

———. *The Two Towers*. 2nd ed., rev. impression. Boston: Houghton, 1987. Print.

———. *Unfinished Tales of Númenor and Middle-earth*. Ed. Christopher Tolkien. Boston: Houghton, 1980. Print.

———. "Valedictory Address to the University of Oxford." Tolkien, *"Monsters"* 224–40.

———. *The War of the Jewels*. Ed. Christopher Tolkien. Boston: Houghton, 1994. Print. Vol. 11 of *The History of Middle-earth*.

Tolkien, J. R. R., and E. V. Gordon, eds. *Sir Gawain and the Green Knight*. 2nd ed. Ed. Norman Davis. New York: Oxford UP, 1967. Print.

Tolkien, J. R. R., and Christopher Tolkien. *The J. R. R. Tolkien Audio Collection*. Harper Audio Caedmon, 2007. CD.

Tolkien's World: Paintings of Middle-earth. New York: MJF, 1992. Print.

Toulmin, Stephen. *The Uses of Argument*. Cambridge: Cambridge UP, 1958. Print.

Toulmin, Stephen, Richard Rieke, and Allan Janik. *An Introduction to Reasoning*. New York: Macmillan, 1978. Print.

Turgon (David E. Smith), ed. *The Tolkien Fan's Medieval Reader*. Cold Spring Harbor: Cold Spring, 2004. Print.

Tyler, J. E. A. *The Complete Tolkien Companion*. New York: St. Martin's, 1976. Print.

Van Engen, Abram. "Reclaiming Claims: What English Students Want from English Profs." *Pedagogy: Critical Approaches to Teaching Literature, Language, Composition, and Culture* 5.1 (2005): 5–18. Print.

Van Hulle, Dirk, and Joep Leerssen, eds. *Editing the Nation's Memory: Textual Scholarship and Nation-Building in Nineteenth-Century Europe*. Amsterdam: Rodopi, 2008. Print.

Vaninskaya, Anna. "Tolkien: A Man of His Time?" Weinreich and Honegger 1–30.

Vink, Renée. "'Jewish' Dwarves: Tolkien and Anti-Semitic Stereotyping." *Tolkien Studies* 10 (2013): 123–45. Print.

Vitaliano, Dorothy. *Legends of the Earth: Their Geologic Origins*. Bloomington: Indiana UP, 1973. Print.

Walmsley, Nigel. "Tolkien and the '60s." Giddings 73–86.

Walter, Brian. "Synthesizing Artistic Delight: The Lessons of *Pale Fire*." *Zembla*. Nabokov Soc., 2007. Web. 6 July 2012.

Walter, George, ed. *Penguin Book of First World War Poetry*. London: Penguin, 2006. Print.

"The Wanderer." *The Norton Anthology of English Literature*. 8th ed. Vol. D. Ed. Stephen Greenblatt et al. New York: Norton, 2006. 111–13. Print.

Warchus, Matthew, dir. "The Cat and the Moon." *Lord of the Rings: On Stage*. *YouTube*. YouTube, 2008. Web. 25 Oct. 2010.

Washington Center. Washington Center at Evergreen State Coll., n.d. Web. 28 Sept. 2013.

Waymeet for Teachers. MLA, n.d. Web. 10 Sept. 2013.

Weinreich, Frank, and Thomas Honegger, eds. *Tolkien and Modernity*. 2 vols. Zurich: Walking Tree, 2006. Print. Cormarë Ser. 9–10.

Weldon, Glen, ed. "Your Picks: Top Hundred Science-Fiction, Fantasy Books." *NPR*. NPR, 11 Aug. 2011. Web. 3 Dec. 2012.

West, Richard C. "Setting the Rocket Off in Story: The *Kalevala* as the Germ of Tolkien's Legendarium." Chance, *Tolkien and the Invention* 285–94.

Whittingham, Elizabeth A. *The Evolution of Tolkien's Mythology: A Study of the History of Middle-earth*. Ed. Donald E. Palimbo and C. W. Sullivan III. Jefferson: McFarland, 2007. Print. Critical Explorations in Science Fiction and Fantasy 7.

Wiggins, Kayla McKinney. "The Art of the Story-Teller and the Person of the Hero." Croft, *Tolkien on Film* 103–22.

Williams, Raymond. *The Country and the City*. London: Hogarth, 1985. Print.

Wilson, Edmund. "Oo, Those Awful Orcs!" *Nation* 182 (1956): 312–14. Print.

———. "The Poetry of Drouth." Brooker 83–87.

Wilson, Edward O. *Consilience: The Unity of Knowledge*. New York: Knopf, 1998. Print.

———. *The Future of Life*. New York: Knopf, 2002. Print.

Wong, Kate. "Rethinking the Hobbits of Indonesia." *Scientific American* 301.5 (2009): 66–73. Print.

Woolf, Virginia. "Modern Fiction." *The Common Reader, First Series*. Ed. Andrew McNeillie. London: Hogarth, 1984. 146–54. Print.

———. *Orlando: A Biography*. 1928. Ed. Rachel Bowlby. Oxford: Oxford UP, 2008. Print.

———. *To the Lighthouse*. 1927. San Diego: Harcourt, 1955. Print.

Yatt, John. "Wraiths and Race." *Guardian* 2 Dec. 2002: n. pag. Web. 31 Jul. 2010.

Your Country's Call. Imperial War Museums Collections. Imperial War Museums, n.d. Web. 25 Oct. 2010.

Zimbardo, Rose A., and Neil D. Isaacs, eds. *Understanding* The Lord of the Rings*: The Best of Tolkien Criticism*. Boston: Houghton, 2004. Print.

INDEX OF WORKS WRITTEN, EDITED, OR TRANSLATED BY J. R. R. TOLKIEN

Adventures of Tom Bombadil, 14, 16, 23, 94, 110, 239
"Ainulindalë," 59, 60–61, 79, 83n6, 228
Ancrene Wisse, 215

"Beowulf: The Monsters and the Critics," 16, 17, 34, 39, 52–53, 55, 57, 89, 92, 102, 102n1, 129, 131, 135n14, 140, 195, 201–02, 204, 211, 213n3
Beowulf: *A Translation and Commentary*, 16
Book of Lost Tales (early versions and parts 1 and 2), 13, 58, 59, 63nn3–4, 75, 78, 79, 80, 81, 82, 82n2, 83n6, 94, 117, 149

Children of Húrin, 13, 43n3, 79, 80, 83 (nn 7, 9)

"English and Welsh," 17, 39, 157, 158

Fall of Arthur, 16
Farmer Giles of Ham, 14, 16, 27n5, 80
Fellowship of the Ring, 5, 14, 78, 108, 111, 112, 113, 118, 127, 128, 129, 165, 169, 170, 173, 191, 192, 193, 194, 195, 196, 197, 198, 210, 225, 231, 232
Finn and Hengest, 63

History of Middle-earth, 13, 26, 28, 37, 75–82, 82n1, 83nn5–6, 96, 137, 179, 182
The Hobbit, 4, 9, 11–12, 13, 17, 21, 23, 24, 25, 26, 27, 27n5, 28 (nn 12, 17), 32, 39, 43n5, 45, 51, 56, 57, 62, 63, 65–74, 74n1, 85, 92, 95, 98, 102n3, 123n9, 128, 140, 151, 158, 159, 177, 179, 195, 201, 205, 210, 211, 225, 228
"Homecoming of Beorhtnoth Beorhthelm's Son," 14, 15, 16, 57, 89, 132

Lays of Beleriand, 76, 80, 81
"Leaf by Niggle," 14, 15, 16, 90, 101, 131, 136n20
Legend of Sigurd and Gudrún, 16
Letters from Father Christmas, 14
Letters of J. R. R. Tolkien, 4, 5, 11, 12, 15, 18, 21, 43, 48, 50, 54, 55, 57, 59, 64, 73, 80, 85, 89, 90, 103, 111, 123n8, 124n12, 132, 136n18, 145, 147, 157–58, 173, 174, 177, 178, 179, 196, 202, 219, 233
Lost Road, 79, 80, 81, 82n2, 83n6, 160

Morgoth's Ring, 76, 79, 83n6, 182n5
Mr. Bliss, 14
"Mythopoeia," 15, 28, 86, 90n1, 173, 239

"On Fairy-stories," 9, 15, 16, 17, 34, 39, 43n9, 45, 50, 51, 52, 55, 62, 83n12, 86, 89, 93, 102, 115, 120, 121, 124n11, 135, 141, 164, 173, 175, 177, 188, 194, 201, 202, 203, 204, 209–10, 211, 213, 213n3, 238, 239
"On Translating Beowulf," 17, 43n9

Peoples of Middle-earth, 80, 148

"Quenta Silmarillion" (various versions), 59, 78, 79, 80, 81, 82, 83n6, 159, 228

Return of the King, 130, 132, 173, 177, 184, 196, 209, 215, 225
Return of the Shadow, 78
Roverandom, 14, 16

Sauron Defeated, 76, 78, 80
"A Secret Vice," 17
Shaping of Middle-earth, 79, 80, 81, 83 (nn 6, 10)
Silmarillion, 4, 9, 12–13, 24, 26, 28n17, 41, 43n3, 56–57, 58, 59, 60–63, 66, 76, 77, 78, 79, 80, 81, 82, 83nn9–10, 89, 139, 145, 158, 159, 162, 177, 178, 179, 180, 181, 182, 201, 203, 210, 211, 218, 225, 228–29, 230n2, 231, 234–36, 237
Sir Gawain and the Green Knight (edition), 92
"Sir Gawain and the Green Knight" (lecture), 17
Sir Gawain and the Green Knight (translation), 16, 17, 215
"Sketch of the Mythology," 78, 80, 81, 82
Smith of Wootton Major, 14, 15, 16, 101

Treason of Isengard, 76, 78, 82n3
Two Towers, 5, 78, 113, 128, 129–30, 132, 133n1, 148, 168, 170, 173, 225, 229

Unfinished Tales of Númenor and Middle-earth, 13, 62, 64, 81, 82n1, 83n9, 87

"Valaquenta," 59, 62, 79, 228
"Valedictory Address to the University of Oxford," 17, 39, 142

War of the Jewels, 80, 81, 82n2, 83 (nn 8, 11)

INDEX OF NAMES

Abley, Mark, 157
Acton, Lord (John Dalberg-Acton), 135n13
Adorno, Theodor, 43n9
"Adventures of the Sons of Eochaid Mugmedón," 88, 91n5
Alter, Stephen G., 147
Amison, Anne, 123n8
Amodio, Mark C., 92
Anderson, Douglas A., 6, 11, 17, 19, 28n5, 74n4, 122n1, 123n7, 207, 208
Ariosto, Ludovico, 45
Aristotle, 220, 223
Arnold, Matthew, 108
Arul, Melissa Ruth, 57–58
Attebery, Brian, 114, 122nn1–2
Auden, W. H., 6, 38, 44–45, 49n1, 128, 129, 130, 132–33, 136 (nn 17, 23), 140, 158, 237
Augustine, 89, 174

Bacon, Francis, 147
Bakhtin, M. M., 114
Bakshi, Ralph, 27
Ballinger, Lucy, 47
Baltasar, Michaela, 209–10, 211, 213n3
Barfield, Owen, 19
Barkley, Elizabeth F., 242n3
Barr, Donald, 128, 135n10
Barrett, Margaret, 213n1
Barthes, Roland, 42
Bass, Jules, 27, 66
Battle of Maldon, 15, 57, 63n2, 89, 90n4, 97–98, 99, 129, 132, 136n20
Beagle, Peter S., 16, 118–19
Beahm, George W., 28n17
Bebb, Angela, 228
Bede, Venerable, 233
Bednarski, Marsha, 177
Benjamin, Walter, 42, 43n9
Bentham, Jeremy, 219
Beowulf, 7, 16, 36, 40, 53, 55, 59, 88, 89, 92, 97, 98, 99–100, 102, 103, 104, 106, 129–30, 131, 133n1, 136n20, 100, 173, 192–93, 194, 195–97, 201–02, 204, 205, 207, 210, 215, 234, 236n9
Berry, Wendell, 113
Bertenstam, Åke, 19
Bible, 32, 174, 175, 186, 201
Blackham, Robert S., 18
Bloch, Ernst, 43n9
Bloom, Harold, 38, 114, 176n1
Boethius, 89, 97, 100–01
Bogstad, Janice M., 27, 48
Bolin, Michael, 176
Bopp, Franz, 147
Boyd, Ian, 176n1
Boyens, Philippa, 218
Brackmann, Rebecca, 149n5
Bratman, David, 13, 48
Brecht, Bertolt, 43n9
Breivik, Anders, 47
Bretherton, Christopher, 57
Brodeur, Arthur Gilchrist, 90n4
Brogam, Hugh, 124n12
Brooker, Jewel Spears, 135n8
Brust, Steven, 122, 125n19
Buchan, John, 209
Burkert, Walter, 209, 211
Burns, Marjorie J., 21, 116, 123n8, 213n2

Cabell, James Branch, 209
Cad Goddeu, 88, 91n5
Cædmon, 233
Caldecott, Stratford, 172, 174, 176n1
Campbell, Joseph, 210, 211
Cantor, Norman, 215
Card, Orson Scott, 48
Carey, John, 91n5
Carneiro, Robert, 181
Carpenter, Humphrey, 4, 11, 18, 19, 27 (nn 2, 4), 37, 55, 85, 122n3, 123n5, 134n3, 138, 139, 140, 173, 199n3, 237, 242n1
Carroll, Lewis (Charles Dodgson), 73
Carter, Stephen L., 222
Carter, Susan, 151, 156n2
Cauty, Jimmy, 41
Chance, Jane, 21, 88, 149n3, 167, 176n1, 210
Charlemagne, 105
Chaucer, Geoffrey, 92, 192, 194
Chesterton, G. K., 116, 123–24 (nn 10, 13), 128, 238
Chism, Christine, 149n4
Churchill, Caryl, 36
Cobb, Christopher, 120
Cohen, Jeffrey Jerome, 149n2
Cohen, Patricia, 164n6
Coleridge, Samuel Taylor, 135n10
Constantine, Mary-Ann, 90n3
Cottell, Philip G., Jr., 242n3
Craig, David M., 218
Crawford, John Martin, 90n4
Croft, Janet Brennan, 18, 21, 27
Cross, Patricia K., 242n3
Crossley, Robert, 35n1
Crowe, Edith L., 218
Curry, Patrick, 28n8, 36, 43n2, 123n6, 144

Darwin, Charles, 146, 147, 183, 184–86, 187, 190n1
Dasent, George Webbe, 86
Dawson, Deidre, 144
"Death of Diarmait Mac Cerbaill," 88, 91n5
de Lint, Charles, 120–21, 122, 124n17
Dickens, Charles, 6, 92
Dickerson, Matthew, 113
Dimond, Andy, 213n2
Donovan, Leslie A., 151
Dorson, Richard M., 209
Drout, Michael D. C., 19, 43n10, 63n5, 134, 199n3
Dubs, Kathleen E., 101
Duggan, Alfred Leo, 128, 135n10
Dumas, Alexandre, 125n19
Dunsany, Lord (Edward Plunkett), 116, 117–18, 123n8, 124n11
Duriez, Colin, 19, 20, 237
Dyson, Hugo, 173

Eddas, 16, 36, 88, 90n4, 102n5, 201, 205, 210. *See also Poetic Edda* and Sturluson, Snorri
Eddison, E. R., 116, 123n8, 124n11
Eliot, T. S., 8, 87, 114, 128, 129, 130–31, 132, 133, 135n8, 136n18
Empson, William, 108
Enright, Nancy, 151, 173, 174, 176n2
Enya, 24
Evans, Jonathan, 113

Farmer, Paul, 176
Fauchois, René, 133
Faust, Cosette, 63n2
Feist, Raymond, 8
Fife, Ernelle, 151
Fifield, Merle, 31
Fimi, Dimitra, 146, 148, 149n5, 164n2
Fisher, Jason, 43n10
Flieger, Verlyn, 8, 15, 17, 21, 36, 39, 63nn6–7, 83n12, 94, 96n1, 123n5, 134n2, 164n3, 167, 169, 171n1, 213n2
Foley, John Miles, 94
Fonstad, Karen Wynn, 26
Ford, Judy Ann, 35n2, 214, 216, 217
Ford, Patrick K., 91n5
Forster, E. M., 126
Foster, Robert, 20
Foucault, Michel, 101
Franson, Craig, 123n3
Frye, Northrop, 114, 200
Fussell, Paul, 193, 196

Gabelnick, F., 213n1
Gaiman, Neil, 122
Garth, John, 18, 27n3, 195, 198, 216
Gay, David Elton, 213n2
Geoffrey of Monmouth, 106, 201
Gianluca, Mezzofiore, 49n4
Gilliver, Peter, 164n4, 215
Glenn, Jonathan, 90n4, 97
Glyer, Diana Pavlac, 19, 27n4, 123n5, 237
Golding, William, 6, 7, 87, 126
Gordon, E. V., 57, 63n2, 92
Graves, Robert, 87
Green, William H., 123n9, 151
Greenberg, Martin, 207
Greenhill, Sam, 49n4
Gresham, Douglas, 173
Grimm Brothers (Jacob and Wilhelm), 123n4
Grindley, Carl James, 171n1
Gurney, Ivor, 196
Gysin, Christian, 49n4

Haber, Karen, 48, 124n14
Hagège, Claude, 157
Haggard, H. Rider, 46, 116, 118, 119, 123n9, 124n13
Haldane, J. B. S., 129
Hammond, Wayne G., 9, 10, 14, 15, 19, 20, 21, 25, 27 (nn 2, 6), 28 (nn 10, 15, 18), 195, 199n3
Hargrove, Gene, 23
Harris, Stephen, 211
Hatlen, Burton, 125n21
Heller, Joseph, 87
Hengest, 59, 63n5
Hesiod, 201, 205, 207
"Hey Diddle Diddle," 197
Hildebrandt Brothers (Greg and Tim), 41
Hobb, Robin, 33
Homer, 93, 103, 104, 131, 207, 210
Honegger, Thomas, 28n9
Hooker, Mark T., 196
Hooper, Walter, 27n1
Horsa, 59
Hostetter, Carl F., 22
Howard, Robert E., 46
Howard, Thomas, 172, 176n1
Howe, John, 25, 28, 41
Hughes, Richard, 128, 133
Hughes, Shaun F. D., 35n2
Hulme, T. E., 133
Hume, David, 222
Hunter, John, 123n4
Hurst, Roy, 47
Huxley, Aldous, 201

Inglis, Rob, 109
Isaacs, Neil D., 21
Iser, Wolfgang, 43n8

Jackson, Peter, 26, 27, 28n17, 36, 37, 40, 41, 42, 42n1, 43n5, 46, 47, 48, 85, 88, 103, 107n2, 111, 128, 144, 148, 165–71,

171nn1–3, 187, 198, 204, 205, 215, 217, 218, 231, 232
Janik, Allan, 190n3
Jauss, Hans Robert, 42
Jenkins, Geraint, 90n3
Johansson, Emil, 26
Johnson, Judith A., 19
Jones, Mary, 91n5
Jones, Tammy, 213n1
Jones, William, 181
Joyce, James, 8, 37, 92, 127, 128
Jung, C. G., 210

Kaissling, Julia, 229
Kane, Douglas Charles, 13, 77
Kant, Immanuel, 222
Kaveny, Philip E., 27, 48, 124nn14–15
Kay, Guy Gavriel, 4, 12, 120, 124n16
Kidder, Tracy, 176
Kilby, Clyde S., 174, 176n1
Kilpatrick, Sue, 213n1
Kim, Sue, 148
Kisor, Yvette, 136n15
Knox, Collie, 157
Koch, John T., 91n5
Kreeft, Peter, 139, 176n1
Kreglinger, Gisela, 123n10
Kristeva, Julia, 57
Kushner, Tony, 36

Lang, Andrew, 86, 209–10
Latham, Robert Gordon, 147
Layamon, 201
Led Zeppelin, 24, 41
Lee, Alan, 25, 28n17, 41
Lee, Christopher, 232
Lee, Stuart D., 21
Leerssen, Joep, 90n3
Le Guin, Ursula K., 48, 87, 114, 118–20, 121, 124 (nn 11, 14)
Lehrer, Jonah, 183
Leiber, Fritz, 121
Lesnik-Oberstein, Karin, 74n1
Levenson, Michael, 136n21
Lewis, C. S., 4, 19, 27n1, 38, 45, 87, 103, 113, 123n10, 124n10, 127–28, 129, 133, 134–35 (nn 3, 6), 136n18, 172–73, 175, 176n2, 178, 205, 213, 237, 238, 240, 241
Lewis, Sinclair, 140
Lindsay, David, 116, 124n10
Lobdell, Jared, 20, 123n7
Long, Josh, 123n10
Long, Kate, 229
Lönnrot, Elias, 90n4, 123n4
Lord, Albert, 93
Lukács, Georg, 43n9
Lyell, Charles, 184
Lynch, Andrew, 123n4

MacDonald, George, 6, 116, 118, 123n10, 124n13, 173, 209, 238
Macintyre, Ben, 132
Macpherson, James, 86, 123n4
Madlener, Josef, 138
Magennis, Hugh, 95
Maher, Michael W., 176n1
Major, Claire Howell, 242n3
Malory, Thomas, 201
Marie de France, 201
Marlowe, Christopher, 192, 195
Marshall, Jeremy, 164n4, 215
Martin, Thomas L., 102n1
Mathews, Richard, 123nn7–8
Mathijs, Ernest, 43n7
Matthews, Dorothy, 180–81
McCarthy, Jeanne, 160
McFadden, Brian, 149n3
McFall, Lynne, 222
McKillip, Patricia, 120
McNees, Eleanor Jane, 135n8
McNelis, James, 123, 135n11
Merritt, A., 211–12
Michaelsen, Larry K., 242n3
Miéville, China, 122, 125n21
Milbank, Alison, 124n10, 176n1
Millis, Barbara J., 242n3
Milton, John, 37, 45
Mitchison, Naomi, 128, 129, 133, 145
Moorcock, Michael, 122, 125n20
Moore, George, 128
Morgan, Francis Xavier, 3
Morganwg, Iolo, 86, 90n3
Morris, William, 6, 116–17, 118, 123n8, 124n11
Mortimer, Patchen, 7, 8, 28n9, 34, 134n2
Muir, Edwin, 128
Müller, Max, 86, 209
Murdoch, Iris, 6

Nabokov, Vladimir, 71, 74n5
Nagy, Gergely, 35n2, 234
Nasmith, Ted, 25, 28n17, 41
Nelson, Dale, 123 (nn 7, 9)
Nettle, Daniel, 157, 161
Newbolt, Henry, 132
Newby, Jessica, 163
Nicolay, Theresa Freda, 134n2
Nietzsche, Friedrich, 87
Nimoy, Leonard, 41, 43n6
Noel, Ruth S., 22
Norman, Philip, 6
Norton, Wil, 227
Novakovich, Josip, 207, 209

Obama, Barack, 236n3
Oberhelman, David, 9
O'Hehir, Andrew, ix
Ong, Walter, 93, 96

Opie, Iona, 193
Opie, Peter, 193
Orwell, George, 7, 87, 126, 127, 128
Ovid, 207, 210
Owen, Wilfred, 87, 132, 196

Parmelee, Dean X., 242n3
Partridge, Brenda, 87
Paul, 175
Pauli, Michelle, ix
Pearce, Joseph, 27n1, 123 (nn 3, 6)
Perry, Lincoln, 47
Perry, Michael W., 20, 123n8
Pettersson, Ninni M., 76
Petty, Anne, 171n1
Plato, 219, 220, 223
Platzner, Gloria, 211
Plimmer, Charlotte, 147
Plimmer, Denis, 147
Poetic Edda, 16, 102n5, 201
Popper, Karl, 186
Pratchett, Terry, 209, 213
Prichard, James Cowles, 147
Prozesky, Maria, 94
Pullman, Philip, 122, 125n21
Purtill, Richard, 176n1

Racine, Jean, 133
Ralegh, Walter, 192, 195
Rankin, Arthur, Jr., 27, 66
Rascoe, Burton, 135n12
Rateliff, John, 28n12
Rawls, Melanie, 151
Ray, Janisse, 187–88
Rearick, Anderson, 148
Reid, Robin Anne, 35n2, 214, 216
Reilly, Robert James, 242n1
Reynolds, James, 144
Rhodes, Roy, 228
Rhys-Davies, John, 47
Richardson, Maurice, 128, 133
Rieke, Richard, 190n3
Ringel, Faye, 8, 124 (nn 15, 18)
Ripp, Joseph, 5, 6, 7, 27n6
Roberts, Mark, 128, 135n10
Rogers, William N., II, 123n9
Romaine, Suzanne, 157, 161
Roos, Richard, 35n1
Rosebury, Brian, 43n2, 123n6, 124n12, 148
Ross, David, 219
Rowling, J. K., 43n4, 120–21, 122, 213
Russell, Gary, 43n5

Saga of King Heidrek the Wise, 88, 102n5
Saga of the Volsungs, 16, 207, 210
Salinger, J. D., 6
Salo, David, 22
Sassoon, Siegfried, 87, 196
Saxon, Wolfgang, 135n10
Sayers, Dorothy L., 238, 241
Schweitzer, Darrell, 122n1
Scott, Walter, 116, 118, 123 (nn 4, 9), 124n13, 131
Scoville, Chester N., 123n8
Scull, Christina, 9, 10, 14, 15, 20, 21, 25, 27–28 (nn 2, 6, 10, 15, 18), 195, 199n3
Seafarer, 88, 90n4, 97, 99
Sears, Neil, 49n4
Seldes, Gilbert, 135n12
Sertillanges, A. G., 241
Shakespeare, William, 21, 36, 131, 147
Shapiro, Stephen, 144, 148
Shippey, Tom, ix, xin1, 7, 16, 19, 21, 36, 39, 49, 66, 74nn2–3, 82, 91n6, 98, 100, 101, 102n5, 114, 123n3, 124n15, 126, 129, 130, 134n2, 135n13, 146, 149n1, 167, 197, 200, 216, 217, 228, 231, 234–35, 236n2, 237
Sidney, Philip, 108
Siewers, Alfred K., 21
Sinex, Margaret, 145
Singh, G., 135n10
Smith, Barbara Leigh, 224n1
Smith, Thomas W., 242n2
Smol, Anna, 152, 196
Snow, C. P., 183
Socrates, 220, 223
Solomon and Saturn, 102n5
Solopova, Elizabeth, 21
Song of Roland, 103, 104, 106, 201
Spaulding, Mira, 161
Spenser, Edmund, 45, 105
Sproul, Barbara, 180
Stanton, Michael N., 35n1
Steinbeck, John, 7
Stevens, Jen, 210, 213n2
Stewart, Fiona, 144
Stewart, R. J., 181
Straubhaar, Sandra Ballif, 144
Stravinsky, Igor, 133
Strickland, Debra Higgs, 149n2
Sturluson, Snorri, 90n4
Swann, Donald, 23, 197
Sweet, Michael, 242n3

Taylor, Sean, 49n2
Taylor, William L., 35n1
Tennyson, Alfred, 123n4, 131–32, 193, 194, 196
Theocritus, 108
Thomas, Melissa, 34
Thomas Aquinas, 222
Thompson, Stith, 63n2
Timmons, Daniel, 171n1
Tolkien, Arthur Reuel, 3, 138

Tolkien, Baillie, 14
Tolkien, Christopher, 4, 9, 10, 11, 12, 13, 14, 15, 16, 17, 18, 24, 25, 26, 28n12, 58, 59, 63nn4–5, 64n9, 74n4, 75–76, 77, 97, 132, 157, 158
Tolkien, Edith (née Bratt), 3–4, 58, 76, 138
Tolkien, Hilary, 3
Tolkien, Mabel, 3, 58
Tolkien, Michael, 147
Tolkien Ensemble, 24, 109, 197
Toulmin, Stephen, 189, 190n3
Turgon (David Smith), 59, 63n2, 90n4
Tyler, J. E. A., 20

Underwood, Michael R., 123n9
Unwin, Stanley, 147
Updike, John, 126

Van Engen, Abram, 31
Van Hulle, Dirk, 90n3
Vaninskaya, Anna, 134 (nn 2, 5)
Vergil, 104, 105, 108
Vink, Renée, 149n5
Vitaliano, Dorothy, 179
Vonnegut, Kurt, 87, 126

Wace, 201
Waldman, Milton, 228, 229
Walmsley, Nigel, 43n7
Walsh, Fran, 218
Walter, Brian, 74n5
Walter, George, 199n1
Walton, Jo, 124n18
The Wanderer, 88, 90n4, 95, 97, 99, 129, 130, 136n17
Warchus, Matthew, 197
Weiner, Edmund, 164n4, 215
Weinreich, Frank, 28n9
Weldon, Glen, ix
West, Richard C., 213n2
Whedon, Joss, 43n4
Whittingham, Elizabeth A., 21
"Wife's Lament," 129
Wiggins, Kayla McKinney, 171n1
Williams, Charles, 19, 136n18, 237, 238, 239, 240, 241
Williams, Raymond, 38
Williams, William Carlos, 192, 195
Wilson, Edmund, 38, 44–45, 49n5, 128, 129, 132, 133, 135n12, 136n18
Wilson, Edward O., 183–84, 186–87, 188, 189
Wong, Kate, 178
Woolf, Virginia, 127, 128, 130, 131–32, 134n3, 135n8, 136n19
Wyke-Smith, Edward, 140
Wynne, Hilary, 19

Yatt, John, 47, 88, 144, 148

Zelazny, Roger, 121, 124–25n19
Zimbardo, Rose A., 21

Modern Language Association of America

Approaches to Teaching World Literature

To purchase MLA publications, visit www.mla.org/bookstore.

Achebe's Things Fall Apart. Ed. Bernth Lindfors. 1991.
Arthurian Tradition. Ed. Maureen Fries and Jeanie Watson. 1992.
Atwood's The Handmaid's Tale *and Other Works*. Ed. Sharon R. Wilson, Thomas B. Friedman, and Shannon Hengen. 1996.
Austen's Emma. Ed. Marcia McClintock Folsom. 2004.
Austen's Mansfield Park. Ed. Marcia McClintock Folsom and John Wiltshire. 2014.
Austen's Pride and Prejudice. Ed. Marcia McClintock Folsom. 1993.
Balzac's Old Goriot. Ed. Michal Peled Ginsburg. 2000.
Baudelaire's Flowers of Evil. Ed. Laurence M. Porter. 2000.
Beckett's Waiting for Godot. Ed. June Schlueter and Enoch Brater. 1991.
Behn's Oroonoko. Ed. Cynthia Richards and Mary Ann O'Donnell. 2014.
Beowulf. Ed. Jess B. Bessinger, Jr., and Robert F. Yeager. 1984.
Blake's Songs of Innocence and of Experience. Ed. Robert F. Gleckner and Mark L. Greenberg. 1989.
Boccaccio's Decameron. Ed. James H. McGregor. 2000.
British Women Poets of the Romantic Period. Ed. Stephen C. Behrendt and Harriet Kramer Linkin. 1997.
Charlotte Brontë's Jane Eyre. Ed. Diane Long Hoeveler and Beth Lau. 1993.
Emily Brontë's Wuthering Heights. Ed. Sue Lonoff and Terri A. Hasseler. 2006.
Byron's Poetry. Ed. Frederick W. Shilstone. 1991.
Works of Italo Calvino. Ed. Franco Ricci. 2013.
Camus's The Plague. Ed. Steven G. Kellman. 1985.
Cather's My Ántonia. Ed. Susan J. Rosowski. 1989.
Cervantes' Don Quixote. First edition. Ed. Richard Bjornson. 1984.
Cervantes' Don Quixote. Second edition. Ed. James A. Parr and Lisa Vollendorf. 2015.
Chaucer's Canterbury Tales. First edition. Ed. Joseph Gibaldi. 1980.
Chaucer's Canterbury Tales. Second edition. Ed. Peter W. Travis and Frank Grady. 2014.
Chaucer's Troilus and Criseyde *and the Shorter Poems*. Ed. Tison Pugh and Angela Jane Weisl. 2006.
Chopin's The Awakening. Ed. Bernard Koloski. 1988.
Coetzee's Disgrace *and Other Works*. Ed. Laura Wright, Jane Poyner, and Elleke Boehmer. 2014.
Coleridge's Poetry and Prose. Ed. Richard E. Matlak. 1991.
Collodi's Pinocchio *and Its Adaptations*. Ed. Michael Sherberg. 2006.
Conrad's "Heart of Darkness" and "The Secret Sharer." Ed. Hunt Hawkins and Brian W. Shaffer. 2002.
Dante's Divine Comedy. Ed. Carole Slade. 1982.

Defoe's Robinson Crusoe. Ed. Maximillian E. Novak and Carl Fisher. 2005.
DeLillo's White Noise. Ed. Tim Engles and John N. Duvall. 2006.
Dickens's Bleak House. Ed. John O. Jordan and Gordon Bigelow. 2009.
Dickens's David Copperfield. Ed. Richard J. Dunn. 1984.
Dickinson's Poetry. Ed. Robin Riley Fast and Christine Mack Gordon. 1989.
Narrative of the Life of Frederick Douglass. Ed. James C. Hall. 1999.
Works of John Dryden. Ed. Jayne Lewis and Lisa Zunshine. 2013.
Duras's Ourika. Ed. Mary Ellen Birkett and Christopher Rivers. 2009.
Early Modern Spanish Drama. Ed. Laura R. Bass and Margaret R. Greer. 2006.
Eliot's Middlemarch. Ed. Kathleen Blake. 1990.
Eliot's Poetry and Plays. Ed. Jewel Spears Brooker. 1988.
Shorter Elizabethan Poetry. Ed. Patrick Cheney and Anne Lake Prescott. 2000.
Ellison's Invisible Man. Ed. Susan Resneck Parr and Pancho Savery. 1989.
English Renaissance Drama. Ed. Karen Bamford and Alexander Leggatt. 2002.
Works of Louise Erdrich. Ed. Gregg Sarris, Connie A. Jacobs, and James R. Giles. 2004.
Dramas of Euripides. Ed. Robin Mitchell-Boyask. 2002.
Faulkner's As I Lay Dying. Ed. Patrick O'Donnell and Lynda Zwinger. 2011.
Faulkner's The Sound and the Fury. Ed. Stephen Hahn and Arthur F. Kinney. 1996.
Fitzgerald's The Great Gatsby. Ed. Jackson R. Bryer and Nancy P. VanArsdale. 2009.
Flaubert's Madame Bovary. Ed. Laurence M. Porter and Eugene F. Gray. 1995.
García Márquez's One Hundred Years of Solitude. Ed. María Elena de Valdés and Mario J. Valdés. 1990.
Gilman's "The Yellow Wall-Paper" and Herland. Ed. Denise D. Knight and Cynthia J. Davis. 2003.
Goethe's Faust. Ed. Douglas J. McMillan. 1987.
Gothic Fiction: The British and American Traditions. Ed. Diane Long Hoeveler and Tamar Heller. 2003.
Poetry of John Gower. Ed. R. F. Yeager and Brian W. Gastle. 2011.
Grass's The Tin Drum. Ed. Monika Shafi. 2008.
H.D.'s Poetry and Prose. Ed. Annette Debo and Lara Vetter. 2011.
Hebrew Bible as Literature in Translation. Ed. Barry N. Olshen and Yael S. Feldman. 1989.
Homer's Iliad *and* Odyssey. Ed. Kostas Myrsiades. 1987.
Hurston's Their Eyes Were Watching God *and Other Works*. Ed. John Lowe. 2009.
Ibsen's A Doll House. Ed. Yvonne Shafer. 1985.
Henry James's Daisy Miller *and* The Turn of the Screw. Ed. Kimberly C. Reed and Peter G. Beidler. 2005.
Works of Samuel Johnson. Ed. David R. Anderson and Gwin J. Kolb. 1993.
Joyce's Ulysses. Ed. Kathleen McCormick and Erwin R. Steinberg. 1993.
Works of Sor Juana Inés de la Cruz. Ed. Emilie L. Bergmann and Stacey Schlau. 2007.
Kafka's Short Fiction. Ed. Richard T. Gray. 1995.

Keats's Poetry. Ed. Walter H. Evert and Jack W. Rhodes. 1991.
Kingston's The Woman Warrior. Ed. Shirley Geok-lin Lim. 1991.
Lafayette's The Princess of Clèves. Ed. Faith E. Beasley and Katharine Ann Jensen. 1998.
Writings of Bartolomé de Las Casas. Ed. Santa Arias and Eyda M. Merediz. 2008.
Works of D. H. Lawrence. Ed. M. Elizabeth Sargent and Garry Watson. 2001.
Lazarillo de Tormes *and the Picaresque Tradition*. Ed. Anne J. Cruz. 2009.
Lessing's The Golden Notebook. Ed. Carey Kaplan and Ellen Cronan Rose. 1989.
Works of Primo Levi. Ed. Nicholas Patruno and Roberta Ricci. 2014.
Works of Jack London. Ed. Kenneth K. Brandt and Jeanne Campbell Reesman. 2015.
Works of Naguib Mahfouz. Ed. Waïl S. Hassan and Susan Muaddi Darraj. 2011.
Mann's Death in Venice *and Other Short Fiction*. Ed. Jeffrey B. Berlin. 1992.
Marguerite de Navarre's Heptameron. Ed. Colette H. Winn. 2007.
Works of Carmen Martín Gaite. Ed. Joan L. Brown. 2013.
Medieval English Drama. Ed. Richard K. Emmerson. 1990.
Melville's Moby-Dick. Ed. Martin Bickman. 1985.
Metaphysical Poets. Ed. Sidney Gottlieb. 1990.
Miller's Death of a Salesman. Ed. Matthew C. Roudané. 1995.
Milton's Paradise Lost. First edition. Ed. Galbraith M. Crump. 1986.
Milton's Paradise Lost. Second edition. Ed. Peter C. Herman. 2012.
Milton's Shorter Poetry and Prose. Ed. Peter C. Herman. 2007.
Molière's Tartuffe *and Other Plays*. Ed. James F. Gaines and Michael S. Koppisch. 1995.
Momaday's The Way to Rainy Mountain. Ed. Kenneth M. Roemer. 1988.
Montaigne's Essays. Ed. Patrick Henry. 1994.
Novels of Toni Morrison. Ed. Nellie Y. McKay and Kathryn Earle. 1997.
Murasaki Shikibu's The Tale of Genji. Ed. Edward Kamens. 1993.
Nabokov's Lolita. Ed. Zoran Kuzmanovich and Galya Diment. 2008.
Works of Ngũgĩ wa Thiong'o. Ed. Oliver Lovesey. 2012.
Works of Tim O'Brien. Ed. Alex Vernon and Catherine Calloway. 2010.
Works of Ovid and the Ovidian Tradition. Ed. Barbara Weiden Boyd and Cora Fox. 2010.
Petrarch's Canzoniere *and the Petrarchan Tradition*. Ed. Christopher Kleinhenz and Andrea Dini. 2014.
Poe's Prose and Poetry. Ed. Jeffrey Andrew Weinstock and Tony Magistrale. 2008.
Pope's Poetry. Ed. Wallace Jackson and R. Paul Yoder. 1993.
Proust's Fiction and Criticism. Ed. Elyane Dezon-Jones and Inge Crosman Wimmers. 2003.
Puig's Kiss of the Spider Woman. Ed. Daniel Balderston and Francine Masiello. 2007.
Pynchon's The Crying of Lot 49 *and Other Works*. Ed. Thomas H. Schaub. 2008.
Works of François Rabelais. Ed. Todd W. Reeser and Floyd Gray. 2011.
Novels of Samuel Richardson. Ed. Lisa Zunshine and Jocelyn Harris. 2006.

Rousseau's Confessions *and* Reveries of the Solitary Walker. Ed. John C. O'Neal and Ourida Mostefai. 2003.
Scott's Waverley Novels. Ed. Evan Gottlieb and Ian Duncan. 2009.
Shakespeare's Hamlet. Ed. Bernice W. Kliman. 2001.
Shakespeare's King Lear. Ed. Robert H. Ray. 1986.
Shakespeare's Othello. Ed. Peter Erickson and Maurice Hunt. 2005.
Shakespeare's Romeo and Juliet. Ed. Maurice Hunt. 2000.
Shakespeare's The Taming of the Shrew. Ed. Margaret Dupuis and Grace Tiffany. 2013.
Shakespeare's The Tempest *and Other Late Romances*. Ed. Maurice Hunt. 1992.
Shelley's Frankenstein. Ed. Stephen C. Behrendt. 1990.
Shelley's Poetry. Ed. Spencer Hall. 1990.
Sir Gawain and the Green Knight. Ed. Miriam Youngerman Miller and Jane Chance. 1986.
Song of Roland. Ed. William W. Kibler and Leslie Zarker Morgan. 2006.
Spenser's Faerie Queene. Ed. David Lee Miller and Alexander Dunlop. 1994.
Stendhal's The Red and the Black. Ed. Dean de la Motte and Stirling Haig. 1999.
Sterne's Tristram Shandy. Ed. Melvyn New. 1989.
Works of Robert Louis Stevenson. Ed. Caroline McCracken-Flesher. 2013.
The Story of the Stone (Dream of the Red Chamber). Ed. Andrew Schonebaum and Tina Lu. 2012.
Stowe's Uncle Tom's Cabin. Ed. Elizabeth Ammons and Susan Belasco. 2000.
Swift's Gulliver's Travels. Ed. Edward J. Rielly. 1988.
Teresa of Ávila and the Spanish Mystics. Ed. Alison Weber. 2009.
Thoreau's Walden *and Other Works*. Ed. Richard J. Schneider. 1996.
Tolkien's The Lord of the Rings *and Other Works*. Ed. Leslie A. Donovan. 2015.
Tolstoy's Anna Karenina. Ed. Liza Knapp and Amy Mandelker. 2003.
Vergil's Aeneid. Ed. William S. Anderson and Lorina N. Quartarone. 2002.
Voltaire's Candide. Ed. Renée Waldinger. 1987.
Whitman's Leaves of Grass. Ed. Donald D. Kummings. 1990.
Wiesel's Night. Ed. Alan Rosen. 2007.
Works of Oscar Wilde. Ed. Philip E. Smith II. 2008.
Woolf's Mrs. Dalloway. Ed. Eileen Barrett and Ruth O. Saxton. 2009.
Woolf's To the Lighthouse. Ed. Beth Rigel Daugherty and Mary Beth Pringle. 2001.
Wordsworth's Poetry. Ed. Spencer Hall, with Jonathan Ramsey. 1986.
Wright's Native Son. Ed. James A. Miller. 1997.